POLITICAL JUNKIES

ALSO BY CLAIRE BOND POTTER

War on Crime:
Bandits, G-Men, and the Politics of Mass Culture

POLITICAL JUNKIES

From Talk Radio to Twitter,
How Alternative Media Hooked Us
on Politics and Broke Our Democracy

CLAIRE BOND POTTER

BASIC BOOKS
New York

Basic Books
Hachette Book Group
1290 Avenue of the Americas, New York, NY 10104
www.basicbooks.com

Printed in the United States of America

First Edition: July 2020

Published by Basic Books, an imprint of Perseus Books, LLC, a subsidiary of Hachette Book Group, Inc. The Basic Books name and logo is a trademark of the Hachette Book Group.

The Hachette Speakers Bureau provides a wide range of authors for speaking events. To find out more, go to www.hachettespeakersbureau.com or call (866) 376-6591.

The publisher is not responsible for websites (or their content) that are not owned by the publisher.

Print book interior design by Jeff Williams

Library of Congress Cataloging-in-Publication Data has been applied for.

ISBNs: 978-1-5416-4499-1 (hardcover), 978-1-5416-4500-4 (ebook)

For Nancy Barnes

CONTENTS

PRESS PASS

I arrived at the Gaylord National Resort and Convention Center in National Harbor, Maryland, after the Secret Service had locked it down. Vice President Mike Pence was giving a keynote, and no one was getting in until it was over. It was the last week in February 2018, and a swelling group of rueful Conservative Political Action Conference (CPAC) attendees had all made the same mistake. I sat down on a bench with a married couple: I learned that Kathy was a minister, and Jake was running for Congress in a Midwestern Republican primary. In addition to her storefront ministry, Kathy also had an internet radio show, which offered a Christian perspective on contemporary politics and culture. They were at CPAC to connect with Christian broadcasters and other alternative media outlets that might support Jake's campaign. The weekend would probably cost them over $2,000.

But what a weekend it is! Almost a half-century after its founding in 1974, CPAC exemplifies the divisive populisms that have been resurgent in American politics since the 1960s, a phenomenon that this book ties to the rise of alternative media.[1] As I chatted with Kathy and Jake, I was exactly where I wanted to be: in a gathering of conservative activists and Donald Trump enthusiasts linked to each other by a network of computers, podcasts, print, and televisions. CPAC is a feast designed for a political junkie like me, one who needs to leave New York City's progressive media, and my own university, behind to immerse myself in conservative activism. My friend Ryan, an alternative media journalist, helped me connect to people in his network; and the live program allowed me to hear entire speeches, not just the decontextualized clips that appeared on the evening news. While the main stage featured numerous members of the Trump administration, as well as the president himself, the keynote speakers who created the most excitement were populist alternative media stars like Laura Ingraham, Ben Shapiro, and Sheriff David A. Clarke (a podcaster and one of fewer than a half-dozen African Americans on the program). *Breitbart News* editor Steve Bannon, a perennial favorite who had just lost his job as White House chief strategist, was notably absent, as were paleoconservatives and neoconservatives, a small coalition of intellectuals and politicians known as "Never Trumpers" who, together, have increasingly opposed the rise of populism in the Republican Party.

And of course, there was also "Prison Hillary," an actor walking around in a striped jumpsuit, a blond wig, and a smiling Hillary Clinton mask, her handcuffed hands held out beseechingly.

"Prison Hillary" is a character we were all familiar with from the memes that showed up in our social media feeds during the 2016 campaign: Clinton's agonized face, photoshopped behind bars. She is a fantasy, born on alt-right electronic forums and promoted by Trump partisans, a post-truth figure who does not represent the "facts" about Hillary Clinton, but rather what many populists *feel* is true about her.[2] And she is a symbol of why political media, and democracy, are broken. *Political Junkies* shows how debates about politics have been reshaped by alternative media; and how this dynamic has created an overheated, populist political atmosphere that offers the greatest challenge to American democracy and government since the Civil War. But this book is also a story about technology: it demonstrates how the rise of opinion journalism, and editorializing, has been replaced by political storytelling designed for "you." Always intended to attract an audience of political junkies and create new ones, in its digital form, alternative media has undermined a common idea of what news really is as well as what role the news should play in constituting a public square where everyone can agree on basic facts.

There is no more persuasive example of the importance of alternative media in contemporary conservative populism than CPAC, which devotes a substantial portion of its programming to alternative media workshops. Some helped students working at conservative campus publications get jobs at digital newspapers and web magazines. Others trained activists to become alternative media producers, offering tips and techniques for establishing and promoting a blog, podcast, or a YouTube channel. The media section in the main convention hall was jammed with correspondents from alternative operations: nearly all the women had long, dyed blond hair in imitation of stars like Ann Coulter, Laura Ingraham, and most of the female anchors on *Fox News*.

I quickly grasped how little of this vibrant and eclectic event was being covered in the mainstream media, even in conservative publications like the *Wall Street Journal*. On Broadcast Row, an exhibit hall of alternative media outlets just outside the main stage, producers like NRATV (a now-defunct operation established by the National Rifle Association, a major CPAC 2018 sponsor) were broadcasting live as crowds of conference attendees looked on. Podcasts of the keynote speakers were dropped on iTunes, Sound-Cloud, and Google Play minutes after they ended. On the lower level of the exhibition hall, I dodged a cardboard cutout of Senator Elizabeth Warren wearing a Plains Indian headdress and bumped into two talkative young women who, as college students, had established a thriving web magazine aimed at the campus right called *Lone Conservative*.

CPAC is an annual event where conservatives of all ages network, and it is a particularly important site for college students to become involved in a Republican Party that has enthusiastically given itself over to the internet, Donald Trump, and conservative populism. But its thriving alternative media exhibits were not unique. At Netroots Nation, the younger, progressive equivalent of CPAC, I would have seen a similar array of alternative media vying for the attention of Democrats. In 2019, the born-digital sites

Alternet, RawStory, and Front Page Live, as well as an array of PACs, unions, and the Democratic National Committee, anchored the exhibit hall as premier sponsors. Lesser sponsors like Bonfire Media (which produces "powerful and creative pieces that raise public awareness"), the Center for Story-Based Strategy ("harnessing the power of narrative for social change"), Firefly Partners ("custom digital solutions for progressive nonprofits"), and SBD Digital ("multiplatform matching to meet audiences where they are") testify to the extraordinary amount of influence that alternative media wields in contemporary American political culture. What progressive and conservative alternative media have in common is that they are explicitly ideological and seek to reach motivated audiences of political junkies.

Alternative media outlets, right and left, also position themselves against the so-called mainstream media, a collection of news outlets that they view as aligned with the interests of corporate and political elites. Also known as "old media," "traditional media," or "legacy media," these newspapers and broadcasting companies are, or have evolved from, family-owned corporations that predated digital distribution. Most importantly, the mainstream media is viewed by alternative media outlets and the activists that patronize them as insufficiently ideological, part of a political, media, and corporate establishment that cannot be trusted to tell the truth or hold the powerful to account. Since its origins in the 1950s, alternative media has sought to recruit readers who were passionate about politics, to jolt Americans alienated from politics out of their apathy, and to cultivate activist information networks. And they have done this in the interests of a more transparent, inclusive, and principled politics that each side, conservative and progressive, believes would represent a fairer political system.

In the 1950s, where *Political Junkies* begins, alternative media producers believed that a more transparent media, a more explicitly ideological media, and a media that positioned itself in opposition to the political establishment could promote a better democracy. By 2016, it seemed that many digital alternative media sites had acquired a sinister power. Sites designed to distribute fake news heightened animosity between the partisans they targeted, undermined the electoral process, and divided voters into acrimonious factions. By the 2018 American midterm elections, over a third of Democrats voted, not to endorse their own party's policies, but to oppose Republican rule; and more than a quarter of Republicans voted, not for their own party's policies, but to keep Democrats out of power.[3]

Ironically, the media that drew us into politics have made us angrier at, and more contemptuous of, our democratic institutions. Although we consume news all day on our digital devices, the vast majority of Americans are more alienated from each other and from a political system that requires citizen participation to function, than they have ever been. From talk radio to Twitter, right and left stay in their red and blue lanes, mainlining ideology, shouting insults across the political divide, and seeing conspiracies everywhere. How has political talk become so extreme and political engagement so anemic? How has a partisan alternative media that is in many cases just as profitable and entrenched come to be perceived by many as equally, or more, reliable than an establishment media that invests billions of dollars a year on reporting, writing, and broadcasting the news?

And how has American democracy, founded on the idea of a free press and free expression, become so broken?

=====

Political Junkies is a history of how Americans got hooked on alternative media and ended up craving satisfaction that politics can never deliver. It is about how, beginning after World War II, some alternative media channels repurposed mass media technologies for political work, imagining new forms of journalism that appealed to a specialist audiences critical of the political and media establishment. *Political Junkies* is also a story about how technology creates communities out of dissidents otherwise isolated from each other, and how it forges majorities out of minorities. And it is about how enterprising alternative media entrepreneurs delivered their message to a chosen public, recycling and refreshing older technologies and adopting new ones that suited their resources, talents, objectives, and imagined public.

But most of all, *Political Junkies* is a story about you and me. It is about the emotional bond that can be created between those who make political news and those who consume it; and it is a history of an identity—"political junkie"—that now binds us as makers and users of political entertainment. It is also about how serving political junkies came to supersede another ideal: that well-reported, objectively written news, organized around facts, could help informed, reasonable citizens make collective choices. These imagined communities, as Benedict Anderson called them, bound together by print, established the emotional and political legitimacy of the modern democratic nation-state by creating a collective understanding of politics that could survive partisanship.[4]

But alternative media outlets, because they gave voice to outsider and minority perspectives within the larger media environment, have also been essential to maintaining the integrity of both the journalism establishment and democracy itself, and to changing mainstream conversations. Because making political decisions mattered, eighteenth-century printers of newspapers, pamphlets, and broadsides were viewed as some of the most influential, and necessary, citizens in the English Atlantic world, each having an organic relation to the other. As the United States broke apart and came back together in the nineteenth century, mainstream partisan newspapers recorded and increasingly drove the conversations that moved politicians, but alternative newspapers and pamphlets, written primarily by white abolitionists, free African Americans, and women, drove political change.[5]

Yet no nineteenth-century reader would have viewed these distinctions as constituting a "mainstream" and an "alternative" media. This was in part because all printed news was partisan until journalism became a profession in the late nineteenth century when, like other literary and scholarly pursuits, it adopted ideals of objectivity.[6] After World War I, newspapers favored the notion that while individual news outlets might be aligned with one of the two parties, democracy, in general, was better served by reporting that did not editorialize or analyze, but rather delivered the facts and stood above the political fray. This idea extended itself to mainstream radio in the late 1920s, and to television in the 1950s, as both mediums became crucial platforms for distributing political news.[7] After World War II, alternative media on the left and the right began to insist on a greater voice for underrepresented political positions, people, and social movements as well as the necessity of criticizing a liberal media and political establishment. After 1952, objectivity itself became increasingly suspect, an unspoken value invoked when liberals lambasted conservative outlets and conservatives assailed the "liberal media" as lacking in fairness or purveying "fake news."[8]

Although both genres seek to inform, mainstream and alternative media have important similarities and differences. Both can be corporate, and there is no one business model: some alternative media have become surprisingly profitable, even as some mainstream media outlets, specifically newspapers and newsmagazines, have steadily lost subscriptions and advertising revenue. Most importantly, while contemporary mainstream media outlets see themselves as institutions whose primary mission is to inform conversation in the public square, purveyors of alternative media are also activists, emanating from, or advocating for, social movements. They emphasize a personal, partisan connection to the reader and often exhort that reader to political action. Whereas twentieth-century mainstream media made a claim, like all mass culture, to educate an undifferentiated audience and to provide a public service for a profit, alternative media outlets were defined by their commitment to a partisan demographic that was already persuaded and needed only to be mobilized with more information and analysis that enhanced their closely held beliefs.[9]

By the twenty-first century, these two distinct genres began to borrow from each other. Partisan media platforms like the *Huffington Post* and *Breitbart News* have become profitable, corporate outlets; while Fox News and MSNBC, two television news outlets owned by mainstream media corporations, deliberately cultivate partisan audiences. This is an ambiguity that readers of this book will have to tolerate, as I have, and it explains a great deal about why Americans sometimes wander to the frontiers of digital journalism to get information they believe they can trust without being sure why that "news" is or is not reliable. But throughout *Political Junkies*, alternative media does retain one distinct characteristic.

While these outlets aren't always populist, populism—which is, by definition, adversarial to the mainstream political and media establishment—thrives in the dissident atmosphere of alternative media. While readers will sometimes see me describe partisan divisions as "conservative" and "liberal," "Republican" and "Democratic," those labels obscure what alternative media have done on both sides: activate "the people" to resist what they perceive as the domination of cultural, economic, and political elites. As Richard Viguerie pointed out in his 1983 book, *The Establishment vs. the People: Is a New Populist Revolt on the Way?*, populism is practical politics, a way of thinking that "identifies with the 'common man,' that is, the man or woman who works for a living . . . it is more than simply a political ideology; it is an attribute of character[.]"[10]

However, twenty-first-century populism is distinctly marked by the power of our media choices to divide us. This was not always true. Dating back to the agricultural movements of the late nineteenth century in the Southern and Midwestern United States, populism often served to unite activists across party, and even racial, lines. While many historians have pegged populism's resurgence to segregationist George Wallace's 1968 presidential bid, Richard Hofstadter saw the right-wing extremism that took Barry Goldwater to the 1964 Republican nomination, particularly in its hostility to the intellectual and political establishment, as a link to the American populist past.[11]

Beginning with the Goldwater campaign, the New Right explicitly claimed the mantle of conservative populism. Left movements—even Occupy Wall Street and Black Lives Matter (now part of the Movement for Black Lives)—rarely used this word until the 2016 election, when the progressive coalition that formed around Vermont Senator Bernie Sanders, and subsequently Justice Democrats, was routinely described as populist.[12] Yet, even without making a claim on the word, by the 1960s, the audiences most dedicated to, and driven by, left alternative media also promoted an antiestablishment "people's politics." Their legacy is today's progressive populism. These political movements are generally horizontal; community-based; seek fairness by reining in, or disempowering, capitalism; and see the Washington political establishment as a barrier to putting government to work for "the people."[13]

Readers will want to keep a keen eye out for the many differences within populisms, not just right and left, but *within* right and left. However, there are broad containers that help distinguish populisms, and the media that promote them, as having roughly aligned with either the Republican or the Democratic Party since 1950. When I use the phrase "conservative populism," I mean movements and organizations bound together by, among other things, a belief in the virtues of small government, faith, family, military strength, anti-Communism, and a retreat from compacts with other nations.[14] The phrase "progressive populism" describes movements and organizations mostly aligned with the historical tradition I described in the previous paragraph, sometimes articulated in the United States today as democratic socialism. Progressive populists believe in *using* government to rein in, and even replace, the capitalist establishment, creating mechanisms for horizontal democracy, mobilizing communities around principles of social equality, and implementing ideas about governance that originate at the grass roots.[15]

In the digital age, alternative media have created new imagined communities increasingly defined by hyper-partisanship, sometimes called "silos," "echo chambers," or "filter bubbles," virtual spaces that now can be found working in tandem with mainstream outlets to create a feedback loop of partisan news.[16] These information silos provide robust, if sometimes unfactual, alternatives to consensus political views promoted in the mainstream, at the expense of pulling us into different ideological corners.[17] Cheap and free digital tools introduced in the 1990s cleared the way for new voices from the political margins to find each other and become visible as audiences. These audiences became new markets for information and advertising, but also new constituencies for politicians. As user-friendly digital media tools—partisan websites, email, blogs, and social media, to name a few—proliferated after 1998, technology that initially promised a more satisfying and productive engagement with the political process produced a world of political talk that many now find uncompromising and vicious, a cauldron of conspiracy theories, propaganda, and fake news that drowns out the information users really want and need.[18]

Importantly, while mainstream media represent a consensus about what news should be and do at any given moment, alternative media are innovative, emerging from the wreckage of mainstream, and even other alternative, media. As an example, political talk radio took advantage of corporate journalism's move to television by amplifying an existing genre and making it more partisan; similarly, newsletters, and then blogging, moved into spaces vacated by newspaper journalism.[19] Although alternative media styles that emphasize rebellion and dissent were learned in mainstream genres like talk radio, alternative media always promised its consumers that it was against the establishment—and *for you*.[20] News and political opinions written by a trusted source for a chosen reader have adapted to new technologies over the years, often drawing on, and recalling, their predecessors. Delivered in partisan newsletters by the 1950s; on public broadcasting by the 1970s; via a talk radio host by the 1980s, and in a blog by the 1990s, each promised a growing audience of dedicated political junkies something unique that could not be obtained in the mainstream. By the 2000s, internet-only news sites, and by 2010, podcasts, often reached millions more consumers than mainstream news sites did—still promising political news personally tailored to readers' needs. And as television, radio, and newspapers struggled to keep their audiences by mastering social media, they, too, sharpened their appeal to the specific, and often partisan, media consumer. In examining the use of social media that helped to elect Donald Trump president in 2016, the *New York Times* discovered that while it was ranked 7 in national shares, *Breitbart News* was a close 14: "Online, Everything Is Alternative Media," the doleful headline read.[21]

The star of this book is, of course, the "political junkie": a person who has a compulsion to immerse herself in politics, political news, and political gossip. It is an identity that mainstream journalists were ambivalent about when it first came into general use in the 1970s. To them, it conveyed an almost recreational lack of seriousness and an unseemly fascination with politicians, rather than with political principles. Differently, alternative media producers, and often political consultants, embraced their identities as political junkies, seeing it as a bond, and a commitment, they shared with their audiences. Although the feelings, and compulsion toward politics, that define the political junkie are clearly visible in the first two chapters, the phrase will barely make an appearance there for the simple reason that it is almost impossible to find it written down, anywhere, until 1973. That year, Hunter S. Thompson, a practitioner of the "new journalism" who was well acquainted with recreational pharmaceuticals, announced that he had become a "politics junkie" during his time as a *Rolling Stone* correspondent on South Dakota Senator George McGovern's presidential campaign. Thompson's sentiment is critical to how twenty-first-century Americans would come to describe the compulsion toward digital alternative media more generally: an almost physical addiction to the adrenaline rush of politics that often overwhelmed reason and objectivity. Being a politics junkie, Thompson explained, was as much about feeding a physical need as being a heroin junkie. "[When] a journalist turns into a politics junkie," he wrote, "he will sooner or later start raving and babbling in print about things that only a person who has Been There can possibly understand."[22]

Sound familiar? It's that sense of politics being authentic at last, not just a bunch of faces on a screen. It's how we feel when we are tweeting a political debate and a pundit or political journalist we admire retweets or @'s us. It's like being—to quote Aaron Burr in Lin-Manuel Miranda's *Hamilton*—in the room where it happens.

Use of the term "political junkie" skyrocketed after 1973.[23] Political consultants used it to describe a passion for politics that caused them to destroy their bodies and marriages to work on campaigns. "A political junkie," consultant Joseph S. Miller wrote in 2008, "is distinguished by one universal characteristic—a fascina-tion-absorption-compulsion-passion for politics that sometimes defies rationality." But the phrase also came to describe political groupies, such as a Capitol Hill astrologer profiled by the *New York Times* in 1977. By the 1980s, journalists both identified with the term and disavowed it. They would coyly use the phrase to invoke their passion for their work, but then explicitly disidentify with it because it connoted partisanship and amateurism. By 1991, the phrase "political junkie" came to describe highly visible anti-establishment alternative media stars, like superstar conservative talk radio host Rush Limbaugh.[24]

But perhaps because of Limbaugh and a new generation of political bloggers giving the mainstream media a run for their money, being a political junkie became cool. Arguably Limbaugh, who had bounced around in the secondary radio market, and Nate Silver, a statistics nerd from the University of Chicago, were radically uncool before discovering a passion for politics. But political junkie also described, not just a passion for politics but a kind of extreme politics fan, and a relationship to that fan, that mainstream journalists and pundits soon tried to cultivate. Beginning in the late 1980s, established media figures like Russell Baker, Chris Matthews, Tom Brokaw, and Gabe Pressman proudly labeled themselves political junkies, and in 2000, National Public Radio's Ken Rudin launched a political news show called—yes, *Political Junkie*.[25] At the same time, the expanding mass audience for political news that was fed by alternative media, and by establishment cable television outlets that offered political entertainment, like Fox News, CNN, and MSNBC, also became known as political junkies. In his 2004 celebration of the role of alternative media in driving the rise of conservative populism, Richard Viguerie looked back on the days when the only media available to political junkies were liberal and mainstream. Around the same time, political bloggers like Taegan Goddard, Ben Smith, Heather "Digby" Parton, and Kevin Drum referred to the audience for their work as political junkies.[26]

By the start of the twenty-first century, both the *news maker* and the *audience for the news product* were embraced by the phrase political junkies. More importantly, alternative media was defined by the needs of the political junkie—and so was democracy itself.

═══

Political Junkies begins at a moment when news values were being challenged by McCarthyism, by advertising-driven models for writing and broadcasting that seemed to favor news palatable to corporate sponsors, and by editorial practices that firmly separated objective reporting from opinion writing. After World War II, the

United States developed "a remarkable form of censorship," critic Paul Goodman commented in 1956. Everyone had the "political right to say what he believes," but American minds were smothered by "newspapers, mass-circulation magazines, best-selling books, broadcasts, and public pronouncements that disregard what he says and give the official way of looking at things." If what an American was thinking was not what other people were talking about, it wasn't considered "newsworthy."[27]

The first three chapters explore the rise of media professionals who began their careers in mainstream journalism and, in some cases, politics, but came to believe that it was necessary to establish an alternative, even independent, method of delivering the news. Chapter 1, "The Political Newsletter," explores the revival of a print format that allowed partisans on the right and the left to distribute news the mainstream media would not report. Left-wing journalist Isidor F. Stone's *I. F. Stone's Weekly* tapped into an audience of left and liberal citizens who craved in-depth news from a political insider. Over the next several decades, Stone became an inspiration to and a touchstone for left alternative media producers. His readers, although they didn't use the term, were among the original political junkies, and Stone's writing retains its power today. Glenn Greenwald, a founding editor of the alternative webzine the *Intercept*, admitted that when he began reading the *Weekly* online, he "instantly became almost an addict[.]"[28] But Stone was not the only alternative journalist to seek a highly personal connection to, and make a good living from, self-publishing. Newsletters, sometimes combined with radio broadcasts and mail-order books, expanded the audience for right-wing ideas as well, creating a powerful grassroots movement for Barry Goldwater's presidential bid in 1964.

The 1960s were characterized by rebellions against the establishment, and journalism was no exception to that. Chapter 2, "Public Broadcasting," explores efforts to create new forms of news targeted at people who wanted to think deeply about politics. It features television news innovator Robert MacNeil who, in 1975, cocreated a highly focused half-hour evening news show with journalist Jim Lehrer. Organized around a few topics selected from the day's news, it was called the *Robert MacNeil Report* and was the first iteration of what is the PBS *NewsHour* today. MacNeil believed that the role of all news was to inform and that the standard evening television format—multiple stories ripped from the headlines and told in 120 seconds or less—failed to do that. In 1968, dismayed by his network's inability, or unwillingness, to report the Vietnam War honestly, MacNeil turned to public television as a place defined by its independence from the political and media establishment. MacNeil and Lehrer produced gavel-to-gavel coverage of the Watergate hearings in 1973 and then proposed a new kind of evening news format that replicated the design of *I. F. Stone's Weekly*: in-depth reporting on a few stories became the basis for analysis, expert commentary, and conversation. Such a show would be produced, not for a mass audience, but for discerning viewers who were passionate about the news, an audience MacNeil characterized after the show's debut as "political junkies."

Chapter 3, "Creating Partisans," focuses on two prominent alternative media experts, Paul Weyrich and Richard Viguerie, who, using alternative media, activated and educated the conservative populist base they named the New Right. They put what had been a fringe minority at the center of the Republican Party, using direct mail fundraising to support political candidates and new conservative institutions like the Heritage Foundation, the Committee for the Survival of a Free Congress, and the American Legislative Exchange Council. Direct mail appeals served as personal, mini-newsletters that explained principles and objectives, hooking recipients on politics and weaning them off "biased" mainstream news. Taking us to the brink of the digital age, the chapter shows how Weyrich and Viguerie amplified their impact with computer technology and the creation of institutions staffed by New Right experts who pumped out news, opinions, and analysis to politicians and a growing national constituency of political junkies on the right.

This first portion of the book describes "one-to-many" communication, in which a trusted voice, or institution, conveyed political knowledge to a devoted audience. The next three chapters describe the rise of "many-to-many" communication, horizontal exchanges of information made possible after 1984 by the affordable personal computers that created a digital alternative media revolution.

Chapter 4, "Electronic Democracy," describes the early years of personal computing, as well as efforts to create engaged citizens, and reverse partisan divides, through the cultivation of a virtual public sphere. Cyber-intellectuals like Howard Rheingold imagined renewed connections and conversations between citizens that expanded the possibilities for community problem-solving and political consensus. Lightly moderated but not edited, Rheingold and other early internet theorists viewed the alternative platforms that hosted these engaged exchanges as supplementing, and eventually even replacing, information distributed by the media and political establishments. These early experiments did create new possibilities for political organizing. But they also demonstrated that the possibility of heightened conflict and division was baked into the design of a medium where users could easily choose others who shared their own views and ignore those who did not.

As the internet became searchable, and alternative media producers migrated to free digital platforms, political junkies discovered a feast of ways to participate in politics from personal computers, at home and at work. Chapter 5, "Scandal," takes a deep dive into a world of escalated partisanship during the Clinton administration, driven by the rise of alternative political media. Here, I focus on freelance journalist Matt Drudge's gossip-laced political news site, the *Drudge Report*. Like Izzy Stone, Drudge promised to tell the truth about the Washington establishment. But the *Drudge Report* did not delve into public documents, relying instead on unnamed tipsters and inside sources. Drudge opened the door to the possibility that digital alternative media could be agenda-setting in a mainstream media landscape that deplored rising partisanship, but was increasingly speeded up by, and forced to respond to, internet sites. Even when Drudge's news was accurate—as it was when he broke the story of President Bill Clinton's affair with Monica Lewinsky— the *Drudge Report* told a story about democracy that was designed to divide, sucking readers into the seamy side of political life and feeding popular suspicions that the establishment was conspiratorial and corrupt.

The political crisis detonated by the Lewinsky affair also demonstrated that the internet could have a larger role in electoral politics:

the first netroots mobilization, MoveOn, organized to defend Clinton, but soon established itself as a permanent, progressive political action committee. By the early twenty-first century, campaign consultants began to experiment with using alternative media to woo political junkies to their clients. Chapter 6, "Netroots," looks at the 2004 Howard Dean campaign, a historic turning point in putting digital media innovators to work in partisan politics. Joe Trippi, Dean's campaign manager, had not only been one of the first political strategists to use personal computing in a get out the vote (GOTV) effort, he had also become immersed in the philosophies of electronic democracy that I discuss in chapter 4. In January 2003, Trippi saw young activists using alternative media platforms—blogs, MoveOn, and the social media tool Meetup—to raise money and rebuild political communities at the grass roots. These political junkies—a mix of left populists, Libertarians, and traditional Democrats—had been drawn to Dean's anti-establishment candidacy and particularly to his early opposition to the Bush administration's wars in Iraq and Afghanistan. Trippi saw these supporters organizing themselves on the internet, just as Howard Rheingold had predicted. As importantly, Trippi understood that web tools could be mobilized as alternative media to amplify outsider candidacies that would otherwise be overpowered by the political and media establishment.

Dean lost his fight for the Democratic nomination, a campaign meltdown remembered for "the Scream," a wild yell that proliferated on cable news networks as the first political meme. He also demonstrated the power of combining alternative media with traditional campaign organizing—as well as its pitfalls. Just as the Scream had zoomed across the internet and cable news channels, social media platforms, then in their infancy, could be used to stoke outrage by distributing unedited video and information about opposition candidates. Chapter 7, "Blogging the News," leads with Virginia Senator George Allen, considered a rising star in the Republican Party, whose 2006 reelection campaign was derailed by a video depicting him taunting a college student with a racist slur. Here, I examine the rise of political blogging, then a form of mostly progressive alternative media, that exploded in popularity that year.

Bloggers did independent research and covered neglected stories so well that they were repeatedly pushed back into the mainstream news cycle. This semiprofessional blogging network was enhanced by a new social media environment. Facebook, YouTube, Twitter, MySpace, and other "many-to-many" platforms allowed political junkies, media professionals, and campaigns to share stories, organize, host political conversations, and generate their own networks among like-minded partisans.

The political junkies who flocked to social media, many of them young, were adept at producing and distributing digital alternative media that could now be made on a desktop. In 2008, Barack Obama, building on the progressive populist appeal of the Dean campaign, lit the spark that mobilized them as an effective real grassroots movement. Chapter 8, "MyBarackObama," looks at how the populist organizing strategies that had fallen short in 2004 carried the first African American presidential candidate to victory amid promises that his media-savvy administration would be the most open and transparent in history. While the Obama team was, in many ways, a very traditional and disciplined machine that sometimes reined in social media activists behind the scenes, it was also the first presidential campaign to embed a social media professional, Facebook cofounder Chris Hughes, into its communications team. In short, the Obama campaign reached out to constituencies, particularly youth and youth of color, who had been historically indifferent to politics, making them into political junkies too.

But social media had expanded the networks of conservative populists too, many of whom were dismayed by Obama's win, and particularly by his plan to create a national health insurance system. The final four chapters explore populist insurgencies on the right and the left, movements driven by alternative media that delivered a seismic blow to the political and media establishments and drove Americans into separate ideological corners by 2016. Chapter 9, "Tea Party Time," explores how conservative populists, activated by Libertarian Ron Paul's 2008 presidential bid, organized to "reboot" the system, as an anonymous columnist in the digital alternative media platform *Breitbart News* described it. The Paul campaign, and its aftermath, reveal the rise of a coherent conservative populist ecosystem that combined many-to-many so-cial media organizing on the part of grassroots organizations like the Tea Party with new digital one-to-many publications like *Breitbart*. These outlets manufactured "news" about the corruption of the liberal establishment that was sometimes relayed, often without basic fact-checking, by mainstream media outlets pushing to keep up with the digital alternative media environment.

These conservative populists also knew that winning elections mattered. While they were determined to remain outside the estab-lishment, they chose to fight their fight by demonstrating against Obama, voting, and endorsing political candidates who exemplified their values, like Minnesota Congressperson Michele Bachmann, who organized a Tea Party Caucus in the House of Representatives. At the same time, the Obama administration sought to replicate its historic victory by creating an unmediated connection between the government and the American people. Chapter 10, "White House 2.0," shows how the Obama administration tried, and failed, to duplicate its campaign success by establishing governance and pop-ular consultation through alternative media. Attempting to capture the social movement atmosphere of the campaign and build on ear-lier ideas about electronic democracy, the Change.gov portal prom-ised to put citizens in direct contact with the president's team and to value citizens' ideas and feedback.

The 2008 campaign caused all politicians and their media con-sultants to take a closer look at the ways social media could effec-tively bypass the need to cultivate the journalism establishment. During Obama's first term, senators, representatives, and New York City real estate developer and reality television star Don-ald Trump, who had been toying with a presidential run since the 1990s, all began to use Twitter to broadcast their opinions. This bare-bones platform, usually accessed on mobile devices in its early years, also became extraordinarily useful to activists dismayed by how little change Obama was able, or willing, to accomplish. Chapter 11, "Hashtag Populisms," examines the particular role that Twitter played in the rising tide of progressive populist groups in the United States following the 2010 social media–driven revo-lutions in the Middle East known collectively as the Arab Spring.

Directly broadcasting their criticisms of actually existing democracy allowed Occupy Wall Street and #BlackLivesMatter to hold the United States political establishment, including the Obama administration, accountable for economic exploitation, systemic racism, and violence against communities of color. Using the # symbol, activists could create narrative threads that conveyed news in the moment, and in an authentic, unfiltered style. Although the hashtag could be used to tell any kind of story—a weather event, a response to a favorite television series, or a firsthand account of an incident—when used to express dissent, it made a new kind of political junkie, the populist activist, hypervisible to potential allies, to enemies, and to the establishment. While organizers' ambitions often outstripped their ability to make the changes they envisioned, their inventive use of social media opened a new chapter in alternative media, one that would turn the 2016 election cycle on its head.

That year, for the first campaign, alternative media—particularly on alt-right and alt-light platforms—seemed to overwhelm the political and media establishment, and Donald Trump rode alternative media into the White House. Chapter 12, "Democalypse Now," shows how the Trump campaign combined Twitter, Facebook, and the alt-right platform *Breitbart News* to construct an alternative media machine and a winning coalition of conservative populist political junkies. Democratic candidate Hillary Clinton organized a disciplined, well-financed campaign that made much of her credentials and preparation for the job and was expected to win. Clinton also had a lively digital presence, replete with self-organized partisans, political junkies who swarmed social media platforms on her behalf. But, attacked by populists from the left and the right, Clinton's alternative media strategy collapsed, her campaign narrative undermined, countered, and overwhelmed by an army of trolls. Supporters of socialist Senator Bernie Sanders—many former Deaniacs, Ron Paul supporters, and activists inspired by Occupy Wall Street—invaded the social media feeds of Clinton supporters to produce some of the most vicious infighting the Democratic Party had seen since 1972. And on Clinton's right, Donald Trump and his campaign advisor, *Breitbart News*'s Steve Bannon, whipped conservative populists into a frenzy at rallies and on alternative media, assuring them that he would tear down the establishment on their behalf, toppling "a rigged system" and a "swamp" that were destroying the America they loved.

When the dust settled on November 9, 2016, a nation of political junkies was exhausted, the mainstream media were in shock, and democracy seemed to be broken beyond repair. This is the story of how we got there—and how we might fix it.

THE POLITICAL NEWSLETTER

On November 2, 1952, the day before the *Daily Compass*, New York's last left-wing, subscriber-supported newspaper, printed its farewell edition, editor Joe Barnes called each of his writers individually to tell them the bad news. A successor to the *Star* and *PM*, the *Compass* was part of a grand experiment in progressive publishing that had lasted only a dozen years. Underwritten by philanthropists like Marshall Field, Anita McCormick Blaine, and Corliss Lamont, these newspapers had been part of an alternative journalism experiment: producing news that was supported by readers and unbeholden to corporate advertisers. But even subsidized by progressive millionaires, with only 30,000 subscribers, the *Daily Compass* had struggled to meet its expenses from the beginning. Every time it broke even, as publisher Ted Thackrey told readers earlier that year, "the rising living costs of our employees, which are of course translated into higher wages, have forced us back into the red."[1]

Alternative journalism in New York City seemed to be failing. Its financial problems were accelerated by declining popular, and government, tolerance for the Communist, socialist, and Popular Front politics that these papers promoted and that had flourished in New York before World War II. By 1952, two years after Senator

Joseph McCarthy had waved a scrap of white paper at the Republican Women's Club of Wheeling, West Virginia, to warn that the State Department was infiltrated by Reds, the purge of so-called radicals in broadcast and print media was well underway. This informal blacklist meant that the veteran journalists released by an unapologetically leftist paper like the *Daily Compass* would struggle to find another employer willing to take a chance on them. If an editor dared to hire one, it was likely that a pair of FBI agents would show up to explain why the decision should be reversed. One of the men fired by Barnes that day, Isidor Feinstein Stone, probably knew when he hung up the phone that this would be his fate: he was already under government surveillance. Known to his readers as "I. F. Stone" and to friends as Izzy, he had been a popular editorial and opinion writer at the *New York Post* and the *Nation* before working for Barnes at the *Daily Compass*.[2]

Despite their accommodation to anti-Communism, and even their willingness to fire accomplished, progressive writers, editors and publishers remained under intense pressure to report news that hewed to McCarthy's conservative populist reality. One tactic the senator from Wisconsin used to harass the press was to intimidate individual reporters from papers that opposed the government's hunt for subversives. At his rallies around the country, the pugnacious senator regularly depicted journalists from prestigious newspapers as enemies of the American people. One regular ritual at these raucous events was to ask a reporter to rise and show the audience "what a reporter from a communist paper looks like." This would prompt the crowd to turn and rain a chorus of boos on the entire press section. As one blacklisted journalist remembered, the range of tactics used to root out subversion and principled opposition took its toll: with a few exceptions, by 1952, the mainstream media had become conformist and largely uncritical in its approach to political reporting.[3]

Urban journalism was also becoming financially vulnerable. Advertising dollars, like newspaper readers, were migrating to the suburbs. When office workers boarded morning trains for New York City from their freshly built, ice cream–colored tract houses in Long Island and New Jersey, they were more likely to have one of the new, local papers touting President Dwight D. Eisenhower's moderate Republican politics, with ads from stores in the local shopping mall, tucked under an arm. The loss of these readers, and the advertising revenue they brought with them, was compounded by a new competitor to legacy newspapers: television. Occupying pride of place in living rooms everywhere, for fifteen minutes every evening, TVs delivered digestible bites of national news, summarizing top newspaper stories, to nearly every home. By 1960, the number of major dailies feeding New York's appetite for news was trimmed to ten; two major strikes would cut that number to four a decade later. Newspapers were dying.[4]

Yet, if advertising dollars were the Achilles' heel of the mainstream press, could refusing corporate advertising still be a model for financing alternative media? Izzy Stone, a reporter's reporter, thought it could, particularly if labor and production costs were low and the product was good. Infuriating to some, beloved by others, rumpled, pudgy Izzy, prematurely deaf and wearing Coke-bottle-thick glasses, was a ball of energy. Unable to compete for attention in, or report accurately from, a press conference because of his disabilities, Stone's specialty was crafting stories from public, government documents that other journalists had no time to find or digest, a form of reporting that also freed him from cultivating entangling alliances with politicians and their staffs. Some of Stone's best qualities as a journalist were infuriating to employers. He insisted on writing the story he wanted to write, regardless of what editors, publishers, and advertisers thought. He was so bullheaded that even Freda Kirchwey at the *Nation*, a left-wing weekly news and opinion magazine almost a century old, had fired him for good in 1947 after he disappeared for several weeks. It turned out he had gone undercover on a Mediterranean freighter for a story about Holocaust survivors being illegally smuggled to Palestine.[5]

After beating the bushes for work, Stone took a step over the cliff: he decided to found and self-finance his own newsletter. Combining his savings with a $3,500 check from the *Daily Compass*, he launched *I. F. Stone's Weekly*, a four-page publication without advertisers whose editorial independence would be supported by reader subscriptions. Unlike the *Daily Compass*, Stone would have only two employees: himself and his wife, Esther. The idea had worked at least once before. In 1940, disgusted with newspaper publishers' subservience to politicians and advertising's "dirty dollars," veteran journalist George Seldes launched the four-page alternative paper *In Fact: An Antidote for Falsehood in the Daily Press*. A reader-supported newsletter, it went out of business in 1950, boasting 176,000 subscribers at its peak. Seldes researched and wrote most of the stories himself; other features came from journalists whose work had been spiked by their own editors (and by advertisers). Part investigative reporter, part newspaper watchdog, in 1941, Seldes became the first journalist to report on a pathbreaking scientific study about the dangers of cigarette smoking.[6]

As he began to plan the *Weekly*'s first issues, Stone knew three things. He knew that he had to make a living; that he needed an outlet for his writing; and that inspiring conversations about politics was an urgent national task, particularly in the midst of McCarthy's war on the media. Stone had start-up money: his severance from the *Daily Compass*. He had an office: the Washington townhouse where he and his wife, Esther (now his production manager), lived. He had a delivery service: a third-class license from the United States Postal Service. He had potential subscribers: lists borrowed and begged from prior employers and at least one union. And most of all, Stone had readers, admirers acquired through a lifetime of writing for the progressive press. On November 25, 1952, a small, paid advertisement appeared on the front page of the *New York Times*. "Former Compass Readers Attention," the headline read, announcing a four-page, advertising-free newsletter that would arrive in subscribers' mailboxes on January 27. "Exciting, exclusive reporting from Washington and independent, hard-hitting commentary," it read. "Send $5 for one yr. sub."[7]

Incredibly, the envelopes began to arrive in the Stones' mailbox. As Esther opened them one by one, coupons, checks, and five-dollar bills piled up on the dining room table. *I. F. Stone's Weekly*, the little newsletter that would bring an audience of left-wing political junkies together and inspire a new generation of journalists, was born.

I. F. Stone's Weekly, as its founder surely knew, followed on a centuries-long tradition of American political dissent that began before the American Revolution. In the eighteenth century, pamphlets and broadsheets were the principal media alternative to the official proclamations handed down by the King of England and his colonial governors.[8] Throughout the nineteenth and twentieth centuries, the newsletter—in its self-conscious ambition to compel an existing audience motivated by ideas, its capacity to urge its community of readers to raise their own voices and take collective action, and its use of public mail—was quintessentially democratic in its design. It was particularly suited to the two decades after World War II, years during which social minorities who lacked the economic or political clout to make themselves heard in the mainstream press were organizing for rights. Produced on typewriters for small audiences, or on mimeograph machines for larger ones, African American civil rights activists and organizations reported to sympathetic Northern audiences about the fight against segregation and racial violence; pseudonymous lesbian and gay activists sought to dispel public myths about their sexuality; and pacifists warned about the dangers of global nuclear proliferation.[9]

As alternative media, newsletters were cheap and often claimed to counter misinformation spread by, or absent from, mainstream media sources. They were written in a personal voice by a trusted source, could be obtained anywhere the United States Postal Service delivered, and were often passed hand-to-hand by readers. The same year that the *Weekly* launched, the homophile organization One, Inc. inaugurated its own newsletter. The group eventually won a landmark free speech case in 1958 when the Supreme Court ruled that it was not inherently obscene to write about, or use the mail to distribute, information concerning homosexuality. The decision shielded other homophile newsletters as well, including the *Mattachine Review*, founded in 1955 to promote the civil and social rights of gay men; and the *Ladder*, a lesbian newsletter founded in 1956. All of these publications, the beginnings of lesbian and gay political media, were supported by volunteer labor, subscriptions, and classified ads taken out by readers hoping to join a community and share ideas.[10]

Although the stigma of homosexuality was different from the political blacklisting that inspired the *Weekly*, homophile publications took on a similar task: disseminating facts about homosexuality to counter misinformation circulated by the political, legal, and scientific establishment.[11] These newsletters were written by self-appointed experts: homosexuals themselves, and a few medical professionals who believed that same-sex desire was a variation on human sexuality. Homophile publications established a privileged, trusting, and personal relationship to their audience by promising them truth. "We earnestly hope that the MATTACHINE REVIEW will go a long way toward giving readers the true facts of the Mattachine Society," the first issue promised in 1955 on its front page. "The truth—good or bad—will be the policy of the REVIEW in helping to make everyone cognizant of the facts."[12]

Where did Izzy Stone and his newsletter fit in this emerging world of dissident and marginalized voices? In the words of one contemporary, Stone was the "quintessential outsider who spent his life with his face pressed up against the window." Perhaps: the child of immigrants, Stone regretted his lack of formal education. His exile from newspapers in 1952 was, he later admitted, isolating. But in other ways, Stone was very much a product of the pre-1950s mainstream journalism milieu, a place where hustle mattered as much as brains and a reporter was more likely to start as a copy boy and move up the ranks than to attend college. Born in 1907, in Haddonfield, New Jersey, Stone began his writing career as a teenager, first as a stringer at the *Haddonfield Public Press* and then at the Camden, New Jersey, *Evening Courier*. By the time he graduated from high school in 1924, Stone was already a self-identified radical and smitten by newspapers. In his first year at the University of Pennsylvania, he went straight to work for the *Philadelphia Inquirer*. Within two years he had married, dropped out of college, and plunged into journalism full-time. By 1939, as Europe was going to war, Stone was an editorial writer at the progressive *New York Post*. Ineligible for the draft because of his age and disabilities, he climbed the career ladder rapidly, sometimes holding several jobs simultaneously. After World War II, Stone became the Washington correspondent for the *Nation*, while writing daily columns first for *PM*, then the *Star*, and finally, the *Daily Compass*.[13]

After founding *I. F. Stone's Weekly*, Stone would never work for anyone else again except, as he would say, his readers. Although he badly missed the camaraderie of a newsroom, the horizontal connection between reporter and subscriber was perfect for the free-thinking Stone. Unmediated by an editor, a corporate style guide, or an advertiser's garish demand for attention, his stories went straight to the reader. "A personal word is in order," Stone wrote on page three of the debut issue, published on January 17, 1953. "I feel as if I am going to work for the best people in the U.S.A." He would choose a few stories to research deeply each week, and he had faith that even at a time when conformity seemed to be the rule, good investigative journalism had a small but vital audience among Americans devoted to politics. There remained "a substratum of good sense and good will in this country," he wrote, "that there are still people willing to listen to an opposing point of view, if fairly, accurately, and soberly presented."[14]

This kind of personal connection, and a confidence in the subscriber's desire for the whole story, rather than the mainstream media's selective editorial choices, would come to characterize the alternative media sensibility. So did good storytelling. Stone's political insights, drawn from Capitol Hill rumors, government documents, and lengthy congressional transcripts, were dense with facts and woven into compelling narratives. Working on one or two stories at a time, Stone had a nose for government documents and read them with scholarly precision. While other journalists scrambled to meet daily deadlines, be recognized at press conferences, and get answers from busy politicians and their aides, Stone spent days deciphering official reports, economic data, and the *Congressional Record*. Producing one main feature and two or three smaller items every week, he often returned to the same issues, reporting a story more deeply over time, following up, and approaching it from different angles.[15]

Stone adapted investigative journalism and opinion writing into something both familiar and different. Designed for lay readers who were unsatisfied with the stilted, objective voice of main-stream journalism, the *Weekly*'s rich four pages also soon appealed to Stone's colleagues in newsrooms around the country.[16] Beginning with a clear articulation of the mainstream media or government perspective on a given issue, Stone would then dismantle that story, not by asking politicians to respond or clarify what they had already obscured, but by bringing documented facts to the table about what had actually been said and done. Stone's writing had a relaxed but authoritative tone, offering a road map to how political decision-making occurred, as well as to sources that any persistent and knowledgeable citizen could obtain from the government. Well aware that independent journalism was too often associated with amateurism, or with gossip columnists and other syndicators whose work was based on planted tips, unconfirmed gossip, and paid informants, Stone emphasized that his independence freed him to share facts with his audience that politicians, advertisers, and editorial boards would prefer they not know. "By now you should have some idea of the kind of newspaper I am going to put out," Stone wrote in a text box on page three of the second edition. "Not the 'lowdown,' sensational even if untrue, but a sober analysis of facts too often left out or buried on the back pages of commercial newspapers."[17]

Stone had placed a bet on Cold War America: that a small, dedicated readership of freedom-loving citizens could support a newsletter that offered the unvarnished truth and would question authority.[18] He was correct. The first wave of subscribers to keep the *Weekly*, and the Stone family, afloat included former First Lady Eleanor Roosevelt and Nobel Laureate Albert Einstein. Movie star Marilyn Monroe bought a subscription for every member of Congress. Even J. Edgar Hoover, the Red-baiting director of the Federal Bureau of Investigation whose agents regularly reported on Izzy's mostly meaningless encounters with others, read *I. F. Stone's Weekly* surreptitiously, obtaining it through subscriptions taken out by others. By the fifth issue, a buoyant Stone could report that "People seem[ed] to like" his new enterprise, not just in the United States, but abroad. English pacifist Bertrand Russell was an early supporter, and by late spring, Stone announced that he had subscribers in all fifty states and a dozen countries, including Japan, Poland, and Hungary. Over the next two decades, while the *Weekly* never equaled George Seldes's numbers, adherents rose steadily. When Stone ceased publication in 1971, he had a respectable 73,000 subscribers, more than enough to support what he called "the old-fashioned poppa-momma grocery store." The staff never grew larger than five, including Esther, Izzy, and at least one college graduate starting out in journalism who wanted to grow up to be some version of Izzy Stone.[19]

An aspect of *I. F. Stone's Weekly* that would come to first differentiate alternative from mainstream media, and then represent a distinctive contribution to commercial journalism more generally, was its pace and its transparency. Stone deliberately slowed the news cycle down, guiding readers through the intellectual process by which a policy paper, a piece of legislation, or a set of documents became a story. In-depth features were complemented by vividly written short pieces that conveyed the excitement of politics and the fun of producing the news. Exchanges on the floor of the House and Senate, or snapshots of life in the heart of the federal government, allowed readers to intuit the nuances of politics, its daily events and decision-making. Some of these sketches also conveyed humorous insights into the *Weekly*'s own operations. "Our research assistant" (probably Esther) "had occasion to go to the Senate last week to page a Senator off the floor," Stone related in one issue. Looking at her card, the page ("cute, she says") asked was that *the* I. F. Stone, who used to write for the *Compass*? "'Gee, he's a terrific writer,' said the page, and was off before our girl could do more than flutter her eye-lashes [*sic*] at him."[20] This otherwise unimportant little story, probably written to fill an empty inch or two, was a funny interlude: but it reminded readers that only Izzy Stone could bring them straight to the heart of government.

This interlude, and others like it, alerted readers that what the *Weekly* lacked in staff and resources, it made up for in the star power of a reporter who may have been kicked to the curb by the mainstream media, but was well known, and well connected, in the Capitol. If Stone could not compete effectively with the comprehensive national and global news coverage that commercial newspapers could provide, a leaner paper with a high focus on a few stories could do a better investigative job than larger papers, particularly when the reporter had good sources.[21] Stone was broadly known and admired in Washington and, as one biographer put it, "shamelessly and happily hustled himself and his product" there. By putting his name in the newsletter's title, he and the *Weekly* became a single authority, a branding technique that numerous bloggers and alternative internet journalists like Matt Drudge, Arianna Huffington, Taegan Goddard, and Andrew Breitbart would later imitate.[22]

The ripple effect from *I. F. Stone's Weekly* was almost immediate. At a moment when newspapers and newsmagazines were still clinging to objectivity, the newsletter adopted an unabashedly partisan stance. Critiques generated on the left, Stone established, were a legitimate place from which to question authority. Thus, the *Weekly* led the way for other alternative media experiments that rebelled against political conformity. Radicals, conservatives, liberals, and countercultural movements also began to publish and broadcast their own news, relying on devoted subscribers that they cultivated through mailing lists, newspaper coupons, radio appearances, and content tuned to readers who were passionate about politics. One of these publications, founded in 1954 by a group of left-wing New York writers and scholars, named itself *Dissent*, and its purpose "to dissent from the bleak atmosphere of conformism that pervades the political and intellectual life of the United States." *Dissent's* politics "would be radical," its tradition "the tradition of democratic socialism," founders Irving Howe, Lewis Coser, Henry Pachter, Norman Mailer, and Meyer Schapiro declared. Mailer, a popular and iconoclastic novelist, would also, along with psychologist Ed Fancher and others, found a new alternative newspaper to cover New York's downtown political and cultural scene. On October 26, 1955, the *Village Voice*, a seven-page "weekly newspaper designed to be read," published its first issue for 5 cents. It did take advertising from downtown movie theaters and cheap furniture stores—along with a back section devoted to classified ads, apartments for rent, and thinly veiled sex work—that supported its left-wing local and national political news coverage for the next sixty years.[23]

In this way, *I. F. Stone's Weekly* helped to launch postwar alternative media in the United States and pave the way for the New Left newsletters and pamphlets that would flourish in the 1960s.[24] One important innovation was to take a proactive stance toward the issues of the day, writing stories about topics that politicians and government officials preferred to downplay or obscure. Setting the news agenda, Stone could take on grand political questions, working on them for as many issues as he liked and publishing in readable, well-researched bites. For example, in 1958, Stone promised to devote himself for the "next five years to the fight for peace," which he believed was "the most important cause of the contemporary era." Using publicly available documents, he reported on the military's nuclear program, not just exposing the cover stories purveyed about the extent and consequences of testing, but also explaining how the government lied. In a series of reports on the Joint Committee on Atomic Energy, Stone noted that statements by this committee were a prime example of the "art of public misinformation," since they "create[d] a false impression by the facts they omitted."[25]

Stone did not work entirely alone. Like Seldes, he was adept at locating public reports, but he was also steered to them by a network of old Washington friends. He received stories and tips from mainstream journalists who knew they wouldn't get them into print at their own publications. But being self-employed gave Stone a protected platform from which to develop a sustained and consistent critique of the political and media establishment. Both politicians and mainstream journalists, he implied, were untrustworthy because each was invested in propping up the other's credibility. Stone was also able to create a new political space on the left that was critical of Soviet-style Communism and articulated American democracy as a radical place from which to critique the Red Scare. "The very fact that I can speak and write as I do," despite McCarthyism, Stone declared in 1953, was proof that the Constitution was strong.[26]

By the 1960s, the civil rights and antiwar movements were making ever more radical demands on the political establishment. Simultaneously, Stone's insistence that analysis and fact-finding were necessary to social change spoke to a new generation of political journalists who wanted to cover those movements and who chafed under their editors' insistence on regurgitating government briefings. The neutral stance imposed on them, many reporters believed, kept necessary information promoted by radical activists, including facts that contradicted, or added complexity to, the official story, out of the newspaper. By the 1960s, younger journalists looked to *I. F. Stone's Weekly* as a model for resistance. As the *Weekly* demonstrated, investigative journalism could change politics by intentionally including the reporter's expertise, authority, and political commitments as part of a story that exposed government lies.[27]

There is no better example of this younger generation than Seymour "Sy" Hersh. Introduced to Stone's work by his mother-in-law in 1964, Hersh was restless and bored with his job writing for the Associated Press. He was, in his own words, "wowed" by the quality of Stone's work—its depth, its bold take on the foreign policy quagmire developing in Vietnam, the lies being told by the administration, and the mainstream press's failure to question those lies. "There was no mystery to how Stone did it," Hersh recalled. "He outworked every journalist in Washington." The two became friends in 1966. As Hersh himself became more outspoken about his opposition to the war, Stone's friendship sustained him, but also helped him understand how the journalism establishment marginalized those who broke the tacit compact not to embarrass the government. "If you supported the war you were objective," Hersh remembered; "if you were against it you were a lefty—like I. F. Stone—and not trustworthy." Hersh soon got his chance to become untrustworthy. In the fall of 1969, a military whistleblower called columnist Geoffrey Cowan at the *Village Voice* to report that the military had covered up a massacre at a village called My Lai. Cowan passed it on to Hersh, who was freelancing in Washington. The resulting story, about 109 civilians murdered in cold blood at the orders of United States military officers, was syndicated to 33 newspapers and won the Pulitzer Prize in 1970.[28]

Journalists like Hersh were emboldened by Stone's insistence that official documents, produced by the people's representatives, should be available for public conversations that exposed government wrongdoing. As domestic resistance to the war in Vietnam escalated, they argued with editors and publishers that mainstream newspapers had an obligation to investigate and expose a violent conflict framed as a defense of democracy. In 1971, reporter Neil Sheehan persuaded his editors at the *New York Times* that the paper had a moral duty to publish the so-called Pentagon Papers, top-secret documents copied and stolen by defense intellectual Daniel Ellsberg, even though it was likely to instigate a lawsuit by the Nixon administration (which it did). A *New York Times* team published a hard-hitting set of articles about the war and efforts to hide its failure from the American public on June 14, and four days later, the *Washington Post* followed suit.[29]

Yet this triumph of reporting, which resulted in a landmark Supreme Court case establishing the right of the *New York Times* to act in the public interest by publishing the stolen, classified documents, also exposed stubborn tensions between mainstream journalists and their editors. The paper's editors did not want to be mistaken for Stone, who they regarded as an activist, and because their reporters were using his techniques they might have been. In the forward to a mass-market paperback containing the Pentagon Papers, foreign desk editor James Greenfield emphasized that even though it strengthened the case against the war, the presentation of the Pentagon Papers had still been objective. The seven-person team that had produced the series "made sure that every sentence written corresponded to a reference in one of the documents," Greenfield wrote. "Adding one's own reporting was unacceptable."[30]

Editors like Greenfield were walking a tight line between acting in the interests of an increasingly antiwar public and clinging to an objective ideal that forbade any expression of antiwar sentiment. Conservatives working for the mainstream press chafed under restrictions too. For this reason, conservative populist readers were also turning to alternative political media, publications that came to be defined in the coming decades by the premise that the "liberal" mainstream media always suppressed and misrepresented conservative ideas. But mainstream conservatives voiced this sentiment as well. While he fell short of calling it a conspiracy, former president Dwight Eisenhower articulated this resentment on the floor of the 1964 Republican nominating convention, while

Eisenhower's vice president, Richard Nixon, made war with the liberal press a recurring theme of his career.[31]

Conservative alternative journalists picked up on these themes, but unlike Stone, viewed their work as a way to fuel a political movement. Long before Nixon reached out to a "silent majority" of conservatives, conservative populists envisioned a community of activist readers that, properly informed and mobilized, would take over the Republican Party, seize the government from corrupt elites, and return it to the people.[32] A classic example of this is Phyllis Schlafly's *A Choice Not an Echo*, a short, self-published pamphlet that Schlafly, at the time a young Republican activist and housewife, sold out of her garage in Alton, Illinois, during the 1964 presidential campaign. A critique of American internationalism and the welfare state, Schlafly's central question for her readers was why, with so many conservative populists in the GOP demanding change, their party routinely nominated moderates. The answer, she told them, was "the kingmakers." Globalist rather than nationalist, this political establishment of largely East Coast corporate leaders rigged politics, Schlafly charged, to serve their interests. These "secret groups of persons" moved in and out of government; traveled around the country and the world on private planes; and leveraged elections by "meeting secretly to make important plans that they do not reveal to the public."[33] The way to stop them, she argued, was for grassroots conservatives to rally around Arizona Senator Barry Goldwater.

For conservatives, alternative media were defined by complete freedom, not just from the government, but from the intellectual and business establishments. For example, Schlafly sought to replicate the successes of populist authors like John Stormer and J. Evetts Haley, who used direct mail appeals to put their books straight into interested readers' hands.[34] Similarly, after sending a few hundred free copies of her book to influencers, Schlafly was inundated with orders from Goldwater activists around the country. In two months, she sold and shipped (with the help of her husband and children) 1.6 million copies of the book, using the family garage as a staging area. As a not insignificant side effect, the experience also left her with 1.6 million addresses, the beginnings of a formidable conservative mailing list.[35]

A second, and more obvious difference, between right and left alternative media was that while *I. F. Stone's Weekly* operated in the absence of a left establishment decimated by McCarthyism, writers like Schlafly often reflected and elaborated on points of view that were routinely promoted by right-wing politicians like McCarthy, published on the editorial pages of conservative newspapers, and funded by corporate conservative sponsors. Stone's output was confined to the newsletter and, by the late 1960s, the occasional guest appearance on radio or television. But as we will see in chapter 3, conservative alternative media outlets had been well financed by businessmen since the 1930s. In these enterprises, newsletters were not the heart of an alternative media enterprise: they were a supplement to broadcasts and paid personal appearances by right-wing stars.[36]

Conservative alternative media's populist bent gradually became its signature feature. Its mission was to mobilize activists through creating political division, often around religion and race. In the 1950s, many older conservatives would have vividly recalled the radio priest Charles Coughlin, whose newsletter and weekly Sunday program—anti-Semitic, anti-capitalist, anti-Communist, isolationist, and, eventually, pro-Fascist—was wildly popular and lucrative until it was shut down by the government as a national security threat in 1939.[37] In 1964, concerned about the resurgence of these tendencies on the right, the Anti-Defamation League (ADL) began to assign staffers to monitor a growing number of far-right alternative media entrepreneurs. The resulting study described the rise of two distinct groups of conservatives: a populist "Radical Right," typified by extreme rhetoric, distrust of political parties, anti-Semitism, and virulent racism; and a non-populist group of "Extreme Conservatives," alternative political media professionals whose education, class background, and comfort with established political parties made them appear to be more mainstream.[38]

Yet both groups were propagandists, the ADL investigators argued: they were conspiratorial and promoted anti-Communism, isolationism, racism, and anti-Semitism. "Since 1960," the ADL concluded, "the Radical Right and the Extreme Conservatives have been pouring millions of dollars into a propaganda campaign aimed at influencing public opinion, often by disseminating pure fright along with distrust of respected American leaders and institutions."[39] The audience for their work, the study pointed out, was also voting. In Wisconsin's 1962 primaries, the extremist John Birch Society had fielded two candidates; and in 1964, five "Birchers" had won ballot lines in California. When, in 1962, a group of Ohio ministers had tried to get conservative populist Carl McIntyre's broadcasts dropped from the local station, 2,500 supporters showed up at a protest rally, with chartered buses bringing listeners from all over the state, as well as from western Pennsylvania.[40]

Conservative media outlets were often backed by wealthy donors. The most successful "extreme right" outlet, William F. Buckley's *National Review*, was supported by the Buckley family fortune, losing money nearly every year and officially becoming a nonprofit in 2015. While conservative alternative media entrepreneurs had paying subscribers, they did not rely on them as *I. F. Stone's Weekly* did. Some also made lucrative careers as political speakers and writers, raking in small donations from thousands of fans. A rally supporting populist radio activist Carl McIntyre raised $4,000 for him in one day. A squad of radio ministers in McIntyre's national network had to bring in a certain sum every month, or they would be dropped. Indiana's Dean Clarence Manion was a similar success story. A former constitutional law professor, America Firster, and member of the John Birch Society, Manion incorporated *The Manion Forum* in late 1954 to oppose Communism, unions, domestic "super-duper planners of the brave new world," and desegregation. Manion had a newsletter, as well as syndicated radio and television shows that were broadcast on local stations. He also published seven books between 1954 and 1964, available by subscription and advertised on his other platforms. In 1963, *The Manion Forum* added youth outreach, offering free prerecorded broadcasts to college and university stations.[41]

Conservative alternative media entrepreneurs were invested in recruiting new listeners and readers, weaving them into a political community. Manion's audience may also have been listening to, reading, and watching Dan Smoot, whose authority was amplified by his previous vocation serving America's top conservative, J. Edgar Hoover. Smoot had begun his media career in 1951 with Texas oilman H. L. Hunt's *Facts Forum*, an operation that produced a newsletter, pamphlets, radio and television shows, and a circulating library of books that included the writing of Senator Joseph McCarthy. By 1964, Smoot had his own platform, broadcasting every week on over a hundred radio and TV stations and receiving $750 for lectures that were sometimes carried live on local TV. Bankrolled by Hunt, in 1955, Smoot launched a newsletter, *Dan Smoot Speaks*, later renamed the *Dan Smoot Report*, which was offered to Congress at a 25 percent discount.[42]

Unlike Stone, conservative populist alternative media entrepreneurs were not yet influencing mainstream journalism in the 1950s and 1960s. They did not have conventional credentials and were thus easy to deride as crackpot extremists. These right-wing voices were, as one report commissioned by the state of California put it, "little old ladies in tennis shoes," paranoid conspiracists wearing tinfoil hats to avert government mind control who believed that a secret network of enemies, buried deep in the bureaucracy of government, committed treason every day.[43]

Perhaps the closest cultural equivalent to Stone on this populist right was the erudite and Yale-educated Buckley, whose influence in publishing and broadcasting did penetrate the mainstream. After the spectacular success of his 1951 jeremiad against liberal higher education, *God and Man at Yale*, in addition to editing the *National Review*, Buckley wrote a weekly column syndicated in thirty-eight weekly newspapers. He made several media or personal appearances a week, in person as a lecturer or debater, or on television. Between 1957 and 1962, Buckley and his siblings purchased two radio stations, and in 1966, Buckley launched *Firing Line* on WOR-TV in New York, an influential show that moved to the Public Broadcasting Service in 1971.[44]

Unlike left alternative media, by the late 1950s, conservative alternative media networks were explicitly geared to organizing a national political movement to take back the government.[45] Newsletters were critical to this vision because each address represented at least one, if not two, voters. Subscription lists were bartered, sold, and consolidated, bringing the relationship between alternative conservative media and right-wing political organizing closer into alignment well before the rise of the New Right in the 1970s. For example, when oilman E. Howard Hunt folded *Facts Forum News* in 1962, the newsletter *Human Events* absorbed his subscription list. Everyone on that list received an invitation to *Human Events'* biannual "Political Action Conferences," launched in 1957, which offered discounted rates to students, teachers, and conservative youth groups. There, an emerging conservative populist grass roots listened to, and mingled with, influential politicians and activists. In 1963, featured speakers included Barry Goldwater, Strom Thurmond, and Dean Manion's daughter Marilyn.[46]

The divide between left and right, as it was beginning to emerge in postwar alternative media, hinged on whether or not the American political system itself was a hoax. Whereas Stone used dissent to make an argument for perfecting American democracy as it existed, conservative populist media figures argued that democracy was a sham and that politicians hoarded power that rightly belonged to the people.[47] This difference, in and of itself, created radically different facts about such things as racial discrimination. "For years," the square-jawed Smoot asserted in one angry 1964 broadcast, civil rights leaders had *claimed* that they sought to eliminate race consciousness, but now liberals were proposing affirmative action programs. "They now admit they *want* racial discrimination in favor of Negroes," Smoot asserted, setting "the American Constitution aside in favor of giving preferential treatment to Negroes."[48] Smoot named the tactic "discrimination in reverse," a program that would steal opportunities from whites.[49]

But there was also one important similarity between left and right. To be indignant about things as they were, to seek a personal connection with like-minded thinkers, and to view the mainstream press as part of a corporate political media establishment committed to the status quo defined what alternative media was by the late 1960s. Freed from the need to woo advertisers or to please the publishers who needed advertisers, alternative media told a story of citizens empowered by knowledge and inspired by the search for the nation that *could be*, if only the truth were told. "I never had to write a word I did not believe," Stone recalled later about the *Weekly*. "I was allowed to fight for whatever cause won my heart and mind." More importantly, across the political spectrum, alternative media producers believed in their readers' intelligence and their desire for truth. It was "more important than ever that this story be told," Schlafly wrote in the closing paragraphs of *A Choice Not an Echo*. "Only in this way will the average voter be prepared for the propaganda onslaught that will be activated by the king-makers against Goldwater."[50]

Alternative media would become ever more influential as the liberal consensus of the 1950s crumbled. Radical movements on the left and the right began to look for intellectual guidance as they confronted what they viewed as an establishment—the government, universities, political parties, churches, and media—that was failing. As Phyllis Schlafly was mailing *A Choice Not an Echo* (1964), Izzy Stone had already turned his critical eye to the United States troops being deployed to Vietnam, an investigation that would bring him to the attention of a new generation of young, mainstream journalists like Sy Hersh.[51] Stone anticipated the general revulsion for the war that would spike as United States violence escalated. "The history of Indochina since the war has been a history of lost opportunities," Stone began, in a double issue published on October 28, 1963, that confronted the failures of the United States foreign policy establishment. The intervention in Vietnam had been "reactive" and not a product of constructive diplomacy. It was a history of bad policies and promises broken, a war that could not be won, "and could, at any time, expand dangerously."[52]

Stone's Vietnam coverage made him "a hero to the young," as one reader remembered it, bringing him a new generation of subscribers who seized on the newsletter to get their own truths before the public. The *Liberation News Service*, founded in a Washington, DC, townhouse by student journalists Ray Mungo and Marshall Bloom in 1967, "viewed Stone and the *Weekly* as models for the underground publications they had established a syndicate for." Five years after it was founded in response "to the incomplete and distorted coverage of the 1967 Pentagon March," *LNS* had grown from a single mimeographed sheet to twenty pages of graphics and articles. Some articles were aggregated from smaller alternative outlets, while original reporting about domestic labor struggles and human rights violations in Vietnam drew the praise of established alternative journalists like Jack Newfield and Izzy Stone. While it only numbered 800 subscribers in 1972, like other New Left alternative newspapers, many copies of *LNS* were passed hand to hand in coffeehouses and prisons, and on military bases.[53]

As government policy became more contradictory, liberal and left readers flocked to Stone as a credible source who reflected, and spoke to, their dismay about the war: subscription numbers doubled by the end of the decade. By 1970, the *Weekly* was still alternative, but no longer marginal to political debates. Journalists named it the fifth most influential publication reporting about Vietnam.[54] Stone's work, written for the people who would be called political junkies two decades later, was not just popular because of rising antiwar sentiment, but because it was exclusively dedicated to telling well-researched truths at a moment when trust in the establishment was collapsing. He did his job so well that the influence of *I. F. Stone's Weekly* seeped back into the mainstream, providing a model for generations of journalists who would use Stone's investigative techniques to change mainstream political coverage. Fifty years later, practitioners of a new digital alternative media form would also look back on Stone's accomplishments and claim him as their godfather. "If he had lived long enough," Stone's granddaughter wrote on her own blog the day after his 2008 funeral, Izzy would have been a blogger. "The targeted, partisan nature of blog readership," she wrote, "would have made a blog the natural heir to the *Weekly*."[55]

As the alternative media world he had helped to create expanded, and mainstream journalists adopted his techniques, Stone's "momma poppa store" was closing down. In 1968, he slowed to a biweekly schedule, and in December 1971, Izzy and Esther dropped their final issue off at the printer. With a nod to the importance of the federal post office as his distributor, Stone also credited simplicity as an important factor in the *Weekly*'s success. "I decided to do a radical paper in conservative format, with lovely typography," he wrote, "to eschew sensational headlines, to document what I had to say from governmental and standard sources," he wrote. "I wanted a paper which a campus reader, in the hostile atmosphere of that time, could pass on to a conservative colleague, without having it dismissed as just another hysterical rag. People on the other side might not agree but, if they read me at all, would have to take my findings and analysis seriously." But perhaps Stone's most important contribution to alternative media was his direct and trusting connection to readers who, like him, were fascinated by politics. "The early years were lonely," he wrote about his exile from the journalism establishment, but after founding the *Weekly*, he said, "No one ever had a more loving audience."[56]

Could that "loving audience" also be assembled in another medium? Robert MacNeil, a young television news reporter from Canada who had worked for both BBC radio and television and NBC's television news division, thought it could—and that the future of American democracy might even depend on it.

But first, they had to get rid of the advertising. And that meant reimagining television news itself.

= 2 =

PUBLIC BROADCASTING

In the fall of 2019, Robert MacNeil and I sat in his dining room, the hub of a prewar New York apartment filled with light and books. I asked him to recall the summer of 1973, when he and Jim Lehrer anchored gavel-to-gavel coverage of the Watergate hearings. Hosted by the Public Broadcasting Service (PBS), the hours of questions and witness testimony, with interviews and analysis during the breaks, compelled millions of viewers. The hearings ended with President Richard Nixon's resignation, something that had never happened before in American history. But they also cemented a partnership between the two newsmen around a shared vision for an alternative to mainstream television news that built on the achievements of public television. It was also the culmination of MacNeil's long journey toward producing news with integrity, a career that had taken him from Canada, to England, and then to the United States. During Watergate summer, MacNeil and Lehrer worked sixteen-hour days, broadcasting a constitutional crisis. Driving back to their homes in Bethesda, Maryland, together after a full day of broadcasting, they would go over what had transpired. "And we would say after John Dean or somebody had really begun to spill the beans"—MacNeil laughed—"'My God, can you believe we're being paid to do this work?'"[1]

Seven years earlier, the Canadian-born MacNeil had not been having fun. An NBC correspondent, he was in the midst of an existential crisis about what, and who, mainstream television news was for, other than to sell advertising for major media corporations. In the summer of 1966, as he was driving his family to the beach, this crisis crystallized. A hearse carrying a flag-covered coffin merged into traffic and traveled side by side with his own car for several miles. The vehicle might have been transporting any veteran, a policeman, or a firefighter. Instead, MacNeil imagined that it was one of the many casualties he saw each week as he combed through battlefield footage for his two-minute nightly segment on Vietnam.[2]

Close to a hundred coffins arrived from Vietnam every week. Why, MacNeil wondered, wasn't the human cost of the war on television? In the next few days, MacNeil and the production staff stumbled onto a monstrous piece of film: American soldiers "pulling safety razors out of their knapsacks and slicing the ears off dead Vietcong, a habit they'd picked up from the Montagnard tribesmen," MacNeil recalled. "We all said, 'Oh God, look at that.' We said, 'Well, we can't run that at suppertime,'" since many Americans watched the news with dinner. Executives agreed that the footage did not belong on the air, although "six months later Walter Cronkite did put the same thing on," MacNeil noted. It would also be Cronkite who shook the political and media establishment on February 27, 1968, when, at the end of a one-hour report on Vietnam, he looked his audience in the eye and told them that it was his "subjective" view that the United States could not win the war.[3]

Cronkite's decision to make this statement may have accomplished what champions of objective journalism feared: he intervened in politics. President Lyndon Johnson was said to have told his aide Bill Moyers after the broadcast that if "I have lost Walter Cronkite, I have lost Middle America," and it cemented his decision not to run for reelection.[4] But Cronkite's frankness did not reveal the violence of a war that would drag on for another five years, nor did he discuss publicly the role television played in editing out its horrors. Few newsmen did. However, MacNeil recalled becoming privately obsessed with mainstream television news's complicity in producing a sanitized "living room war," even though NBC staff on the ground, and other reporters, were trying to get the story out. When a group of "extraordinarily brave cameramen" were caught in the midst of a firefight, MacNeil recalled, they kept filming, even as American shells—so-called friendly fire—screamed in on top of their position. One direct hit smashed a soldier's legs. The cameraman zoomed in on the victim, who was, MacNeil recalled, "lying facedown, screaming, trying to claw and bite his way into the earth." He and the editors were undone by it and understood why it could not be broadcast. But that also interfered in politics. By editing the scene out, they understood that "without intending to, we were making the war more bearable to watch."[5] Alternative journalists like Izzy Stone, freelancers like Sy Hersh, and even mainstream pictorials like *Life* were finding ways to get the story of Vietnam to their readers. Television, which reached the most Americans, was literally leaving crucial facts on the cutting room floor.[6]

Yet the rapidly growing alternative media world, and changes in investigative journalism inspired by alternative media, suggested there might be an audience for alternative television news too. Broadcasts that were not sanitized, that appealed to serious viewers, might be able to thrive on public television. The time, and the editorial independence, to produce alternative media would require getting out from under television's advertising structure and its perhaps equally profitable relationship with the political establishment. But unlike print alternatives, TV could not be produced easily and inexpensively from home, nor was there the equivalent of the state-subsidized British Broadcasting Corporation (BBC) or its Canadian equivalent, the CBC. American alternative broadcast media consisted of a single, as yet decentralized network, National Educational Television (NET). These public access channels, commanding very small, local audiences, were linked by satellite in 1954 and would not become the Public Broadcasting Service (PBS) until 1969. Even then, while PBS featured documentaries and a news roundtable, it had no nightly news show. Between 1965 and 1975, MacNeil would be among a group of mainstream journalists, critics of commercial broadcasting, who imagined and created this alternative world of television news. A not-for-profit model, it would seek to inform, not entertain. Based on in-depth interviews, investigative journalism, and lengthy conversations with experts, it would connect viewers straight to the sources of political news and then let them decide what to think.

MacNeil believed that public television provided a "genuine alternative to the business-oriented television which has dominated our screens" and that it could be a platform for the deep conversations about politics and world events that might have made a difference in ending the Vietnam War. Others had already taken steps in this direction. In 1967, NET had created the National Public Affairs Center for Television (NPACT) as a Washington news bureau, recruiting an award-winning reporter from the *Dallas Times Herald*, Jim Lehrer, to establish reporting and production standards. NPACT recruited other print and television journalists, creating *Washington Week in Review*, a show for viewers who wanted to dig more deeply into the week's newspaper headlines. The network also brought in programming produced by conservatives. In 1971, at the suggestion of a South Carolina affiliate, the network added William F. Buckley's *Firing Line*, a one-hour talk show where liberals and conservatives debated the issues of the day under Buckley's guidance, his head cocked back and a smile flickering around his mouth that anticipated, for viewers, a witty takedown. In the name of balanced debate, Buckley cannily persuaded liberal audiences to listen to the points of view promoted in conservative alternative media by putting his conservative guests in conversation with flamboyant representatives from the Black Power, women's liberation, and antiwar movements.[7]

However, PBS would not launch a real news show until 1975. That year, the fact that MacNeil and Lehrer's Watergate broadcasts had drawn unprecedented audiences persuaded the network that an interview-style show similar to what the pair had done during the hearing breaks could bring those viewers back. *The MacNeil/Lehrer Report* (today the *PBS NewsHour*), which debuted in 1975, wouldn't be for everyone. It would be for all of us who canceled a summer of swimming pools and sunshine to sit in front of the television, waiting for bureaucrats formerly unknown to us to reveal, as Senator Howard Baker famously put it, what the president knew and when he knew it. It was television for, as MacNeil told an interviewer in 1978, after *The MacNeil/Lehrer Report* was a breakout success, political news junkies.[8]

—

The Vietnam War was a turning point for MacNeil, as it was for many Americans, and it was also a turning point for the news. The war shook the journalism establishment, producing demands for reform that reflected a crisis of authority and the growing attention that alternative print media were paying to the causes of this political and foreign policy crisis. Izzy Stone quietly led the way, both in uncovering the facts of the war and in rebuking the mainstream media's complicity with the Johnson administration's false justifications for ramping up the US troop presence there. "The process of brainwashing the public," Stone wrote in 1964, began with "off-the-record briefings for newspapermen in which all sorts of far-fetched theories" were promoted by government officials and obediently conveyed to the public by reporters sent to cover the government's version of events.[9]

Until 1965, when the Berkeley Free Speech Movement and the March on Washington against the war both grabbed public attention, mainstream reporters were also cursory in their coverage of the antiwar movement. Radical organizers viewed journalists as condescending and even dangerous: for example, Black Panther Party activists were "typically portrayed in the media as thugs," Kathleen Cleaver, the group's communications secretary, recalled. Mainstream news stories ignored the ideas expressed in demonstrations activists had worked hard to organize. Instead, they tended to feature the reporter's journey to a strange America, where naive idealists wore ragged clothes, grew their hair, and sympathized with the Vietcong. Reporters, activists charged, deliberately undercounted attendance at demonstrations, overemphasized conflict in the movement, and—in a self-interested desire to seem objective— gave equal time to far less numerous, and sometimes decidedly marginal right-wing opponents.[10] Worst of all, in the eyes of these activists, commercial media covered for the political establishment's lies. When Black Panthers Fred Hampton and Mark Clark were murdered by a squad of Chicago police in 1969, reporters claimed that the dead men had initiated the shootout. "But we didn't buy the official story, even for a minute," white radical educator and former Weatherman Bill Ayers recalled.[11]

Because student radicals believed that the mainstream media channeled government propaganda, they immersed themselves in the rich collage of alternative media produced by comrades, and by disillusioned, feminist, gay, and countercultural journalists.[12] New Yorkers read the *Village Voice*, *Dissent*, *Rat*, the *Nation*, and the *East Village Other*; Californians read *Ramparts*, the *Black Panther*, and the *Berkeley Barb*; and nearly every university town had an array of its own feminist, queer, Marxist, Black Power, and insurgent alternative weeklies. All of these papers could be received by mail, with a several-day lag time, in other parts of the country; or be found in coffeehouses, where antiwar youth sometimes mingled with draftees stationed nearby. Any reader, politician, or journalist who wanted to understand the mobilization of radical youth would have also turned to the *Liberation News Service*, which viewed people embedded in the movement as the only qualified reporters.[13]

Mainstream reporters literally inhabited a different world from the alternative press. Many were well aware that their access to powerful men implied a quid pro quo from politicians who worked hard to cultivate them. MacNeil recalled that during his time covering President John F. Kennedy, as the press plane prepared for takeoff "flight attendants began dispensing the Bloody Marys that [were] traditional on press planes." Sometimes the deal was more explicitly tied to professional advancement. At one point, President Johnson pulled MacNeil and another reporter on the plane aside to promise that in return for positive coverage, he would pass on "special information" that would "make those guys up in New York think you're the smartest sons of bitches they've ever seen." Afterward, although MacNeil had not agreed to this arrangement, Johnson's press secretary Bill Moyers would contact him after his nightly appearances on the *NBC Evening News* to say that Johnson was either "pleased" with the segment or "awfully disappointed."[14]

MacNeil wasn't the only journalist who saw something wrong with this: so did a new, and more socially aware, generation of reporters. In Izzy Stone's day, most journalists had not finished, or even attended, college, but by the 1960s, a novice reporter was expected to have a bachelor's degree, had usually worked on a college paper, and would probably have come to the newsroom from a campus roiling with activism. By 1970, the mainstream news establishment was also beginning to hire women and people of color in significant numbers, some of whom had gotten their start freelancing for alternative papers and had activist pasts. Charlayne Hunter-Gault was hired by the *New York Times* in 1968 to cover the violent resistance to racism in African American urban communities. One of the first students to integrate the all-white University of Georgia in 1961, she was prosecuted by that state in 1963 for marrying a fellow student who was white.[15] These newcomers inaugurated "a quiet revolution" against mainstream news practices. As Gay Talese described it in 1969, while veteran editors and reporters at the *Times* "feared that the paper was losing touch with its tradition," younger journalists like Hunter-Gault and Sy Hersh "felt trapped" by such traditions, knowing that they were inadequate to the task of reporting on a rapidly changing culture, the New Left's challenge to the political establishment, and a political system in crisis.[16]

These younger journalists sometimes just walked away from establishment media in disgust. In June 1968, Joe McGinniss, a twenty-five-year-old reporter for the *Philadelphia Inquirer*, filed a story about Bobby Kennedy's assassination, bitterly describing the United States as a "cesspool." He arrived home a few days later to learn that the *Inquirer*'s publisher, Walter Annenberg, had written a column publicly apologizing for McGinniss's words. Angry, and sick of covering politics, McGinniss took a leave from his job and, to distract himself, went to New York City to write a profile about Howard Cosell for *TV Guide*. There, he ran into an advertising executive who proudly told McGinniss that he just landed "the Humphrey account." Thus, McGinniss learned that techniques invented to market commodities were now being used to market political candidates, creating a cynical new form of manufactured television "news"—without the journalism. By setting Vice President Hubert Humphrey up in realistic encounters with voters that were intended to make him seem sympathetic, the ad man planned to sell the Democratic presidential nominee to voters "like so much toothpaste or detergent."[17]

McGinniss quit his job to write about this ever-more-cynical bond between the media and political establishments. Although the Humphrey team rejected the idea, McGinniss arranged to shadow Harry Treleaven and Len Garment, ad men who were running a similar media blitz for Richard Nixon. Treleaven and Garment's challenge was to minimize the candidate's frequently hostile encounters with the press and his discomfort with voters, while, at the same time, conveying Nixon's carefully scripted views to a mainstream television audience. As he shadowed the team, McGinniss also met a charismatic, conservative media cowboy, Roger Ailes. Popular talk show host Mike Douglas's twenty-eight-year-old producer, Ailes would use his experience creating fake news for political campaigns to jump to CNBC in 1993, where he was instrumental in launching a second all-news cable channel, MSNBC. In 1996, he became the CEO of Fox News.[18] In 1968, Ailes's job was to create a series of talk shows around Nixon, organizing groups of "representative citizens" for live, televised conversations with the candidate based on scripted questions. Ailes, Treleaven, Garment, and Nixon's speechwriter Patrick Buchanan were simulating an in-depth news event, one that almost never occurred on a mainstream broadcast. They hoped it would persuade the audience that they had experienced actual news: an extended, candid experience with Nixon.[19]

While other political reporters speculated about whether the former vice president, returned from the political wilderness, was a "new" Nixon, McGinniss was privy to these alternative media strategy sessions. He saw, and published a post-election book about, the techniques by which mainstream journalists were manipulated by advertising and public relations professionals working for politicians. Nixon wasn't new, and he didn't need to be new. Instead, because his team had crafted a "new approach to television," a half-hour that simulated in-depth news coverage, the "new" candidate was a Nixon-like character, who, unlike the testy, unscripted Nixon, had been coached into being a plausibly pleasant human being. As Nixon's speechwriter Patrick Buchanan put it, to succeed, his boss only had to pretend that connecting with ordinary Americans was "one of the great joys of seeking the Presidency." He must never be tired, impatient, or dull, never offer complex explanations that would cause a bored viewer to switch the channel. Carefully rehearsed and focus group tested phrases could be repeated, "because they were not really answers," just statements that "were exactly the same, phrase for phrase, gesture for gesture, from state to state." Maintaining this illusion meant that Nixon also had to avoid actual television reporters, whose camera crews were permitted to film him no more than once a day.[20]

Published the year after the election, McGinniss's *The Selling of the President 1968* described how professionals produced the modern mediated candidate by simulating news events. In fact, these orchestrated television encounters and campaign speeches staged before an audience chosen to represent a diverse voting public had been evolving for over fifteen years. In 1952, Dwight Eisenhower's handlers organized them because unexpected questions made their candidate unusually incoherent, while the 1964 televised speech about Barry Goldwater that launched Ronald Reagan's political career was simply a rehashed version of one he had been giving to live audiences for years. In 1962, political historian Daniel Boorstin named these scripted productions pseudo-events. "Every American knows the anticipation with which he picks up his newspaper at breakfast or opens his evening paper before dinner," Boorstin wrote, "or listens to the newscasts every hour on the hour as he drives across country, or watches his favorite commenter on television interpret the events of the day."[21] These media spectacles, assembled by campaign consultants, kept audiences addicted to staged, political performances that left them craving more.

=====

Like Izzy Stone, before his career in alternative media Robert MacNeil was a card-carrying member of the journalism establishment. Growing up in Nova Scotia during World War II, his early experiences with the news were the rich broadcasts of the CBC, publicly funded Canadian radio modeled on the BBC. Beginning his career as an aspiring actor and playwright, MacNeil began to do some radio work, both at the CBC and on commercial stations, and he had a brief stint at a CBC television station in Ottawa, Ontario. Moving to London in hopes of selling a play, MacNeil found himself suddenly stranded with a wife and a child to support when the production failed to materialize. He parlayed his writing and radio news experience into freelance journalism, doing rewrites for Reuters and broadcasting for England's Independent Television Network (ITN). "One day there was a phone call from NBC," MacNeil recalled, asking him to substitute for television correspondent John Chancellor. When Chancellor was reassigned to Moscow, MacNeil took over the job permanently.[22]

From the perspective of journalists like MacNeil, networks' desire to entertain and seduce audiences with the news (some called these broadcasts "infotainment") was guaranteed to prevent Americans from thinking. Although the evening news was a source of pride and prestige for television networks, these nightly pseudo-events offered little information, and no analysis, mostly summarizing what had appeared in print that day. Anchormen, and for the first three decades of television they were all men, were a voice of authority that channeled the choices of mainstream news institutions into American living rooms as the official account of the day. Although evening entertainments were the real moneymaker, news was the prestige product by which networks competed with each other. To create a more compelling account of the day, CBS and NBC expanded their evening shows from 15 to 30 minutes in 1963 (which meant about 22 minutes of actual news); ABC followed their lead in 1967.[23]

Like Nixon's media team, these polished shows managed and massaged reporting to produce a soothing product called "the news" that aggregated audiences for prime-time shows and their lucrative advertising buys. The task required muting news that challenged the audience to think or caused viewers to change the channel. Television reporters, editors, and producers understood that Vietnam was exactly what protesters and the alternative press said it was: a cauldron of suffering, a war already lost, and a foreign policy quagmire that required a political solution. In the face of an alternative press willing to dig deeply into accounts of the war promoted by the government, conversations about the ethical obligations of reporters intensified and divided newsrooms.[24]

These debates had begun during the civil rights movement. Journalists' experiences of being targeted by white mobs in the American South had been radicalizing and caused them to align with African American activists. But Vietnam was far more divisive for newsrooms. Worse, challenging official military accounts threatened the alliance between journalism and the political establishment that reporters counted on to do their jobs. Sometimes politicians, bureaucrats, and military commanders threatened to ice out an entire news outlet in retaliation for negative coverage. This was particularly enraging to reporters on the ground in Vietnam. They struggled to learn basic facts about the war at government briefings, received the information they needed through back channels, and put their lives on the line traveling to battle zones, only to see their stories spiked or edited to support the government's sanitized account of the war. "All governments try to control the news, especially in crises," *New York Times* correspondent Sydney Schanberg commented as the war was winding down. "But I for one have never been in a reporting situation quite as frustrating as the one in Vietnam."[25]

As MacNeil intuited, because they had close to 25 million viewers a night, the television establishment was particularly complicit in numbing the public's response to a brutal war. By contrast, alternative media were reporting to far smaller audiences at a bare-bones cost. Even conceding the wisdom of exposing the country to mass casualties at the dinner hour, there were other, better ways to tell the story that were not pursued. "The networks did not do specials regularly," on Vietnam, MacNeil pointed out, "as they did on most other things." As he wrote after he left NBC, "The world's most powerful nation was informing itself through a medium that was essentially flawed."[26] In 1968, MacNeil mapped out the consequences of a television news environment driven not by the commitment to inform, but by advertising dollars, powerful political interests, and an entertainment economy. "Television *is* the Machine through which American people are now reached, persuaded and nominally informed more extensively and homogeneously than ever before,"

MacNeil emphasized in his book *The People Machine* (1968). Because of this, there was "a pressing need for more public attention to the commercial structure and journalistic independence of television, as well as its relations with government and its exploitation by politicians." Television technology had achieved one of the most radical transformations in political media history, and the media establishment had squandered it.[27]

By the 1960s, networks had become particularly reluctant to broadcast live political events like nomination conventions, fearing loss of advertising revenue should audiences find democracy boring. Here, the television and political establishments had also found common ground. The "mass of trivia," the often "dull proceedings," and the unscripted and "kaleidoscopic switching from, say, a floor interview to a civil rights demonstration to a platform speaker to an anchorman's anecdote to a candidate's hotel corridor to a floor demonstration" undermined the clean candidate narratives prized by political parties. By 1968, shooting scripts provided by each party's television consultants dictated how the networks would cover conventions, with the most handsome and telegenic politicians scheduled for prime time. And there was no going off-script. "When television pries too deeply they grow worried and want to ban the cameras from sensitive areas," MacNeil wrote.[28]

MacNeil left his job at *NBC News* in 1968 to write a book and to explore how journalists living in the shadows of corporate broadcasting might nevertheless tell a more complete story. He took a job at NBC radio, an alternative within the news industry and a place where reporters enjoyed less scrutiny from network executives. *Emphasis* was a news and opinion show, where MacNeil wrote and produced three original three-minute spots every week, one minute longer than the typical television story, each airing repeatedly. A script was 450 words, "roughly equivalent to a newspaper column—room to develop an idea," MacNeil remembered. But he also continued to seek out possibilities for doing alternative television news. A second job as an American correspondent for the BBC's television documentary series *Panorama* allowed him and a production team as much as three weeks to develop a story that would air for between twenty and fifty minutes.[29] MacNeil also freelanced for the only existing alternative television net-work, NET. A string of affiliated stations around the country that produced and shared nonprofit educational and public interest programming, NET emerged as a viable alternative for good jour-nalism when Fred Friendly, a visionary television newsman at CBS, coproduced a TV documentary, with Edward R. Murrow, that was credited, in part, with persuading the public that anti-Communist purges had to end. Stymied in his attempt to continue this work in commercial television, Friendly persuaded McGeorge Bundy of the Ford Foundation to fund NET in 1966.[30]

Anyone old enough to remember NET also remembers its eclec-tic offerings: children's shows, university extension courses, farm reports, interviews with local celebrities, and occasional dead air time. Nevertheless, NET was soon referred to in television jour-nalism as the "fourth network," a set of affiliates that were inde-pendent but coordinated, dedicated to public access, and, most importantly, funded through public spending and donations. In 1967, NET scooped the corporate networks for the first time, broadcasting President Lyndon Johnson's State of the Union ad-dress on all its affiliates, followed by two hours of discussion and analysis. The civic value of broadcasting an agenda-setting polit-ical speech made the case for "removing commercials altogether from news programming," MacNeil wrote in 1968, as in shows like the monthly *News in Perspective*, which featured *New York Times* journalists Tom Wicker, Max Frankel, and Lester Markel in a discussion that took viewers beyond the headlines. By 1970, when NET had become PBS, MacNeil had begun to take on short freelance assignments for *Public TV Lab*, a Sunday night magazine founded in 1967 that featured short documentaries about urgent contemporary issues.[31]

One of these was, of course, the Vietnam War, and as the 1972 election season approached, Nixon—who had promised to end the war in 1968—became the object of fierce attacks in left alternative media. One antiwar pamphlet lampooned him as "Hitler Nixon," while the *Berkeley Barb* simply substituted a picture of Hitler for a photograph of the president.[32] In this extreme atmosphere, Mac-Neil decided to report on the election by telling the story of the ordinary voter. In partnership with Sander Vanocur, he launched *A Public Affair—Election '72*, in which the pair traveled around the country speaking to Americans about the candidates. But public television, funded by tax dollars, was not free of political pressure. Tensions between the media and the Nixon administration were escalating, as the president and his staff fought off media queries about a group of burglars arrested while breaking into Democratic headquarters at Washington's Watergate complex on June 17, 1972. PBS's discussion shows had been following the story, and suddenly the network became vulnerable *because* of its public funding. In an attempt to ease tensions, the director of news programming, Jim Karayn, proposed that although the network had only provided a half hour of news each evening from the Democratic convention, MacNeil and Vanocur would anchor gavel-to-gavel coverage of the Republican convention. They refused. "We felt it was quite inappropriate for a news organization under attack by the Nixon White House to cover his re-nomination convention in full when we had not covered McGovern's," MacNeil wrote. Instead, Bill Moyers, Lyndon Johnson's press secretary from 1965 to 1967, did the show, while MacNeil anchored gavel-to-gavel coverage for the BBC.[33]

Predictably, the Nixon administration was not mollified by Karayn's decision, and after the election, tensions with the media escalated. Both Congress and a team of reporters, Bob Woodward and Carl Bernstein from the *Washington Post*, began an investigation into the burglary, now simply called Watergate. The Corporation for Public Broadcasting, a government oversight board composed entirely of the president's appointees, announced that the budget for all PBS news programs would be eliminated. At the end of one *Washington Week in Review*, MacNeil announced this funding cut as news. He appealed to the public to write and tell PBS "what they felt" about the loss of these shows. The station received 13,000 letters from viewers, 80 percent of which were passionate PBS fans. Despite this evidence of public support, in March 1973, although the network continued to produce, distribute, and share other kinds of programming, its news shows—*Washington Week*, *Bill Moyers Journal*, and for good measure, the conservative *Firing Line*—were all defunded.

In the wake of this loss, however, came a sudden opportunity: Congress announced public hearings to investigate the Watergate break-in and a possible cover-up by the White House. "The way was open," MacNeil remembered about this watershed moment in American politics, "for public television to win the kind of credibility that the new ABC network had by preempting all daytime programs to cover the Army-McCarthy hearings in 1954."[34]

MacNeil approached Jim Lehrer, who agreed immediately to coanchor gavel-to-gavel coverage of the hearings, a job that turned out to entail being on the air all day and at the studio into the evening. "We were here to do what no one else would do," Lehrer recalled thirty years later. Both journalists believed that public television should "always be pushing the envelope" for what all broadcast news, corporate and alternative, aspired to. The pair flew to Dallas to get the stamp of approval from the chairman of PBS, businessman and philanthropist Ralph Rogers. "We had dinner with him and his wife," Lehrer remembered, "and we said, 'Mr. Rogers, we think the Watergate hearings are going to be an important thing and we think PBS should broadcast them gavel-to-gavel, and possibly even rebroadcast them at night.' And he said, 'You guys, *you guys*! You don't know what the news is. There's going to be an energy crisis like nothing we have ever seen,'" and then launched into a polemic about oil. "And we could barely stay *awake* while he was talking"—Lehrer laughed—"and of course, a year later, there was the biggest energy crisis we'd ever had." Nevertheless, when the pair left they had secured Rogers's support for broadcasting the Watergate hearings.[35]

But there was one potential hitch: unlike commercial networks, PBS affiliates chose what they would purchase and broadcast. Would they elect to replace local programs and national favorites like the popular children's show *Sesame Street* with live political broadcasts? The team arranged to poll the stations one by one, beginning with those in large, urban, liberal markets where Nixon was especially disliked. As soon as 51 percent of the stations had agreed, the decision to carry the hearings was announced, which "meant that the people who were wavering had to come on board," Lehrer explained, so that their viewers wouldn't feel left out.[36]

There could have been no better contrast to the pseudo-events that McGinniss had exposed in 1968. The Watergate hearings were almost 250 hours of riveting television, breaking news, and expert analysis. MacNeil began every broadcast by reading the Special Committee's charge, both to "set the tone," as he put it, and to highlight the fact that this was democracy in action, not a media attack on the president. On May 17, 1973, the first day of the hearings, Lehrer spoke straight to the viewers and explained why PBS had taken the extraordinary step of preempting regular programming. This would be, he reminded them, the first time congressional hearings had been broadcast in their entirety since 1954. "We are running these hearings because we think it is important," Lehrer explained, "and because we think it is important that you get to see the whole thing and make your own judgments." He also emphasized what it meant for viewers to get the whole story and why the broadcasts were different from receiving summaries and highlights from mainstream newspapers and networks. It was an experiment, Lehrer emphasized in his soft Texas accent, in telling the whole story by "temporarily abandoning our ability to edit . . . however many hours it may take."[37]

The nation watched a drama unfold that might have led to only the second presidential Senate impeachment trial in American history, and the first in over a century, had the president not resigned. There was no question that liberals would watch. Enraged by the war and by Nixon's easy stroll to victory in 1972, PBS's core audience was transfixed by the prospect of learning the full truth about a man nicknamed Tricky Dick since his 1950 Senate campaign. PBS took no breaks unless the committee did and rebroadcast sessions in the evening when most working people could view them. When the hearings were not in session, airtime featured commentary and analysis by experts, as well as interviews held outside the hearing room by correspondent Peter Kaye. "For the first time in history, it seemed that the whole nation knew what public television was," MacNeil recalled. The broadcast also showed that an energized public would pay for alternative television. Although there was no appeal of the kind public television is famous for now, viewers spontaneously sent donations and affiliates like New York's WNET tripled their membership. More importantly, MacNeil had proved that a broadcasting model that trusted the public's intelligence and ability to think about the news would earn the faith of the public in return.

The success of the broadcasts, and the willingness to give viewers all the facts and as much context as possible from both sides of the aisle, "revealed to doubters that public television journalism could be vital, fair, and trenchant when dealing with the most sensitive political matters," MacNeil remembered. This, in turn, allowed the two journalists to fantasize about an evening show that could win the public's trust in alternatives to commercial TV journalism. "Only news," MacNeil believed, "would give PBS programs an air of *indispensability*" that would allow the network to survive future political attacks.[38]

MacNeil and Jim Lehrer had figured out how to sell, on a broad scale, Izzy Stone's insight that Americans wanted to know how their government worked. The Watergate broadcasts offered a dramatic preview of how channels like C-SPAN, Court TV, and other 24-7 cable news programming would enthrall political junkies ten years later. The hearings also began to shift how politicians, who normally stayed under the national radar, related to a public newly fascinated with them as actors in a drama about democracy. Little-known senators like North Carolina Democrat Sam Ervin, a Harvard graduate and segregationist who presented himself as a "country lawyer" and told folksy stories from his seat as chair of the Senate Watergate Committee, became television characters who played to the camera. Tennessee Republican Howard Baker's insistent question—"What did the president know and when did he know it?"—initially intended to provide a path to Nixon's exoneration, became an iconic phrase that ultimately led to the president's downfall. As the hearings ground on, Nixon's staffers dropped one bombshell after another, live, sending simultaneous shock waves through viewers, committee members, and journalists crammed into the hearing room, as well as MacNeil and Lehrer, watching from the studio. When John Dean delivered prepared remarks, in which he revealed that Nixon had known about the cover-up and that he, Dean, had told him that the Watergate investigations were "a cancer on the presidency," it was "a showstopper," Lehrer recalled: so was Alexander Butterfield's revelation that the Oval Office had secret recording devices. As Lehrer characterized it, the broadcasts "showed the government of the United States at its worst—and then it showed it at its best."[39]

In other words, alternative television showed government *as it was*, mainlining the excitement of democracy to a dedicated and growing group of political junkies. At the same time, seeing the investigation play out live provided reassurance that Watergate was a constitutional crisis but not, as Nixon characterized it, a plot against American democracy.

Working together for the entire day, and into the evening, Robert MacNeil and Jim Lehrer became good friends. But they also had the opportunity to watch public television news emerge as a legitimate alternative to its corporate counterpart, supported by a viable audience of educated liberals who cared deeply about politics. In 1975, WNET, the New York PBS affiliate, invited the pair to launch an evening news show, airing from 7:30 to 8:00, after the end of the major network broadcasts. It was a time slot that as MacNeil characterized it, was normally "full of rubbish, a wasteland for intelligent viewers." The show, they imagined, would "slow down" and make sense of the rush of information that viewers had already absorbed on the commercial networks. Initially named *The Robert MacNeil NewsHour*, and the following year renamed the *MacNeil/Lehrer NewsHour*, the show offered the two journalists absolute independence. PBS "told me how much money I had to work with—1.4 million dollars for nine months—and then left me alone," MacNeil wrote. "Nobody told me what the program had to be or what it had to achieve. They did not ask what I intended to do and they did not come and look over our shoulders, as we began to put it together." Instead of losing seven minutes of airtime for commercials as the networks did, they had the full half hour. And instead of trying to meet the demands of an undifferentiated national audience, they would address a single segment of that audience: the political news junkie, who wanted facts, the inside scoop, and expert opinions.[40]

The show was also honest about what it did not do: give a comprehensive report on the day's events. Early advertising for *The*

Robert MacNeil Report proposed that viewers watch their favorite evening network news and then shift to PBS to study a single issue with politicians, scholars, policymakers, and guests drawn from across the political spectrum. In this way, the show removed the editorial filter between the news source and the audience, encouraging viewers to decide what *they* thought, rather than accepting what producers, network executives, and the hosts had decided they *should* think. MacNeil also flipped the normal staffing, hiring fewer production personnel and more researchers. The show couldn't afford established journalists, and so it hired young people willing to innovate, each of whom had a beat to cover. Most importantly, in the early years of the show, no one was assigned to the White House press pool, an elite group of reporters who covered the president. But actual news rarely happened at the White House, and proximity to power, MacNeil knew from experience, intensified pressure to please the administration. "We cover the issues, not the buildings," MacNeil deadpanned when asked about this decision.[41]

In its early years, the show also featured ordinary people who gave a face to otherwise abstract news. A program about the economic recession began with a graph showing sharply rising unemployment rates topping out at 8.6 percent. MacNeil explained that this meant eight million people in the United States were currently unemployed, with African Americans three to four times as likely to be out of work as whites. "Well, what do these figures really mean?" MacNeil asked. "How is the nation going to live with what's starting to look like mass unemployment on a scale only exceeded by the Great Depression?" The camera angle widened to reveal four unemployed New Yorkers—a female teacher and three men: a secretary, a policeman, and an electrician. Shifting to the Washington studio, Jim Lehrer introduced Republican House Minority Leader John Anderson and Democratic Congressman Jim Wright, who laid out their parties' economic philosophies. Cutting back to the New York studio, MacNeil turned to his "living statistics," who explained why they held President Gerald Ford responsible for their plight. They also exchanged views with the Congressmen. "Throughout the Great Depression, not one New

York City police officer was laid off," the policeman pointed out. The secretary, an African American man, reported that when his unemployment benefits ended, he was told to apply for welfare, a humiliating experience.[42]

It was riveting television that would not have appeared on any other network in 1975. The half hour was filled with unscripted news and substantive information; and it put politicians in direct conversation with citizens, rather than an anchorman speaking for both. By "eliminating the last filter, the reporter's own synthesis," MacNeil and Lehrer had also created a journalistic style that was perceived by its viewers to be more ideologically balanced than mainstream news shows. This worked to reassure the show's mostly liberal audience that despite escalating partisanship in Washington, *they* could be passionate about politics and still be open-minded people.[43]

Television critics saw *The Robert MacNeil Report* as a breakthrough. "There's a new public-affairs program in town, and it is rapidly proving to be one of the more significant and solid developments in television news," wrote John J. O'Connor of the *New York Times* soon after the show launched in January 1976. MacNeil had created "his ideal television forum. His control over the material and program 'flow' is immediately apparent. He is well prepared. His material and questions are remarkably to the point. In fact, within the present context of broadcast journalism, he is unique and is making the most of it." O'Connor applauded both journalists as models of nonpartisanship, experts at "saying everything and revealing nothing."[44]

An instant hit among its New York viewers, in January 1976, the show—now renamed *The MacNeil/Lehrer Report*—was offered to the PBS affiliates. In March 1976, it debuted in Washington. It was relegated to an 11:30 p.m. slot, but it nevertheless drew 450,000 viewers every evening. By 1978, when it was reaching 235 stations, the show was so popular that conversations began about expanding it to an hour, something that occurred in 1983. By then, they had nine reporters on staff, including Charlayne Hunter-Gault, still one of very few African American women working in the news business, who also served as a substitute host. Judy Woodruff left

NBC to become chief Washington correspondent. MacNeil and Lehrer also began using the hour-long slot to do longer investigative features, producing short films, not unlike the ones MacNeil had done for *Panorama*, often followed by a roundtable discussion. In a 1978 interview with the *Los Angeles Times*, MacNeil claimed they had found a niche audience: political "news junkies," a subset of the viewing population that was never bored by hearing about a political story in detail.[45]

=====

That MacNeil used that exact phrase was no accident: since Hunter Thompson had coined the phrase "politics junkie" in 1972, the idea that a person could be hooked on political news was gaining currency. But Thompson had used it to describe only himself: MacNeil was using it to describe a collective and a shared excitement about politics that connected the alternative news producer to the audience as members of the same media community. MacNeil and Lehrer built a project that would last for at least the next half-century, alternative journalism nestled securely inside the television news and the political establishment. But liberals were not the only political junkies out there in the 1970s. Nixon's defeat had proved, for many, not that investigative journalism was good for democracy, but quite the opposite: that the left-wing media, now amplified by thriving alternative media outlets, had it in for the right. As conservative book publisher Henry Regnery put it: "Modern communications—the mass press, television, and radio—have given the 'scribblers,' as they were once called, the people who dominate the popular dissemination of ideas and information and presume to speak for us, unprecedented power and influence." Nixon's whole career had been a successful "attack on the credibility of the whole liberal position," Regnery wrote, "and no one understood that better than the liberals themselves."[46]

Which was why, by 1973, conservative alternative media were poised to strike back.

= 3 =

CREATING PARTISANS

O n November 3, 1964, the young reporter and his wife, both conservative activists, voted early. Paul Weyrich was twenty-one, a local radio celebrity now making a career in television news. After voting, Weyrich headed down to the WISN studios, Milwaukee's CBS affiliate, to prepare for his first live election broadcast. As a longtime member of the Wisconsin Young Republicans (YGOP), he knew state politics—every district and every seat—inside and out. The national contest between incumbent President Lyndon Baines Johnson and Arizona Senator Barry Goldwater would be handled in New York, and Weyrich, a passionate Goldwater supporter, may have already known when he voted that his candidate would lose.

The word was certainly out among those in leadership positions in the Republican Party. In a meeting with college conservatives a few days earlier, William F. Buckley gently prepared Goldwater partisans for the strong possibility that their standard-bearer would lose to Johnson. But even in failure, Goldwater's candidacy was a turning point, Buckley insisted. It laid the ground for the Republican Party's transformation into a conservative populist movement. As Buckley wrote in the *National Review* after the election, conservatives needed to develop a massive public information campaign to find others like them. It would build on core ideas advanced by Goldwater, ideas that the mainstream media would never report on honestly.[1]

It was time, Buckley said, to take account of the Goldwater insurgency's successes and to launch an offensive against the liberal consensus in both parties that had defined the political process in the United States since World War II. One of those successes was a robust alternative media network that was beginning to be noticed by the conservative political and media establishments.[2] When Phyllis Schlafly arrived at the San Francisco nominating convention, she was already a star: hundreds of delegates had a copy of *A Choice Not an Echo*, a book carried door-to-door like a talisman by canvassers that made the case for Goldwater. Buckley's own first book, *God and Man at Yale* (1951), which decried the absence of religious values in the liberal educational establishment, and paid for by Buckley's father, was also a bestseller. The publisher, independent bookman Henry Regnery, learning there was an untapped audience, and a lucrative market for, conservative ideas, followed Buckley's bestseller with another hit in 1953, Russell Kirk's *The Conservative Mind*. In 1960, Buckley's brother-in-law, L. Brent Bozell, ghosted Barry Goldwater's manifesto, *The Conscience of a Conservative*. Commissioned by Dean Clarence Manion and privately printed, it was sold in bulk to conservative businessmen for free distribution, until it became so popular that bookstores demanded copies to sell. By June 1961, it sat proudly on the *Time* and *New York Times* bestseller lists and made a tidy profit for Manion.[3]

By 1964, alternative book publishing was a cornerstone of a new conservative media offensive that, among other techniques, repurposed familiar forms of print to reach audiences by mail. Books conveyed intellectual seriousness in a way that talk radio, newsletters, and personal appearances before the conservative populist faithful did not. Books allowed activists coalescing around, and looking beyond, Goldwater to see themselves as a movement based on common ideas, a "New Right," as direct mail entrepreneur Richard Viguerie would name these partisans in 1973.[4]

But books wouldn't topple the establishment by themselves. Morton C. Blackwell, a conservative youth organizer who would ride the New Right insurgency into the White House with Ronald Reagan in 1980, asserted that electoral success, not being "philosophically correct," was what changed laws and the legislative bodies that made laws. Conservative populists needed their own alternative political networks, a counter-establishment supported and amplified by a robust alternative media. When Viguerie convened an informal meeting of conservative populists to chart the future of this movement in 1972, Blackwell was there: so was the young broadcaster—now a congressional aide—twenty-eight-year-old Paul Weyrich. "Central to our plan," Blackwell recalled decades later, in a tribute to Weyrich, "was to create new, effective, conservative groups" and link them together through an alternative media strategy that included newsletters, direct mail, pamphlets, radio, and television. Because it would rely heavily on the postal service and be explicitly aimed at voter turnout, their movement needed to know where conservatives were. Addresses and telephone numbers would be their infrastructure. Using existing technology, this alternative media network would bring conservatives together in coalition, raise the money to nominate populists within the Republican Party for offices at all levels, and defeat Democrats in the general election.[5]

The new organizations and the alternative media mobilization imagined at this meeting became the nerve center of a conservative populist movement that remade the Republican Party. In doing so, it also launched a decades-long challenge to what Weyrich, Viguerie, and others saw as a compact between the mainstream media and the political establishment to control information. Weyrich became the institution-builder of the New Right, creating think tanks like the Heritage Foundation and fundraising engines like the Committee for the Survival of a Free Congress to counter the influence of liberal universities, labor unions, and civil rights organizations on the electoral and policy-making process. Viguerie, who had already built a peerless, computer-driven direct mail operation to fundraise for conservatives and to distribute alternative conservative print media, would turn networks of names and addresses of known conservatives into mailing lists targeted to specific issues: abortion, foreign policy, and school prayer, to name a few.

Viguerie's computers would be a real game changer, and Weyrich knew it. In 1964, when Weyrich was reporting the election, computers were newly available to political consultants, newsrooms, and direct marketers like Viguerie, and the information they processed in minutes revealed the political landscape as it was. As liberal Republicans repudiated Goldwater that day, Weyrich had been standing not twenty feet away from the Monrobot Mark XI, from which, WISN-TV promised, Milwaukee viewers would get their results faster than any other station could deliver them, using a form of exit polling that CBS gave a scientific polish by calling it voting precinct analysis. Using computers, the New York newsroom had called the election for Johnson even before precincts in the West, where Goldwater's support was strongest, had closed, perhaps discouraging conservative voters from going to the polls at all.[6]

To conservative populists CBS's premature prediction may have seemed like perfect evidence of an establishment conspiracy against Goldwater. But if a computer could rig an election by discouraging partisans from voting, with careful planning, computer-driven direct mail could also make sure those partisans saw voting as a moral responsibility. In his Falls Church, Virginia, office complex, where one of the rooms already contained banks of computers, Richard Viguerie already knew that these machines—the data that they organized, the new ways that such data could help candidates locate and target supporters, and the power of computer-driven direct mail to energize partisans to go to the polls and vote against the status quo—would be a crucial tool for this new conservative populist movement. Two decades before the internet, and three decades before campaigns would go online, computer technology reshaped the world of alternative political media. Marrying politics to the sciences of data analysis and direct marketing, Viguerie, Weyrich, and their allies nurtured and disseminated conservative populist ideas in easy-to-read pamphlets, books, newsletters, and fundraising appeals. This printed alternative media would be issued by institutions with dignified names like "The Heritage Foundation," tucked into the heart of Capitol Hill, not personalities like Manion who had been successfully tarred as extremist in the liberal press. They aimed this alternative media at a partisan audience, targeting conservatives in both parties for their populist revolution.[7]

And, when Ronald Reagan won the presidency in 1980, it happened faster than anyone in that room in 1972 could have hoped for.

===

Paul Weyrich was the youngest of Viguerie's group of collaborators. In retrospect, Morton Blackwell said that he was the only one of the three men to truly grasp how institution-building, fundraising, and alternative media could work together to reframe Republican politics around conservative populist principles. Weyrich's strategy required reincorporating marginalized voters: for example, attacking the liberal insistence on keeping religion out of public life as an affront to constitutional guarantees of free speech and freedom of religion. It required, as Weyrich told reporters in the 1980s, raising money so that conservative populists could challenge well-funded incumbents; and making research available to publicize their liberal voting records. It meant organizing voters around an uncompromising, winner-take-all approach to politics. After Weyrich and his "political technicians," as he called them, succeeded in electing Ronald Reagan and winning a Senate majority in 1980, Democratic political consultant David Frum identified these tactics as not just an attack on liberals, but as a concerted attempt to divide a political establishment committed to ideological compromise. These tactics were, Frum commented as Weyrich worked to recruit a challenger to Senator Ted Kennedy, "a whole scheme to deal in a negative, nasty, uncivil way, alien to the political tradition of this country and to Massachusetts."[8]

But partisanship was very much in line with Weyrich's political tradition as a Midwestern populist: his conservative Catholicism, working-class background, and devotion to Senator Joseph McCarthy were all part of the package. Born on October 7, 1942, as the only child of working-class Catholic parents, Weyrich grew up in Racine, Wisconsin, a historic hotbed of populism, progressive and conservative. The Church was the cornerstone of Weyrich's upbringing and where he learned his first lessons in effective, personal mass communication. Notes sent home by the nuns at his parochial school challenged the whole family to improve its faith practice; and when Paul was thirteen, his church-sponsored Boy Scout troop distributed flyers that urged fellow Catholics to disavow consumerism and "Put Christ Back into Christmas."[9] Weyrich's idol, McCarthy, also grounded his populism and anti-Communism in his Catholic faith, a bond that linked the young man ever more closely to the Cold War drama playing out on a national stage as McCarthy and his allies exposed and disgraced suspected leftists. As a teenager in July 1953, Weyrich organized a trip to Washington for a group of schoolmates: the teenagers sat in the galleries of the House and Senate to see their representatives, including McCarthy, in action.[10]

Weyrich's professional career in politics would not begin until the mid-1960s, but from an early age, he was a budding political junkie. A star debater, an A student, aspiring journalist, and civil defense volunteer, Weyrich became an officer of his high school's YGOP club and volunteered for local Republican campaigns. In 1959, he was chosen as a delegate to the annual statewide YGOP meeting where, in a speech to the convention, he called for his fellow delegates "to reject all socialistic and communistic ideas," to keep their goals in sight, and to be vigorous in "selling our principles to the Nation."[11] Selling these principles became more difficult when *ABC News* broadcast the Army-McCarthy hearings in gavel-to-gavel coverage, and the liberal critique of McCarthy's populist tactics broke the anti-Communist consensus. A key turning point was when Joseph Welch, representing a member of the progressive Lawyer's Guild, characterized McCarthy's methods as unfair and anti-American. His words "Have you no sense of decency, sir? At long last, have you left no sense of decency?" were rebroadcast and reprinted repeatedly, a moment that marked the beginning of the end of McCarthy's political career.[12]

Yet to Americans like Paul Weyrich, McCarthy was, and remained, the essence of decency, a man brought low, not by his tactics, but by the liberal media and political establishments.[13] However, even after McCarthy's fall, Weyrich did not see his own conservative commitments as a stumbling block to a career in media or politics. In high school, he wrote for the student paper, wrote and performed in radio shows, won a national high school broadcasting championship, and openly contemplated a life in politics.[14] In January 1960, he went to Washington for the fourth national YGOP leadership training school, where he networked with conservative Congressmen and posed for a photograph with Barry Goldwater. In the fall, Weyrich enrolled at the University of Wisconsin–Racine, where he volunteered for political campaigns and worked broadcasting shifts at WLIP in Kenosha.[15]

Although television was becoming popular in the early 1960s, AM radio still held its own as a broadcast medium for political news. Every car came with a radio, and although 90 percent of Americans owned a television by 1960, audiences were still more likely to listen to the news on the radio—both in their cars and on the smaller, portable transistor models invented in 1954 that became especially popular with teenagers. Political junkies would have been particularly attuned to radio: national television news came on once a day for fifteen minutes, but the radio listener was likely to hear breaking news as it happened, as well as talk shows featuring local and state officeholders.[16] This latter fact created an opening for Weyrich to combine his interests in politics and broadcasting, and earn a little cash, by becoming a local media consultant. In July 1961, the nineteen-year-old Weyrich helped his congressman Henry Schadeberg, whom he had met through the YGOP, connect directly with voters by producing five-minute tapes describing Schadeberg's policies on federal spending and the national debt. Weyrich produced these spots in the family basement, then drove around the district delivering the recordings to local radio stations.[17]

Weyrich also learned a new political strategy: creating controversial media events that would be covered by others, garnering publicity that made conservative issues visible. In June 1961, as Director of Racine YGOP, he organized a small group to picket a local appearance by the now-elderly former First Lady Eleanor Roosevelt, who had recently expressed support for reopening trade with the revolutionary regime in Cuba. Weyrich called the local papers, but wouldn't tell them the event's exact purpose. Reporters would have to show up to see what the story was.[18]

The demonstration got into the news and the ensuing controversy uncovered the tensions that were already emerging between populist conservatives and the Republican Party establishment. Weyrich was rebuked by the YGOP leadership for having embarrassed the former First Lady. But he was also invited to join a more private group, "a stag meeting for a selected group of Racine and Milwaukee men" that invited William Worthy, an anti-Communist CBS correspondent who had been posted in China, to speak to them. Later that year, Weyrich was chosen to attend a Midwestern mock nominating convention for YGOP, where he spoke passionately about the need for conservatives to take over the party. He chastised "ultraliberal" senators like Alexander Wiley of Wisconsin and New York's Jacob Javits, warning them to "end their close association with Democrats" or leave the GOP altogether.[19]

As Weyrich tried to use his leadership position to align YGOP with conservative factions within the party, his relationship to the group, an organization mostly controlled by the state Republican establishment, frayed. YGOP abruptly canceled an event he had planned and rejected Weyrich's demand that its leadership be elected, not appointed by older Republican stalwarts. In response, Weyrich resigned from the organization.[20] He dropped out of school and accepted a broadcasting job at WAXO-Kenosha, taking over the 6:00 to 9:00 a.m. slot, a "fast-paced morning show designed to start your morning right." In the lead-up to the 1964 elections, he started broadcasting interviews with local conservative Congressmen.[21] He learned how to tell a policy story clearly and persuasively, and he embraced opportunities to debate liberals. Senator William Proxmire, a liberal Wisconsin Democrat who had won McCarthy's seat in 1957, found Weyrich to be "a truly unusual young man," an intellectually curious and open-minded person "with a strong viewpoint which he unabashedly and vigorously expresses." A few days later, Congressman Schadeberg invited Weyrich to join his "Freedom and Information Committee," a group dedicated to promoting anti-Communist alternative media.[22]

Weyrich, like conservative organizers and media professionals elsewhere, also saw women as an important conservative voting constituency, "home executives" who were particularly attuned to the radios that kept them company through long hours of house-work and childcare. In September 1963, he created a 9:00 a.m. to noon slot called "Home Executive Club," where political inter-views were interspersed with popular music.[23] In turn, this cata-pulted him into a network of conservative media professionals. Along with the publishers of the Manchester *Union-Leader*, the New Orleans *Times-Picayune*, and the Tucson *Daily Citizen*, Wey-rich was asked to blurb *Disarmament: A Blueprint for Surrender*, a pamphlet distributed by the Conservative Society of America, and he was increasingly asked to speak at local Republican clubs. On November 1, 1964, Weyrich became a political and special events reporter for Milwaukee's WISN-TV, a CBS network affiliate, arriv-ing just in time to see Barry Goldwater take one of the worst drub-bings in the history of modern presidential elections.[24]

The defeat mobilized Weyrich. His speeches at Republican clubs were increasingly focused on criticisms of a corporate media that as he argued, functioned to empower the political establishment and deny the people access to knowledge and influence. His top-ics included "Is the Communications Media Becoming a Political Tool?," "Managed News," and "Liberal Control and Influence in the Press."[25] Two years after Goldwater's defeat, Weyrich would leave journalism entirely, determined to put his media skills to use to make the Republican Party a home for movement conservatives like himself. He began this effort by helping Gordon Allott win a Senate seat from Colorado. Weyrich would uproot his family and leave the Midwest forever, first to work for Allott in the Senate and then to work with Richard Viguerie and other conservative populists to create some of the most powerful grassroots conserva-tive organizations in history in the heart of Washington's political establishment.

Despite their ten-year age difference, Paul Weyrich and Richard Viguerie lived almost parallel lives. Born outside of Houston, Texas, in 1933, Viguerie also came from a working-class family. The Vigue-ries were conservative and Catholic, "but we didn't sit around the dinner table talking politics," he remembered. Viguerie's childhood heroes were "the two Macs—Douglas MacArthur and Joe McCarthy," and, like Weyrich, he was a staunch anti-Communist from an early age. Both men were first-generation college students and volunteered for Republican political campaigns in the 1950s. What's more, like Weyrich, Viguerie "always knew I was going to do things, important things, that would make a difference in people's lives. And I knew I would do them through politics."[26]

As a young activist, like Weyrich, Viguerie also ran into trouble with the YGOP establishment because he imagined the possibility that all conservatives, at a time when many Southern conservatives were Democrats, could find a home in the Republican Party. When Viguerie invited Jack Cox, a conservative Texas Democrat suspected of having ties to the John Birch Society (he became a Republican to run for governor in 1962), to speak at a YGOP barbecue, Viguerie was soundly rebuked by his elders.[27] But he knew what he was doing. The turnout for the event was huge, causing Viguerie to understand that the political party establishment might be inhibiting the growth of a conservative populist *movement*. "I see now I practiced coalition politics without realizing it," he said later. During the 1960 election, Viguerie served as county chairman for John Tower's challenge to Senate Majority Leader Lyndon Baines Johnson, who was also running for vice president. Tower lost, but respectably. "I did all the usual things," Viguerie remembered, including helping "to write a one-page fundraising letter for Tower that worked pretty well."[28] In 1961, Viguerie's reputation had exceeded Texas. In the spring of 1963, he was hired by Buckley's Young Americans for Freedom (YAF), a new competitor to the YGOP that was organizing conservatives on college campuses—but outside the structure of the Republican Party establishment. Hiring Viguerie was, as one historian pointed out, a power play by William Rusher, the publisher of the *National Review*, to push Buckley's youth organization even further to the right than its founder originally intended.[29]

Viguerie's assignment was to improve grassroots organizing and to work with a public relations consultant, Marvin Liebman, to fundraise and raise YAF's profile through direct mail and other alternative media appeals. While his effect on the organization was said to be transformative, Viguerie was undoubtedly transformed by the experience of working with a major media professional. He also came to political organizing at a moment when the technology for reaching voters, and intuiting their preferences, was changing. In 1961, political media consultants and the public were abuzz about the Kennedy campaign's strategic use of computer data modeling in the 1960 election, a contest Kennedy had won by a hair and a victory dogged by accusations of voter fraud.[30] This sort of modeling, rarely seen outside a scientific laboratory at that time, was particularly interesting to a campaign concerned about whether anti-Catholic bias would prevent independents, and even Democrats, from voting for Kennedy. In 1959, the campaign approached Ithiel de Sola Pool and Robert Abelson, two political scientists at MIT, and asked them if they could do a computer simulation about *how* Americans decided on a candidate. Known as the "Simulmatics project" and using more than two decades of Roper polling data stored on computer punch cards, de Sola Pool, Abelson, and their graduate student, Samuel Popkin, got to work.[31]

What the Simulmatics team learned was that trying to persuade the vast majority of Americans was a waste of resources, because they almost always voted on a straight party line. Elections were won by getting registered voters to the polls and then swinging votes from independents, as well as irregular, or new voters. The team also confirmed what local conservative organizers like Phyllis Schlafly already knew: that uncommitted voters were less persuaded by parties than by neighbors, friends, co-workers, and relatives. Creating a sense of momentum around a candidate, with media buys and press coverage, was essential, but getting the right information to the right voters provided the margin of victory.[32] For this reason, as the Simulmatics project came to light, it bred paranoia that a political establishment could invisibly manipulate voters and even rig the nominating process to choose a candidate that would match predicted voter preferences. On the first page of their book, the Simulmatics team deplored these "sensational" and "lurid" accounts: the team had only observed voter behavior using old polling data, not done anything to change it in Kennedy's favor.[33]

Americans may also have conflated the Simulmatics project with what they did know about the potential power of computers to change minds: these machines had become important tools for collecting and analyzing data about consumer behavior, creating advertising campaigns, and making direct marketing appeals. In January 1965, Richard Viguerie decided to fuse his interests in alternative political media and public relations to launch a political direct marketing company.[34] At the time, direct marketing was a relatively young field that was a kind of advertising backwater. Intended to get products to consumers without going through a third-party retailer, direct sales had existed since the early nineteenth century. Marketing products through catalogs or ads that promoted merchandise not available in stores, the technique invited interested consumers to make contact. Individually mailed solicitations were not considered especially productive until the 1950s, however. Without the endorsement of a trusted publication, many consumers worried that the product was difficult to evaluate, or even fraudulent; as importantly, consumers rarely opened envelopes sent by strangers. In 1955, however, the circulation manager of *Reader's Digest*, Walter Wentz, created a mailing that contained two real pennies, visible in the envelope's glassine window. Unable to throw money away, the recipient invariably opened it. Out of twenty million mailings, *Reader's Digest* acquired one million new subscribers, more than paying for the cost of postage and the coins.[35]

Such mailings were known by their senders as direct mail or advertising mail; and by irritated or uninterested recipients as "unsolicited letters," or junk mail. Two factors led to the success of this alternative media genre: targeting recipients who were known to be interested in what was on offer, whether political ideas or a consumer product; and making a personal connection with that recipient. A key figure in creating mail strategies later repurposed for politics was Lester Wunderman, known to some as the "father of direct marketing." Wunderman pioneered innovative techniques and technologies that would make it possible to engage quickly, efficiently, and personally with consumers through the mail. An ambitious ad man from the Bronx, Wunderman began his career during the Great Depression when, unable to find a job, he and his brother decided to market themselves to employers through a common advertising ploy: the two-for-one deal. Any employer who hired one brother got the other for free. It worked. Wunderman launched his career in what was then called "direct selling," in which a returned coupon from a magazine invited a representative of the company to call on the customer at home.[36]

But Wunderman was also responsible for the success of a media innovation that would make direct mail advertising a profession by the 1960s and create new tools for political fundraising: the zip code. While numerous people have claimed credit for the five-number code at the end of addresses that made machine sorting possible, the Zoning Improvement Plan (ZIP) code was originally imagined by postal inspector Robert Moon in 1944. It was taken up by a federal committee in the early 1960s as the sheer number of magazines, advertisers, and direct mail appeals threatened to overwhelm the Postal Service.[37] Americans regarded the zip code with suspicion and irritation: Why should the government need to locate them with laser accuracy? Why were people being replaced by numbers? And how were they to know what zip codes were assigned to friends they had known for years? Businesses also groaned, seeing zip codes as an extra expense as they updated their databases. But Wunderman realized that it was a potential boon for direct mail professionals. In an hour, the Post Office's optical character reader, introduced in the mid-1950s, could separate and direct 36,000 bulk mail items equipped with computer-generated labels. Furthermore, the zip code itself would allow direct marketers to create demographic profiles matched to geographic locations that would then permit businesses to target customers more accurately. In 1965, Wunderman accepted an assignment from the Ad Council, a nonprofit public service organization, to popularize the zip code. Within three years, a promotion campaign that included an Ethel Merman tune persuaded Americans to adopt this technology as part of their regular mail practice.[38]

It is hard to overemphasize the importance of the zip code, not just to the technology of direct marketing, but also to a moment when politicians were being, as Joe McGinniss put it, sold by alternative political media experts. To men like Lester Wunderman, there was no such thing as "junk mail": only opportunities and information directed to the wrong people or written in an impersonal way. Sending the right solicitation to the right person told them that you knew "something about their needs, wants and lifestyle," Wunderman pointed out: "You're doing them a service." Wunderman also saw computers, which many consumers deemed suspicious and impersonal tools for surveillance, as critical to maintaining the personal connection between a direct marketer and the recipient. A computerized letter could not only be sent to a recipient known to be receptive, but it could also be tailored to that person. A computer could insert a personalized salutation, using the recipient's name throughout the letter. Political professionals were watching: a 1967 speech that Wunderman gave to the American Marketing Association at the Massachusetts Institute of Technology, the most important computer science research center on the East Coast, entered into the Congressional Record, easily suggested that techniques invented to sell consumer goods could also sell politicians.[39]

This emphasis on the personal appeal would become extraordinarily important to political direct mail, and to telephone fundraising, something that campaigns did for decades by cold-calling voters registered with the party. But again, this could be personalized. By the 1970s, Wunderman was also the acknowledged leader in using the 1-800, or toll-free, telephone number that allowed a client—or a contributor to a political campaign—to make contact on their own initiative and at no cost to themselves. Like direct marketing, the 1-800 number allowed a reverse solicitation: instead of receiving an annoying telephone call from a company, the potential consumer was invited to initiate contact, through a print or television advertisement. This created a sale, but it also allowed the company to collect that consumer's information and demographics, a technique that predated the capture of consumers' online data over the internet. Politicians were slower than direct marketers to experiment with the power of a 1-800 number to create a personal connection, invite contact from supporters, and collect voter data. In 1992, populist third-party presidential candidate Ross Perot would establish a toll-free number that supporters could call to get information about his campaign stops; and Bill Clinton created one that allowed supporters and journalists to listen to campaign speeches they could not attend. Clinton's was both wildly successful and a failure: so many people called in that the line was frequently jammed.[40]

Wunderman's theory, that direct marketing was about highly individualized, personal appeals sent to the right people, was a natural turn for politics, since voter turnout rates flatlined and then declined after 1960.[41] More worrisome was the expansion of that volatile category of voter that the Simulmatics team had identified in 1960: independents, who were driving successful third-party candidacies at the national level. In part because of this phenomenon, both major parties saw more dynamic communications with voters as part of a "new politics" that would better address the desires of constituents and shore up the two-party system. As Gordon Wade, director of communications for the Republican National Committee, put it, the collapse of political patronage and traditional party discipline was not replaced by an effective way of commanding voter loyalty. In its essence, wooing voters back to party politics was a sales problem, but the "salesmen"—politicians and the party leadership—were "unclear about the clients on whom they are calling or the products they are selling." By the mid-1970s, John Stewart, director of communications for the Democratic National Committee, saw a similar problem, but believed that both parties needed to look for ways to "humanize" their approach to voters, balancing advances in computerization and marketing techniques with approaches that appealed to "human judgment" and respect for an "electorate possessing a remarkable degree of common sense."[42]

This was Richard Viguerie's challenge when he launched his own company, American Target Strategies, in 1965: to marry commercial direct marketing appeals to political media in order to raise money for conservative candidates and causes. Furthermore, Viguerie saw alternative media as a way to build a movement and only wanted the right kind of clients, those who would be supported by conservative populists. Republican mailing lists would not be sufficient to identify this demographic: many conservatives rejected Goldwater's vision for the future of the party, either by not voting or by defecting to Johnson. However, Viguerie could identify Goldwater donors because that information was public. One of his first tasks was to go to the office of the Clerk of the House of Representatives where, by law, the names of all contributors who had given more than $50 to the 1964 presidential campaign were recorded. Since no photocopying was permitted, Viguerie "copied down their names and addresses," he remembered, "until my fingers were numb." He got about twelve thousand before they kicked him out.[43]

Viguerie's lists, kept on giant magnetic reels of tape in the 1960s and '70s, became a fundraising engine for the political institutions that Paul Weyrich built in the early 1970s after he left Gordon Allott's staff. These institutions and collaborations were initially bankrolled by conservative brewer Joseph Coors, an Allott donor. Subsequently, Viguerie's powerful direct mail appeals allowed candidates to counter the influence of major party donors by raising money from conservative populists themselves. Giving money also gave Viguerie's voter base a sense of ownership and connection to campaigns, a way to take action, and a common language to discuss politics with each other. Weyrich's membership organizations—the Heritage Foundation, the Free Congress Foundation, and the American Legislative Exchange Council (ALEC), powerful think tanks that pumped out policy and position papers to members of Congress, also raised money through Viguerie's lists. In other words, the institutions themselves, their members, and the candidates they sponsored, became Viguerie's clients—not the Republican Party itself. Small-donation fundraising from advertisements taken out in alternative print publications gave conservative populists a sense of ownership over their own movement, and they gave Viguerie names to add to his database. Furthermore, Viguerie retained ownership of all mailing lists that he generated for every political client or activist group, names that could be resold to other clients and causes. When Weyrich persuaded evangelical minister Jerry Falwell to join the new conservative movement in 1979, suggesting that he bring a group of religious leaders in under the name "the Moral Majority," Viguerie stepped in to help the new group raise funds. In turn, Viguerie accessed a whole new database of Christian voters from lists curated by evangelical megachurches.[44]

Viguerie's tweak to the conventional direct marketing contract had ramifications beyond profit. Direct mail operations like Wunderman's generated lists that were then owned by the client, while Viguerie's standard contract made his firm and the client co-owners of the list. Thus, each client was pulled into a larger conservative populist alternative media universe, and each list could be cross-referenced for future direct mail campaigns, weaving a range of causes and constituencies into one large conservative populist media strategy. Long before the networked world of the internet created communities of activists, this practice, as one scholar has observed, "cultivate[d] a network of like-minded Americans," creating an alternative media matrix that distributed news, perspectives, and knowledge that conservatives would never receive from the political or media establishment.[45]

Because of this, a cause could be valuable to the movement even when it failed. A good example of this was the fight over the Panama Canal in 1976, the first year of Jimmy Carter's presidency. The imminent expiration of the Canal Treaty that guaranteed United States control over the passage between the Gulf of Mexico and the Pacific Ocean became a hot issue during the Republican primary when Ronald Reagan made it part of his strategy to challenge incumbent President Gerald Ford for the nomination. When, after the election, the Carter administration announced its intention to pursue Ford's plan to relinquish sovereignty over the Canal in 1978, the infant New Right seized on it as an issue that spoke to the emotions of grassroots Reagan supporters and might reorient them to the nationalist principles of conservative populism. The campaign to "save the Canal," Viguerie recalled, "gained conservative converts around the country" and generated a list of over 400,000 names. Campaigns like this were a worthy investment for the future, Viguerie explained, even if the cause failed, because they helped him locate voters and contributors, articulate and publicize a vision for conservative populism, and link specific partisans to an aggressive theory of national defense.[46]

In addition, the Canal struggle helped Viguerie and Weyrich identify Reagan as an imperfectly conservative, but acceptable, candidate that might mobilize their network in 1980. Seven years after Viguerie had convened the meeting with Weyrich and other leaders of what he would soon call the New Right, he had twenty-five million names. Those voters and donors were now the engine for Weyrich's conservative institution-building project, as well as the base for a wide-ranging political media project and conservative populist revolution that could upend the liberal establishment. They were also extremely profitable. As Viguerie's lists grew, and computers could parse the names more accurately, he sold them to conservative political activists, evangelicals, and entrepreneurs who were capitalizing on consumer niche markets within conservative populations: gold bugs, survivalists, anti-pornography and anti-union campaigners, and those interested in generating independent income from home.[47]

Yet the Republican establishment was more resilient than either Viguerie or Weyrich knew. In 1980, Viguerie and Weyrich believed that their alternative media methods helped to elect the New Right's first president, Ronald Reagan, but they found themselves quickly stymied by a revived GOP power elite that quickly insulated the president-elect from his conservative populist supporters and their policy objectives.[48] The New Right's hopes that Reagan, an intellectual protégé of William F. Buckley, would move quickly on at least some conservative populist priorities were quickly dashed. True, the Reagan administration immediately went to work on a tax cut package, but it walked away from many of the social issues that motivated conservative populists—opposition to gay rights, ending abortion, and reasserting prayer in schools—and deferred these issues indefinitely. Worse, with the exception of Morton Blackwell, outreach to the transition team intended to place conservative populists in administration posts was rebuffed, and Reagan surrounded himself with senior members of the Republican establishment.[49]

Having been part of almost two decades of struggle, it was painful to Weyrich and Viguerie that Reagan, now part of the political establishment, was holding them at arm's length. Viguerie reached out to the White House directly in mid-January 1981 to set things right before the inauguration. Pointing out the obvious, "that some New Right spokesmen have been critical of your transition effort," Viguerie assured the president-elect that his own views "intended to be constructive have been transformed by some of the press into comments that sounded harsh and shrill." As usual, the establishment media was distorting things, eager to see conservatives turn on each other. Viguerie proposed that "our feeling that things are not going well for conservatives in the new administration" might be only a misimpression created by "our relative lack of contact with you and your top advisors." To solve that problem, he proposed a dinner with the Reagans, top advisors Edwin Meese and James Baker and their wives, and "9-10 New Right conservative leaders and their spouses at a time convenient to you." Three weeks later, the White House declined. Similar efforts on Viguerie's part were rebuffed over the course of the first term and virtually abandoned in the second.[50]

Viguerie saw his alternative media work as part of the fight against the establishment, and what he learned after 1980 was that Phyllis Schlafly's "kingmakers," who rigged not just the political system, but the media, education, and every other institution in favor of elites, were still in charge. When Reagan became part of that establishment, Viguerie began openly calling himself a conservative populist, a political designation, he explained, that described those "who seek political power only so they can return it to the people." The establishment, Viguerie believed, was neither Democratic nor Republican, liberal nor conservative (although liberals had particular power in the media), but both. It consisted of those with "unusual access to the political process, whether gained through economic power or social status or through an old-boy network." Members of the establishment were not even necessarily rich, but included "professors, bureaucrats, or TV commenters." The establishment consisted of anyone who looked down their nose at the people, or believed that "Washington's values [should be] imposed on the rest of America, instead of the other way around."[51]

But the nexus of this rigged system, Viguerie emphasized, was the liberal media. While in totalitarian countries, government elites would impose their views on the media, in the United States, a media elite had succeeded, he wrote later, in "impos[ing] its views on government and on society as a whole." Newspaper bestseller lists excluded books about religion. Journalists covered pro-choice, but not pro-life, rallies and excluded conservative media stars like Phyllis Schlafly from prestigious speaking engagements. Worse, by referring to conservative populists in panicky language like ultra-conservative, far-right, and ultra-right, the liberal media framed them as extremists, not patriots. Most insidiously, because members of the "big media elite" moved in and out of politics and government, promoting their views at the highest level of power, the power elite controlled the media narrative, "establish[ing] certain opinions as legitimate and others as foolish."[52]

Creating an alternative media apparatus even more compelling than the successful effort to put Reagan in the White House would be the key to implementing Viguerie's proposed populist program, or what he called in one chapter heading of his 1983 book *The Establishment vs. The People*, "100 Ways to Make America Great Again." The government would never operate fairly as long as it was controlled by elites. Therefore, conservative populists had to support alternative media that would counter the "preconceptions and prejudices" of the establishment narrative. Making sure that public discussion was informed by facts would "normally [be] the job of the communications media in a free society," Viguerie wrote, but that could not happen under current conditions.[53]

＝＝

Disappointed though they were, Viguerie and Weyrich knew they had not failed, and it is worth returning to the months prior to the 1980 election to see why. They had, instead, pioneered ways to alter the media environment so that future political campaigns, and political conversation could target conservative political junkies for appeals intended to bind them to each other in opposition to liberals and even to the Republican Party itself. In late August 1980, prestigious members of the New Right gathered at the Religious Roundtable, an evangelical association that was mobilizing itself, and all of its media resources, for the coming election. There, Phyllis Schlafly warned that without a conservative in the White House, the threat from "godless communism" would only intensify. Another speaker promoted the idea to the audience of ministers and people of faith from forty-one states, many of whom were radio and television personalities, that to not vote in this atmosphere was "a sin against Almighty God!" The network that Viguerie, Weyrich, and their allies had created, financed, and institutionalized after 1964 was actually poised to elect a president.

Most importantly, a GOP campaign consultant visiting the meeting told a *Washington Post* reporter that most of the audience no longer watched mainstream television news. Instead, they chose to get their information from the alternative religious media, particularly radio and TV broadcasts by megachurch leaders like Pat Robertson and Jerry Falwell. In his own remarks to the *Post* reporter, Paul Weyrich downplayed the ability of Christian voters to affect the looming presidential election between President Jimmy Carter and his challenger, Ronald Reagan: they just weren't that well organized. However, in his remarks to the meeting, Weyrich sang a different tune. "How many of our Christians have what I call the 'goo goo' syndrome?," the former national debate champion, and now a powerful conservative organizer and media personality, boomed, using the infantile nickname turn-of-the-century Republican reformers had been given by political machines in both parties. "*Good government*," Weyrich said mockingly. Regardless of how many people voted, democracy did not become more perfect in a society where the culture war had been lost; voter participation by the wrong people was dangerous to the conservative populist cause. "I don't want everybody to vote," Weyrich said emphatically. "Elections are never won by a majority of people, they never have been, from the beginning of our country, and they are not now." Simply put: conservatives did better, not when all the people voted, but when the *right* people voted.[54] And those people were on Richard Viguerie's lists.

The story of Ronald Reagan's victory was the story imagined by the Simulmatics project. That story was voter mobilization: targeting conservative populists and independents with information and issues, activating them, and getting them to the polls. All this could be done through alternative media, which was not only more effective than trying to tell the conservative populist story in a hostile mainstream environment, it also had the advantage of being nearly invisible to the establishment. As Viguerie noted a year later, the only reason that liberals were so stunned by Ronald Reagan's victory was that they had "depended on the establishment media for their forecasts." Conservative populist alternative media had kept their voters informed and energized, and Viguerie knew where they all were. The "people's right to know," he declared, unhindered by establishment falsehoods, "had finally become a reality." Using alternative media, conservatives had "been able to bypass the Left's near-monopoly of the national news media" and, at last, won the election they had wanted to win so badly back in 1964.[55] And the computers that had helped them do it were about to take center stage.

= 4 =

ELECTRONIC DEMOCRACY

In the middle of the 1984 Super Bowl, an advertisement for a personal computer (PC) made history. The spot, which cost $800,000, appeared during a third-quarter time-out. Partygoers and fans suddenly saw a gray screen crisscrossed with what looked like fiber-optic cable. A harsh voice shouting polemic began to rise slowly in intensity. Minute objects moving through the cable revealed themselves to be shaven-headed automatons, gender and race obscured, marching obediently past wall-mounted monitors. Suddenly, a blond female athlete wearing a white singlet and red shorts and carrying a hammer pushed through the gray crowd, chased by storm troopers. As phrases like "pure ideology" and "we are one people, with one resolve" spewed from an older male figure depicted on a large screen, the athlete rushed into the auditorium and flung her hammer. When the male voice said firmly, "We shall prevail," the screen exploded, spewing dust, glass, and light over the assembled crowd, now jarred from its complacency. In two days, a voice intoned, Apple Computer would "introduce Macintosh. And then you'll see why 1984 won't be like '1984.'"[1] For the first time, PCs were being sold as tools for enhancing democracy and fighting the establishment.

Prior to the Macintosh, personal, or home, computers, might not have seemed equal to such an important task. The screens of early PCs were tiny and filled with blinking letters and numbers in amber or green. Documents and spreadsheets required hand-coding and the use of function keys to produce the simplest formatting. Users had to type in strings of characters to locate the address of a listserv, or the bulletin board systems (BBS) that some users were setting up on their home servers. By contrast, Macintosh's new graphical interface was a breakthrough: its digital environment simulated the real world. Its screen featured colors, illustrations, sound, and crude characters that moved. True, using a Mac still required the user to swap discs in and out to load programs every time the machine was booted up or switched to another task. But a writing program, instead of looking like a computer screen, simulated what letters would look like on a page. A graphic of a calculator, which did simple arithmetic, was nestled next to a spreadsheet. Had Izzy and Esther Stone still been producing the *Weekly*, they could have produced it at home in one of several hundred fonts, with digitized illustrations or graphs inserted. BBS's, which the user could dial in to over a telephone line, showed nested threads that could be collapsed or enlarged, depending on what topic the user wished to pursue. A game of chess, which could be played with someone sitting at another computer across town or across the country, looked like a three-dimensional game board. And the machine was even programmed to speak for itself. "Hello, I'm Macintosh," the machine growled when CEO Steve Jobs unveiled it at an Apple shareholders' meeting held shortly after the Super Bowl. ". . . NEVER TRUST A COMPUTER YOU CAN'T LIFT."[2]

Access to the internet made PCs a conduit for unmediated information and conversation within like-minded communities, transforming them into a platform for both one-to-many and many-to-many alternative media. Although computers were not yet capable of steering users to ideologically friendly information, computer users were far more likely to do this on their own than they ever had been. New Right organizing that culminated in a sweeping victory for Ronald Reagan and the Republican Party in 1980 sparked liberal fears that powered by conservative religious organizing, gender, economic, and racial equality measures championed by the Democratic Party for two decades would be reversed. Although many Americans who had crossed party lines to vote for Reagan in 1980 frustrated conservative aspirations by voting in a Democratic Congress in 1982, populist values such as shrinking the federal bureaucracy and lowering taxes were on the rise.[3] As significantly, by 1984, trust in government, although it had risen from an all-time low of 27 percent at the end of the Carter administration to around 40 percent, was still a little more than half of what it had been in 1964.[4] At the same time, Americans seemed increasingly underinformed about public life. As one 1986 study showed, partisans tended to identify political positions they supported with a politician in their own party, regardless of whether that particular politician actually shared that view.[5]

The groundswell of conservative populist support for Reaganism, and the coalescing of a liberal Democratic opposition, concealed a disturbing trend as January 1, 1984, approached: ideologically committed activists were more politically engaged than ever but the average American was retreating from politics. As one example, Ronald Reagan's 49-state landslide reelection the following November was the largest electoral college victory in history. But voter turnout was only up slightly from 1980: 52.9 percent of Americans eligible to cast a ballot actually went to the polls. Conceding that some voters may not have turned out because television networks had called the election before polls had closed, it was nevertheless "a disappointing outcome," Curtis Gans of the Committee for the Study of the American Electorate told the UPI, particularly given heightened political polarization and the resources that the Democrats had sunk into voter registration.[6]

Could computers reverse political disengagement by rebuilding democracy in online communities that were easy to access from home? One might, of course, imagine the opposite: that a machine-mediated public sphere would accelerate passivity. This was a problem that critics across the political spectrum had long laid at the door of mainstream television news, broadcasts that distracted and entertained but often failed to make viewers think. Were George Orwell, the English author of the dystopian 1949 novel *1984*, able to survey the United States at the end of Ronald Reagan's first term, one journalist wrote, he would see a nation of passive citizens enthralled with media pablum. Americans had forgotten that democracy was "a precious gift," one that, a philosophy professor chimed in, needed to be cultivated. Conservative evangelical Tim LaHaye, himself a writer of popular dystopian science fiction and an advocate for small government, emphasized that citizens had been less disempowered by Washington than by the real "Big Brother": ABC, CBS, and NBC, "the most powerful corporations in America as far as influencing the thinking of people."[7]

Those engaged in the PC revolution emphatically disagreed that digital technology would make Americans more passive. This smaller and less visible group of intellectuals and engineers had already begun to see personal computers in every home as a renewed conduit for democracy, one powered by interactive alternative media created at the grass roots. What they called "networked communities" challenged the "one-to-many" model of media production, in which a single corporate producer distributed to a passive audience, with "many-to-many" production, in which a crowd conducted and published its conversations on the internet. Networked communities imagined information independence from media giants, corporations that would be replaced by convenient, horizontal, and trustworthy news distribution within an unlimited community of users. Best of all, in this period before algorithms nudged the user to particular sites based on their past choices, liberation from advertisers in internet newsgroups meant that information was unmediated, and uncorrupted, by corporate and political manipulation.[8]

As political junkies made the turn into the 1990s, they would increasingly flock to the internet for serious talk that was also a kind of entertainment—except that users experienced these conversations as far more informative, unguarded, and wide-ranging than those the mainstream "infotainment" news environment could offer. Best of all, by getting credentials to an internet community and paying a nominal fee, every user could be their own publisher.

Despite alternative innovations like *The MacNeil/Lehrer News-Hour*, mainstream commercial news grew, but changed very little, by the end of the twentieth century. Between 1980, when cable news channels began to establish themselves, and 1993, when the Mosaic browser made the internet fully searchable, Americans experienced a rapidly expanding news and commercial broadcast environment that seemed to pull them in—only to tell them very little. As one television critic put it, being "more informed" did not necessarily mean being "better informed." Broadcasts continuing from the site of an event, and political conversation shows on cable, chewed up time for twenty-four hours a day, regardless of whether there was anything new to say. And yet people watched. On June 17, 1993, an estimated ninety-five million Americans were mesmerized for over forty-five minutes while Los Angeles police conducted a low-speed chase of former football star O. J. Simpson, evading arrest for the murders of his wife, Nicole Brown Simpson, and bystander Ron Goldman.[9]

While such events were exciting for the new cable entrepreneurs, this passive fascination with pseudo-events amplified existing concerns that popular commitment to civic and political life was deteriorating. Personal computers, available to middle-class Americans for between $300 and $2,500, a cost that could be financed on a credit card or through a manufacturer's installment plan, promised to change this. Empowered users, PC enthusiasts argued, would go out into digital space to seek meaningful information, not spectacular events that producers or editors had chosen for them.[10]

Techno-utopians imagined that participation in electronic, virtual forums, and access to unmediated knowledge, would also nurture a more democratic off-line culture. Users working together could gather information and act on it as a collective, much as digital developers themselves were likely to do. Digital technology would allow Americans to tell their own stories, and listen to each other. These moderated—but unedited—conversations would transform and democratize the political environment, reduce partisanship, and bring otherwise disconnected citizens together in a single experience. And for a short time, for some people, that became a reality. As national security specialist–turned–whistleblower

Edward Snowden recalled about his teenage years exploring virtual space, "for one brief and beautiful stretch of time . . . the internet was mostly made of, by, and for the people. Its purpose was to enlighten, not to monetize." A collective project of peer-to-peer users, the 1990s internet was, to Snowden, "the most pleasant and successful anarchy I have ever experienced."[11]

What this electronic democracy, powered by a PC in each home, would look like was impossible to know, a representative of Apple's advertising agency Chiat/Day explained as the creative team was inundated with questions about what their 1984-themed Macintosh commercial really meant. Their Super Bowl spot wasn't intended to sell an object, but an idea: that through personal computing Americans could "free our lives" from powerful influences that hoarded vital knowledge.[12] This message was ubiquitous in the PC industry. Digital alternative media would, user by user, reinvigorate democracy through distributed, peer-to-peer conversations. Furthermore, because a consumer could enter the PC market for less than $1,000, far lower than the professional cost of producing and distributing a single paper newsletter, the machine was viewed by many as increasing access to core democratic values outside formal politics, such as education and activism. This was a particularly important selling point for Apple, since its 1983 product, the Lisa, had bombed at a sticker price of $10,000. "This is a machine that a lot of people are going to be able to afford," Bill Gates said in a promotional video for the Apple II, sold with a Microsoft Z80 SoftCard coprocessor. That turned out to be correct. By February, Apple had doubled production, signaling a decisive turn to servicing the consumer market.[13]

The PC boom of the 1980s laid the ideological groundwork for the next wave of alternative media by demonstrating what computers could do: bring Americans into direct, unmediated conversation with each other and make every citizen a potential alternative media entrepreneur. The early inhabitants of the internet saw their emerging political culture as a real alternative to the Cold War political violence, committed by activists and the state in the name of expanding democracy, that their parents' generation had experienced. "Democracy could never be imposed at the point of a gun," Snowden wrote about the lessons of Vietnam, but peer-to-peer networks could model a new politics of reason, powered by information and "sown by silicon and fiber."[14] That proved to be too optimistic. Instead, as Republicans and Democrats became more ideologically divided in the 1990s, alternative media platforms became places where subcultural partisan communities flourished. While reporters still used the term "political junkie" to describe their perennial zest for the ins and outs of life in Washington, it soon became popularized to describe an audience for politics in a computerized world where like gravitated to like and every citizen had the potential to be an expert.

The PC's transition from specialized machine to domestic media appliance took several decades. By the early 1980s, no longer confined to the lab, military base, or university, "word processors" had begun to displace typewriters at the office. Hobby computers built from kits purchased for as little as $400 infiltrated homes. The 1984 Apple II advertising blitz marketed the machine as the perfect bridge between home and office, work and play, and the next essential domestic media technology. More generally, manufacturers entering the PC market promised that these beautifully designed, affordable machines would break barriers and unleash creativity. With the addition of a graphics program and the help of a local copying franchise, groups of any size could publish professional-looking newsletters, pamphlets, and broadsides. Computing companies like Apple, IBM, Xerox, Commodore, and Tandy competed throughout the decade to reduce the size and price of PCs, marketing them as a portal to the technological future children would be living in as adults, as well as devices that could ease daily life, paying for themselves by facilitating household budgets and investment strategies. Toward the end of the decade, many of these companies were selling access to the internet, billed as an information highway developed from the military ARPANET and a world of linked virtual communities of choice unfettered by rules, gatekeepers, and limitations on speech. Connecting users to news, libraries, and government agencies, manufacturers promised, the internet would create a new kind of democratic public sphere that anyone, at home, at school, or a public library, could access through a computer terminal.[15]

Like radios and televisions before them, the information available on this new digital alternative media was free, but unlike traditional broadcasting, gaining access to it was not. A basic Apple II, about $700 in 1988, opened the door to other necessary purchases: floppy disks, cables, peripherals, games, software, and additional memory as the user's needs and desires grew.[16] Most importantly, electronic democracy was only available to those willing to pay for access to other users, initially via local or long-distance calls placed through a telephone provider. As an open internet replaced the closed, noncommercial, government-funded ARPANET in the mid-1980s, internet service providers (some of whom also sold computers) worked to lower the cost of access by marketing fee-based systems that could bring users together for a single monthly price. Quantum Computer Services was the earliest provider to try a monthly subscription that created one networked community, reachable through a single portal. Renaming itself America Online (AOL) in 1989, the platform featured news, weather, person-to-person chat, instant messaging, community groups organized around identities and interests, and email. By January 1994, AOL announced that it had six hundred thousand subscribers and anticipated one million by the end of the year.[17]

The internet would soon facilitate sites that revolutionized reporting, broadcasting, and publishing, as well as daily activities like teaching, shopping, banking, travel, and dating. After the first commercially available browser, Mosaic 1.0, was released in 1993, the system itself, its searchable environment, its emphasis on transparency, its low cost of entry (AOL subscribers paid $17 a month by 1995, $11 less than a subscription to the Sunday edition of the *New York Times*), and its potential for limitless free distribution amplified the idea of what alternative digital media could achieve.[18] Alternative media was no longer just a publication or newsletter received through the mail, but a digital *place* where Americans sampled whatever news they liked and responded to it; where they had access to limitless information and conversation;

and where they could distribute their own ideas and organize for political and social change. Instead of being targeted by direct marketers, users could take the initiative to choose what products or services they wished to engage with and avoid what they did not. Instead of passively receiving news from a television, radio, or newspaper, they could share news items that sparked discussions, questions, and criticism. Alternative digital media indulged those who were already consumed with the national or local political scene and enticed new subscribers into an expanding world of political junkies on BBS's and in chatrooms. Participants in online political forums did not just receive a publication; they actually participated in writing, researching, and reporting news stories in threaded conversations where debates over facts and interpretation accrued through the days, or weeks, that the topic remained interesting to the group. Long before legacy news organizations went online in the mid-1990s and began to market themselves to segmented political audiences, internet service providers (ISPs) were, perhaps unknowingly, exacerbating partisan divides: the digital environments they designed could be wholly or partly devoted to particular political communities and viewpoints, while discouraged dissenters could easily migrate and thrive elsewhere.[19]

Alternative media forums designed for discussion and the exchange of information became particularly important at a moment when mainstream media initiatives like cable were increasing the volume of news, and talk *about* the news, as their only form of programming. Beginning over a decade earlier, American viewers increasingly tuned into channels where they could experience politics live, much as journalists and politicians did, whetting their appetites for speedy, unfiltered access to political news and news makers. The Cable-Satellite Public Affairs Network (CSPAN), conceived a year after the Watergate hearings ended, began broadcasting live, and without commentary, in the House of Representatives in 1979 (a second channel, CSPAN-2, debuted in the Senate in 1987). Ted Turner's Cable News Network (CNN), initially broadcast out of his Atlanta "Superstation" via satellite, was the next out of the gate in 1980, offering commentary and interviews from the halls of Congress and other breaking news sites twenty-four hours a day.

The Financial News Network, underwritten by the brokerage firm Merrill Lynch, launched in 1981; CNN introduced a subsidiary, Headline News (HLN), in 1982; and CNBC, a cable affiliate of the legacy NBC network, in 1989. By 1990, almost fifty-seven million Americans had access to CNN, and half of American homes had cable news subscriptions of some kind. Between 1995 and 1996, MSNBC, a partnership between Microsoft and NBC, and Fox News, a spin-off of the entertainment corporation Twentieth Century Fox, joined the party.[20]

Unlike legacy news channels, these new cable news shows, even those that ultimately settled on a liberal editorial viewpoint like MSNBC and CNN, saw conservative populists as a potential market to be cultivated. Rupert Murdoch, the Australian newspaper entrepreneur who bankrolled the channel, under the direction of CEO Roger Ailes, described Fox News's editorial approach as "fair and balanced," insinuating that other news channels were ideologically slanted to a liberal viewpoint. Established media outlets presumed that because Murdoch himself was conservative, and he had hired Ailes, the channel would be explicitly conservative, even before a single broadcast had aired. And it was. Fox News would quickly come to own this conservative audience, forcing other networks like MSNBC to quietly release conservative commenters and tack left.[21]

While internet conversations were open to anyone approved by a moderator (which, in practice, meant anyone), threads—which designated a topic and then separated it into subtopics as the interests and knowledge of the users identified discrete areas of debate—gave participants the opportunity to divide themselves into focused groups. Because modems used dial-in telephone systems, most internet communities also mapped onto "in real life" (IRL) communities, defined by area codes. "To call a BBS was to visit the private residence of a fellow computer fan electronically," journalist Benj Edwards reminisced about the 1980s and early 1990s, while anonymous usernames permitted frank and experimental exchanges. Using these forums also required an initiation into the special language and skill set of the PC hobbyist. "After signing up or logging in, the service might present a list of bulletins," Edwards explained, such as a message from the systems operator, or "sysop," who had built the community on his own server. Proceeding to the main menu, the user would then see threads of conversations, games, open source coding, programs, and other items of interest. Then, a user would make "single character selections like 'R' to read messages, 'E' to send email, 'T' to see the file library (to download programs), or 'G' to log off."[22]

Although these users had access to an alternative news environment in selected threads and, as yet, only a small fraction of viewers, these platforms were designed to facilitate a slower, more deliberate and participatory approach to conversation than the rapidly expanding mainstream broadcast news environment could, or would, accommodate. Interfaces read as menus of simultaneous, and parallel, conversations that permitted deep engagement with some topics and complete disengagement with others; within threads, conversation that paused on issues rather than moving on to the next item in the news cycle.[23]

By contrast, despite the positive response to PBS's in-depth reporting on the Watergate hearings, television news, and cable news in particular, continued to specialize in repetition, duplication, and round-the-clock coverage of sensational events. And it worked. CNN, on the air in 1980, was first noticed by a mass audience in 1987, when first responders in Midland, Texas, worked for almost three days to free an eighteen-month-old girl who had fallen down an abandoned well.[24] The network's live coverage of the first Gulf War in 1991, and particularly the aerial attack on Baghdad, cemented techniques that would shape cable news as a genre: having journalists and camera crews on-site for extended periods of time, talking heads in the studio to provide commentary, and an anchor directing traffic with help from producers. But more news, accompanied by titillating visuals, was not better news. The cable broadcast model was characterized by speed, a voracious demand for content, and recycled stories with often trivial updates, a technique that would be mimicked by corporate internet news services by the end of the 1990s.[25]

The sense that the mainstream media could be everywhere, broadcasting everything to everyone, made the cable news format an exciting but newly flawed genre, even by comparison to traditional broadcasts. To paraphrase CNN founder Ted Turner, it was important to get a story right—but it was *as important* to get it on the air *fast*. Fast was not always accurate, or even a sign of a news item's urgency, but rather a phenomenon produced by the need for content. In its early years, legacy news broadcasters mocked CNN as the "Chicken Noodle Network" for its low-budget look, technical screwups, and endless human interest stories featuring cats and babies. However, as they tried to compete with these interlopers, and legacy networks expanded the time slots allotted to news divisions with hour-long magazine-style shows, they wooed political junkies, not with more informed broadcasts, but sensationalism, exposés, and human interest stories about politics. By the 1980s, only one out of three segments on the prestigious CBS newsmagazine *60 Minutes*, first aired in 1968, was an investigative story. The network also drew repeated criticisms for its "gotcha journalism," lack of fact-checking, and prosecutorial questioning style adopted by hosts drawn from CBS's stable of evening news anchors.[26]

Like traditional evening broadcast news, cable news relied on trustworthy voices, a need that grew as the number of stories covered every day multiplied. By contrast, alternative digital media formats were perceived by their users as more democratic: as news coverage expanded on the internet, ever-more authority in choosing, and even reporting, news items to feature on a BBS devolved to users, not designated truth-tellers. Digital alternative media prided themselves in these early years on having no establishment and no authoritative voices. Despite its reliance on corporations, universities, and the federal government for its infrastructure, the internet was anti-corporate in its ethic, its aspirations, its language, and its conventions. Its practices emerged outside corporate media in an earlier period when most people who subscribed to listservs (applications that delivered messages to subscribers by electronic mail) and bulletin boards were members of a collaborative, horizontally organized scientific community. *Whole Earth Catalogue* founder Stewart Brand described this early network of participants to *Rolling Stone* in 1972 as "a mobile new-found elite, with its own apparat[us], language and character, its own legends and humor." This new breed referred to its members as "hackers," code-savvy people who discovered, invented, and repurposed things they found on the internet. Hackers were, Brand believed, "scouting a leading edge of technology" and inhabiting an "outlaw country, where rules are not decree or routine so much as the starker demands of what's possible."[27]

Brand's use of a sentimental language, one that invokes the potential for personal transformation in exploring territory beyond the reach of the state, is telling. Many of these early designers, users, and digital philosophers are now thought of as being the quintessential techno-utopians. They were people who firmly believed that new forms of digital alternative media would transform, from the bottom up, a society that had been divided by political strife in the 1960s and rendered passive by establishment media and politics in the 1970s. Many of them first cohered as a community on the Whole Earth 'Lectronic Link (WELL), founded in 1985 by Brand and New Age technology pioneer Larry Brilliant.[28] Few discussion groups on the WELL were focused on formal electoral politics: participants were consumed with numerous topics that they understood to be both political and urgent, but which received little or no coverage in the mainstream. Issues like composting, marijuana legalization, recycling, underground radio stations, feminism, traveling to Cuba and other countries embargoed by the United States, and communities made up of yoga, meditation, and other New Age practitioners fueled lively discussions that were only lightly moderated, even when they became nasty and sexist. Whereas mainstream media were vertical and structured around the authoritative voice, the WELL emphasized what it called "distributed learning," horizontal conversation in which all participants learned from each other. Inaccurate information would naturally be corrected by others who were better informed. Problem-solving was accomplished by the "hive mind," a virtual town square where many people gathered to bring multiple skill and knowledge sets together.[29]

Digital alternative media's news and discussion platforms were built with the conviction that politics, as it was, was alienating and had failed to enhance personal freedom. Because users divided themselves into communities and threads by choice, the WELL also anticipated the algorithmic divisions that would characterize social media and the searchable web. By the mid-1990s, it served as a crossroads where intellectuals who had come out of prior left social movements thrived, and it began to take on some of the characteristics that would later be typical of MySpace, Blogspot, and other early social media sites. For example, feminist socialist Barbara Ehrenreich and gay comedian David Sedaris maintained pages that updated followers about their appearances and writing. Radical political cartoonist Dan Perkins (aka Tom Tomorrow), whose weekly cartoon about Washington politics, "This Modern World," was syndicated in alternative newspapers around the country, used his page as a multimedia environment, linking to radio, television, and newspaper interviews about his work and his books at the new digital bookseller Amazon.com. Perkins also encouraged his readers to lobby their local alternative papers to carry his work or, in some cases, not bow to political pressure to drop it.[30]

The WELL hosted a remarkable amount of civic activity, as well as conversations about how a digitally connected world might promote democracy and free speech in a rapidly changing society. Feminists for Free Expression (FFE), a national group founded in 1992 to end restrictions on the production and sale of erotic materials, promoted its real-world mission on the WELL. But FFE also used its access to digital community to explain the importance of the struggle against censorship and why it mattered to the future of digital alternative media. In "Feminism and Free Speech: the Internet," FFE explained that the WELL community should care about zoning and civil forfeiture laws to restrict adult sexual materials. Would-be censors argued that pornography would proliferate online, giving children easy access to dangerous ideas about sex. But violent sexual materials that were illegal to produce and sell in the real world would also be illegal online, FFE explained. The solution to keeping inappropriate content out of the hands of children was not censorship, but enhanced vigilance by parents. Adults needed to recommit to monitoring children's virtual lives as they would their real-world ones and, most importantly, discuss sex honestly. "FFE believes most Americans would prefer to do this themselves," the authors wrote, in phrasing that gestured to Libertarianism, "rather than let a government committee decide what their children read, watch and think."[31]

Unlike one-to-many mainstream broadcasting, which identified market segments for its broadcasts, the many-to-many WELL expanded distribution across geographical boundaries. Online spaces occupied by activist editors and print journalists created a bridge between the old world of newsletters and community newspapers and a new form of writing emerging in the mid-1990s called the "web log," or blog, at the time a rare digital platform because it required the technical skills to code and manage a website. The *San Francisco Flier*, founded by independent journalist John Hutchison in 1987, went online via the WELL in 1995. Early issues included well-researched critiques of United States foreign policy, international economic affairs, an interview with radical organizer Harry Bridges's daughter about local labor history, and the Iran-Contra scandal. Like FFE, the *Flier*'s very presence established the WELL's democratic commitments. It also scrutinized intimate ties between the Democratic Party and Silicon Valley, particularly emerging environmental and labor issues. One article debunked corporate assertions that technology promoted a cleaner environment and a stronger economy. Computer industry waste, the *Flier* noted, had serious health consequences, and corporate lobbyists had "been leaders in efforts to undermine the existing protections of labor laws." Furthermore, states and municipalities were covertly creating tax incentives and eliminating local regulations to attract these industries to communities, without concern for the public interest.[32]

Most early internet intellectuals agreed that while technology could create and serve democracy, it was not itself inherently democratic. Rather, digital technology could be put to the work of democracy in a way that mainstream media could not because it would be designed from scratch to that goal and reflect the non-digital alternative media ethic. As computer hacker Kevin Kelly recalled the original design goals of the WELL in 1985, critical principles were that the community be inexpensive, open, self-sustaining, and governed by its users.[33]

Simultaneously with the launch of the WELL, Stewart Brand created an alternative print publication to push these ideas and conversations out into the nondigital world. The *Whole Earth Review: Tools and Ideas for the Computer Age* was a publication meant to serve as a nerve center for the intellectual work of the developing digital alternative media system. While the magazine reviewed equipment, advertised computer peripherals, and kept up with new ideas in computing, it also proposed that ideas were tools, activated by technology, that promoted real democracy. One of these tools was the principle of self-organization. As one writer explained, "The vitality of democratic politics depends on people's willingness to act together, to appear together in person, speak their minds, deliberate, and decide what to do."[34]

Yet self-organization of the kind techno-utopians imagined implied that users would leave behind their preexisting ideological attachments. It is worthwhile to pause and ask how activists so deeply steeped in internet communities miscalculated a future in which widening political divides in the real world actually mapped onto, rather than being neutralized by, the virtual world. One answer is that a surprisingly small number of people were involved in early conversations about digital alternative media. By 1991, although PC ownership was growing rapidly, fewer than 1 percent of Americans participated in any kind of BBS or virtual community. A second explanation is that although these visionaries represented a range of political viewpoints from left to right, and many were Libertarian, internet intellectuals associated with the *Whole Earth Review* saw themselves as a self-appointed vanguard who were inventing technology's democratic future and remaking the culture to match their own insights.

These visionaries did not foresee that as the internet became more popular and populated, mainstream media and politics would come to dominate and divide digital spaces. Instead, they anticipated a future similar to that of the community radio movement of the 1960s that produced the government-funded network of stations called National Public Radio in 1971. The demise of the 1985 Fairness Doctrine, which required politically balanced programming, produced stations that were uniformly conservative, liberal, or progressive, thereby fragmenting audiences. But deregulation also opened radio to voices across the political spectrum, enhancing the ability to speak freely over the airwaves. Radio did not in the end devolve into chaos, but rather "a new order, far more simple and perfect and porous than the old system of government fiat," as community radio activist Lorenzo Milam in the *Whole Earth Review* wrote. Now, anyone could start an alternative radio station: "You go to your local equivalent of Radio Shack and buy an FM or television transmitter and you are on the air."[35]

Those who promoted electronic democracy believed that imbalances of power were created, and enforced, by the mainstream media's inherent tendency to stifle dissident ideas. They did not foresee that listeners might simply choose media that supported what they already believed and screen out whatever did not. Instead, they envisioned that the expansion of digital alternative media would make Americans more eager to participate in "the wisdom of the citizenry," as social scientist Duane Elgin put it in 1991. "If we don't know what our fellow citizens think and feel about the issues," Elgin asserted, "then we don't know what is possible[.]" Some community activists, knowing that computers were not yet universally accessible, developed prototypes for the connected world they envisioned by repurposing analog technology. In 1987, the League of Women Voters and the ABC affiliate station in San Francisco created an "electronic town meeting," in which select viewers watched the event on television and "voted" by telephone six times during the proceedings, giving policymakers rapid feedback about proposed policies. Similarly, the Detroit school board worked with a local public television station to equip 22 schools with cameras, screens, and broadcasting equipment, creating a giant "town hall" for 1,500 participants debating and voting on proposals to reduce the school dropout rate.[36]

Cumbersome as it was to make multiple electronic technologies work together, they nevertheless modeled an alternative democratic process. Horizontal decision-making might be replicated more efficiently on digital platforms, allowing engaged citizens to represent themselves rather than working through a political establishment. In 1987, the San Diego Board of Supervisors installed a $16 million videoconferencing system that allowed citizens and municipal employees to participate in meetings from numerous remote locations. Users trained by watching mainstream televi-sion newsmagazines would understand how to participate. "The result will be the legislative equivalent of 'Nightline,'" one reporter wrote, "with supervisors and the public talking, not face to face, but through large television monitors, miles apart from each other." In 1989, the idea moved to the internet, when the Santa Monica City Council created an electronic bulletin board, the Public Elec-tronic Network (PEN), accessible from home, work, or from free public terminals, to facilitate asynchronous public debate.[37]

The intellectuals gathered around the *Whole Earth Review* fol-lowed these developments closely. Few would be more engaged with the future of electronic democracy than Howard Rheingold, one of the earliest to use the phrase "virtual community"; and to accurately predict the impact of PCs on white-collar work, as well as political campaigns, organized in online environments that sup-ported traditional activities such as canvassing and fundraising.[38] An early member of the WELL, Rheingold saw that PCs and the telephone networks that linked them could be the "great equalizer" that allowed citizens to stand up to the political and media estab-lishments. Public policy formation was "essentially communicative in nature," Rheingold wrote. The BBS was not only the most basic and accessible form of digital alternative media, but it also gener-ated lists that could be put to the purpose of encouraging people to vote, attend political meetings, or protest. Registration also gave the user access to electronic mail, or email, which could "give a small organization big leverage" by linking a group of citizens to distant communities of activists who could contribute resources, knowledge, and publicity to a civic campaign. What's more, digi-tal media could reform the political system. Rheingold pointed to one Colorado activist who had successfully used a BBS to organize his community to challenge a rigged city bidding process and un-seat a corrupt politician. A new city councilman "was elected, and the councilman continued to use the BBS to communicate with his constituents."[39]

Rheingold saw electronic democracy as a plausible response to the heightened ideological divisions of the 1980s, not a force that would deepen them. Picking up on criticisms of the political process by thinkers as dissimilar as Phyllis Schlafly and Joe McGinniss, Rheingold believed that who was selected as a candidate was less of an issue than the fact that candidates were preselected by political parties and sold to the electorate in the media. "The time has come," he wrote, "for us to work toward a less simplistic dialogue in which a larger portion of the citizenry can have real input into the decisions about which candidates will appear on ballots."[40]

Digital alternative media promised a more just distribution of political power, one linked to a transparent, horizontal production and distribution mechanism for the news. The biggest media story of the first Iraq War was CNN's coverage of the bombing of Baghdad that began on January 16, 1991. The network's reporters had refused to be evacuated, live broadcasting the terrifying aerial attack, something Americans had never seen. Yet the idea that the news of the war would be equally transparent was an illusion. The Pentagon had learned from the Vietnam experience that journalists required management. As the war progressed, the US military's practice of embedding reporters in combat units, and not permitting them to move freely from sector to sector, made it difficult for news organizations to have a grasp of the whole war, or know whether press briefings were accurate. But a service called PeaceNet, founded in the San Francisco Bay Area in the 1980s to support peace activism, became the digital home for a "thriving alternative press corps." Composed of freelance and amateur journalists not registered with the military, PeaceNet was able to get news out of Kuwait and Iraq by bypassing official channels and posting reports online. Mainstream syndicates, newspapers, and television networks found themselves playing catchup with these independents as PeaceNet itself became a major news source on the war, with over 10,000 subscribers and five conferences, subcommunities where users gathered to discuss specific topics.[41]

Similarly, as Eastern European countries broke their ties with the Soviet Union and moved toward independent governance after 1989, BBS services sprang up as an alternative to mainstream newspapers, controlled for years by the Communist party, which few citizens trusted. By 1993, *Wired*, a new American print magazine dedicated to reporting on the digital and new media world, reported that billionaire George Soros opened offices in four major Eastern European cities. A major project was rebuilding media institutions to support democratic politics and governance in the new nations that were emerging from the post-Soviet era. Soros-funded institutions were training journalists, updating radio stations, and establishing Balkans-based BBS's.[42]

During the first Iraq war, digital alternative media proved itself not only more nimble than mainstream media, but also better capable of evading the Bush administration's narrative about the war. But Rheingold saw these journalism innovations as only a first step toward transformation of the entire political establishment. Instead of the world as it was—primarily run by political parties, powerful economic forces, corporate media, and nation-states— Rheingold imagined an electronic democracy powered by "civic networks" that lived on the internet and took real-world action. Society would be governed not by institutions but by ideas, conversation, and the people who were committed to political change, not the status quo. Theories of governance, instead of being imposed from above, would emerge spontaneously from below, having been already debated by the crowd. Digital alternative media also provided the means to implement good ideas far more quickly than establishment institutions permitted. Something as basic as delivering services to the homeless, Rheingold argued, could be debureaucratized, linking those in need directly to benefactors via the internet.[43]

A few politicians were also grasping the possibility that civic networks could create solutions to problems that governments could not, or would not, address. In 1993, North Carolina Democrat Charlie Rose sponsored a bill to put all public government information—including opportunities for funding and congressional records and hearings—on the internet. As he told a reporter for *Wired* magazine, personal computers had ushered in an era of "in your face democracy" that would permanently disrupt the Washington establishment's stranglehold on information. "Access to power and access to how things get done are the main commodities bought and sold in Washington," Rose said. That could be "swept away, and replaced with simple, open, electronic access by the people, to their government." In a 1995 profile in *Whole Earth Review*, California Governor Jerry Brown also remarked that the successful politician of the future would be embedded in community networks, be "able to provide example and direction to different people with differing skills and [get] them all to work in support of what they have come together to accomplish." Critical to realizing this vision would be to transcend the mainstream media "sound bites" that only gestured at campaign coverage, and to use technology to promote "sustained conversation" among and between citizen networks.[44]

Yet, these visions for a democracy revived by digital alternative media arose at precisely the moment when the real-world partisan divide was becoming increasingly bitter and Americans were beginning to retreat to spaces, virtual and real, where others shared their values. More involved in political talk, they were increasingly less interested in political action and community engagement. In January 1995, this phenomenon acquired a name when a sociology article escaped from its obscure academic journal and began to circulate around the mainstream media: "bowling alone." The strong ties between individuals that American democracy required, Harvard political scientist Robert Putnam argued, had frayed. Americans were more religious than ever before, but attended church less; they had become political junkies, but local political parties had few volunteers. The organizations that had structured civic life for decades were also in decline: union membership was at its lowest ebb since before the Great Depression; local parent-teacher associations had collapsed, as had fraternal organizations like the Lions, the Jaycees, the Elks, and the Masons. Bowling was not just a metaphor in Putnam's work: bowling leagues, an excuse to socialize, were disappearing: without face-to-face contact, the social capital built up in conversations over "beer and pizza" had all but evaporated.[45] *Bowling Alone: The Collapse and Revival of American Community*, the book Putnam developed from this article, became an instant bestseller in 2000, as Americans turned the corner into a new century defined by the internet.

The ideas about transforming democracy through alternative media that Howard Rheingold and others at the *Whole Earth Review* promoted did not occur in a vacuum, and they were not just about technology. They were a response to the decline of the establishment institutions that had defined most of the twentieth century, particularly corporate media and political parties that seemed static, weakened, or unable to respond to Americans' real lives. Like Rheingold, Putnam also saw a set of institutional changes promoted by campaign professionals like Richard Viguerie that could target and inform voters so precisely that even political activists no longer talked to the voters they wished to mobilize. There was no perceived need to contact a neighbor personally because that person was likely to receive multiple rounds of direct mail or "an anonymous call from a paid phone bank. Less and less party activity," Putnam wrote, "involves volunteer collaboration among committed partisans. More and more involves the skilled (and expensive) techniques of effective mass marketing. This trend goes hand in hand with the explosive growth of direct-mail fundraising and political action committees (PACs) formed to channel financial support to party organizations."[46]

As it turned out, the internet was part of the problem and part of the solution. In the next decade, media experts would begin to experiment with remaking mainstream institutions—journalism, politics, social networks, and civic organizations—to look more like alternative media projects, gradually moving politics and establishment political media online. They learned how to slice, dice, and segment the online audience for political news, exacerbating political divisions rather than bridging them. But Rheingold's ideas would also survive, as outsider candidates tried to energize grassroots support that would help them compete with handpicked establishment officeholders.

= 5 =

SCANDAL

Few people had heard of Matthew Drudge before January 17, 1998, the day that he printed a story about a twenty-four-year-old woman and her paramour, Democratic President William Jefferson Clinton. Between 1995 and 1997, a female White House staffer, Drudge wrote, had been "a frequent visitor to a small study just off the Oval Office where she claims to have indulged the President's sexual preference."[1] The events that followed—an investigation, a salacious public report with pornographic details about the president's "sexual preference," an impeachment, and a Senate trial averted by only a few votes—unfolded as political history. But Drudge's bold move was also a turning point for the history of journalism. It legitimized alternative digital media as a source for breaking news, and it demonstrated how internet platforms could be used to exploit a widening partisan divide between left and right. Most importantly, Drudge's scoop challenged the mainstream media's unwillingness to tell the truth about the politics. Alternative media could be an effective way of holding both the media and political establishments to account.

The story was an extraordinary scoop for a relatively obscure, alternative digital media site. In the tradition of George Seldes and Izzy Stone, Drudge had only obtained the story because *Newsweek* had pulled it from the weekly issue at the last minute—and someone who has never been named gave it to him. Drudge's lede was not the president's extramarital dalliance, nor did he identify Monica Lewinsky as the president's lover. Instead, he highlighted the fact that a top political reporter had researched and fact-checked the story, but *Newsweek* refused to publish it. "**World Exclusive**," the dispatch began, in a hyperbolic style that Drudge fans were accustomed to. "At the last minute, at 6 p.m. Saturday evening, NEWSWEEK magazine killed a story that was designed to shake official Washington to its foundation: A White House intern carried on a sexual affair with the President of the United States!"[2] Two decades later, *Newsweek* would primly characterize Drudge's news item as "technically a scoop of a scoop."[3]

For almost six months prior, Drudge had leaked bits of gossip about what reporter Michael Isikoff was working on. Monica Lewinsky, the daughter of a Clinton donor and a former White House summer intern, had begun her job in the Office of Legislative Affairs on November 15, just as the Republican-led Congress shut down the federal government rather than pass a budget. The "atmosphere of crisis" and the unusual intimacy of a West Wing reduced to a skeleton staff had immediately thrown Clinton and Lewinsky together. After exchanging a few smiles, their flirting intensified, ending in a tight embrace and a kiss. Their affair, such as it was, proceeded until senior White House staffers, concerned about Lewinsky's trips in and out of the Oval Office, moved her to the Pentagon. Clinton, who had been dogged by rumors of extramarital affairs in 1992, promised her that this arrangement would only last until the 1996 campaign ended. The election came and went, and Lewinsky was no closer to resuming her relationship with the president. She poured her heart out to a coworker, Linda Tripp, a Bush appointee who disliked the Clintons and secretly taped telephone conversations with her friend. Imagining that she might write a book, Tripp shared the tapes with literary agent Lucianne Goldberg, and then with special prosecutor Kenneth Starr, who was tasked with investigating the Clintons' finances. Now Starr extended the inquiry into the president's private life and what he might have done to protect himself from further gossip.[4]

Matt Drudge—email newsletter entrepreneur, professional scandal seeker, midnight scrounger of office trash cans, and a man who, until he broke the Lewinsky story, literally had nothing to lose—was the First Couple's nightmare come true. There is perhaps no better proof of this than the fact that in neither Hillary Clinton's 576-page autobiography, *Living History* (2003), nor in Bill Clinton's 1,008-page doorstop of a memoir, *My Life* (2004), does the name of Matt Drudge, the man who gave every Clinton conspiracy theory on the internet legs, appear once. In fact, Drudge's decision to publish the Lewinsky story nearly toppled the presidency. Arguably, he also helped to ensure that at least two other Democrats—Al Gore in 2000 and Hillary Clinton in 2008 and 2016—never became president. In addition, Drudge, whose thin knowledge of technology beyond simple publishing tools made him an ideal consumer for the burgeoning personal computer industry, launched a new chapter in alternative media, becoming a bridge between the era of the political newsletter and the dawn of blogging. A man with little formal education, but a genius for media, Drudge took old things—gossip, news, the newsletter format, email—and made them new.[5]

The Lewinsky affair was also something new: a classic piece of tabloid gossip crossed with political news that ignited an impeachment. The real possibility that the Starr investigation would become a constitutional crisis emerged when Linda Tripp's tapes revealed that Lewinsky might have been instructed, by the president, to lie about their affair under oath. When Drudge, who had been sniffing around the story for months, learned that *Newsweek* would not print their own reporter's investigation, his decision to run it was a kind of alternative media manifesto: the mainstream media should not be allowed to decide what, and what not, to reveal about a political figure. But who leaked the story in the first place? Was it an as yet unknown actor? Was it Isikoff himself, who neither confirmed nor denied it to me, and whose own account of the breaking story begins when he received a call from Drudge near midnight on the night before the story zoomed out over the internet? Was it Goldberg, who had been in direct contact with Drudge, or was it Tripp's lawyer, Jim Moody: both of whom were notified by Isikoff when *Newsweek* pulled the story? Or was it one of the "Elves," a cadre of conservative activists who had explicitly stated their determination to topple the Clinton administration by leaking every piece of dirt about the Clintons they could find? The Elves included lawyer George Conway and beltway pundit Ann Coulter, a close friend of Drudge's.[6]

What all of these possible leakers knew was that although no mainstream outlet would break the story, Drudge would. This was not because he was a committed conservative populist (he has always identified as Libertarian), but because he was an outsider to the establishment. Imagining himself as an old-school muckraker, Drudge redefined digital alternative media as a new frontier for feeding the growing American hunger for political news. While most journalists still shied away from covering politicians' private lives, Drudge saw it as an opportunity for exploring the hypocrisy of the mainstream establishment and reinventing political infotainment as a partisan enterprise. Drudge's revelations, and the congressional investigation that ensued, cemented the growing hostility between Republicans and Democrats that has characterized national politics ever since.

But the scandals roiling the Clinton administration didn't just inform and fuel political conflict, they entertained. A few months after the Lewinsky story made Drudge an alternative media star, the following story made the rounds: Drudge and Coulter boarded a plane together. As Coulter drew the *New York Times* out of her bag, Drudge smiled and said, "You aren't going to learn anything from *that*," and reached for a copy of the *National Enquirer*.[7]

═══

Matt Drudge wasn't the first person to establish a political tip sheet. Raised in the Washington suburb of Takoma Park by middle-class parents, it is hard to imagine that he had not seen a tip sheet at some point before he began to write one. But by his own account, early on, Drudge was fascinated by the news. "Talk radio tucked me in at night and the police scanner was my unconditional best friend," he recalled. In junior high school, Drudge got a job delivering the *Washington Star*, but rarely completed his route, partly because he would take time off to read the paper, pretending he was the editor. "I noticed how *their* lead story was not really *the* lead story," he wrote, perceiving that the most interesting news was hidden on the inside pages. "I just knew I'd do better if I were in charge."[8]

Newsletters like the one Drudge began to distribute by email prior to launching his site in 1995 were a common resource for mainstream political reporters. One was *Capitol Hill Blue*, a nonpartisan Washington news and gossip internet site established in 1994.[9] But newsletters aimed at journalists and pundits were a pre-internet phenomenon. Some news publications offered closed circulation, numbered newsletters, circulated to their political writers, providing background that could never be printed, but context for news that should be reported. Prior to the internet, the Washington press corps had two other ways of staying broadly informed about national politics: *Congressional Quarterly*, which cost several thousand dollars a year and kept them up to date with all of the news in the Capitol; and clipping services, which provided deep background about state and local politics around the nation. Journalist Susan Glasser recalled reporters gathering around a table once a week in the mid-1980s "to sift through a large stack of clips from local newspapers across the country, organized by state[.]"[10]

Drudge was fascinated by journalism and politics, but an indifferent student. After he graduated from high school, he passed on college, heading to Los Angeles, where he got a job in the CBS gift shop. At night he snooped in trash cans, looking for bits of gossip about the television industry. His father, "in a parental panic" about his son's apparently aimless life, flew out one day and, in an aspirational gesture, bought him a personal computer. After that, Drudge began posting his stolen tidbits on an internet news group. "I collected a few email addresses," he wrote. "I set up a list." By 1995, thousands of people had joined. "The ensuing website," he wrote about the early years of the *Drudge Report*, "practically launched itself."[11]

Other than *Capitol Hill Blue*, the *Drudge Report*'s most immediate inspiration was *The Hotline*, a bipartisan newsletter full of backroom Beltway gossip, polling stats, and political jokes. Founded in 1987 by Doug Bailey, a liberal Republican political consultant who was widely admired by liberals and conservatives alike, *The Hotline* was faxed to subscribers every business day. A dedicated political junkie, Bailey, as one friend recalled, "had an amazing ability to always be modern, always be of the moment, always be thinking about what the next big thing is." *NBC News* anchor Chuck Todd, a former editor at *The Hotline*, agreed. Bailey fostered "an addiction to political reporting" in everyone who worked for him there. Many journalists saw *The Hotline*, which could be delivered instantaneously to an entire subscription list by preloading a list of fax numbers, as the inspiration for the political e-newsletters and born-digital political journalism sites that would emerge in the 1990s. "We were addicted to it," said Susan Glasser, echoing Todd.[12]

A year shy of thirty years old, Drudge was addicted to the news too. He came home from CBS at night, pockets stuffed with paper, to write his newsletter and connect to Capitol Hill sources online, styling the *Drudge Report* as a gossip sheet about Washington and Hollywood. Soon, *Wired*, launched as a prototype web magazine in 1994 by writers who worked for *Whole Earth Review*, noticed the *Drudge Report* and hired him to write a column that drew on material from the newsletter. It was one of only two times (the other was a short stint for *Fox News* after the Lewinsky scandal broke) that Drudge would work for anyone else as a journalist. Between November 1996 and May 1997, his jazzy, mash-up style put utterly unimportant information next to potentially seismic political gossip. In one column, he began with a short description of fans waiting outside the Virgin record store on Sunset Boulevard for the release of Madonna's *Evita* album; jumped to a few lines about a Fleetwood Mac reunion; segued to a paragraph about getting a massage in a grocery store; and ended with a tip that Maine's former senator George Mitchell would come out of retirement to become Secretary of State (he didn't). In his next column, Drudge mused about when the "privacy zone" that the Clintons had created around their daughter Chelsea would collapse, since "she was already viciously gossiped about at Washington dinner parties." Later that day, alongside inside info about Oprah Winfrey and news anchor Barbara Walters, Drudge reported that Hillary Clinton was pushing to have her friend, Massachusetts Governor

William Weld, appointed as attorney general; and—more importantly—that the Starr investigation was leaking like a sieve.[13]

Long before he broke the Lewinsky story, Drudge surely saw the media circus around the Clintons as a potential opportunity, since a sizeable and lucrative publishing industry on the right had already sprung up around them. David Brock's bestselling *The Seduction of Hillary Rodham* (1996) portrayed the First Lady as a dangerous radical, hungry for power yet unsure of her own identity. The conservative *American Spectator* routinely produced salacious, often anonymously sourced stories about the Clintons' Arkansas years, authored by Brock and others.[14] Drudge played to this audience in his persistent reporting on the Clintons, portraying the First Couple as bumbling, out of touch, angry, underprepared for national office, and under siege from their own unforced errors. In spring 1997, Drudge reported with glee that Clinton—whose vice president Al Gore was an internet evangelist—had no idea how to use a computer, despite a White House photo op in which the president appeared to send an email on a military laptop. A PC, connected to the internet, had been installed in the president's office a year earlier, Drudge wrote, but "as exclusively reported in this space last year, Clinton is completely computer illiterate. He also faces the block of very poor typing skills."[15]

Written in an intimate, confiding tone, Drudge's work invited readers into the backstage of the political and media establishment. As it transitioned from an e-newsletter to a website in 1997, the *Drudge Report* stuck to the traditions of the tip sheet and anticipated an alternative media genre that did not yet exist: political blogging. Focused on original reporting and opinion pieces based on mainstream media reporting, Drudge updated the site several times a day. Drudge reported a few original stories, but provided a dizzying number of links to other publications and sites. This design encouraged other journalists to keep his site open in their browsers all day, if only to navigate easily to the other sites that they needed to read. The top link, labeled "Matt Drudge," led to a page that either had a story, or hinted at an investigation in progress. "Matt Drudge is out in the field," said one short message. "His Report will return when he does." Underneath was a claim to copyright, and the message: "The REPORT is issued when circumstances warrant."[16]

Drudge's design was also a conceit, one that situated himself where he didn't yet belong: among the nation's most accomplished and popular political writers. The center column of the *Drudge Report* linked to forty-seven different columnists and opinion-makers, from Patrick Buchanan on the far right to liberal Mike Barnacle and gossip columnist Liz Smith. One link, labeled "Arianna," led to AriannaOnline.com, where Drudge's new friend in Los Angeles, Arianna Huffington, then a Republican married to millionaire Michael Huffington, provided contrarian commentary such as: "Exorcising Newt [Gingrich] is GOP's Only Hope." Huffington's own selling point was her access to the political movers and shakers in her elite circle, which gave her readers an inside track to what policymakers were thinking. But like Drudge, Huffington's political news was also written as gossip. "Dick Morris and I have a bet," Huffington wrote in 1997. "He's convinced that Al Gore will be president. And I am convinced that he will not. The winner gets dinner and, my money says, the deep pleasure of never having to say those frightening words 'President Gore.'"[17]

While Huffington's money and celebrity lifestyle yielded access to inside scoops, Drudge's readers were his sources, leaking items they had an interest in making public. And it may have been one of those sources—a disgruntled reporter, a book agent with a pending deal, a lawyer, or a conservative partisan with an axe to grind—who handed Drudge the Golden Fleece in January 1998. Claiming an inside source at *Newsweek* itself, Drudge published the allegations about Clinton's affair with Lewinsky under the banner, all-caps headline: "NEWSWEEK KILLS STORY ON WHITE HOUSE INTERN."

The story hit the White House, and the Washington media establishment, like a truck. Not only did a major national newsmagazine decide not to publish a fully sourced and vetted feature about these serious allegations, written by one of its top political reporters, but also, this was the second time that the same reporter had been shut down on a story about Clinton's extracurricular sex life. Previously, Isikoff left the *Washington Post* in part because his editors refused to publish "a meticulously researched investigative report" on Paula Jones, an Arkansas state employee, who charged Clinton with sexual harassment. But the powerful did not, and could not, shut down Drudge. As of 11:52 p.m. Pacific time on January 17, 1998, the piece was whizzing its way to personal computers all over the country, ending with a reminder to the establishment about who, however temporarily, was in charge: Isikoff and *Newsweek* were unavailable for comment, Drudge wrote, and "The White House was busy checking the DRUDGE REPORT for details."[18]

═══

With the Lewinsky scoop, alternative political media temporarily knocked the mainstream journalism establishment off its axis. Speculation and punditry were flourishing, supported by conventional advertising, at new corporate networks dedicated to political talk, like Fox News, CNN, and MSNBC. But Matt Drudge showed that internet click-based advertising, and an alternative digital media site that aggregated an audience of political junkies, could also pay. Amassing readers for internet advertisers, the *Drudge Report* laid the groundwork for twenty-first-century sites like the *Huffington Post* and *Breitbart News*. Drudge frequently described himself as a journalist with the ethic of a computer hacker: an ordinary guy, stripped down to his shorts in a shabby West Hollywood apartment as he churned out his stories, tips, and links while talking to his cat. But the Drudge everyone saw, once he became famous, was rarely, if ever, in public without a coat and tie and a 1930s fedora tipped back over his handsome, slightly crooked face. This retro look caused him to be instantly characterized, not as a visionary but a throwback, by a mainstream media world that was both fascinated and repelled by him. He was the "new" Walter Winchell, the mid-century gossip columnist, who mixed Hollywood and Washington, delivering scoops often planted by political insiders like FBI Director J. Edgar Hoover.[19]

The collision between the Clinton White House and Matt Drudge was, in a sense, the culmination of the rocky relationship that evolved between the First Couple and the mainstream media after 1992, when the complexities of their personal life in Arkansas were exposed, bit by bit, during the campaign. Rumors of Bill's extramarital affairs, alleged financial hanky-panky, lurid conspiracy theories about the assassination of enemies, and Hillary Clinton's justifiable anger about her husband's misdeeds, bubbled up from conservative alternative media to broadcast news shows. By 1995, the Clintons were also aware of bizarre rumors about them being asserted as factual on internet bulletin boards like FreeRepublic .com. Furthermore, the Little Rock Arkansas milieu that the First Couple dominated for over a decade gave the Clintons little of the experience they needed to navigate the Washington press corps, and they never got better at it. "In their view," writes historian William Chafe, "the press were scandal seekers, going after 'character' issues such as Bill's sex habits, or the draft, or whether he inhaled when he smoked marijuana."[20]

But the Clintons also underestimated the mainstream media's professional reluctance, prior to the Lewinsky scandal, to publish stories that would interfere in politics or be seen as a partisan attack. In his published account of the scandal and political crisis, Michael Isikoff claims that one of the reasons *Newsweek* killed the original story about the president's affair with Monica Lewinsky was that he himself expressed concerns that it might be unethical to print it. The reporter worried—not about whether the story was true (he was sure it was)—but *what it was for*. That a president who was lying about sex could deceive the public about other things was a legitimate concern, Isikoff thought. But would printing such a story change the course of American history by undermining, or even ending, a presidency, over a sexual dalliance? Were his sources simply using him as a political weapon? Most of all, Isikoff worried about putting himself at the center of the story (something that by contrast, delighted Drudge). The Sunday after the scandal broke, Isikoff found himself on NBC's *Meet the Press* and was horrified to learn that Drudge would also be a guest. When he asked host Tim Russert why he would have a "reckless gossip merchant" on the show, Russert shrugged and said: "He's part of the story too."[21]

Although they would not have admitted it, once the cat was out of the bag, the mainstream media let loose a flood of pent-up resentment toward a White House that failed to be transparent, treated them like an enemy, and then berated reporters for doing their jobs.[22] And yet, journalists who knew about it still kept the rumors about Lewinsky under wraps. Although they began to report political sex scandals in the 1970s, reporters were still reluctant to delve too deeply into politicians' private lives because of what many felt was the disproportional blowback from sexual revelations. There was no better example of this than a scandal that ended, not just a presidential bid, but a public career. In 1987, Democrat Gary Hart's campaign went off the rails when his refusal to answer questions about alleged adulteries led *Miami Herald* reporters to stake him out until they found him in a compromising position with a woman friend. Because Hart's political career was destroyed by the scandal, by the time Clinton ran for president in 1992, the rules were still in flux. Although serial accusations of affairs and at least one allegation of sexual assault (all of which Clinton denied), became a partisan political weapon during the campaign, mainstream reporters kept their distance. Nevertheless, over time, the president's private life joined the Whitewater land development deal, Hillary Clinton's former law firm's billing practices, the tragic suicide of White House aide Vince Foster, and a mass firing at the White House travel office, not just as objects of official investigation, but of unofficial investigation on internet bulletin boards frequented by conservative partisans and conspiracy theorists.[23]

It is also significant that the *Drudge Report* debuted in 1995, a year after the Republican House leadership sought to mobilize a growing populist constituency led by former Nixon speechwriter Patrick Buchanan, and declared a formal culture and media war on the Democratic Party. The GOP's "Contract with America," a pledge to reinvigorate the conservative and values politics of the Reagan years, resulted in Americans electing the first Republican House of Representatives in forty years. Led by conservative firebrand Newt Gingrich, who vowed to bring federal spending and national morals under control, the campaign relied on dramatic media stunts, such as the 367 GOP Representatives who gathered to sign a "contract" with the American people on the steps of the Capitol.[24]

Gingrich was the perfect man for his time and had a particular flair for dramatic gestures that expanded the public's appetite for political news. In 1995, in an appeal to anti-tax populists, he refused to pass a budget that did not repeal a 1993 tax increase, effectively shutting down the federal government twice over the next seven weeks—and inadvertently creating the hothouse atmosphere in the West Wing that brought Clinton and Lewinsky together. The success of these tactics, Clinton's budget director Alice Rivlin recalled, created an atmosphere of hostility between the parties that left a permanent, partisan divide in place. "There are just some things that are very hard to turn off," she commented later.[25]

Gingrich, a technology geek, also understood that the political establishment was no longer fully in control of the media. The increased volume of news that now traveled over cable and the internet privileged dramatic headlines, eventually called "clickbait," was designed to grab a political junkie's attention. And by 1998, it wasn't just alternative political media that traveled fast: all news was in a race for time, competing for the many eyeballs now trained on personal computer screens. Although CompuServe began distributing newspaper content in 1980, the *New York Times*, the *Los Angeles Times*, and the *Washington Post* (which had established a telephone number that subscribers could call for news in 1990) all went online in 1996, the year after Drudge founded his e-newsletter.[26]

Political alternative media entrepreneurs were also moving their work out of the bulletin board and subscription systems I described in chapter 4, and onto their own sites. These hand-coded online diaries, dubbed "weblogs" in 1997, or "blogs," were available to anyone with a browser and facilitated by the release of a series of commercial platforms—Ty, Inc.'s Online Diary in 1995; Open Diary in 1998; and LiveJournal and Blogger in 1999. Although it wasn't a blog, the *Drudge Report* benefitted from this growing interest in homemade digital alternative media, growing to a few hundred subscribers, then to a thousand, and then to tens of thousands of subscribers by 1998. Like the *Drudge Report*, the roughly 450 blogs online by 1998 (nine times the number than had existed two years earlier) were, with a few exceptions, written in a highly personal voice by self-trained journalists, most of whom wrote as a hobby. Like their electronic democracy predecessors, the blogger community believed that the essence of digital alternative media was openness. With every byte added to every blog, "however mundane or extreme, the more accessible the essence of mankind is," blogger Ophelia Z told *Wired* in 1998. Filmmaker Doug Block saw the phenomenon as connected to the reality television boom of the 1990s. "You don't have to earn fame with talent anymore, you just have to get a name," he said. "People are dying for attention."[27]

It was in this context that Drudge's story about the Clinton–Lewinsky affair broke. Mainstream sites scrambled to catch up and report the story. January 17, 1998, was Christmas all over again for political junkies, but sparked a genuine constitutional crisis for a White House in damage-control mode. Ken Starr, and the Republican House majority, demanded explanations for testimony Clinton, and others, had already given about the Lewinsky rumors. As the House of Representatives began to explore impeachment, Drudge became a mainstream media sensation. Now a competitor and a colleague, he was hailed as the journalist who had broken one of the biggest political scandals since Watergate, even though he had not reported or researched a word of the story. But Drudge's scoop also pointed to how the new alternative digital media, or what some called "technojournalism," was redefining mainstream print and broadcast media.[28]

Journalists were, in fact, some of the earliest professional adopters of computer technology, and many had been reading the *Drudge Report* for several years. Terminals used for writing, editing, and filing stories began to appear in North American newsrooms in the 1970s. By 1995, reporters relied on the internet for research and distributing their work globally; they also checked bulletin board services, listservs, and blogs for leads. Yet mainstream media professionals had not seen these electronic technologies as fundamentally altering what news was. Therefore, Drudge's willingness to turn gossip into a political story, and himself into a sought-after expert, raised disturbing questions. Would retraction statutes, which had historically protected journalists from libel suits but that a Wisconsin court had recently ruled did not apply to bulletin boards or chat rooms, apply to any internet writer declaring that he was a journalist? Did they apply to mainstream journalists publishing online? As journalists increasingly communicated with sources by email and in chatrooms, how would they verify the identities of people they had never met? "In cyberspace, anyone can claim to be a journalist," Denise Caruso wrote at the *Columbia Journalism Review*, "or at least a publisher, creating his or her own publication and distributing it around the world with a single keystroke."[29]

The internet transformed the news cycle into a rolling series of scoops. Often these were stories of little value but presented as breaking news. Sometimes a channel or internet site would simply announce that another outlet was reporting a story, as their own reporters scrambled to the phones to get a unique angle on it. "News is no longer reported once in the evening, on television, and again, in the morning, in newspapers," wrote one journalist, concerned that the pace of production was affecting accuracy and analysis. "CNN and its around-the-clock cable successors, MSNBC and Fox News Channel, along with the Internet are dramatically recasting how journalists do their jobs by shortening news cycles down from daily to hourly to sometimes 10-minute cycles." What was often missing in this frantic news cycle was the opportunity to reflect and report deeply. Journalists not only had to worry about being scooped by someone reporting the story more quickly, but also about trying to be accurate and fair while absorbing new information coming in every minute on television and the internet. Computerized research was a boon, but reporters suffered from information overload and "first and fast" was edging out the obligation to be "first and right."[30]

Technojournalism also presented a category problem: Were digital alternative media writers, who worked without editors and fact-checkers, actually journalists? Or were they just political junkies with an internet connection? When Drudge began his round of television appearances in January after breaking the Lewinsky story, a *Los Angeles Times* reporter seemed to resent what he saw as Drudge's impersonation of a journalist, since he reported on news few journalists respected. "He casually pontificated about sex and the White House as though he were Walter Cronkite," the reporter fumed. "The mainstream media treated him like a cockroach that had skittered out from under a sink. And in that perceptual chasm was born a question that continues to rankle traditional reporters: Who is this guy and why can't we just squish him flat and get back to business?" A Canadian journalist, who interviewed Drudge on one of his then-rare trips out of his Hollywood apartment, admitted that no one was quite sure what he was. "He is courted by news programs such as *Meet the Press*, a terrific honor for the average ink-stained wretch," Charles Laurence wrote, "and is invited to lunch at the National Press Club, but there he is rudely reminded that he is not a journalist."[31]

In a day and age when newspapers were cutting their staffs, and more writers were establishing their own sites and personal brands, these were urgent questions. In June 1998, when Fox News announced that Drudge would have a half-hour show on the network, CEO Roger Ailes, then chairman of Fox's news division, brushed off reservations about Drudge's professionalism. "Sure, he's a journalist," said Ailes. "He's a citizen journalist. I don't think Ben Franklin ever went to [journalism] school, did he?" Granting that Drudge's look was a little eccentric for television, Ailes indicated that it might be time for television news, not Drudge, to change. Drudge was "unique in terms of the way he looks, sounds and thinks," Ailes said. "Whenever you have someone come on who is unique and fearless and says what is on his mind, I think that attracts people." Not everyone was buying it. Drudge's show wasn't news, another critic said, but a tribute to "goofy guys everywhere." Putting him on TV "in this day and age" was almost a parody of journalism and a symptom of the celebrity culture television news had become.[32]

Drudge not only succeeded because he uncovered a scandal. He also succeeded because, however much *Newsweek* agonized over not printing Isikoff's story, the revelation that they had withheld it confirmed popular suspicions that there were things going on in the White House they needed to know, and the mainstream media could not be trusted to report them. The appeal of alternative political reporting was not that readers believed that amateurs would do a better job, but that they would be less subject to establishment pressure. As Bill Kovach of the *St. Petersburg Times* wrote, "even in carefully reported stories journalists tended to accept interpretations from their sources, uncritically helping perpetuate the hopeless feeling that there was no truth to be found in Washington."[33]

But alternative media also had the potential for producing a stream of partial, or unvetted, information that would be sucked up by mainstream editors in constant need of new content. The consequences of this potential free-for-all were quite serious for those who were the subjects of stories that began on platforms like the *Drudge Report*, made their way to cable news networks and were repeatedly broadcast in hours of daily news shows. Discussing the events that changed her life, and changed the news, in 1999, Monica Lewinsky was far more critical of television's role in keeping the salacious story about her affair with Clinton alive than of Matt Drudge's role in making it public. "Our tabloid TV has now spawned tabloid government," Lewinsky later observed about the months in which she became the target of official investigations and unofficial, humiliating publicity. For some, particularly late-night talk show hosts, Lewinsky became a cruel joke; for others, she was symbolic of the worst abuses of presidential power.[34] But she was never just herself: a young woman who had fallen in love with a powerful, married man.

Drudge's scoop had many unintended and intended consequences. Perhaps the most significant was that the constitutional crisis he triggered also created the first internet political advocacy group intended to push back on organized conservative partisanship by mobilizing partisans on the left. MoveOn.org, an email list, membership organization, and fundraising vehicle, was a progressive alternative media platform that, by the twenty-first century, came to rival Richard Viguerie's famous mailing lists. Many of us remember the day in 1998 when, sitting at our office computers, we received an email forwarded from a friend concerned about the impeachment crisis who asked us to visit the MoveOn site. Drawing its name from its stated mission—mobilizing a critical mass of voters to instruct Congress to "censure" Clinton for his misbehavior and then "move on" to "pressing issues facing the country"—

MoveOn reinvented what political scientists call the "organizational layer of politics," in which interest groups serve as an intermediary between voters and parties, using alternative digital media to empower partisans to organize themselves on a national scale.[35]

MoveOn founders Joan Blades and Wes Boyd were best known as a married Silicon Valley couple whose company, Berkeley Systems, created popular screen savers that prevented graphic display computer terminals from burning out when left idle. Their most famous was "Flying Toasters," a fleet of—yes—toasters with little wings that gracefully flew across the screen, surrounded by pieces of toast, released with Windows 1992. The whimsical quality of their products (the flying toasters could be programmed with musical accompaniment, most notably, Wagner's "Ride of the Valkyries") contrasted sharply with Blades's and Boyd's serious commitment to politics and their long history as Democratic fundraisers. Once it became clear that the Republican Congress might actually remove a sitting president, the couple threw their weight behind ending what they thought was an absurd, and potentially destructive, spectacle. Echoing Clinton's insistence that he was being kept from the work of the American people, Blades and Boyd made returning to political normalcy their goal. Determined to find out "how powerful" the internet could be "as a political tool," on September 22, 1998, they founded MoveOn.[36]

MoveOn was a paradox: in the name of opposing excessive partisanship, Blades and Boyd used alternative digital media to cultivate and mobilize progressive partisans. The website instructed users how to take action: adding their email addresses to the MoveOn database, reaching out to their network of internet contacts to do the same, and signing up as a volunteer organizer to lobby Congress. A message sent through the MoveOn portal automatically notified each respondent's congressperson that the impeachment process should be concluded. The site's resources included press releases for media coverage of the campaign, bumper stickers that could be printed out for those with access to a color printer, and downloadable petitions that could be printed "for your friends without email or web access." For Blades and Boyd,

Lewinsky herself, and the president's affair, were footnotes to history. What was more important was ending what they regarded as an unnecessary constitutional crisis, manufactured for partisan gain—and getting the government back to the people's work.[37]

MoveOn.org was a website with numerous resources, but the activists decided to mobilize a digital tool nearly every professional working adult knew how to use by 1998 as a form of alternative media: email. As one group of internet researchers noted in 1998, email was now like the telephone, "an increasingly pervasive means of communication" that was used in most workplaces and many homes. Because of its "speed and immediacy," email created a sense of intimate, democratic exchange between senders and recipients otherwise unknown to each other. And it was becoming ubiquitous. In 1998, if only a little more than twenty-six million American households had internet access, many more sat in front of computers all day at work. Although many of these users expressed frustration with slow connections and clunky search engines, seventy-four million Americans were online every day. They were going to online sources for news and politics, and they all used email.[38] In the ensuing weeks, the MoveOn petition spread through friendship and work networks throughout the United States, calling on "Congress to 'immediately censure President Clinton and move on to pressing issues facing the country,'" as Katie Hafner reported in the *New York Times*. "Once a visitor to the site endorses the petition, it is automatically transmitted to 'key members of Congress' and the President." What Hafner did not mention, or perhaps did not know, was that the petition also stored the signer's email address and added it to the MoveOn database. By 2002, when 62 percent of American workers had access to the internet, and over half used email at work, MoveOn had already built a powerful database of Democratic loyalists, a resource that would prove to be as powerful an alternative media tool, and distributor of political news, as Richard Viguerie's famous computerized mailing lists.[39]

═══

With the Lewinsky story, Drudge handed the press a gold mine. This was particularly true of Rupert Murdoch's young Fox News channel, a network that was building its reputation and market share by speaking exclusively to conservative populists.[40] After two decades of struggling to reclaim her life, Monica Lewinsky came to understand that driven by the internet and television, the scandal that enveloped her in 1998 signaled a definitive shift for political news away from journalism and toward a form of popular political entertainment focused on personalities, not issues. Unable to leave her home during the crisis, Lewinsky watched *Fox News* caricature her around the clock. "No rumor was too unsubstantiated, no innuendo too vile and no accusation too abhorrent," she recalled about this dark time. In her view, Matt Drudge had not only broken the story but made tabloid news a signature feature of the digital alternative media environment. "Just as television news was devolving into a modern coliseum," she recalled, "the internet came along and compounded this culture of shame and vitriol." However, others saw MoveOn, which soon became the first progressive digital PAC, as a hopeful sign that the internet could self-correct. Yes, alternative media troublemakers like Matt Drudge were cultivating the internet as a space to feed the public's taste for gossip. But MoveOn was "a counterforce" that showed the power of digital tools to demand accountability from Congress.[41]

In the wake of the Lewinsky scandal, Drudge was catapulted into a journalism world where, formerly an outsider looking in, he was now an object of fascination to the elite institutions he scorned. In late May, Drudge, who barely graduated from high school, addressed a conference on the internet and society at Harvard. On June 2, 1998, a little more than five months after he broke the Lewinsky story, he was invited to the prestigious National Press Club to explain to a room full of Washington journalists, none of whom would have hired him, what the future of journalism looked like. The internet, Drudge told them, was not just a faster information delivery system: it was changing what Americans wanted from the news and who they wanted to hear it from. "Clearly there is a hunger for unedited information, absent corporate considerations," Drudge told men and women who spent their lives reporting the news and no one knew how journalism would evolve to meet that need. Experts at all of the places he had been invited to speak since he had broken the Lewinsky story did not yet "appear to have a clue what this Internet's going to do," he said, "what we're going to make of it, what we're going to—what this is all going to turn into. But I have glimpses," he said. "We have entered an era vibrating with the din of small voices. Every citizen can be a reporter, can take on the powers that be. The difference between the internet, television and radio, magazines, newspapers is the two-way communication. The Net gives as much voice to a thirteen-year-old computer geek like me as to a CEO or speaker of the House. We all become equal. And you would be amazed what the ordinary guy knows."[42]

Matthew Nathan Drudge has remained a mysterious figure, becoming ever more reclusive even as his site has become a valuable media property. In 2011, when Facebook, Google, and other internet giants had become major distributors of political news, *New York Times* media journalist David Carr learned to his surprise that the *Drudge Report* still provided "7 percent of the inbound referrals to the top news sites in the country," twice as many as Facebook. And these were not just conservative populist political junkies. As Carr discovered, 15 percent of the traffic to WashingtonPost.com was driven there from a link on the *Drudge Report*.[43]

By 2012 *Business Insider* ranked Drudge as perhaps the most influential figure in political news. At 1 billion page views, 14.4 million readers per month (2 million fewer than the *New York Times*), and with only four employees including Matt Drudge himself, the *Drudge Report*'s gross income was estimated to be between $15 and $20 million a year.[44] And yet, one of the most extraordinary things about its popularity is that a reader who went to sleep one night in 1997 would wake up today to find the *Drudge Report* largely unchanged. The vast majority of its content still consists of links to other publications, listed neatly in three columns under a screaming red headline, several hundred links to mainstream and alternative media sources across the political spectrum, and the occasional original story written by Drudge himself.

The *Drudge Report*'s shabby, cluttered, retro digital storefront belies its history as one of the great alternative media success stories in American journalism, one that helped to mobilize conservative populist partisans against the political establishment and, most importantly, notified mainstream journalists that those partisans did not trust corporate news outlets. Digital alternative media had been a low- or no-profit operation before 1995, but Drudge proved that an entrepreneur on the margins of the internet could watchdog the mainstream media and win big. He proved that there was money and fame in putting political gossip on the internet that informed mainstream journalists and entertained political junkies.

As journalists feared, Drudge was, in fact, a changemaker. His success inspired numerous internet-only alternative media sites that reinterpreted the mission of journalism as the leaking of secrets from behind the scenes: everything they printed, no matter how trivial, was presented as a scoop since clicks meant advertising dollars. In 2002, tech entrepreneur Nick Denton launched *Gizmodo*, a site dedicated to the hacker culture's love for digital toys. He soon added niche gossip sites, including *Valleywag*, *Gawker*, and *Fleshbot*, a site that specialized in leaked celebrity sex tapes. Other new sites were more political. In October 2006, a former Australian cyberpunk named Julian Assange founded a bare-bones, searchable platform called *WikiLeaks*. Billing it as a news site, in part to seek the protection of free speech laws that covered whistleblowers and journalists in the United States, Assange became famous in the next decade for publishing, without commentary or analysis, leaked digital documents about, and stolen videos from, the Iraq War, as well as material about government and corporate corruption around the globe, hacked from the governments' own computers. While the two men had very different goals in mind, both Denton and Assange shared a similar ethic: the public was entitled to information, regardless of the consequences to the powerful.[45]

What Matt Drudge looked like was what he was: a transitional alternative media figure, who came to the front step of the political and media establishment in 1998, rang the doorbell, and tossed a digital Molotov cocktail inside when it opened. And he did this without ever really becoming a reporter. Instead, Drudge was a super-aggregator, a specialist in driving readers to stories reported by others, and a master of innuendo, gossip, and breaking news. Drudge became a person who took a piece of information and literally *made it into news* in a style that by the end of the twentieth century would be recognizable as a specific genre, political blogging. As the Lewinsky scandal demonstrated, when Drudge did present an original story, it was usually—like most gossip—*a story about a story*, and one that put himself, and a vast audience of partisans, at the center of a drama called politics.

= 6 =

NETROOTS

In the 2000 presidential field, no one typified the unfiltered speech that would characterize twenty-first-century digital alternative media like Senator John McCain. The gruff, testy Arizonan—a Navy veteran, one of the most prominent prisoners of war held in North Vietnam's "Hanoi Hilton," and the man whom voters sent to succeed Barry Goldwater in 1987—was as likely to challenge his own party as he was to challenge the Democrats. He pushed for campaign finance reform, condemned congressional pork, and disavowed right-wing populist Patrick Buchanan, who had abandoned the GOP to run for president on the Reform Party ticket. His campaign consultants transformed this style into a brand. When McCain snapped at reporters, or went off the GOP script to say that evangelicals opposed him "because I don't pander to them," it wasn't rude or shocking, it was "straight talk" from a Western "maverick."[1]

Occasionally the straight talk went over the line. McCain habitually used the racial slur "gook" when speaking about his former captors. A Democratic opponent might use such remarks "to string him up later," one mainstream journalist told readers, then explained neutrally that McCain had been tortured in Vietnam, after all. But digital alternative media, where marginalized voices controlled the conversation, did not think this was an excuse. Asian American political junkies condemned McCain's words as racist, a calculated dog whistle to white, conservative populists. As one participant in the internet bulletin board soc.culture.vietnamese commented, Asian American voters just weren't well enough organized to make McCain, or the GOP, "wary of offending them."[2]

Mainstream journalists so delighted in McCain's accessibility and newsworthy sound bites that they didn't dwell on the occasional racist remark.[3] When McCain used a word like "gook," it made the press corps uncomfortable, but not enough to condemn him for it. Nothing typified the clubby, establishment relationship between mainstream journalists and official Washington like a presidential campaign, and these reporters were having too much fun to risk making the candidate mad. McCain's campaign bus, named the "Straight Talk Express," and the novelty of his internet-powered fundraising effort, were thought to be so newsworthy and engaging that the junior reporters initially assigned to cover the campaign were soon replaced with seasoned colleagues who were usually unwilling to leave home for a long-shot primary candidate. "Middle-aged pundits clamber on McCain's bus, and he rides them around, with free doughnuts," wrote a disgusted Bob Somerby of the *Daily Howler*, a take-no-prisoners political blog that advertised its comments section as a "bull session."[4]

McCain's people probably read that blog post. They knew the internet and were among the first political consultants to take a campaign to the place many voters now spent the most time: in front of a computer screen.[5] The McCain campaign's direct appeals, and its creative small-donation fundraising at mccain2000.com, became the talk of a primary season that should have been dominated by the impending battle between two scions of American political dynasties, Texas governor George W. Bush and Vice President Albert Gore.

For a few months, McCain's openness to the mainstream press, his internet strategies, and his fundraising temporarily overshadowed these establishment candidates. In the first two weeks of October 1999, mccain2000.com boasted over one million visitors.[6] The senator was also savvy to the conservative voters listening to talk and shock-jock radio, populists who had tired of what they saw as liberals' demands for "politically correct" speech. While 29 percent of Americans went online for news, and 34 percent watched the evening news on a mainstream network, an astounding 43 percent of Americans knew what they knew about politics from talk radio. Because of this, McCain regularly called in to these shows from the Straight Talk Express, sparring in a belligerent, irreverent style that delighted listeners. Teen heartthrob Leonardo DiCaprio, he said on one show, was "an androgynous wimp." McCain then facetiously bemoaned the loss of "the thirteen-year-old vote."[7] He cursed constantly, nicknamed one staffer "the Ferret," commented that the politically influential evangelicals Pat Robertson and Jerry Falwell were "evil," and referred to the Washington lobbyists on K Street as "the bazaar."[8]

It was an unusual style for a presidential candidate. But after McCain cleaned George W. Bush's clock by eighteen points in New Hampshire's primary, GOP party leaders, solidly behind Bush, were said by one political blogger to be "in a state of panic."[9]

The victory in New Hampshire showed that a campaign that appealed to partisanship on alternative media could upend a better financed, establishment candidate. But McCain's high-touch, internet-driven campaigning style was not yet ready for an old-school, Southern, dirty-tricks operation that blended old and new media tactics. By the time the Straight Talk Express arrived in South Carolina, the Bush campaign had purchased every second of television time. False information about McCain and his family was emanating from mysterious and not so mysterious sources allied with Bush. At Bob Jones University in Greenville, South Carolina, where McCain was scheduled to give a talk, a viral email sent by a member of the faculty alleged that McCain's adopted Bangladeshi daughter, Bridget, was actually the child of an extramarital affair with an African American woman. Bob Jones himself wrote an article, published in Bush advisor Marvin Olasky's *World Magazine*, describing McCain as an adulterer with "Clintonesque"—even Marxist!—tendencies, who had driven his wife to drug abuse.[10] At McCain rallies, anonymous xeroxed flyers repeating these charges appeared on attendees' cars. Rumors about McCain's mental health and war record were spread by telephone push polls: "Would you vote for McCain if you knew . . . ," the caller would ask, and then plant a rumor.[11]

McCain lost South Carolina badly, and although he won two more states, the campaign collapsed after Super Tuesday. But his candidacy demonstrated that by blending politics with entertainment and using digital alternative media to raise money and pull new voters into politics, an outsider could activate grassroots voters—the netroots—to challenge the political establishment. But new strategies tested by the McCain team also raised new questions about the role of alternative media in political campaigns. What did it mean to *engage* a voter who was pulled in multiple directions by talk radio, the internet, newspapers, and cable news? How might Americans who thought they had given up on politics be a constituency *for* politics?

In 2000, strategists for the leading candidates understood that a web presence was vital in a world where voters spent more and more time online. The internet was not yet changing how campaigns were run, but putting technology to work to do a traditional task: mobilizing the party faithful and wooing independent voters. The Al Gore/Joe Lieberman Democratic campaign headquarters in Nashville boasted a website that when visitors clicked on icons, transported them to a town hall meeting occurring thousands of miles away, pictures from a campaign stop, or games for children about democracy. A "NashvilleCam" displayed new stills of campaign headquarters shot every ten seconds, creating "a campaigner's utopia" that could, as one observer described it, "transcend geographical boundaries and unite Sally in Boise with Joe in Biloxi." Similarly, the Bush campaign website boasted personal invitations to "study the issues, try our hand at daily trivia or board the Bush news e-train and win prizes." Answering four questions about their finances, voters could also preview a prospective Bush tax cut.[12]

But McCain's strategists believed that the route to the Republican nomination was through the energy of a populist appeal amplified by the internet. "McCainiacs," as the senator's followers came to be known, were often from the political margins: military veterans, independents, and first-time voters. McCain, an evangelist for campaign finance reform, committed himself to small-donation fundraising, a technique first deployed in 1972 by Democrat George McGovern to emphasize the candidate's independence from special interests. In 1974, McGovern's campaign manager Gary Hart actually did win a Senate campaign on an average donation of $17 (for other Democratic Senate challengers that year it was around $370).[13] In 1992, California governor Jerry Brown positioned himself as a man of the people by making the same pledge. He established a toll-free 1-800 number where supporters could charge donations to their credit cards. This allowed Brown to use any broadcast medium to raise money, and he did, reciting the 1-800 number on radio and television, during debates and interviews like, as one journalist put it, a "schmaltzy late-night salesman." And, as Richard Viguerie had intuited, small donations mined valuable data about voters, allowing them to be contacted repeatedly by the candidate—and by any subsequent campaign to which the list was sold.[14]

In 1998, campaign fundraising was revolutionized when it became legal to use a credit card to make a political donation over the internet. This opened the door for advocacy organizations like MoveOn to become major political players by bundling small donations for a cause or a candidate, but it also opened the door to the multiple solicitations for five dollars that many Americans now receive by email and text messaging every day during campaign season.[15] By binding voters to a candidate through multiple, easy-to-deliver donations, a campaign was not just raising money, it was creating a grassroots organization that could be activated, at a far lower cost and greater speed than direct mail, volunteer labor, and reminders to vote could achieve.[16] Furthermore, as MoveOn had intuited, these appeals could be shared in friendship networks. The potential donor base for an outsider candidate could now exceed the direct mail and voter registration lists jealously guarded by party officials and campaign consultants. An outsider candidate could reach out to independents, populists, first-time or infrequent voters, identity groups, and even voters registered with another party. Republican A-listers could still only give $2,000 to a candidate, but twenty middle-class Americans could equal that donation with $100; two hundred working-class voters with only $10 each. In the two days after he won the 2000 New Hampshire primary, McCain's online fundraising tool sucked in $18,000, with an average contribution of $100, every hour. The campaign's final haul that week was $2.7 million, to which McCain added $1.4 million in federal matching funds.[17]

McCain's political consultant Mike Murphy was tinkering with a few digital tools that he combined with a high-touch campaign, exposing his brash candidate to mainstream journalists and voters in as unfiltered a way as possible. Murphy hoped to seize the nomination from George W. Bush by creating news: intensifying media coverage of McCain, as well as making him seem more personal by putting him on alternative media—the internet, talk radio, and cable news shows. Online tools incorporated in the McCain website allowed the campaign to sign up volunteers, identify pockets of support, collect information, and solicit donations. Murphy released policy proposals directly to the website, where McCain himself occasionally appeared live, something that digital video technology now supported.[18]

McCain's failure to win the nomination has overshadowed how innovative these ideas were, and how well this blend of virtual and live appearances worked in New Hampshire, a bastion of populist and independent voters. For example, McCain held 114 live town hall meetings in that state, and in the days before the New Hampshire primary, he starred in the first internet-only town hall. For 60 minutes, he sat in a bare-bones studio answering questions from 500 virtual supporters, each of whom donated $100 to join a chat room. McCain's terse, direct style, which sometimes made him seem abrupt, and even nasty, on television, was well suited to the fast pace of an internet forum.[19]

The alternative press was particularly struck by how genuine McCain seemed. As novelist David Foster Wallace wrote for *Rolling Stone*, McCain's calls to national service and patriotism were not "just one more piece of the carefully scripted bullshit" that voters expected from presidential candidates. There was something "un-spinnable" about McCain's promise to tell voters the truth, whether they liked it or not, something that made him cool at a moment when the vast majority of Americans were increasingly partisan but alienated by elections. Wallace also enjoyed the spirit of the campaign, its experimental quality, and its willingness to bypass the mainstream media with its internet and talk radio strategy. McCain was willing to take risks to "[pull] more voters *in*, especially those who'd stopped voting because they got so disgusted and bored with all the Negativity and bullshit of politics."[20]

The loser, not the winners, provided the lessons for 2004. McCain's iconoclasm, and his internet tactics, pulled both political junkies and the mainstream press to McCain like rubberneckers at a traffic accident. "I held my breath that year," recalled campaign consultant Joe Trippi, a Californian who had steeped himself in the lessons of electronic democracy, "terrified" that the McCain team would succeed at creating the first full-fledged internet campaign "before I got the chance."[21]

Three years later, Joe Trippi mined the McCain campaign for ideas as he worked to assemble an alternative media strategy for Vermont Governor Howard Dean's 2004 presidential bid. Trippi envisioned a horizontal, networked community built around the candidate that would allow supporters to shape the campaign they wanted to be a part of: one that harnessed the new enthusiasm for free social media and blogging; that harvested the enthusiasm of a rising tide of political junkies, hungry for an antiestablishment progressive populist; and that engaged the vibrant digital alternative media communities who would never engage in the grind of a traditional campaign.[22]

=====

Joseph Paul Trippi was a born political junkie. Growing up in a working-class, Los Angeles family during the television revolution of the 1950s and '60s, he was mainlining politics from broadcast news by the time he was ten. "I can still see Bobby Kennedy walking into that packed ballroom at the Ambassador Hotel in Los Angeles—just a few miles from my house," Trippi remembered. "I was cheering in front of the television as he was led out of the ballroom through his supporters, and into the kitchen, and I was stunned watching the confused reaction—people running, pointing, crying—after Sirhan Sirhan shot him."[23]

Trippi first became involved in an election in 1974. After enrolling at San Jose State University to study aeronautics, he agreed to run for student council and won, eventually becoming student body vice president. Soon he was working on a city council campaign, and then another. By 1989, Trippi quit school and was walking precincts in Des Moines, Iowa, going door-to-door to persuade voters to caucus for Senator Edward Kennedy's bid to unseat incumbent President Jimmy Carter. He was happier than he had ever been.[24]

Trippi was also obsessed with computers. He returned to San Jose State's computer labs regularly after dropping out, fascinated by the room-sized behemoths that ran on IBM index cards. As computers became smaller, Trippi purchased everything he could afford. He became a "gadget-obsessed geek," and as he matured into a strategist and media consultant, he came to understand "the singularly democratic and open network" of the internet as a model for what electoral politics could be. He bought a Radio Shack portable TRS-80, a modem, and even an Apple Newton, the clunky personal communication device that in 2007, would evolve into the iPhone. Trippi began to explore how his two worlds, politics and technology, might mesh. The politically engaged people who were creating internet culture weren't necessarily engaged with elections, after all. But "the world that *could be*," as Trippi put it, was taking shape in their imaginations, and in his. This network of computer users sharing information, life stories and computing tips, recipes for cookies and petitions to abolish apartheid, seemed perfect for campaigning.[25]

As computers became more portable and inexpensive, data analysis, direct mail, and voter turnout strategies that had previously been the province of big firms like Viguerie's were now available to consultants working on a smaller scale. In 1981, Trippi agreed to run Los Angeles mayor Tom Bradley's campaign for governor of California. He used computer data to find out who was already likely to support his candidate so he could target his appeals and turnout strategies at them. Taking out a loan for $17,000, Trippi bought a personal computer to process data from prior elections to find out who those people were. "I can't say for sure," he recalled, "but it had to be one of the first computers used in-house for a political campaign." And it was on that same computer that Trippi, as he watched the precincts report in real time, realized that his candidate, the projected winner according to mainstream media exit polling, had lost. As Bradley prepared to give his acceptance speech, Trippi dashed over to the "victory" party to tell him the bad news.[26]

Throughout the 1980s, Trippi moved up the chain of political consulting. He worked on the 1984 Mondale campaign; did a stint with consultants David Doak and Bob Shrum, and one on the doomed 1987 Gary Hart presidential campaign (he was given a quick promotion to chief of staff to the candidate's wife as she weathered the storm of her husband's alleged extramarital affair). Trippi also ran the 1989 campaign that made Doug Wilder the first African American governor of Virginia. Throughout, Trippi continued to think about how computers could transform political campaigning.[27] He was particularly influenced by internet theorist Howard Rheingold. Following the work of Rheingold, Stewart Brand, and other digital innovators at Xerox PARC and Stanford, Trippi became particularly intrigued with the possibilities for human brains working together on a campaign—not as they normally did, in large rooms buzzing with fluorescent light and littered with old pizza boxes—but in their own homes and communities, linked by technology into one gigantic, super-computing, decentralized grassroots organization.[28]

Trippi was the ultimate crossover political consultant for the digital age. He read *Newsweek*, but he read *Wired*, too. He was skilled in navigating mainstream media on behalf of establishment candidates like Vice President Walter Mondale and Senator Barbara Mikulski; at the same time, Trippi thought deeply about how digital alternative media might change American journalism to promote outsider candidates. He read political blogs, media platforms that by 1998 could be created for free in minutes. Even as data analytics played a more and more important role in predicting voter turnout, Trippi knew that the missing link was how to get people who *didn't* vote as excited about elections as they were about talking politics on the internet. And people were excited about talk. Startups as varied as MySpace, LiveJournal, Blogger, Friendster, and a new college social networking platform launched in 2004 called Facebook were building new online communities and, as Trippi recalled, "making people *talk to each other* again."[29]

Trippi got it, and all he needed was a candidate who got it too. In January 2003, he received a call from Vermont, where Howard Dean was drawing together antiwar activists, progressive Democrats, and Libertarians, a staff that included internet activists Zephyr Rain Teachout and Nicco Mele, to make a run for the presidential nomination that the Democratic establishment had earmarked for Massachusetts Senator John Kerry. A few days later, Trippi was climbing the steps of a rickety building in downtown Burlington.

=====

Howard Brush Dean III was not a likely pick for the leader of a progressive populist insurgency powered by alternative media. Born and raised in tony East Hampton, New York, he graduated from Yale University and Albert Einstein College of Medicine before moving to Burlington in the 1970s to start a medical practice with his wife, Judith Steinberg. Dean entered politics in 1980, organizing a grassroots coalition of environmentalists to stop a condominium development, then volunteering for the Carter campaign. In 1982, he was elected to the Vermont House of Representatives, becoming lieutenant governor in 1988. In 1991, when Governor Richard Snelling died in office, Dean suddenly became the chief executive of a small state with a big deficit.

He implemented progressive policies on health care, early childhood programs, and LGBT civil rights, pairing these issues with fiscal conservatism, lower taxes, reduced teen pregnancy, and an A rating by the National Rifle Association (NRA). This made Dean a rising star in the Democratic Party. He was elected chair of the National Governors Association in 1995. "Leadership must come from Washington," Dean insisted as Bill Clinton's national healthcare plan foundered in 1993, but "innovation from state-level policymakers who understood local needs." When he floated the idea of a 2000 presidential run, however, Dean was called to the White House for a lesson in establishment politics. It was Vice President Gore's turn. The Clintons, as journalist Carey Goldberg reported it, "plucked Howard Dean from the chorus line and made him a star"; if he didn't behave they could bury him too.[30]

But Al Gore's devastating loss to George W. Bush in 2000 opened the 2004 Democratic field up to new challengers to a sitting president who had saddled himself with an unpopular, and unsuccessful, war in Iraq and Afghanistan. Dean wasn't asking permission this time. By late 2002, the prospective Democratic candidates included Kerry, Missouri senator Richard Gephart, North Carolina Senator John Edwards, and Connecticut Senator Joe Lieberman. Only Dean made a commitment to finance his campaign with small donations, a decision that political bloggers noticed. But the campaign was not yet a sophisticated digital operation. In January 2003, a year before the Iowa caucuses, when Trippi met with Dean, there were only six people on staff; a computer that wasn't turned on; a slim war chest of $300,000; and a prospective donors list that consisted of a shoebox full of papers labeled "Friends of Howard."[31]

Trippi noticed something else, however. The mainstream media had Dean polling at about 4 percent, but in the ecosystem of blogs, chatrooms, and an early social network called MeetUp.com, where strangers met in real time to talk, organize, and bring the ideas cultivated in alternative media spaces to life, Dean was a star. Mainstream polls had little access to the world of alternative media, where political junkies were now gathering. Jerome Armstrong, the founder of the political blog *MyDD*, called this online progressive populist energy "the netroots." There, Dean's support was growing rapidly: the Dean group at MeetUp.com had 426 members in January 2003: by mid-February, there were 2,600 members. Dean supporters were already organizing themselves organically, without any help from the campaign. One group committed to raising a million dollars and brought in $300,000 in online donations in four months. In March, when Trippi announced that the candidate himself would come to a MeetUp event in New York City, so many people flocked to see him that Dean could not get into the building. Instead, he took a lap around the block to cheers from fans who also couldn't get in the door.[32]

Like McCain, the Annapolis-educated son of an admiral, Dean looked like an establishment candidate and talked like a populist. He had grown up wealthy, gone to Yale, and had risen through the ranks in a state Democratic party. But he also had an instinct for the outrageous and for expressing his convictions so vigorously that he was routinely described as "passionate," a man with, as one reporter put it, a "smackdown style."[33] Furthermore, the huge crowds at events like the New York MeetUp were great publicity. They demonstrated that the campaign was a real grassroots alternative to the top-down establishment model driven by polls, data, and press releases. The excitement about Dean and the willingness of activists to create their own organization seemed like the next stage of an electronic democracy that was dispensing with political parties altogether. Traditional campaign organizations and journalists began—in a less-than-friendly nod to the 2000 McCain campaign—to refer to these fervent supporters who carried laptop computers everywhere as "Deaniacs," a name that one of the Dean blogs cheerfully adopted. "Deaniacs wonder why the main criticism of Howard Dean is that he is angry," wrote "Linda," who had organized the blog. "We're more than angry—we're furious that George W. Bush is smashing core American ideals of freedom, liberty and the rule of law." The anger was rational, she argued, and she urged fellow Deaniacs to infiltrate local Democratic club meetings to spread the message.[34]

Where a traditional political consultant might see a disorganized mess, Trippi saw a plausible path to the nomination, powered by an energized, progressive populist base that the Democratic establishment didn't even know or care about. Trippi arranged for a Dean Facebook page to encourage comments and conversation from supporters, using the company's data tools to find out where undiscovered pockets of support were. In addition to several pro-Dean blogs, a website that showed campaign goals and achievements, and a blistering email fundraising operation, the official campaign site had its own internet broadcast operation. The tool was called

DeanTV, where supporters could interact with and ask questions of the candidate in real time. In one famous fundraising gimmick, Dean mocked a $2,000-a-plate Bush–Cheney event by eating a turkey sandwich online: Deaniacs ate sandwiches at their desks too and sent in campaign donations. In 1956, the Eisenhower campaign had done something similar: fundraising dinners were held simultaneously in fifty-two cities, and the president "attended" all of them through a television hookup. But this idea had a populist twist: no one had to dress up, be invited, or cough up a minimum donation. It was a fundraiser designed for ordinary Americans, using machines that increasingly dominated work and home.[35]

Because of alternative digital media, the Dean campaign became a financial juggernaut, turning first-time volunteers into serious fundraisers and committed political activists. After hearing Dean speak, a stay-at-home Pennsylvania mom began to visit the campaign blog, add to the conversation there, make virtual friends in other states, and give money. When she maxed out her own legally permitted donations, she didn't want to stop. So she became an amateur bundler: she started tapping friends and relatives and holding fundraisers in her own home, using the campaign's free tools to raise even more money for her candidate. By July 2003, numerous Deaniacs setting their own fundraising goals had raised almost $15 million, a single-quarter record for a Democratic candidate.[36]

Although the McCain campaign experimented with streaming video and internet fundraising appeals, by 2004, free commercial applications like MeetUp.com (2002), Friendster (2002), MySpace (2003), WordPress (2003), and Facebook (2004) shifted the balance even more toward alternative media activists and created digital spaces where the campaign and the netroots collaborated.[37] This signaled a shift in media culture that the front-runners in both parties had not yet grasped. While Bush advisor Karl Rove was weaving together a network of conservative talk show hosts to support President Bush's reelection, Trippi invested in an army of bloggers. Two rising stars in alternative media came right onto the campaign staff: Ezra Klein, an undergraduate at UC–Santa Cruz; and Markos Moulitsas Zuniga, a military veteran, lawyer, and Republican-in-recovery, who had just launched a politics blog called the *Daily Kos*.[38]

A second difference was that innovative as the McCain campaign was, like MoveOn's 1998 email blasts, it was still "one-to-many" communication: broadcasting to supporters on alternative digital media, but not creating channels for them to talk back. By contrast, the appropriation of social media by the Dean campaign, and particularly Trippi's enthusiasm for grassroots organizers' launching their own platforms and websites, created a horizontal "many-to-many" network. This principle, a legacy of the electronic democracy movement, allowed progressive populist ideas and enthusiasm to flourish in nonhierarchical conversations shared with the campaign. Many-to-many platform designs promoted the idea that technology did not connect people; rather, people used technology to facilitate connection *to each other*. Howard Dean may have been the candidate, and Trippi the campaign manager, but within the alternative media ecosystem of the campaign, they were each simply one person in the crowd.[39] Technology was not the hero of the campaign, either: the netroots was, and they weren't always online. Volunteers knocked on doors, wrote letters, made phone calls, attended local Democratic Party events wearing "Deaniac" T-shirts, and signed up new volunteers by hand. At one point Teachout, the ultimate alternative media whiz kid, checked in on all the campaign offices by taking "an old renovated Airstream bus on a city-by-city tour to meet Dean supporters face-to-face," a move she called "an almost anti-internet approach."[40]

Ultimately, over half a million Americans volunteered time or money in the 2004 election through the Dean campaign alone, and well over half of them remained active after Dean dropped out of the race in March. But organizing a high-adrenaline campaign of political junkies also came at a cost, which ultimately undermined Dean's ability to compete successfully for the nomination. Having launched a national online organizing effort, the campaign was unprepared for the intensive face-to-face effort required for the Iowa caucuses. It was also a labor-intensive way to run a campaign, and it is hard to overstate how fragile, and improvised, many of the Dean campaign tools were, often collapsing with spikes in internet traffic; or how much human labor it took to maintain communication with supporters. Emails, for example, were answered personally, and new addresses entered into the database by hand. The blogs, powered by Blogger, a commercial platform now run by Google, did not require the endless tweaking and coding that the campaign's own tools did. But blogging was still work done by human beings. "We would read the blogs," Howard Dean recalled in 2007. "[W]e would respond to the blogs, we had a bunch of people whose job it was to read the blogs and respond. And people felt like we cared [about] what they had to say."[41] Blogs were an alternative media network, connected to each other through hyperlinks and blog rolls, and because they were not professional journalists, bloggers could be paid bonuses to work harder, and produce favorable posts, at key moments.[42]

The blogs also became a tool for crowdsourcing campaign work and for allowing the campaign's thousands of participants to experience political rituals that they could not attend. At the Dean for America official campaign blog, supporters were enlisted to perform tasks that were now part of normal blogging practice: fact-check other candidates, praise Dean endorsers, and rain disapproval on mainstream journalists in the comments sections of stories unfavorable to Dean. The blog provided daily reports about campaign activities across the nation, position papers issued by Dean, and links to the larger network of other Dean bloggers. The opportunity to communicate directly with top campaign brass was a reason to come back over and over to get a backstage glimpse of campaign headquarters. "Ok, so I am sitting in Des Moines, Iowa munching on my favorite Pork Tenderloin sandwich," Trippi wrote in one post, as he stopped for barbecue and beer. "Sorry folks, that has been a habit I've had on every trip to Iowa since 1979—and I've made more than my share of trips, and no need to tell you what I am washing it down with either."[43]

In establishing an alliance between progressive populists and a centrist politician with an elite background, Trippi also demonstrated that the Democratic Party could change. Dean promoted progressive causes that he had worked for successfully in Vermont, such as universal health care and gay civil unions, and he was staunchly antiwar. But he also argued that these were not left-wing issues but rather "common-sense solutions," consistent with family values and fiscal restraint, values that conservatives and Libertarians could find compelling, even as the partisan divide was widening. Because of this, some saw the populist energy of the campaign, its fundraising power, and Dean's relentless and often impolitic honesty as a possible third-party threat. "On the left, there has been a hunger for authenticity detectable for some time," one analyst wrote; "a weariness and even anger at being told that their causes weren't yet ripe for prime-time political action. That's why Ralph Nader," the Green Party candidate whose strong following in Florida had bled voters from Gore, "attracted such huge crowds during the 2000 election, despite being perhaps the worst stump speaker in American history."[44]

Trippi found a lot of eager, young partisans where, increasingly, they lived, learned, socialized, dated, and looked for political news: the internet. While there was a blog for every interest, blogging was a particular magnet for a new breed of political junkies. Volunteer death-row defender Tom Sawyer, who had worked on Dean's gubernatorial campaign, established his blog to get the story out about a cause, and people, who had been virtually forgotten. Jerome Armstrong, the founder of *MyDD*, had been watching the way right-wing media had kept negative stories about Bill and Hillary Clinton in the news "through FreeRepublic.com, DrudgeReport.com, and Lucianne.com, working with conservative talk radio, into the mainstream press," he recalled. Armstrong "felt outrage and disgust," for what Republicans had done to the Clintons and was "ready to kick some spine into the Democratic Party."[45] He decided to fight back by taking his readers to the Dean campaign.

Mainstream journalists who were skeptical of Dean suddenly found themselves in a defensive posture as often hostile commenters, coordinated by the bloggers, showed up in their comments sections to troll them. Making no pretense about their partisanship, bloggers challenged mainstream reporters and editors to admit that they were biased too, and that they shaped elections with the news they reported—or didn't report. When, only days before the 2003 California governor's election, the *Los Angeles Times* published allegations that Republican movie star candidate Arnold Schwarzenegger had had an affair, bloggers and conservative partisans saw it as clear evidence of collusion between the paper and Democrat Gray Davis's campaign. Conservative radio talk show host Rush Limbaugh, now commanding a national audience of twenty million listeners, exhorted Californians to vote for Schwarzenegger to strike a blow against "dastardly political assassins who use ink instead of bullets to hit candidates under cover of objective journalism." As one Republican growled, the scandal "made me want to vote for him more." Other voters agreed: Schwarzenegger, whose campaign labeled the story "puke politics," actually won. The outgoing populist governor of Minnesota, former wrestler Jesse "The Body" Ventura, saw Schwarzenegger's victory as proof that "the people are becoming savvy to the media. . . . They're realizing the media's dishonest."[46]

Dean supporters also thought the mainstream media had led the country into war. Major newspapers had failed to detect the Bush administration's invented pretext for invading Iraq, so antiwar partisans turned to blogs like history professor Juan Cole's *Informed Comment*, founded in 2002, for critical news and analysis, rather than to the *New York Times*, which had published the administration's evidence against Iraq—information that later turned out to be false. Cole was receiving a million page views a month in 2004; his blog posts were being reblogged and included in antiwar newsletters, and he became a frequent guest on CNN.[47]

In this atmosphere, Dean bloggers could keep pushing out stories about their candidate and know they would be read by the people who counted most: other Dean supporters. They were also unapologetic about adding a fundraising appeal when interviewed by mainstream journalists. "My $2,000 counts as much as George Soros's $2,000 or Ken Lay's $2,000," a Dean supporter told one reporter. "I may be just a mom in Pennsylvania, but I can be just as much a participant. That makes me feel powerful. That makes me feel like I'm participating in this country again." This woman returned to Dean for America over and over again to see how her donations were helping a cartoon baseball bat fill in with red ink as the campaign closed in on its fundraising goals. "It makes it fun," she said. As Teachout also pointed out, the campaign didn't just take supporters' money: organizers wanted ideas, too. The "red bat" had been suggested by a supporter, as had the candidate's nickname, "People-Powered Howard," and the orange wool hats organizers wore when they descended on Iowa in January 2004.[48]

The campaign developed an idiosyncratic lore and language, not messaging and branding imposed by image-makers. It was a culture that distinguished Deaniacs from establishment Democrats, but it also made the campaign appear stronger, and more influential outside the circle of Dean supporters, than it ultimately was. In addition, what mainstream journalists rightly saw as an effort to circumvent them became a source of resentment. Reporters portrayed Dean supporters as fanatical, nicknaming them "Birkenstock voters," after a pricey sandal associated with the white, educated constituency that did, as it turned out, make up a substantial portion of the Dean base.[49]

But by November 2003, when the campaign had broken multiple fundraising records, a grudging press corps snapped to attention. Suddenly, there were fewer stories about hippie sandals, pizza MeetUps, and energized moms, and more digging into a campaign where the policy positions did not always fit together and the "burn rate"—the speed at which the campaign spent money—was unusually high. Trippi restrained himself, but warned mainstream journalists that Deaniac bloggers would defend their candidate. When NBC's *Meet the Press* host Tim Russert poked holes in Dean's policy positions, making the candidate visibly irritable, bloggers responded by soliciting a wave of donations that tripled the amount collected on any prior Sunday. As Trippi explained, the netroots had "a real feeling of ownership." When mainstream media and political elites went after Dean, "It's not just Howard Dean that's getting attacked. It's them," Trippi explained. "They want to change the country, and you're trying to stop them from changing it when you attack them."[50]

Veteran political journalists' continued emphasis on the weirdness of the alternative media–driven campaign obscured the fact that like McCain, Trippi and Dean were both seasoned, pragmatic campaigners who knew that populist organizing that reached out to marginalized voters was their only real chance to seize the nomination. Initially, it even looked like it might work. In early November

2003, a candidate who had little name recognition outside his state a year earlier was sitting on $25 million, more than half the spending limit required for federal matching funds, as they had been established by the McCain–Feingold Act in 2002. Confident that he had unlocked the secret to small-donation fundraising, and that he could burst through federal limits without establishment donors, Dean announced that he would be the first Democrat to opt out of public financing. Using the campaign's tools, Trippi consulted supporters and was able to report back to journalists that 105,000 Deaniacs were supporting the decision so that the campaign could "go toe to toe with George W. Bush." This was a statement that could not, of course, be corroborated. But it made an impact. On December 9, former Vice President Al Gore, "enthralled" by how the campaign had mobilized the netroots, stunned the Democratic field by endorsing Dean.[51]

Yet little more than a month later, the Dean campaign was in pieces. Digital alternative media had powered the netroots and created a national political phenomenon. But heavy reliance on the internet had also concealed weaknesses, like insufficient boots on the ground in Iowa and New Hampshire, and, importantly, Dean's lack of visibility to voters not on the internet. Despite an endorsement from Iowa Senator Tom Harkin, on January 19, 2004, Dean scrambled to a third-place finish in that state's caucuses behind Kerry and Edwards. Supporters crowded into a Des Moines ballroom that evening, stamping, screaming, and calling for the candidate. Dean, who had never lost an election, had not prepared any remarks. Harkin urged Dean not to let his young supporters down: "Go out there, throw me your jacket, and let 'er rip!" he said.[52]

Dean did just that. As he built to a crescendo, he answered the crowd's energy with a bellowing cheer of his own. There was only one problem: the podium mic was directly wired into the mainstream television network feeds, and the result was an eerie, crazed yowl.[53]

What was known ever after as "Dean's scream," accompanied by a vigorous fist-pump, ripped around the mainstream media like wildfire. Playing over and over again on 24-7 cable news channels, as news anchors smirked, it made Dean appear not just unpresidential, but unhinged. Who *celebrated* a third-place finish in Iowa? Were Dean supporters out of their minds? Was Dean? Because it occurred on Martin Luther King Jr. Day, mainstream journalists snidely renamed the moment Dean's "I Have a Scream" speech. Late-night host David Letterman compared the candidate to a crazed Vermont "hockey dad." The *Tonight Show*'s Jay Leno deadpanned that Iowa cows now feared that they would contract "mad Dean disease" and advised that when a campaign staffer was "shooting you with a tranquilizer gun," a candidate should pay attention. Deaniacs themselves arguably did their candidate just as much harm by not understanding what a disaster it was and causing the Scream to go viral over the internet, as they did for all of his speeches. Some created mash-up versions, mingling Dean's words with popular beats, that also went viral. A campaign that empowered supporters to act on their ideas independently, and network with each other, now found itself in an endless echo chamber of political delirium that was impossible for Trippi to shut down.[54]

Dean's scream, although most Americans saw it on television, was the first viral political gaffe of the internet age. Although the mainstream media deliberately overplayed and misunderstood what had motivated Dean, there was a kernel of reality to their approach: the loss in Iowa raised serious questions about Joe Trippi's Rube Goldberg digital alternative media campaign. Dean supporters had been talking to each other all along, and it wasn't enough to win a nomination. Raising money was one important aspect of a presidential race, and the netroots did that well, but so was educating and motivating voters outside the candidate's most enthusiastic base. Worse, a third-place finish for the best-financed candidate in the race did not make Dean seem like the results-oriented politician he claimed to be. Nine days later, in New Hampshire, where Dean had led Kerry by almost fifty points, and in a state where he had high name recognition, he suffered a double-digit defeat. Again, campaign workers celebrated. Onstage at the University of Southern New Hampshire on primary night, Dean held the microphone out into the crowd for a full three minutes as they stomped and roared. "This time," a journalist deadpanned, "it was the crowd that screamed, not the candidate." When Dean finally spoke, sleeves rolled up and pointing his finger like a World War I poster of Uncle Sam, he roared: "We really are going to win this nomination, aren't we!"[55]

Veteran campaign watchers wondered if everyone in the room was hallucinating. Dean had spent eighty-two days in New Hampshire over two years and come in second to one of the least charismatic candidates in modern political history. As donations slowed to a trickle, the Dean campaign unraveled. Trippi was fired and replaced by former Beltway lobbyist Roy Neel; most of the campaign staff was laid off; and those that remained worked unpaid. Despite a whirlwind tour of Maine, on February 8 Dean again came in second to Kerry, who never made an appearance in the state, sending Robert F. Kennedy Jr. as a surrogate.[56]

It all came to a grinding halt after a final, humiliating defeat in Wisconsin on February 18 where Dean came in a weak, and disappointing, third. Yet many supporters blamed, not themselves, or the campaign, or Dean for this loss, but the establishment. As one Dean partisan wrote to the *New York Times* following the defeat, Dean had been "inspirational" in his outreach to "the many people who feel disenfranchised by the administration in Washington," but had been brought down by "blistering criticism from many in the media as well as in his own party."[57]

Wisconsin was the end, but also a new beginning: electoral politics had undergone a seismic change by incorporating alternative digital media into a campaign. On the morning of February 19, reading from a speech he had written on a few pieces of lined paper ripped from a spiral notebook, Dean dropped out. As supporters waved hand-lettered signs and wiped away tears, Dean, his voice breaking with exhaustion and emotion, vowed to hold his delegates together into the convention to press for change. He urged his supporters to remember what they did well and use it to reform the Democratic Party. "Use your network to send progressive delegates to the convention in Boston," he told them as he threw his support behind Kerry, the presumptive nominee whom he once characterized as "the senator who took more special interest money than any other senator in the last 15 years."[58]

Dean supporters blamed the establishment media for the disaster: as one Dean partisan reproached NPR's Juan Williams, reporters seemed too eager to see someone who was not "a plastic candidate" fail.[59] But having invested almost exclusively in relationships with bloggers, the campaign neglected relationships with the boys—and girls—on the bus, and any other member of the media that trivialized Dean and Trippi's innovations. Postmortems in the mainstream press focused on the Scream and what they characterized as a disorganized and spendthrift campaign. Sure, Trippi raised money at a record rate, but of the $41 million war chest accumulated in 2003, almost $32 million had been spent by the end of the year, leaving little to mobilize voters in Iowa and New Hampshire. In fact, the campaign learned that the vast majority of voters were not even reachable over the internet: $7.2 million in direct mail and other advertising had been required "just to introduce Dr. Dean" to primary voters who relied primarily on television, radio, and newspapers. That was "a lot of money," Al Gore's 2000 campaign manager noted piously. "I can't imagine spending that much."[60]

The harvesting of ideas from supporters, the so-called Perfect Storm of orange-hatted Iowa organizers, the red bat, and other innovations now looked too much like the campaign was throwing spaghetti against the wall to see what would stick. In the final days before Dean withdrew, campaign workers rolled out new ideas, almost using failure as an opportunity to experiment. Teachout and Mele inaugurated a web-based radio show, modeled on a technique that some practitioners called "audio blogging" and others, because these sound files could be downloaded on Apple's popular iPod personal music devices, called "podcasting."[61] Another staffer wrote an algorithm that analyzed news stories to detect their political bias.[62]

Some mainstream observers appreciated the innovation, but couldn't imagine why these initiatives would be unrolled by a sagging campaign. "I can't help but think that the web radio show, which would have seemed like another groundbreaking campaign tactic just a few weeks ago, now seems hopelessly out of touch," wrote political reporter Ryan Lizza, "a sign that the campaign and its followers are becoming further and further isolated from what's actually happening in the election." Attempts to bypass the mainstream media in its search for supporters had caused the campaign to become "caught in an echo chamber populated by Dean partisans."[63] Comparisons to Silicon Valley in the mainstream press were now scornful. Like the collapse of the dot-com economy a few months earlier, one observer noted, the Den campaign had been a mirage. The claims to innovation, the excitement, and the hyperbole had masked the fact that the campaign had no "business plan." One journalist compared Deaniacs to "online investors that promoted a company's stock before a single profit—or vote, in this case—has been booked."[64]

However, Dean and Trippi understood how to mobilize progressive populists who had never cared about politics before. "We are not going away. We are staying together, unified, all of us," Dean vowed, as other political teams began to quickly pick the campaign's carcass for talented digital organizers. This, in turn, spread the Dean network across the campaigns of more conventional candidates, giving them valuable experience that resulted in the creation of new political consulting firms like Blue State Digital, and the fundraising PAC ActBlue, all founded by former Dean organizers and supporters.[65] Campaign workers Amanda Michel, Zack Exley, and Aaron Myers brought many of the Dean tools directly into the heart of the establishment, the Kerry campaign. These innovators, and other Dean veterans, became the backbone of the Obama campaign in 2008. Zephyr Teachout became a professor at Fordham Law School, ran for office three times herself, and would be ready when another progressive Vermonter, Bernie Sanders, announced his first presidential bid in 2015.[66]

Mainstream media postmortems underestimated both the campaign's achievements and what was learned from failure. Dean would be only the first politician taken down by a misstep broadcast virally over the internet: Mississippi Senator Trent Lott would be the next and Virginia's George Allen after him. More importantly, by assembling progressive populists over the internet, the campaign forcefully injected new ideas into the Democratic Party mainstream, such as a principled antiwar stand, and it reinvigorated policies, such as gay rights and universal health insurance, that had been abandoned by the Clinton administration's failure to pass them. While in retrospect, the Dean mobilization seemed almost shockingly unprepared for the resistance to these policies, and to internet organizing, by the Democratic and media establishments, they also learned valuable lessons about what a national progressive populist campaign might look like. As Nicco Mele later observed, the crucial insight was that digital media mobilized and sustained real connections between partisans that superseded traditional party networks. "People who thought they lived in conservative Republican neighborhoods," he remembered, "would go on MeetUp.com and discover a group of Deaniacs meeting right by their house." These voters, formerly overlooked by traditional Democratic canvassers, had become visible.[67]

===

Joe Trippi got his chance to do it first. He harnessed alternative digital media to bridge the world of electronic democracy and party politics. He brought activists into the political process and turned them into political junkies. And he helped to revive progressive populists as a constituency that over the next fifteen years, would redefine the Democratic Party as an organization committed to a social movement style, unmediated connection to voters, and small-donation fundraising. As the editors of the *New York Times* conceded once Dean had withdrawn, Trippi, Teachout, Dean, and thousands of bloggers and bulletin board denizens had been an "object lesson in daring and tactical innovation" who "transplanted spine into the campaign" and into a party still aching from its defeat in 2000. The Deaniacs left "party leaders . . . salivating over the Dean machine's trailblazing knack for attracting hundreds of thousands of newcomers to politics via the internet, as well as prodigious amounts of campaign money."[68] While the Scream was an enduring symbol of Dean's failure, Trippi's experiment would be remembered "both for its revolutionary use of the Internet and its swift collapse."[69]

But Dean's movement didn't actually collapse. Digital alternative media networks survived the failure of a single campaign, and so did the progressive wing of the Democratic Party. "You have the power to take our country back," Dean had told his campaign workers on the final day of the campaign, words written months earlier by Joe Trippi.[70] This new progressive populism, which glued together unlikely allies against a growing discontent with establishment politics, would be nourished in the next decade. Dean himself salvaged and strengthened his internet operation as Democracy for America and, in the wake of Kerry's defeat, had enough support within the party to be elected DNC chair in February 2005. His internet-powered "fifty-state strategy" became a crucial foundation for Barack Obama's successful campaign for president, raising more money from small donors than in any prior election cycle.

After 2004, as *New York Times* columnist David Brooks would write, the Democrats were not bound together by a vision, but by the internet. The netroots had "mobilized new networks of small donors," Brooks wrote, "and these donors have quickly become the money base of the party. . . . The energy and the dough are in the MoveOn.org wing, which is not even a wing of the party, but the head and the wallet." By 2006, it would no longer be possible to run a campaign without an even newer alternative media ecosystem called social media, or without knowing how to run damage control on a gaffe gone wild.[71]

When he was elected party chairman, the *New York Times* cited Dean's energy, "talent for working across the political spectrum, and his ambition to compete nationally" as qualities the soul-searching Democrats, eight years out of power, needed. Dean had an opportunity "to be remembered as someone other than that presidential candidate who yelped defiantly in the face of defeat" and "be judged on the results of the presidential election of 2008."[72] That same year, someone else was getting ready to make history, someone who may have been too busy coding and raising venture capital to vote in November 2004, but whose rudimentary platform Trippi had tapped to map where his young supporters were.[73]

Not registered in either political party, this skinny, gawky kid had an idea that his spare and easy-to-use platform could be a new kind of alternative media company. When, a few months after Dean's election as party chairman, Mark Zuckerberg drew a second major investor to Facebook, valuing a company that had never turned a profit at $98 million, could he have dreamed that Facebook, along with MySpace, YouTube, and Twitter, would become the next alternative media platform to make political history.[74]

= 7 =

BLOGGING THE NEWS

For years before the 2006 campaign, there had been talk about Virginia Republican senator George Allen's casual racism. It hadn't affected his political career, but the evidence was there. Allen had repeatedly displayed, and been photographed with, Confederate flags, dating back to 1970, his senior year in high school. In 1993, three local newspapers, including the *Washington Post*, reported Allen's failure to condemn an anonymous flyer comparing a political opponent to Adolf Hitler. In 1996, then-governor Allen had been photographed with movie star Charlton Heston and several officers of the white supremacist Council of Concerned Citizens (CCC). Known as the White Citizens Council until 1985, and an influential conservative donor organization, the CCC published the photo in the summer issue of their newsletter, the *Citizens Informer*. Allen had a long-term relationship with the group, as well as with the Sons of Confederate Veterans and the United Daughters of the Confederacy. In 2005, numerous news outlets reported on a twisted loop of rope hanging outside Allen's law office between 1998 and 2000 that he vaguely described as a "lasso," a symbol of law and order. Right before the election, however, the *Philadelphia Jewish Voice* reported that in a May 2006 interview on MSNBC, Allen admitted that the rope *could* be perceived as "a little old noose"; and in mid-September, when asked about it by NBC's Tim Russert, Allen did not deny that it was a noose.[1]

The Republican establishment seemed not to care. Allen's political trajectory from local to national candidate had been unimpeded by these disturbing alliances and actions. The son of a legendary Washington football coach, Allen was popular in Virginia and spoken of as a presidential contender long before he first ran for Senate in 2000. In 1997, an editorial in the *Richmond Times-Dispatch* praised him for his conservative accomplishments and, without mentioning race or racism, alluded to "misinformation and hyperbole" about, and "misportrayal" of, Allen by biased leftists. "Tall, dark-haired and ruddy," as the editorial described him, "Allen has drawn widespread comparisons to Ronald Reagan." Allen seemed to encourage comparisons to Reagan by affecting Western dress and mannerisms. A second biographical article in September 2000 echoed references to Allen's good looks, along with his penchant for country music, chewing tobacco, cowboy boots, and fiscal conservatism. But there was no mention of nooses, Confederate flags, or hobnobbing with white supremacists.[2]

Although Allen's racial views and neo-Confederate sympathies were well known, they were mostly dismissed by the mainstream media as allegation or rumors. On the evening of December 5, 2002, it turned out he wasn't the only one who was being protected, and it wasn't only the local press that was looking the other way when politicians let their hair down. That night, Mississippi senator Trent Lott, the Republican minority leader, got up to toast Strom Thurmond, a segregationist senator from South Carolina, on his hundredth birthday. Lott expressed pride that Mississippi had voted for Thurmond's segregationist States' Rights Party bid in 1948. "And if the rest of the country had followed our lead we wouldn't have had all these problems over the years either," Lott finished, to cheers from the other guests. As a reporter for the *Guardian* wrote two weeks later, these "incendiary comments" were not reported by either the *Washington Post* or the *New York Times*. Both papers had reporters at the event.[3]

At least, they didn't report the story until political bloggers did, eventually forcing Lott to resign his position as minority leader. On

December 6, historian Josh Marshall, the founder of *Talking Points Memo*, reported Lott's praise for Thurmond, as well as the senator's own prior membership in the CCC. As Marshall's post launched reporting about Lott in the mainstream media, a Richmond reporter sounded the alarm about Allen too: drawing a veil over politicians' past and present ties to racist groups might no longer be possible. "Lott's problems call attention to the question of others in the Senate Republican leadership," Jeff Schapiro wrote. "Allen's history, as a private citizen and public official, is replete with utterances and actions that inflamed racial sensitivities." Clearly, the mainstream media still didn't get it: Schapiro's framing made it seem as though the sensitivity of others to racist statements was the problem, not Allen's actions, speech, or beliefs. Perhaps it was no surprise that as Allen contemplated a national run in 2008, subsequent feature articles buried the topic again. A 2004 article about Allen syndicated by the Associated Press made no mention of race, or racism. A 2005 *New York Times* article, which acknowledged Allen as a cosponsor of a bipartisan bill apologizing for the Senate's role in blocking anti-lynching legislation, noted vaguely that Allen had been "accused in the past of insensitivity on race issues" and "racial callousness" for displaying a noose and a Confederate flag.[4]

Both stories framed Allen's racial attitudes as accusations, without stating that reporters knew these allegations to be factual. But political bloggers had no such scruples. "It looks like George Allen is trying to clean up his image on race prior to a presidential run," reported politics and media blogger Brendan Nyhan, a public policy professor at the University of Michigan, detailing all the charges that had been made over the years on May 15, 2005. This was why Nyhan was still skeptical, when Allen was captured on video making a racist statement on August 11, 2006, and the video began to circulate on YouTube, that it would dent his viability as a presidential nominee.[5]

═══

As information about campaigns—schedules, donors, a candidate's past, and analysis from self-appointed bloggers—became easily searchable on the web, unanticipated consequences of publishing political information freely and without filters emerged. In October 2000, New York City architect Fred Bernstein drew attention to a new website, created by a former FEC employee from public information, that made political campaign donations over $200, as far back as the Reagan administration, public. By entering his zip code, Bernstein could investigate his neighbors' political views, as they were expressed through campaign donations. "A man down the hall had given $1000 to a Senate hopeful I despise," he learned. Another had given to Ralph Nader's third-party challenge for the presidency. "True, a donation isn't a ballot," Bernstein wrote, but now he did not know whether he would "contribute again. Because in doing so, I'll be broadcasting my beliefs to anyone who has a modem."[6]

Broadcasting one's own beliefs, and the beliefs of others, was the essence of blogging, the most public form of digital alternative media. The first web log had been coded by hand in HTML by a first-year Swarthmore College student named Justin Hall in 1994. Hanging out in a student lounge, he had picked up a newspaper and read about the searchable web. Hall had been on the internet since his early teens, but "the whole concept" of using a mouse "to surf information was a wild idea." By spring, he had created his own site, "Justin's Home Page," hosting it on the Swarthmore server and inviting friends to read his thoughts. The first hit outside the Swarthmore system arrived on January 23, 1994, and as his readership grew, Hall renamed the web log "Links from the Underground," a hint of how inherently subversive and antiestablishment blog culture would become. It was an eclectic site, showing the breadth of what could be published: "links to HTML information, some stuff about my college, a photo of me and Oliver North, a sound clip of Jane's Addiction's lead singer saying, 'Well I'm on acid too, and I ain't throwin' shoes at you,' and a list of my favorite websites," Hall recalled. A year later, he was getting tens of thousands of hits a day and won an internship at *Wired*. "I created it all on a PowerBook," he wrote in 1995. "It cost me nothing. I can maintain it from anywhere I can be on the Internet. And for better or for worse, no one edits me, or has control over the content I provide. It is a self-publishing dream."[7]

By 2006, free commercial blog platforms meant that almost anyone could publish on the internet, opening the door to thousands of would-be Drudges eager for content and eyeballs. Enter University of Virginia senior S. R. "Sid" Sidarth, the American-born son of Indian immigrants who, on August 11, 2006, was at Breaks Interstate Park, following George Allen around with a video camera. Supporters expected Allen to win reelection to the Senate easily. Virginia was heavily Republican, and his opponent, James Webb, a decorated Marine veteran, writer of military thrillers, and fierce opponent of the Iraq War, was trailing. Sidarth wasn't a reporter or a blogger: he was a "tracker," a campaign worker assigned to surveil a candidate to identify possible lines of attack. Was it an accident that the strategists for the Webb campaign sent a brown-skinned volunteer to track a man who had a reputation for using racist slurs? Probably not: and, as Sidarth later wrote, when he had joined the Allen bandwagon five days earlier, he had been spotted immediately. The candidate, Sidarth asserted, even "knew my name."[8]

If he knew Sid's name, Allen, who had declared that he intended to run a "positive campaign," should have used it when he decided to have a little spontaneous fun in front of the all-white crowd at the Breaks Point event. Pointing at Sid patiently recording, Allen asked the group to give him a "welcome to America," addressing Sid as "macaca" several times. It isn't clear who put the video online four days after the confrontation: Sidarth said that it wasn't him.[9]

Yet there it was. On August 14 the video was moving through the blogosphere, and by August 15, it was uploaded to YouTube, pulling down increasing numbers of views. "What the hell does 'macaca' mean?" blogger Phil Yu fumed at the top of his story on August 14. He answered his own question later in the day, linking to a story from the *Daily Kos* that identified macaca "as a racial slur, and a reference to the macaque monkey, originating in French Tunisia, where Allen's mother had been born." Yu, who had been blogging since 2000 and had launched *Angry Asian Man* in 2001, helpfully posted the campaign's telephone and fax numbers, its address, and a link to the senator's email form. "Do what you think is necessary," Yu suggested, unleashing his readers on Allen's staffers.[10]

By 2006, journalists who covered politicians like Allen still played by the old rules, but mainstream outlets were no longer fully in control of the news. As Brendan Nyhan, one of the bloggers who published the story the next day, argued, it was YouTube that made all the difference, providing tangible, unmediated evidence of Allen's race-baiting. Before the Sidarth video, Nyhan recalled, there seemed to be a tacit agreement that Allen's questionable past, however well documented (by, for example, yearbook photographs) could be ignored as a youthful indiscretion or a rumor. However, the Sidarth video made it clear that the past was actually the present. It "created," Nyhan speculated, "a focusing event that made his history common knowledge and thus made it hard for other elites to deny knowing about." As Nyhan pointed out in a later article, when the mainstream media reversed its practice of excusing Allen's racism, digital alternative media came of age as a source of breaking news.[11]

Unlike the Trent Lott scandal, there were no national reporters at the Allen event, nor is there any record that the local journalists, who had brushed off questions about Allen's racism as they touted his future as a rising GOP star, were covering it either. But they didn't have to. YouTube made posting a video like Sidarth's the work of a moment, while blogs, and the increasing popularity of social media, highlighted issues muted or ignored by the journalism establishment. Although neither platform yet supported video streaming, Twitter launched in March; and a little more than a month after the Allen campaign's long, painful death spiral began, Facebook opened its platform to anyone who provided a valid email address and was over thirteen. But in August of 2006, it was blogging that was shaking up the mainstream media environment the most. On the day of Allen's "macaca moment," coders and designers at Blogger, the free tool used by the Dean campaign in 2004, and by Phil Yu since 2001, were readying a spiffy, easy-to-use template that allowed subscribers to post by email. By June 2007, when Apple introduced the iPhone, no one would even have to carry a video camera or a computer anymore: users could film an event, or a political gaffe, and upload it to a blog from the same device.[12]

Sidarth's video was released at a moment when interest in digital alternative media was on the rise, for makers, consumers, and the mainstream media alike. These new, user-friendly platforms meant that political junkies could more easily write for other political junkies, linking to and commenting on each other's work and constituting themselves as expert communities. Many reflected deeply on mainstream news stories; others reported what establishment journalists would not, or could not, write about. Video grew just as quickly. By August 2006, political junkies, advertisers, politicians, networks, wanna-be celebrities, and aspiring filmmakers were uploading an average of sixty-five thousand videos to YouTube a day, while visitors to the site watched an average of one hundred million a day. Unlike television programming, visitors never knew what, or who, they would find on YouTube. Sometimes it was someone entirely unknown, trying to capture the collective imagination: actress Lena Dunham's first video, "Pressure," a conversation between young women describing their orgasms, was filmed in the Oberlin College library and first uploaded in 2006. Political junkies became mesmerized by YouTube, as it became a source for watching and listening to past, as well as present, events. *Wired* magazine predicted the end of mainstream broadcasting as it had been understood since the launch of radio in the 1920s. YouTube, the reporter mused, tapped into something "primal," the "hunger for something we can discuss."[13]

By 2006, blogging was also making the news because of its capacity to promote discussion. In comments sections, followers could talk back to, correct, and add information to a post. To their readers, bloggers were the new trusted voice. A blogger could stay doggedly on one story, activating readers to dig up more information and calling attention to a news item until mainstream journalists were forced to report on it—and report it again, and again. In December 2002, for example, it was not that Lott's praise of Thurmond became public, but that bloggers refused to let the story go, forcing mainstream journalists to report new facts as they emerged. Political blogs like *Atrios* and *Talking Points Memo* predicted, as

TPM's Josh Marshall put it, that Lott's career was "toast," and then worked hard to make their prediction come true. While mainstream reporters tried to move on to the next story, bloggers like Marshall continued to dig into Lott's history, affirming that he had made similar remarks in front of white audiences for years.[14]

Writing for openly partisan audiences of political junkies like themselves, and using no- or low-cost distribution networks where they could develop the story together, political blogs soon had a reputation for producing more thorough coverage than the Washington press corps. Using blogrolls (a list of favored blogs) and links, they created alternative media networks, pushing readers to each other's sites and raising their results in search engines with the sheer volume of clicks they received. Good bloggers prided themselves on putting inside information in front of readers' eyes and sticking with stories longer than a corporate journalist usually could. As Marshall explained, "The way daily journalism works, a story has a twenty-four-hour audition to see if it has legs, and if it doesn't get picked up, that's it."[15] Bloggers could keep an important political issue alive, and they could put rumors or gossip in the digital record so that speculative information could be investigated collaboratively. "Bloggers," an I. F. Stone biographer wrote in 2006, when these freelance investigative journalists had become a permanent part of the alternative media scene, "bill themselves as the next Izzy."[16]

Independence was the essence of the blogging ethic, even for bloggers with partisan commitments. Soon mainstream journalists began to create spaces where they could moonlight as alternative media producers and evade editorial control. Andrew Sullivan, a conservative, out, gay journalist who was a writer and editor at the *New Republic*, and then at the *New York Times Magazine*, recalled the leap of faith it took to become a blogger. Sullivan was distinctive among the small cadre of publicly gay journalists for his outspoken conservatism and his belief that in the face of AIDS, adhering to mainstream values like monogamy and marriage was the only route to acceptance, dignity, and happiness for gay men.[17] Sullivan began the *Daily Dish* in 1999 as an outlet for views that were regarded unfavorably by his liberal editors. Steeped in the one-to-many culture of traditional journalism, he liked aggregating his work in one place and receiving comments from readers. "But still, I kept asking myself, as I stared at the laptop screen," he remembered, "What is this new medium really *for*?"[18]

That year, Blogger developed its first free platform that allowed anyone with rudimentary computer skills to establish a site. Like the famous music file-sharing site Napster, suddenly there were no gatekeepers to keep writing away from readers and no barrier to audiences reading what they wanted and screening out the rest. Blogger had over 150,000 sites by January 2002 and was adding over 40,000 a month. The sheer variety of what could be found online was staggering. Journalism was in transformation, as digital alternative media went head-to-head with the mainstream outlets that had gone online in the mid-1990s. Writers were free to choose their own style: informal, cranky, ironic, obscene, scholarly, or humorous. Sullivan imagined the *Daily Dish* as more like a "broadcast" or a "performance" than his mainstream writing, with reader comments providing him with doses of "instant gratification." While he couldn't afford to leave his job, Sullivan learned how to make a small income by adding a subscriber button and hosting ads. But mostly it was just, as he described it, "an online community, reading and thinking and paying for itself." Best of all, it freed Sullivan from what he experienced as the tyranny of liberal editors who disagreed that lesbian and gay equality could be part of a conservative moral agenda.[19]

Like BBS users, ordinary people who had something to say saw blogging as a way to enter public life and create community with others who shared their interests. Bloggers were younger and less white than the general population, and the "blogosphere," as it was called, was far more gender-balanced than the average newsroom.[20] It was proudly partisan and a medium where identity politics flourished. A 2006 report by the Pew Research Center showed that while only 11 percent of blogs were political in their orientation, 72 percent of bloggers (in contrast to 58 percent of the general population) consumed news online. The assumption that was built into blogging from the beginning was that these alternative journalists would write in good faith, and would be trustworthy, not because they were unbiased, but because they were transparent about their political biases. In addition, hyperlinks to evidence, scrutiny by other bloggers, and answering readers in the comments section created a dynamic reading and writing atmosphere in which bloggers' assertions and interpretations could be contested. For all these reasons, according to another study, political junkies, antiwar activists, media skeptics, and so-called information seekers believed that bloggers were more credible than mainstream sources.[21]

Blogs had the capacity to get news out quickly, providing details and views that contradicted or supplemented the official story and anticipating how commercial platforms like Facebook and Twitter would become sites for breaking news and commentary. The attacks on the World Trade Center and the Pentagon by Al-Qaeda-trained terrorists on September 11, 2001, were a clear turning point in the larger public's awareness that blogging was an alternative news system that could be superior to mainstream news. Television networks broadcast images of the tragedy over and over again and hastily brought in talking heads to speculate about the origins and meaning of the attacks. But anchors had to acknowledge that they had little new information, even when they interviewed eye-witnesses, as CBS's Bryant Gumbel was able to do ten minutes after the first plane struck the World Trade Center. Bloggers, however, were piecing together and relaying information from all over the city. "People have been getting onto sites, on the web, which is a very good thing to do," ABC's Peter Jennings acknowledged as he covered the grisly scene from the studio.[22]

People who turned to blogs after the attack needed to talk, and they wanted information. "While phone networks and big news sites struggled to cope with heavy traffic," the editors of *Wired* recalled five years later, "many survivors and spectators turned to online journals to share feelings, get information or detail their whereabouts." Others vividly recalled the differences between what was "broadcast at us" and the stories that spread from person to person on digital alternative media. While members of the "broadcast public" were "invisible to one another and to the person talking to us," the horizontal, internet public was "conversing.

We may not have been in the same room, but we were in some real sense face to face."[23]

Blogs were an extension of electronic democracy. Best of all, in a media world that was repetitive, dull, and often superficial, bloggers' capacity to entertain and inform, offering tools and suggestions for learning more, kept readers absorbed in a story longer. The use of hyperlinks was blogging's greatest news innovation, one that was not fully accepted in mainstream journalism until 2008, in part because of the fear that readers would simply leave the news site and not return. Hyperlinking reflected a strong ethic of transparency and horizontal cooperation among bloggers, forcing them to reveal sources of information and even connect readers to views they were attacking. Radio, television, or print sources held audiences captive to a single narrative, but the hyperlink took readers away from a story to teach them something, allowing them to return to the original post with a single keystroke, better informed and prepared to engage critically.[24]

As blogging expanded, it developed numerous subgenres: blogs catered to mothers, deployed soldiers, academics, disabled people, or combinations thereof. But political blogs soon became prominent because establishment politicians, and media consultants like Joe Trippi, saw them as a way to reach an untapped audience of partisans. In early summer 2004, as the Republicans prepared to renominate George W. Bush and the Democrats unified behind John Kerry, Marlon Manuel of the *Atlanta Journal-Constitution* announced that "Politics has gone to the blogs." Many of the top bloggers—Taegan Goddard of *Political Wire*, Ana Marie Cox of *Wonkette*, Markos Moulitsas Zuniga of the *Daily Kos*, Andrew Sullivan, and *RealClearPolitics*, founded by former options trader John McIntyre and advertising executive Tom Bevan, to name a few—were granted press passes to the nominating conventions. Yet blogging was still new enough that Manuel had to explain, using frequent scare quotes, what a blog was, reminding his readers that bloggers were not journalism professionals. "Web logs—'blogs'— are chatty cyberdiaries posted on the Internet by often irreverent, free-speaking 'bloggers,'" he wrote. "Political blogs have crawled from the Web's primordial ooze, evolving into a mutant strain of journalism. In the freewheeling online world, bloggers—often partisans—can spin the news till they get vertigo, free from the clutches of (a) an editor and (b) the truth."

Seeing these writers as descended from the *Drudge Report*, Manuel believed that gossip—not investigative reporting—was political bloggers' value added. Ana Marie Cox, "satirizes the D.C. scene with the libido of a Viagra-charged teenager and the judiciousness of a drunken blowtorch operator," Manuel wrote; she toggled between rumors of Capitol Hill affairs and "assessing the size of John Kerry's (non-tax) package." Cable news channels embraced entertaining bloggers like Cox as fellow travelers in the 24-7 news cycle. Hired to report from the floor for the cable music channel MTV, Cox built on previous appearances on CNN, Fox News, and CNBC, as well as feature stories in the *New York Times* and the *Washington Post*. Even veteran political reporters were embracing the new medium. Pulitzer Prize–winning journalist Walter Mears was persuaded to come out of retirement to blog the conventions for the Associated Press: What did he think of Cox's *Wonkette*? Manuel asked. "I'm a 68-year-old man," Mears deadpanned. "I can't allow my heart to race that much."[25]

The idea that bloggers could hold establishment journalism to account was graphically underlined during the bruising 2004 presidential campaign. Weeks before the election, CBS newsmagazine *60 Minutes* ran a story charging that President George W. Bush had dodged his Vietnam-era military service in the Air National Guard. Based on a document given to a producer by a Texas Democrat, CBS returned to a story first broken by the *Boston Globe*'s "Spotlight" investigative team in 2000: the Bush family had, the team charged, pulled strings to get Junior into the Guard to keep him out of Vietnam. In addition, a year of that time, 1972 to 1973, was unaccounted for. Bush neither reported for drills in Houston, nor did he report to the Alabama air base where the Houston command presumed he was.[26] Yet the night of the broadcast, on the conservative site FreeRepublic.com, Vietnam veterans started asking questions about the leaked memos: the style, the format, the location of the signature—even the typewriter font. The story was picked up by a Minneapolis political blog, *Powerlineblog*, run by a lawyer with a day job at a bank, who launched an independent investigation. Helped by hundreds of other bloggers and a volunteer staff of "Freepers," he researched the documents' provenance in excruciating detail. Bloggers raised enough compelling doubts about the document, and CBS's verification process, that the network had to retract the story.[27]

Stories like this, and the attention paid to the thirty-four bloggers that had been credentialed for the nominating conventions, sent political junkies out onto the internet to find blogs to read and to start their own.[28] Although journalists were themselves becoming frequent blog readers, many resented scrutiny from this freebooting alternative media class, the partisan attacks that emanated from popular blogs, and the armies of "trolls" who demanded explanations and retractions from establishment journalists. As Jim Rutenberg of the *New York Times* wrote a week before Election Day in 2004, conservative media bloggers had become obsessed with issuing constant corrections or pointing out examples of bias. "But the most personal critiques arise in the political blogs—especially from the left—run by individuals who use news media reports for their often-heated discussions." Some blogs, Rutenberg noted, included email addresses and telephone numbers for reporters whose work they objected to. A targeted journalist might receive hundreds of messages, many harassing, every day. A reporter for *Newsweek* chimed in to say that criticism could be productive, but comments on his personal appearance and intelligence were a drag. On the *Daily Kos*, now drawing 500,000 readers a day, he had been accused of being homophobic, "'wimpy,' a 'slime' and worse."[29]

Blogging fueled partisanship and made it more visible; and while they made conversations about politics more vigorous, bloggers made political culture more uncivil. As Paul Burka of the liberal *Texas Monthly* wrote in March 2005, "Blogs are the talk radio of cyberspace: entertaining, provocative, and usually identified with one end or the other of the political spectrum. The main difference between themselves and the mainstream media (MSM), the bloggers say, is that they own up to their biases, while the MSM masquerade as objective." But Burka saw the ideology expressed on blogs as too naked and too extreme: bloggers' "belief that they own the future is Maoist in its fervor," he wrote.[30]

The lines between blogging and other forms of alternative media blurred and changed the nature of broadcasting. In 2004, Rush Limbaugh moved his radio show to an internet platform, where fans who missed his broadcast could listen later, read a transcript, search his archives, and prepare questions for the following day. Former talk radio host Rachel Maddow, a rising star on MSNBC in 2005, described what she did on cable television as blogging over the airwaves. There was also a synergy between these conversation news shows and the blogosphere that Maddow dubbed the "tweety" effect: a talk news star would express an opinion, discussions about it would spread to the blogosphere, and then to a mainstream news outlet: suddenly an opinion piece reemerged as a political issue. No one was better at this than Limbaugh or Glenn Beck, a former shock jock, who would emerge by 2008 as "an apocalyptic yet strangely ebullient conspiracy theorist" on *Fox News*, leading viewers through "crazy Venn diagrams exposing the hidden links between 1960s radicals and Barack Obama."[31]

Like bloggers, this new breed of broadcasters were outsiders in different ways: Maddow, an out lesbian, had a PhD in political science from Oxford and brought incisive, liberal analysis to discussions of the news. Differently, Rush Limbaugh, a proud Midwestern college dropout who had begun his broadcasting career as a sportscaster and disc jockey, positioned himself as a "man of the people" with a particular disdain for establishment "experts" who told his listeners what to do. "If it were up to the 'experts' in government," Limbaugh wrote in 1993, "which of them would have selected my show for success?"[32] Glenn Beck, who created his own media company in 2002 to produce his radio show, as well as books, internet content, and live events, had a particular disdain for the higher education establishment, "sites of indoctrination" where liberals learned to have contempt for common people. "As far as formal education goes," he boasted, "I went from high school right into radio and never looked back."[33]

Blogging had arrived by 2004, but something else had arrived with it: the exodus of both politics and journalism from their establishment moorings. Born in its place was a world where little people broke big stories, no campaign gaffe went unrecorded, and mainstream media and alternative media looked more and more similar. As one journalist observed, the 2004 campaign had been historic because audiences were now rewarding partisanship in the media. "For the first time, a cable news channel—Fox—attracted more viewers than a broadcast network when they were competing head-to-head, covering the Republican National Convention," Tom Rosenstiel wrote. Viewers were rejecting news "built around the carefully written and edited story" in favor of highly partisan opinion-based journalism and the cable news networks' "live and extemporaneous medium built around talk. Only 11 percent of the time is devoted to edited stories" on these channels, Rosenstiel wrote. Most of the broadcast time was devoted to shouting matches in the studio, "'anchor reads' and live reporter stand-ups, in which correspondents talk off the top of their heads or from hasty notes." In this culture of talk, arguments about the news drew more attention than the news itself.[34]

Soon, journalists also began to recognize bloggers as colleagues. In 2005, conservative journalist Jeff Gannon urged liberal blogger Garrett M. Graff, a veteran of the Dean campaign, to apply for a White House Press pass. With the support of USA Today and the White House Correspondents' Association, he got it.[35] But letting bloggers in the door had consequences. In February 2005, Eason Jordan, the head of CNN's news division, was forced to resign after "being pounded for days" by conservative bloggers protesting his reported assertion that US soldiers "had targeted" twelve journalists killed in Iraq. The statement, made at the annual World Economic Forum in Davos, Switzerland, had been ignored by the mainstream journalists present. But it was picked up by both conservative and liberal blogs, forcing editors to print the story. Whether the statement was actual news or not was only one of the issues: Jordan's character and the elite establishment of Davos were also under attack. Absent the "lightning-quick and unregulated 'blogosphere,'" one reporter concluded, both Jordan, and Rather's faulty story about Bush's National Guard service, "probably would have escaped unscathed."[36]

While covering the Dean campaign, mainstream journalists had resented bloggers as intruders and partisan hacks. By the summer of 2005, the two groups were bonded in a symbiotic relationship, each depending on the other for content. Bloggers looked to journalists for stories to dissect, attack, and editorialize about, while journalists looked to blogs, not just for commentary on their own profession, but for political conversations at the state and local level that they might be missing. Florida, in the midst of a political upheaval following the state's starring role in the 2000 election controversy, was one place where national political reporters tracked blogs like *Florida News*, *Sayfie News*, *Florida Politics*, and at least one subscription blog, *Florida Insider* (available at $149 a year, a rate equal to most newspapers). New political blogs about Florida, mostly written by angry liberals after the Supreme Court ended a recount, effectively awarding the presidency to Bush, seemed "to be popping up every week," as the *St. Petersburg Times* reported. Some took on a role formerly filled by local newspapers that had folded. More importantly, bloggers refused the mainstream media's exclusive prerogative to set the news agenda. Because of this, alternative media became more influential in the post-Dean era, as candidates sought to craft antiestablishment images. In 2005, Senator John Edwards, urged on by his blog-reading wife, Elizabeth, hosted a dinner party at his Georgetown home for a select group of bloggers in an attempt to win their support.[37]

Analysts who saw Al Gore as a possibility for 2008 pointed to his unfair treatment by the mainstream media in 2000 and wondered how a campaign powered by digital alternative media could put him back on the stage. Since his loss in 2000, the former vice president had mostly withdrawn from mainstream media, citing its superficiality and lack of openness to serious, well-researched debate. Instead, Gore had taken to publishing his speeches and ideas on the internet, "making full use of what today's techies call 'viral marketing,'" one journalist explained, noting sarcastically that Gore believed that the establishment media, particularly television, was "too shallow for his substantive concerns." But supporters argued that should he choose to run again, Gore could simply refuse to engage major outlets, publicizing his views on climatecrisis.net, a site that he created for his film about global warming, and on MoveOn. Students, as the Dean campaign had shown, could organize on Facebook. Liberal political bloggers liked Gore better than they liked Hillary Clinton, another rumored front-runner for 2008, and promised that they would help him raise the funds he needed outside the Democratic Party establishment.[38]

Blogging enthusiasts believed that the possibilities for enhancing democracy on digital alternative media were limitless. "Instead of disappearing, people's communities are transforming," one set of researchers reported in 2006: "The traditional human orientation to neighborhood- and village-based groups is moving towards communities that are oriented around geographically dispersed social networks." Yet readers were quietly secluding themselves on the blogs that reflected their own views. Looking ahead to 2008, skeptics of this transformed media landscape also detected a disturbing lack of concern for the truth in some digital alternative media. Pointing to the numerous conspiracy theories circulating in conservative populist blogs and BBS's, one reporter warned that, "Coming from a print culture where the rule was check, check, source, source, I was chilled, in the early days of the blogosphere, by the easy dissemination of lies."[39]

Media scholars Brooks Jackson and Kathleen Hall Jamieson agreed. Despite bloggers' faith in the crowd's ability to self-correct, these scholars expressed concern about some digital alternative media platforms' "outright dishonesty, misrepresentation, and a lack of respect for facts." By manipulating language, images, and information, bloggers and candidates could, working from the same set of facts, tell dramatically different stories while technically telling the truth. Like cable news, where guests rambled on unchecked and put countless uncorroborated assertions into circulation, the internet was, in Jackson and Jamieson's view, a conduit for "informational sludge" across the board. But this could change. Political junkies could be trained to become smarter and more critical media consumers. If they were already on the internet, it was but a click of a mouse to check stories on sites like Factcheck.org, a site the authors had developed at the University of Pennsylvania as a clearinghouse for political claims.[40]

For reasons cited by Jackson and Jamieson, some mainstream media outlets continued to insist that gatekeeping mattered. "We filter out writing that doesn't meet our standards," Paul Burka of *Texas Monthly* wrote. "We filter out stories that we think readers won't find interesting. We filter out lack of objectivity (though not the author's point of view). Hopefully, we filter out mistakes. We see this structure as something of a Good Housekeeping seal that promises a certain level of quality." Accountability mattered. "Who do the bloggers think they are," Burka fumed, "hiding behind pseudonyms, denouncing the very concept of the filter as anti-democratic, insisting that their unfiltered, unfettered, unaccountable, uncommercial way is better?" In fact, *Texas Monthly* had thought about establishing blogs on their site, as so many newspapers and magazines were doing, but they didn't, "because we couldn't guarantee that our postings would live up to the magazine's standards."[41]

In April 2005, an alternative media platform took it one step further: bringing bloggers together to create a new kind of opinion-based journalism site. The site would sponsor no investigative reporting and would encourage discussion about stories already in the mainstream by asking political and cultural celebrities to provide commentary on the week's news. Arianna Huffington, friend to Matt Drudge and aspiring journalist Andrew Breitbart, and a recent candidate for governor of California, imagined a future in which mainstream journalists would be more like bloggers. Now a liberal, Huffington also sought to push back against conservative talk radio and *Fox News* by creating an arena where liberal politicians and their supporters would blog to popularize their ideas and policies. Huffington met with Southern California liberals, Hollywood stars, and political bloggers to raise money, hoping that this new alternative outlet could counter the growing power of conservative alternative and mainstream media, click for click. She ran the *Huffington Post* out of her home in Southern California, where it would live for years, with interns and low-wage assistants scattered around the floor editing and posting essays. She had three partners, all of whom, in one way or another, later claimed to have invented the site. Two were Jonah Peretti and Kenneth Lehrer, experienced internet entrepreneurs; the third was Breitbart.[42]

On May 9, 2005, the *Huffington Post* debuted a digital newspaper/blog hybrid, where celebrity writers were encouraged to post (mostly unpaid), and readers were encouraged to respond in the comments section, an opportunity most mainstream newspapers didn't yet offer. Huffington had, she boasted to the *New York Times*, assembled the 250 "most creative minds in the country," mostly on the left but some on the right, to write what she imagined as a more sophisticated version of the *Drudge Report*. Although it joined *Salon* and *Slate* as a born-digital publication, it also drew on the spontaneous excitement that was blossoming around blogging, cable and reality TV, and talk radio. Covering topics from politics and entertainment to sports and religion, it was, as journalist Kathryn Seelye wrote, "a nonstop virtual talk show that will also serve up breaking news around the clock." The fact that so many prominent people, many of them journalists and academics, had agreed to blog for her, including the eighty-eight-year-old Walter Cronkite, proved that blogging had really come of age, Huffington declared. Cronkite agreed. After a life of telling stories in under two minutes, the *Huffington Post* gave him "an opportunity to sound off with a few words or a long editorial," the former news anchor explained. "It's a medium that is new and interesting, and I thought I'd have some fun." Whether the *Huffington Post* was actually a blog or not, however, was still up for debate. Like mainstream publications, posts promoted to the main page were fact-checked and copyedited. Furthermore, although bloggers believed that sparring in the comments section made them accountable, Huffington, aware that readers could be abusive and nasty, did not require her writers to engage them.[43]

Blogs had come a long way in the short time since the Dean campaign. By August 2006, when George Allen found himself at the center of a national firestorm over the Sidarth video, for better or worse, bloggers were a trusted source to their own readers. They were capable of not just amplifying a story, but researching it and insisting that the mainstream media report the things they had always known about Allen. What was also clear was that multiple forms of digital alternative media could work together to get a partisan story out to voters. Sidarth's video began to travel around the internet, spreading virally over YouTube and Facebook, as bloggers launched a months-long campaign to dig up and publish the details of Allen's past behavior and alliances. "The political world exploded," wrote Jake Tapper and Betsy Kulman of *ABC News* on a blog established for the ABC newsmagazine *Nightline* a few days after the video was published. Allen's racism was finally news. As celebrity journalists weighed in on what the slur revealed about Allen, Tapper and Kulman reported, "Chris Matthews of MSNBC's *Hardball* asked, 'Is George Allen committing suicide?'" They quoted Rich Lowry of the conservative *National Review*, who said that while calling Sidarth "macaca" might not have been racist, it certainly revealed that Allen had "a mean streak." It was only paragraphs down in both of these stories, a place where many internet readers never arrived, that Allen's agonized personal apologies to his Indian American constituents appeared. Meanwhile, Webb, Allen's opponent, seemed to have an innate sense of what to do in a news environment where unanswered questions caused bloggers to renew their efforts. Refusing to say why Allen had called his campaign volunteer "macaca," or why it was racist, Webb directed journalists back to his opponent. "George Allen knew what he was saying," Webb told ABC tersely, "and he's the one you need to talk to about why he said it."[44]

That summer the campaign trail must have seemed spooked to seasoned politicians who were used to reporters' simply ignoring the occasional outburst or faux pas, or respecting a zone of privacy around supporters. Media strategies in the 2008 cycle would be "all about control," worried incumbents told a *Politico* reporter blogging for CBS.[45] Politicians were going down like bowling pins. A video of Montana's Republican Senator Conrad Burns checking his watch during a hearing on a farm bill, and finally falling asleep, had surfaced on YouTube with the song "Happy Trails" playing winsomely in the background. In an airport grin and grip, Delaware's Democratic senator Joe Biden, preparing a presidential run for 2008, was recorded chatting with an Indian American man. Referencing the corporate franchises through which some South Asian immigrants established themselves in the United States, Biden asserted cheerfully that in his state, "You cannot go to a 7-11 or Dunkin' Donuts unless you have a slight Indian accent." Eventually chosen by Barack Obama as his vice presidential candidate, Biden's own bid fizzled. Journalist Ryan Lizza, who had been one of the most significant skeptics about the Dean campaign's use of alternative media, worried that candidates would soon "retreat to a scripted bubble" and lose their last shred of authenticity: "Will YouTube democratize politics or destroy it?" he asked.[46]

YouTube and blogs may not have broken politics in 2006, but they broke George Allen. While many remember the effect of the video on Allen's campaign as instantaneous, in fact, the real damage was delayed, as bloggers mobilized to keep the story alive. Allen's multiple apologies only caused them to double down. On the *Daily Kos*, where readers could establish their own mini-blogs, one activist posted a sample letter for Virginians to send to mainstream media outlets and numbers to call to harass Allen's staff. "Again, the more information that gets out, the more votes Webb will get," Ivan Carter wrote. Admittedly, the facts that bloggers fed back into the mainstream seemed to speak for themselves. Suddenly voters knew that as a member of the Virginia House of Delegates, Allen had opposed the creation of a holiday for Dr. Martin Luther King. He had been photographed with a Confederate battle flag. Although Allen continued to deny allegations that he had ever used racial slurs as "ludicrously false," his denials only triggered more reports from his past. Two former friends reported that they had heard Allen use a derogatory word meant to describe African Americans. The wife of the University of Virginia rugby coach reported that she had heard Allen use "the 'n' word" and that the Sidarth video had encouraged her to speak up about it. And a photograph surfaced: as an office holder, Allen had posed for a photograph with white supremacists at CPAC.[47]

It wasn't that alternative media commanded a bigger audience that was more likely to vote. Rather, bloggers commanded the eyeballs of tens of millions of political junkies who wanted to follow a story to what they saw as its logical endpoint: the termination of Allen's political career.[48] As blogger Nate Silver analyzed the impact of the "macaca moment" eight years later, it was the drip-drip-drip of the story that gradually mobilized activists to work for, and donate to, the centrist Democrat Webb, draining the life from the Allen campaign. The race had been almost competitive prior to the gaffe, with Allen holding an edge because he was an incumbent with excellent fundraising power and name recognition. Webb's campaign "wasn't a lost cause, but Allen was not an easy target," Silver wrote. "Webb probably needed some catalyst to generate more attention for his race and push him over the finish line," and the viral gaffe provided it. It also drew out-of-state money to Webb. Although the national netroots already favored Webb, Allen's remarks "dramatically increased their attention on Virginia. And the netroots maintained their heightened attention right up through the November election."[49]

As the United States made the turn into the new election cycle, with John McCain determined once more to seize the Republican nomination and Hillary Clinton almost sure to be anointed by the Democrats, this question of how a candidate controlled their campaign narrative became more fraught than ever. Was it even possible for a politician to be gaffe-proof? Or to account for a long history in politics without having ugly facts uncovered? The answer was no. The new alternative media would demand an entirely new kind of candidate—a fresh face, perhaps one who had barely been in politics at all.

In fact, at that moment, Illinois's freshman United States senator Barack Obama was trying to convince his wife, Michelle, that running for the Democratic presidential nomination was the right thing to do.

= 8 =

MYBARACKOBAMA

In 2008, the unstated question was: Would the next Democratic candidate be the first woman, or the first African American, to be nominated by a major party? On January 5, toward the end of the final New Hampshire debate, the three remaining male candidates battered New York Senator Hillary Clinton all evening.[1] The moderator, *ABC News* anchor Charles Gibson, then asked Clinton what she would say to voters who did not find her likable. "They seem to like Barack Obama more," Gibson elaborated as the auditorium grew tense. Clinton acquired a bright, slightly fragile smile and took a deep breath. "Well that hurts my feelings," Clinton answered, as the crowd began to laugh.

"I'm sorry, Senator—I'm sorry," Gibson backpedaled.

"But I'll try to go on," Clinton continued with a comic headshake. "He's—he's very likable. I agree with that." Obama stared down at his notes as the audience laughed. "I don't think I'm *that* bad," she appealed. The crowd began to applaud, as the camera switched back to Obama.

"You're likable enough, Hillary, no doubt about it," the junior senator from Illinois cut in curtly.

"I appreciate that," Clinton said brightly, in her best Midwestern "nice" voice, as the audience applauded loudly.[2]

Women voters were particularly outraged by the exchange. They heard Obama's faint praise as a put-down, the kind that jocks use to humiliate unpopular, brainy, high school girls. And when, the day before New Hampshire voted, Clinton seemed to hold back tears at a campaign stop, sympathy for her grew.[3] "This wasn't 1972," veteran media consultant David Axelrod later wrote, emphasizing how quickly the television clip had migrated from a local news station to YouTube, then posted to the progressive blog *Talking Points Memo*, where thousands of views made it news, pushing it onto cable and mainstream evening broadcasts. Although Obama had been between 11 and 14 points up in the polls, momentum abruptly shifted to Clinton. New Hampshire handed the former First Lady a surprising three-point win; women voted for Clinton by a 13-point margin.[4]

By 2008, digital alternative media encompassed more than just campaign tools or networks of political blogs: 44 percent of all adults went online for their political news during the 2008 campaign, as many as read newspapers. Fewer Americans turned to magazines, while sharing news electronically was on the rise. Younger voters were "not just consumers of news and current events, but conduits as well," wrote *New York Times* reporter Brian Stelter, "sending out e-mailed links and videos to their friends and social networks." Only 25 percent of voters under 30 turned to television for campaign news, compared to 40 percent in the 30- to 49-year-old bracket and 50 percent who were older than 50. Two-thirds of web users under 30 used social networking sites, and 4 out of 10 watched campaign events and speeches on YouTube. In retrospect, the outcome of the 2008 election was foretold by new statistical categories: "friends," "followers," and "likes." Obama had one million followers on the two top social media sites, MySpace and Facebook; his Democratic rival, Clinton, 330,000, and John McCain, the Republican nominee, 140,000. As Stelter observed, "MySpace and Facebook create a sense of connection to the candidates." As of March 2008, three million voters under thirty—most of whom had grown up on the internet—had voted in a primary, compared to one million in the entire 2004 primary season.[5]

Just as Joe Trippi imagined, digital alternative media was driving campaigns now. Political junkies were not just watching, but uploading, posting, reposting, texting, and sharing, as they sought to make a difference in the 2008 election. Emotional moments, like Clinton's, became ubiquitous mainstream media stories that moved voters, while campaign events, populated to YouTube, became an ongoing advertisement for the candidate. When Barack Obama became the first African American to win a presidential primary in January 2008, his Iowa Caucus speech became a "YouTube moment," the Pew Research Center's Aaron Smith wrote, a video that took on a "campaign-altering life of its own" as it zipped around the internet. Of course, it was a "great speech," Smith admitted, although "relatively few people, outside of the most inveterate political junkies, actually *did* watch the speech live in its entirety." But on YouTube, the speech garnered 160,000 views in the 12 hours after it was posted—and that didn't count the myriad views on blogs, Facebook, MySpace, and Twitter.[6]

As subscribers to these platforms multiplied, digital alternative media could also turn on a dime to do unprecedented damage. Campaigns now feared what happened to George Allen in Virginia, and what may have happened to Obama in New Hampshire: when disparaging views of a candidate were voiced by an establishment figure and played in an endless online loop, it so enraged independent, and even apathetic, voters that they showed up in droves to defend the other person with their votes. There were no safe spaces left. In April 2008, when Obama characterized rural conservatives as "clinging to their guns and religion," that ungenerous comment also went viral. "Barack would get into a room of wealthy supporters and, thinking he was among friends, offer remarkably candid, if impolitic, observations," Axelrod recalled, "except this time there was a blogger for *The Huffington Post* in the crowd, recording the entire disquisition on her digital recorder."[7] Rush Limbaugh urged his listeners to wear the phrase proudly and gave his fans—who usually referred to themselves as Dittoheads—a new campaign nickname: Bitter Clingers. "To liberals, if you're proud of your country, there's something wrong with you," Limbaugh snarled on his daily show a few days after the gaffe. "You are a jingoist, or you cling to religion and guns. Or you're a NASCAR fan and you're stupid."[8]

Increasing numbers of political junkies had migrated online, and as a result, political news had become intensely personal, served up for an audience of "you." In 2008, 25 percent of Americans and 60 percent of internet users got all their political news, increasingly tailored to their personal tastes by algorithms, from the internet. Political conversation also moved online: 38 percent of internet users had regular online exchanges with each other about the 2008 election. With the addition of social media platforms like Facebook, YouTube, MySpace, and Twitter, alternative media delivered an ongoing feast of political news, gossip, opinions, and gaffes straight to journalists, campaign staff, and political junkies, via laptops, desktops, and new mobile smartphones. By the end of the campaign cycle, 59 percent of internet users had shared a video, message, fundraising appeal, or news about a candidate at least once. However, users were increasingly declining to discuss their differences: 33 percent of internet users admitted that when they went hunting for political news, they chose sites that shared their point of view. Blogs were particularly prone to this dynamic. While these sites provided opportunities for "healthy debate," they also served as refuges that "enable[d] people to avoid information that may be unpleasant or unwelcome."[9]

As television had been, digital alternative media was now a place where Americans sought knowledge and entertainment. Many internet users discovered in 2008, when the Democrats were likely to nominate a "first," that politics could be extraordinarily entertaining. Partisan videos posted to YouTube, and then circulated on Facebook or MySpace, had the potential to reach constituencies who were, as yet, indifferent to politics, wooing them with something similar to what they might see on MTV or cable TV comedian Jon Stewart's *Daily Show*. A signature moment for the Obama campaign was a music video posted to YouTube, produced by the digital humor shop *Barely Political* in February 2008. Titled "Crush on Obama," it featured an aspiring singer-actress named Amber Lee Ettinger, subsequently dubbed "the Obama Girl." The video told the story of a beautiful young political junkie. She supported John Kerry in 2004, but upon watching Obama's convention keynote, she "put down my Kerry sign, knew I had to make you mine." In a month, the song "Crush on Obama" had over 2.3 million YouTube views, spread to late-night television, and was written up in the *New York Times*.[10]

In 2004, the Dean campaign failed at converting a digital alternative media community into a voting plurality that could win a nomination. Still, Howard Dean, chair of the Democratic National Committee from 2005 to 2009, made sure that the 2008 political establishment would incorporate a rapidly developing digital alternative media toolbox in its quest for the White House. Dean enlisted Blue State Digital, the political consulting firm created by former Deaniacs, to create a fifty-state strategy that helped the Democrats to run the table in the 2006 midterms, creating a powerful organization that Obama would inherit in 2008. But Dean did not imagine the candidate who took the nomination as the establishment candidate of the past. Rather, that person would represent a new Democratic Party, reshaped by progressive populism and repackaged as a movement, massed behind a youthful former community organizer, with a charming, accomplished wife and two cute daughters. Digital alternative media, and videos like "Crush on Obama," worked to veil Obama's membership in the Democratic political establishment. It created a historic candidacy, turned a political campaign into a social movement, and made promises about inclusion and hope that would, in the end, run up against the wall of an ever-more-partisan political landscape.[11]

=====

Barack Obama wasn't expected to be the internet star of 2008. In 2006, Adam Nagourney of the *New York Times* identified John Edwards as "the most Web-savvy candidate," the one campaign watchers would be looking to for "insight into how campaigns are adapting to the pressures of the internet."[12] One of those pressures that became evident in the 2006 midterms was how to respond swiftly to attacks on digital alternative media that moved quickly into a competitive, mainstream media environment and were then amplified by partisan cable television opinion and talk radio shows. Partisan talk also moved to a new platform: podcasts, radio shows that could be downloaded to a digital listening device to be enjoyed at leisure. In 2005, the liberal digital politics and culture site *Slate* launched the first political podcast, the *Political Gabfest*, an hour-long conversation between journalists David Plotz, John Dickerson, and Emily Bazelon.[13]

The modern political candidate didn't just need a media team. He, or she, needed sympathetic digital alternative media allies who were not formally associated with the campaign, political junkies willing to spend their time countering negative stories on blogs, social media, cable television, radio, and mainstream news outlets. This had been a crucial flaw in Senator John Kerry's 2004 campaign, which was unable to overcome attacks from the 527 political group, funded by a Bush donor and organized on the internet, "Swift Boat Veterans for Truth" (SBVT). The group posted stories alleging, among other things, that Kerry lied to his commander about an action that had resulted in his being awarded the Bronze Star; and that his third Purple Heart, which sent him home from Vietnam early, was awarded for a faked wound.[14] Despite the Kerry campaign's vigorous effort to get the facts on the record, slurs that originated on the SBVT site circulated, often uncontested, on conservative blogs, talk radio, *Fox News*, and even the *Wall Street Journal*. In 2007, Rush Limbaugh was still telling his audience that SBVT's allegations had never been disproved. "The problem that the libs have with that," he explained, is that "you don't dare tell the truth about them." Except, of course, that it was Kerry's story that was true.[15]

Because of the scandals that had rocked her husband's administration, Hillary Clinton was particularly vulnerable to accusations that she was hiding the truth about herself and her motives for wanting to be president. This was not because she had actually done anything wrong, other than make political decisions that some voters disagreed with, but because she had been the target of elaborate antiestablishment conspiracy theories promulgated in alternative print, digital, and broadcast media since the 1990s. In fact, prior to her 2000 Senate run, Clinton benefited from a surge of sympathetic popularity because of the Lewinsky affair. But as her ambitions turned to the presidency, conservative and progressive populists targeted her with conspiracy theories. Recast as a collaborator in her husband's centrist policies and an enabler of his undisciplined sexual behavior, she was also censured by populists on the left and on the right for her Senate vote to authorize the war in Iraq.[16]

Even the mainstream media were skeptical of Clinton's ambitions, an attitude many supporters viewed as sexist. On July 18, 2007, C-SPAN was broadcasting Clinton as she gave a speech on education from the well of the Senate, when female *Washington Post* fashion writer Robin Ghivan noticed an irregularity in the Senator's otherwise plain business attire. "The cleavage registered after only a quick glance," Ghivan wrote. "There wasn't an unseemly amount of cleavage showing, but there it was. Undeniable." It was "like catching a man with his fly unzipped. Just look away!" It had to be deliberate, Ghivan concluded. "It means that a woman is content being perceived as a sexual person in addition to being seen as someone who is intelligent, authoritative, witty and whatever else might define her personality. It also means that she feels that all those other characteristics are so apparent and undeniable, that they will not be overshadowed." Bizarrely, journalists speculated that the candidate was trying to raise money by looking sexy. The *Washington Post*'s Howard Kurtz sniggered about "Clinton's Campaign Chest," Megan Garber of the *Columbia Journalism Review* deadpanned about her "war chest," and Kenneth Bazinet of the *New York Daily News* proposed that Clinton was "hot and bothered" about the cleavage talk. The Clinton campaign's response, a 746-word email rebuttal sent to mainstream journalists with the single word "cleavage" in the subject line, earned further derision. "I'll take things I didn't expect in my inbox for 500," wrote the *National Review*'s Jim Geraghty, spoofing the popular TV quiz show *Jeopardy*. "Dear Hillary campaign: Don't ever, ever do that again."[17]

Driven in part by the mainstream media's desire to imitate the snarky humor and edgy attacks that made alternative digital media sites popular, these sexist attacks trivialized Clinton. At the same time Obama, aspiring to be the first African American president, was gaining traction in digital alternative and mainstream media as a grassroots, progressive populist. Suddenly, in the post–Howard Dean moment, being a populist was making a comeback on the left. In 2007, blogger Peter Levine identified both Obama and rival John Edwards as populists, and Ben Smith of *Politico* compared Obama to populist Henry Wallace.[18] The *New York Times* published a photo a few months before Obama officially announced his candidacy showing the lanky senator as a man of the people. Smiling happily and with shirtsleeves rolled up, Obama waded into a crowd of white Iowa voters. The story made a point of his "celebrity buzz" and cited one supporter's view that Obama did not need the Democratic Party establishment's approval to succeed. "He's telling us he's got to pay his dues," said an Illinois man who had pushed through the crowd to meet his idol, "and we're telling him, 'Learn as you go.'"[19]

By contrast, Clinton's actual qualifications, and her experience, caused her to be depicted as a card-carrying member of the failed Washington establishment. After listening to Bill Clinton give a speech on his wife's behalf in New Hampshire, journalist Matt Bai asked peevishly, "I found it hard not to wonder why so many of the challenges facing the next president were almost identical to those he vowed to address in 1992. Why, after Clinton's two terms in office, were we still thinking about tomorrow?" In a New Hampshire stump speech, Edwards did not name, but was clearly referring to, Clinton when he urged voters to reject "establishment elites" who offered "outdated answers" that were "rooted in nostalgia." Meanwhile, liberal bloggers not only slammed Clinton for her vote on the Iraq War, but viewed her as too groomed, overly strategic, and inauthentic. Arianna Huffington told one reporter for *Politico* that bloggers were shunning Clinton because "she has been so calculating you can smell it. Every thought has been processed through multiple channels in her and her consultants' brains. It's so fabricated."[20]

Ironically, Clinton had embraced the language, styles, and techniques of digital alternative media from the beginning of her campaign in an attempt to connect with voters where they were: online.

On January 20, 2007, she announced her campaign on YouTube and proposed a digital listening tour. Filmed in the living room of her elegant Chappaqua, New York, home, the two-minute video outlined a progressive agenda and named the numerous failures of the Bush administration. She then looked into the camera to propose an intimate conversation. "Let's talk. Let's chat," Clinton said with a smile. "Let's start a dialogue about your ideas and mine. Because the conversation in Washington has been just a little one-sided lately, don't you think? And we can all see how well that worked," Clinton continued. "And with a little help from modern technology, I'll be holding live, online video chats as of this week, starting Monday."[21]

Notably, Clinton made her campaign about "you." But it was Obama whose live announcement, delivered a few weeks earlier and immediately posted to YouTube, seemed to capture the magic of old and new, speaking personally to each voter by constantly repeating the words "you," "us," and "we." Striding onto a stage built on the steps of the Old State Capitol in Springfield, Illinois, where Abraham Lincoln had first been sworn in to elected office, Obama surveyed the cheering crowd with apparent wonder. "Look at all of you," he greeted them: "Look at all of *you*." Remarking on how cold it was and how far people had traveled to be there, he said, "We all made this journey for a reason. . . . You didn't just come here for me. You came here because you believe in what this country can be." He challenged the crowd to think about a new political world, driven by what the people, not politicians, wanted. The campaign couldn't "only be about me," Obama insisted. "It must be about us. It must be about what we can do together. This campaign must be the occasion, the vehicle of *your* hopes and *your* dreams." As the crowd cheered, he ended in a way few politicians would: "I love you," he said. "Thank you."[22]

The insistent use of these intimate second-person and collective pronouns matched the spirit of an increasingly personal alternative digital media. YouTube's very name insisted that videos uploaded by and for everyone were really created by you, and for you. MySpace was your own personal spot on the internet. Not surprisingly, bloggers and the netroots coalition spearheaded by MoveOn leaned toward the progressive populist Obama, not Clinton who, as a woman, had fought her way into establishment success. But strangely, even though the candidate did, the political operatives on the Obama campaign didn't seem to immediately understand what role internet activists should play. Axelrod, Obama's senior strategist and a former journalist, was most comfortable promoting his candidate through newspaper contacts and his own appearances on political opinion shows. He didn't join Twitter until 2011 and did not seem to trust bloggers. One clue as to why is that Axelrod liked to refer to himself as "the keeper of the message," a centralized approach to the campaign narrative that was at odds with the spirit that grassroots alternative media had displayed in 2004.[23]

But the same passion that brought Axelrod to Obama also drew a much younger, but equally successful, digital alternative media professional to the campaign. When twenty-three-year-old Chris Hughes took leave from Facebook, the company he had co-founded with Mark Zuckerberg three years earlier, to work with the Obama campaign, he found that despite its eighteen million users, Axelrod and his seasoned operatives neither knew nor cared about the alternative media platform devoted to personal story-telling, friendship, and community building. And yet, everyone in Obama headquarters used digital tools nonstop. Speechwriter Ben Rhodes remembers the young digital natives on the campaign routinely "communicating by Instant Messenger even when we were sitting next to each other." However, Hughes was warned not to speak of Obama as a "Facebook candidate," and to instead say that he was an "organizer," like everyone else, because "the campaign and its energy were not about Facebook at all." Undaunted, Hughes spent his early weeks building a social network around the candidate, using all the digital tools available. Most crucially, he brokered the purchase of a popular MySpace page, MyBarack-Obama, that a supporter had built after Obama's 2004 convention keynote. It had already accrued 160,000 subscribers.[24]

While they made an establishment campaign consultant like Axelrod nervous, he knew these techniques were the future. Net-roots volunteers had ideas about how to "brand" their candidate and "sell" him to their peers, and they were not shy about sharing them with the campaign chiefs. Axelrod had interacted with these activists before when he ran Deval Patrick's 2006 campaign for Governor of Massachusetts. These "young insurgents, some of whom were refugees from Howard Dean's failed presidential bid . . . had glimpsed the potential of the Internet," Axelrod recalled, "and tech-savvy Massachusetts proved to be fertile ground for their new, expansive digital strategies."[25]

Obama's 2008 victory would later be framed in terms of the campaign's mastery of digital alternative media channels, but its leadership, drawn from the political consulting establishment, was reluctant to give authority to progressive populists at the grassroots who might be difficult to control. The many successes of the Dean campaign, such as DeanLink and CivicSpace, built on the early popularity of social networking sites like Friendster and Facebook. But its failures—the high burn rate of campaign funds, overreliance on digital outreach, failure to cultivate mainstream media outlets, and supporters' often eccentric and unrestrained sense of humor—told a cautionary tale about progressive populism's potential for sending a campaign off the rails. Hughes struggled to persuade Axelrod and campaign manager David Plouffe that social media networks were made up of real people, a new generation of potential political junkies who influenced each other. Making good on Obama's promise that "this campaign is about you," Hughes argued, was more important than Axelrod's insistence that the campaign, not a network of digital volunteers, control the message. Initially rebuffed as "the crazy tech guys in the corner," Hughes and his team began to prove their point with results. By the end of the campaign, the MySpace platform Hughes bought had racked up 2 million friends. Supporters had "planned 200,000 offline events, formed 35,000 groups, posted 400,000 blogs, and raised $30 million on 70,000 personal fundraising pages."[26]

While Obama did not seem to have to work hard to be liked by Democrats, despite her extensive digital outreach, Clinton was saddled with a perception that she was unlikable, stiff, and inauthentic. As cultural critic Susan Bordo reflected later, even Clinton's accomplishments were used against her. Her "polish and poise" were read as insincerity, her familiarity with a broad range of issues as ambition and opportunism. The liberal and feminist blogospheres split bitterly on this issue. Obama and Clinton partisans littered each other's blogs and supporters' social media with vicious comments. While bloggers at the *Daily Kos*, journalist James Wolcott wrote, "faced off like the Jets and the Sharks," a reference to the 1957 Broadway play about gang rivalries, *West Side Story*.[27]

Unquestioningly, the Obama team owned YouTube, and that, too, became a vehicle for creating suspicion about Clinton as conspiracy theories circulating about her on conservative populist sites leaked into the Democratic primary. In March 2007, Obama supporter Philip de Vellis created a mash-up of the now-classic Apple "1984" ad. Now titled "Vote Different," it superimposed Clinton's campaign launch speech on the screen that had displayed Big Brother in the original version. Designed to emphasize Clinton's establishment credentials and association with a controlling federal government, by implication, it promoted Obama's antiestablishment, even revolutionary, potential. As Clinton spoke, the same torpid audience listened, but the hammer thrower wore a singlet with the Obama campaign logo. The final screen read: "On January 14th, the Democratic primary will begin. And you'll see why 2008 won't be like '1984.'" Like the earlier Macintosh ad, this video went viral. One media scholar, blogger, and confessed political junkie remained unsure about how such interventions would reshape the campaign, but admitted that he found "the underlying message of citizen empowerment" in the video "irresistible."[28]

Clinton partisans continued to resent what they saw as mainstream and alternative media bias against their candidate. Indeed, the *New York Times* assigned newcomer Amy Chozick to Clinton, perhaps believing that her gender was more important than experience: Chozick had never covered a single political campaign and never fully connected with the candidate. Worse, as younger female voters migrated to Obama, some older progressive white women, whom Clinton had imagined to be her core constituency, cooled on her as well. In 2007, a multigenerational group of women writers, journalists, and academics agreed that Clinton was not resonating with them. *Thirty Ways of Looking at Hillary* was a collection of essays published as the campaign was getting off the ground:

in them, feminists agreed that Clinton did not meet the challenge of authenticity, which was "shaping up to be the buzzword of the 2008 campaign." Why was she simultaneously so well known and so unknowable? they asked.[29]

How had professional media women who had supported Clinton through the eight years of her husband's presidency and worn buttons that asked voters to "Elect Hillary's husband" come to dislike and distrust her? How did media women fail to identify with an establishment candidate whose life, successes, and challenges, in many ways, paralleled their own. One answer was that feminism was no longer a sufficient bridge between generations, nor did it speak to the growing partisan divide between establishment liberals and progressive populists in the Democratic Party. Novelist Lorrie Moore saw Clinton's public persona as "too often in pragmatic retreat, overmanaged, increasingly botoxed and schoolmarmish." Political journalist Jane Kramer, reflecting on the Cleavagegate controversy, wanted Clinton to be "a good, generous, and loving person *and* a steely, scary, effective person." According to novelist Lauren Collins, compared to Obama's direct online connection to voters, Clinton's budding social media presence was "frumpy," just an online version of her managed mainstream media image. Ignoring Obama's thin history as an elected official, Judith Thurman charged that Clinton had paid her political dues, but "not from her own account," running for Senate in a state "where she had no roots" (something that was far from unprecedented, particularly in New York). Some of the authors remarked that Clinton's feminism was simply outdated. "There's something about the reality of Hillary Clinton, the accommodations she's made and the roles she's played, that leaves many of us cold," grumbled Dahlia Lithwick of *Slate*.[30]

At a moment when progressive populism was on the ascendant in the Democratic Party, Clinton's inability to persuade voters that as a woman, she, too, was an outsider to the establishment, was fatal to a national candidacy. By contrast, the Obama team, however reluctantly at first, successfully leveraged digital alternative media support to redefine the race as a generational contest and capture everyone outside the establishment, regardless of gender or race. The Democratic National Committee helped to push this narrative by reframing traditional political rituals. On July 23, 2007, the eight candidates in the race—Clinton, Obama, Joe Biden, Edwards, Christopher Dodd, Mike Gravel, Dennis Kucinich, and Bill Richardson—debuted in a debate broadcast on CNN and YouTube, where viewers were invited to send in their questions. The United States Department of State billed the event as a triumph of American political values, inspired and facilitated by the internet. "Politicians accustomed to controlling discussions saw people in T-shirts pose cheeky, incisive questions from all over the country and the world," one press release read. "One question came from an aid worker surrounded by children at a refugee camp in Darfur, Sudan." YouTube was becoming a primary destination for all populist political junkies that year. When they learned that Libertarian presidential candidate Ron Paul was receiving more hits on YouTube there than any Democrat or Republican, the Republican National Committee quickly announced a YouTube debate for November.[31]

Social media was now a routine tool for political campaigns and for the political establishment. Politicians used it not only to capture the grassroots zeitgeist but also to reach demographics beyond the youth vote, as older people increasingly adopted Facebook. And yet, although the internet was still cheap, it was also still a labor-intensive site for strategizing a campaign. Before turning over the Barack Obama MySpace page to the campaign, its creator had invested thousands of unpaid hours administering it. By March 2007, he sometimes spent his entire evening just approving friend requests. Perhaps this was why one marketing professor who reviewed the sites and apps being used by every campaign in 2007 found many of them hard to navigate, disconnected, and sometimes abandoned.[32]

While maintaining control of their message, the Obama team found creative ways to keep the netroots occupied and energized, while generating content that had a fresh, antiestablishment look. Midway through the primary season, the campaign launched a contest that invited supporters to produce their own political commercials. Sponsored by MoveOn, the "Obama in 30 Seconds" contest was inspired by an earlier, far more divisive 2004 MoveOn contest, "Bush in 30 Seconds," in which political junkies had been invited to create attack ads. This time, makers were carefully instructed to create a positive message. Of course, both worked, since the secret to YouTube virality was to inspire emotion in viewers that caused them to want to view the video repeatedly and share it with others. Videos created by the grass roots were likely to meet that standard; carefully crafted and focus-group-tested videos generated by the Clinton campaign were not.[33]

Organizations like MoveOn, Blue State Digital, and ActBlue, which emerged from the 2004 campaign with powerful email lists of progressive populists, played a game-changing role in 2008 as digital alternative media moved to center stage for fundraising and voter outreach. Well in advance of primary voting, MoveOn, now a political action committee, endorsed Obama, the first time it had ever explicitly supported a candidate. It was also a sign that the netroots alternative media apparatus was throwing its weight behind a challenge to the Democratic political establishment whose most influential, often invisible fundraisers and power brokers were used to picking the candidate they planned to support. MoveOn was now a fundraising and digital alternative media giant. Yet the organization still insisted on its grassroots identity, the importance of small-donation fundraising, and on acknowledging its constituency as collaborators from whom it solicited advice and ideas, not just money. By extension, Obama became the grassroots candidate, a brand that was, ironically, strengthened by his thin political experience.[34]

Why not invite voters with no experience in campaign advertising to join the party? The MoveOn contest rules stated that the ads were not for profit and could not be copyrighted. Instead, the group encouraged the use of the Creative Commons license developed by Harvard Law School professor Lawrence Lessig. Capitalizing on the cultural obsession with reality television contests, the crowd would vote to choose the finalists. The winners would be chosen by a jury of celebrity Democrats that included blogger Markos Moulitsas; progressive actors Matt Damon, Ben Affleck, and Adrian Grenier; feminist Naomi Wolf; and civil rights leader Jesse Jackson.

Running the contest allowed MoveOn to identify even more potential Obama supporters as they registered with the site to view the videos and choose their favorites, adding 5.5 million emails to their supporter list. Data collected during those visits also identified the digital profile, and physical location, of each participant. The winner, "Obamacan," featured John Weiler, an Air Force veteran and Republican crossover voter. It ended with a catchphrase that gestured to the growing political divisions between right and left that digital alternative media were accelerating: "Bringing America Together."[35]

In contrast to the Clinton campaign's one-to-many digital approach, the Obama campaign was consistently designed as many-to-many communication. Both approaches allowed the campaign to build its fundraising and voter outreach capacity through data collection and analysis, practices that companies like Facebook refined significantly after 2004. But a many-to-many approach promoted far more engagement. This, in turn, helped the Obama campaign appeal to the Democratic Party establishment in the most traditional way possible: money. Hillary and Bill Clinton were masterful fundraisers and easily secured commitments from big donors. But in first-quarter fundraising, 100,000 donors contributed $25 million to Obama, making it possible for the campaign, like Dean's, to reject public financing. The online souvenir store was also immensely profitable. Each T-shirt, hat, and mug identified a supporter whose physical, and email, addresses could be used for voter outreach.[36]

If the campaign's internet presence continually emphasized Obama's reliance on grassroots energy, it also effectively concealed how much he was wedded to, and embedded in, the Democratic establishment to begin with. Half of the Obama war chest would actually come from the same big-money sources as Clinton's. The investment firm Goldman Sachs ultimately bundled over $1 million for Obama, as did Citigroup, JPMorgan, and major universities like the University of California and Harvard. Yet because of the volume of small donations, the Obama campaign narrative continued to emphasize its antiestablishment credentials. "By throwing open the convention doors," Axelrod explained about the decision to have Obama accept the nomination in an outdoor stadium, "we had kept faith with the grassroots supporters who had propelled us to that moment."[37]

Obama went on to face John McCain and his conservative populist running mate, Alaska governor Sarah Palin. Palin's squeaky voice, garbled syntax, and inability to grasp basic facts were pilloried in the mainstream media, but her profile as a "hockey mom," her homemade look, and her love for hunting and other outdoor sports made her the darling of the Republican Party's growing populist alternative media channels.[38] Prior to Election Day, up to 10 percent of American voters reported to pollsters that they had not yet decided on a candidate. On the morning of November 4, *Minneapolis Star-Tribune* reporter Randy Salas unveiled a digital tool to help Minnesotans determine how to cast their vote. He directed readers to a site called the "Glass Booth," where they could find eighteen issues "such as immigration, health care, and education," and select the ones that mattered most to them. The voter would then go on to step two, a series of questions about a range of "hot topics" in the campaign. "Your answers are evaluated on a weighted scale that factors in your stance on the issues from the first step," Salas wrote, "and then the site shows which candidate is most aligned with your views, by percentage."[39]

It was almost as if each voter had the opportunity to choose a candidate that was customized—just for *you*. But voting at the direction of an algorithm was only one way in which this historic election had brought the full weight of the internet to bear on the election process. *Yahoo! News* reported that a quarter of its traffic in 2008 had been driven by the election, particularly its Election '08 Political Dashboard. The site delivered analysis, real-time polls, projections, campaign contribution data, and odds to the voter's desktop. It also contained expert political analysis from online-only political sites like *Politico* and *RealClearPolitics*; and an online collaborative called "Video the Vote," where citizens were encouraged to document local election activity to combat voter suppression. For the first time, internet companies Digg and Twitter offered election night coverage on CurrentTV, an online-only channel.[40]

Obama's improbable victory over not one, but two, seasoned establishment politicians solidified digital alternative media's prominence in political campaigns and reporting. At 10 p.m. central time, the telephone rang at Obama headquarters in Chicago. It was John McCain, the Republican nominee and the first primary candidate to experiment with internet-driven grassroots campaigning, conceding the election to the candidate whose team had finally harnessed the internet successfully. "To the very end, Mr. McCain's campaign was eclipsed by an opponent who was nothing short of a phenomenon," wrote Adam Nagourney of the *New York Times*, "drawing huge crowds epitomized by the tens of thousands of people who turned out to hear Mr. Obama's victory speech in Grant Park in Chicago." Obama's victory was so sweeping that for the first time since 1995, Democrats would be in control of both the House and the Senate, making the kinds of changes Obama had promised during the campaign, particularly national health insurance, a real possibility.[41]

However, as the president-elect addressed the massive crowd standing outdoors in Chicago's Loop that night, he never mentioned the internet once, nor the many digital tools that had propelled him first past Clinton, and then past McCain. Instead, recounting the principles of electronic democracy, he spoke to the real celebrity of the campaign, the individual that *Time* magazine chose as its Person of the Year in 2006: You.[42] "I will never forget who this victory truly belongs to—it belongs to you," Obama said, after thanking his campaign advisors and his running mate, Joe Biden. "I was never the likeliest candidate for this office," he continued. "We didn't start with much money or many endorsements. Our campaign was not hatched in the halls of Washington—it began in the backyards of Des Moines and the living rooms of Concord and the front porches of Charleston." It was, he said, "built by working men and women who dug into what little savings they had to give five dollars and ten dollars and twenty dollars to this cause. It drew strength from the young people who rejected the myth of their generation's apathy; who left their homes and their families for jobs that offered little pay and less sleep; from the not-so-young people who braved the bitter cold and scorching heat to knock on the doors of perfect strangers; from the millions of Americans who volunteered, and organized, and proved that more than two centuries later, a government of the people, by the people and for the people has not perished from this Earth. This is your victory."[43]

Without using the word, Obama described a successful populist campaign.

=====

But was it as sweeping a victory as it seemed? Was America united, as Obama imagined, or divided? Were populisms driven by digital alternative media, progressive and conservative alike, pulling Americans further apart? As John McCain gave his concession speech in Arizona, his supporters seemed unwilling to concede. When McCain mentioned Obama's name, boos rose up from the crowd, and McCain raised his voice to insist that they stop, something he had to do repeatedly on the campaign trail. On the same internet that powered the Obama campaign's progressive populist brand, disturbing misinformation had spread: Obama was not really born in the United States; he was a Muslim, he had attended a madrassah as a child; he was allied with the anti-Vietnam war group Weatherman and had ties to East African terrorist networks. McCain, himself a victim of dirty campaign tricks in 2000, forcefully and consistently rejected these claims. But at a rally not a month before the election, his running mate, Sarah Palin, openly accused Obama of "palling around with terrorists." As McCain struggled to finish his concession speech in Phoenix, many in the audience seemed to reject the outcome of the election altogether, shouting "No!" when McCain mentioned Obama's name again and drowning him out with loud chants of "USA! USA! USA! USA! USA!"[44]

The demonstrated hostility to Obama was not new among conservative populists. The gun-toting, conspiracy-minded Palin, Axelrod believed, had been deliberately added to the ticket to bring out the antiestablishment, conservative populist vote that had become increasingly visible on alternative media sites like *Breitbart News*, FreeRepublic.com, and *Infowars*. Toward the end of the campaign, Palin had "ramped up the ferocity of her attacks, to the delight of the angry throngs who streamed out to greet her,"

Axelrod recalled. "Some chanted vile epithets about Obama, and they all seemed to share an enmity toward a government they viewed as overweening, wasteful and corrupt."[45]

These disgruntled McCain supporters were not the only dissenters from the consensus that Obama was the legitimate president of the United States. Fiscal conservatives who began to organize in the 1990s as a populist anti-tax group turned away from McCain long before Election Day. They met each other online, and in real life, as volunteers for Libertarian Ron Paul's bid for the 2008 Republican nomination. In December 2008, they began to talk about a resistance. On January 24, 2009, the day after Obama was inaugurated, a group of these citizens met in Binghamton, New York, to protest the new taxes proposed by David Patterson, New York's African American governor, as well as the forms of big government that they believed Barack Obama and the Democratic Party stood for.[46]

They called themselves the Tea Party.

= 9 =

TEA PARTY TIME

Two days after Barack Obama's inauguration in 2009, the Dane County, Wisconsin, Libertarian Party held its monthly meeting in Madison. The agenda was packed. There were reports on gun shows, upcoming political races, and a screening of *Waco: A New Revelation*, a ten-year-old documentary about an alleged government conspiracy to cover up the FBI's deadly attack on the Branch Davidian compound in 1993. Door prizes included two books about Waco and *The Portable Nietzsche*. Anyone running for office received David Alexander's 1993 guide to generating media coverage, *How You Can Manipulate the Media: Guerrilla Methods to Get Your Story Covered by TV, Radio, and the Newspapers*. The group also discussed its possible participation in a day of national tax protests planned for April 15. Still angry about President George W. Bush's $700 billion bailout of troubled financial institutions in 2008, this loose coalition of conservative populists and Libertarians discussed the likelihood of "creeping socialism" under the new Obama administration.

Conspiracy mongering wasn't new in the United States. In the 1950s, activists like Paul Weyrich and Phyllis Schlafly believed fervently that Communists infiltrated the federal government, that establishment elites either tolerated or were blind to them, and that patriots like Joe McCarthy were doing important work to expose them. But the Communist threat was over. The Soviet Union crumbled in 1989, and by the twenty-first century, conservative populists were ready to defend their personal freedom from their own government, particularly Barack Obama's plan to create a national health-care system. Groups like the Dane Country Libertarians were already networking with each other on digital alternative media sites: they were on MeetUp.com and FreeRepublic.com, email, blogs, and web pages. They were also being egged on by conservative radio talk show hosts. Rush Limbaugh, now sponsored by Weyrich's Heritage Foundation, urged his listeners to be uncompromising in their opposition to Obama. They shouldn't just be the party of no, Limbaugh emphasized. They should be the party of "HELL, no!"[1]

But the Republican Party, the establishment that had given conservatives twelve years of Bush presidencies, was also an uncomfortable fit for these activists. When they voted, they voted Republican, but the ties of the Bush family to international elites, and John McCain's reputation for working across the aisle, had Libertarians casting around for a third option in 2008. Many supported Ron Paul's bid for the Republican nomination, a robust digital alternative media campaign that had allowed groups like the Dane County Libertarian Party, a pocket of conservative populism in a liberal university town, to network with other groups like themselves around the country. In 2009, these political junkies determined to stop big government and protect personal freedom began calling themselves the Tea Party, after the colonial-era anti-tax movement that helped to spark the American Revolution.[2]

Pairing mass rallies with the same tools that had powered Obama's historic victory, instead of mounting third-party candidacies, Tea Party activists challenged moderate Republicans from the right and won. Being defeated in this way, as many Republicans were in the 2010 primary season, soon had its own verbs: being primaried, or Tea Partied. The movement's principal achievement was to organize everyone who was alienated from the political establishment. Only 54 percent of Tea Party activists were registered Republicans: 41 percent were independents, and a small but significant 5 percent were Democrats. "With the emergence of the Tea Party movement, I sense for the first time that it may be possible to shrink the federal government," Richard Viguerie wrote optimistically in 2010.[3]

The Tea Party drew in people who were alienated from the party system more generally, drawing attention from big-money donors who realized this could be the swing to the right that conservative populists had been looking for since the 1970s. And a new digital alternative media ally emerged to embrace them and tell their story: Andrew Breitbart, now the editor in chief of a powerful new platform, *Breitbart News*. Together, this conservative populist movement and Andrew Breitbart would widen the gap between left and right, pose an ongoing challenge to President Obama's legitimacy, and intensify partisanship by making it nearly impossible for Republicans to compromise with Democrats unless they were willing to lose their seats.[4]

Stunned by the apparently sudden emergence of a political tsunami unafraid to push the rankest conspiracy theories into the mainstream, the liberal *New Yorker* dubbed this phenomenon "the rage machine."[5] The Tea Party believed in limited government, free-market ideology, constitutional originalism, isolationism, and low taxes. Some turned up at protests wearing tricorn hats and Continental Army gear to signify their ideological roots in the eighteenth-century American resistance to English taxes that triggered revolution. These conservative populists vowed to "take back America" from both the Democratic Party and a GOP that had lost its way. Some groups would remain independent, while others became affiliated with incorporated national groups funded by conservative mega-donors, like Tea Party America, Tea Party Express, and FreedomWorks. On February 19, when the Obama administration announced that it would expand the Bush financial bailout, CNBC financial correspondent Rick Santelli, who was broadcasting from the Chicago Mercantile Exchange at the time, launched a six-minute, spontaneous rant that galvanized these activists by calling for a "modern-day tea party," similar to the vigilantes who dumped tea from British trading ships docked at Boston's harbor in 1775. On February 27, a new generation of

Tea Partiers stormed Twitter's virtual public square, started Facebook pages, built websites, and organized forty-eight live anti-tax protests around the country for April 15, the day that Americans traditionally pay their taxes.[6]

Born as a spontaneous mainstream media event, the Tea Party became a movement powered by digital alternative media. Protests were also featured regularly on *Fox News*, which immediately saw the conservative populist candidates the Tea Party promoted in the next several years as, among other things, a ratings gold mine and branding opportunity.[7] Glenn Beck, who had come to Fox from talk radio in 2008 became, along with Breitbart, a de facto national spokesman for Tea Party principles. Rush Limbaugh was also thrilled. As he told his audience, the Tea Party wasn't just about taxes: it was about opposing "the destruction of the foundation of the country" and "restoring individual liberty and freedom" by putting an end to the taxation and spending policies that supported big government. Republican politicians, still stunned that the seasoned McCain had been defeated by a political newcomer, also started paying attention. It was a genuine conservative populist movement, not coming out of Beltway think tanks, but out of the living rooms, community centers, and social media feeds where angry populists gathered to talk. On September 9, 2009, three days before a massive Tea Party march on Washington to protest the Obama administration's proposal for health insurance legislation, South Carolina Representative Joe Wilson brought the revolution into a joint session of Congress. In the middle of the president's assertion that Americans could keep health-care plans they liked, the Republican shouted, "You lie!"[8]

Wilson was factually correct, but accusing the president of deliberately lying was a shocking break in decorum. Although the Congressman later apologized, his outburst encapsulated the anger against the establishment that Tea Party activists sought to turn into political action. At the same time, as even the conservative *Washington Examiner* noted, the health-care debate had become an opportunity for populist media, alternative and mainstream, to exploit ordinary Americans' fears about the erosion of health care. *Fox News*'s Glenn Beck falsely asserted that 129 million, or half, of insured Americans would find themselves with no health coverage at all under the administration's proposed Affordable Care Act (ACA). Meanwhile, Wilson's protests became a partisan meme. Two months later, the internet was still "abuzz with Joe Wilson sites, Joe Wilson Tweets, and Joe Wilson hate groups" on Facebook, wrote the *Huffington Post*'s Alex Leo. "You dissed America, we'll diss you right the f*ck back," read the tagline of one anti-Wilson site that Obama supporters created and populated with insults, literally overnight.[9]

The collective fantasy among Democrats that by electing Obama voters had repudiated both a long history of American racism, and the political establishment, vanished. Among conservative populists, Obama came to personify the rule of an illegitimate political establishment over the common people. Tea Party organizers sought to create a definitive break with the political and media establishment through their activism, even as, by 2010, they began fielding candidates in Republican primaries and adopted *Fox News* as their official network. Obama campaign aide and speechwriter Ben Rhodes, who came into the administration with such hope, remembered a meeting several years later in which Estonian president Toomas Ilves explained to Obama that his Russian counterpart, Vladimir Putin, was tightening his grip on Eastern Europe with fake news and disinformation "intended to turn Estonia's Russian speaking minority against Europe." These populist forces were made up of extremists who, he said, "fundamentally rejected the liberal order." Obama understood the problem instantly: the Tea Party, and alternative media figures who supported it, like Beck, Limbaugh, and Breitbart, were a parallel force.[10]

Ironically, the Tea Party was powered by the same alternative media technologies that had lifted Obama himself to power. Differently from the liberal bloggers who had embraced Obama, however, *Breitbart News* promoted manufactured, decontextualized, or heavily massaged news, intended to portray the political and media establishments as liars and Obama as an undemocratic usurper. The Tea Party also won a new champion the day after the 2012 election. As New York real estate developer Donald J. Trump tweeted angrily after Obama was reelected with 51.1 percent of the popular vote, "He lost the popular vote by a lot! We should have a revolution in this country!" and in a second tweet, "Our nation is totally divided!"[11]

＝＝

Although the Tea Party seemed to come from nowhere, it was a successor to, and fed off of, the conservative populisms that had been percolating in alternative media since the 1950s. By 2008, populists hated liberals for all kinds of reasons, but mostly because they believed liberals and leftists to be chronically dishonest. "They were lying then AND they're lying now!" Limbaugh said in December 2009 about AAUP lobbyists' attempt to expand Medicare funding under the ACA. "They're liberals!" Similarly, populists hated a GOP establishment whose most senior members were now, Limbaugh charged, colluding with Obama. "Reason number 248 why I am no longer a Republican," Limbaugh grouched after the inauguration when Senator Lindsey Graham and other senior members of the GOP promised to help Obama resolve the financial crisis triggered by the bank failures of 2008. "As you know, Graham is the bootlicker friend of Senator McCain," Limbaugh informed his audience. Republicans who "caved" and decided to work with the administration were "going to face more trouble from their own party voters than they will ever face from the Democrats and the left," the broadcaster vowed.[12]

Tea Party meetings and rallies were personal: they were where Limbaugh's listeners, people who felt abandoned by establishment conservatives, fought for personalized things called "my freedom," "my country," and "my Constitution." Because it was largely homed on digital alternative media, the Tea Party seemed to create genuine opportunities to be heard in a system where the political and media establishments seemed more exclusive and complacent than ever. Members of the John Birch Society, Libertarians, and evangelicals began to come to Tea Party meetings, where middle-aged activists recalled the broken promises of the 1995 "Contract with America" and Republicans' failure to remove Bill Clinton from office. Younger activists were galvanized, both by the trauma of 9/11, and by their revulsion for the Bush administration's open-ended war on terror launched in 2001. When George W. Bush was reelected in 2004, a Libertarian journalist and political consultant told me, "If you were a conservative who was against the war, there was no *air* to breathe in Bush's Republican party. You couldn't get a job in a conservative organization. Even Patrick Buchanan was shut out: he couldn't get on Fox News, and he had to go on MSNBC to get work as a commentator."[13]

If there was ever a fate worse than death for a conservative pundit, it was to be driven to the increasingly liberal MSNBC—now hosting popular evening opinion shows with Rachel Maddow; Keith Olbermann, a sportscaster turned progressive political blogger; and former Capitol Hill staffer Chris Matthews. After 2004, the conservative populist wing of the GOP seemed to be in shambles: Limbaugh called 2008 "the no choice election," and his callers agreed with him. "I am not voting for the lesser of two evils again," one said firmly, and said he was writing in Ron Paul, who had run a fierce primary campaign, mostly on social media. Limbaugh agreed that the caller had "no choice" but to cast a vote for Paul.[14]

For many conservative populists, the Tea Party was about having a choice. It was also about "trolling the libs" by rejecting anything that smacked of feminism, anti-racism, and other forms of "political correctness." On September 13, 2009, when Tea Party activists mustered on the Washington Mall for a march and a rally, offending liberals was, in part, the theme. At the time, I was in DC on business. I left the meeting I was attending as quickly as possible and rushed onto the National Mall, joining a sea of white people carrying many American flags: Revolutionary War flags, Confederate battle flags, and the yellow Gadsden flag, with its snake cut into thirteen parts and the warning: "Don't Tread on Me!" There were posters depicting Barack Obama as the devil, and in "whiteface" as Batman's nemesis, the evil Joker, as well as signs that said: "Liberals carry the race card in their wallets."

The movement drew organizations, and sketchy characters, who hadn't been seen out in the open in a national political movement in decades. Marchers came in costume: there were Revolutionary War minutemen (also a common costume to wear at CPAC), a white person dressed as a Plains Indian, and another in blackface, with fake dreadlocks, dressed as Uncle Sam. Others showed their solidarity with Joe Wilson by wearing T-shirts, manufactured a few days after the event, that read, "YOU LIE!" Other T-shirts, many decorated with American flags, commanded Congress to "get your hands off my Constitution." They proclaimed that the wearer "loves my country but fears the government," and some proudly advertised white supremacist groups. Participants that I talked to emphasized that the Tea Party marchers would act on their Libertarian credentials by committing to leave the Mall as clean as they found it, unlike "freeloader" groups on the left whose mess had to be cleaned up using taxpayer dollars.[15] In my admittedly cursory observation, Tea Party activists did clean up after themselves.

Who were these people? I wondered at the time, and where had they come from? As I later learned, some had joined through so-called Astroturf conservative groups that simulated grassroots organizations, such as FreedomWorks and Tea Party America, organizations funded by donors that had quickly sprung up after the tax protests. Some activists responded to invitations from conservative political operatives who used conventional direct mail and email messaging. Some attended because of the economic issues that had always mobilized populists: Tea Party activists I talked to were not infrequently older professionals who had been laid off or forcibly retired during the 2008 financial meltdown. Some were "gold bugs," believers in hard currency; some were underwater on their mortgages; and most believed that the government was committed to corporate profits, not ensuring that the American economy was working for ordinary people.

But many were there because they had connected to each other on digital alternative media managed by Ron Paul's 2008 presidential campaign. Later, I read a study commissioned by the Libertarian Cato Institute that confirmed my informal survey: whether sponsored by so-called dark political money or local fundraising, much of the early energy for the Tea Party movement had come from Paulites' attempt to wrest the Republican nomination from John McCain.[16]

Although the seventy-two-year-old Texas congressman never came close to winning, Paul was the *other* digital alternative media star of 2008. A man of ironclad principle who saw electoral politics as a form of activism, Paul launched his first campaign for Congress in 1971 because Richard Nixon took the United States off the gold standard. Throughout his career, Paul consistently championed small government, low taxes, hard money, deregulated markets, a restrained foreign policy, and a strict constructionist view of the Constitution. Paul's votes against the war in Iraq, the USA Patriot Act, and the federal Real ID Act, and his belief that marijuana should be decriminalized, also drew young progressive populists into his orbit. Like the Dean campaign in 2004, Paul supporters coalesced on MeetUp. More than 7,000 subscribers regularly accessed Paul content on YouTube, more than for any other candidate, and in 2007 "Ron Paul" was the most-searched-for phrase on Technorati.com, a search engine capable of accessing 82.6 million blogs. Internet gamers were also Paul enthusiasts. In fact, so many Paul supporters organized on gaming sites that in January 2008 *World of Warcraft* forbade players from discussing "real-world politics."[17]

Paul, as one conservative political blogger put it, "was the Howard Dean of the 2008 campaign cycle." Declining to identify with the party whose nomination Paul was trying to win, supporters dubbed their movement "The Ron Paul Revolution." They organized themselves and shared information on Facebook and Twitter, countering the mainstream media's lack of interest in their candidate with a lively alternative media network and providing a rapid response when Paul was criticized on establishment outlets. A dismissive article in the *Pittsburgh Post-Gazette*, posted to a Paul site, triggered a blizzard of comments from conservative populist political junkies around the country. For those who loved freedom, "Ron Paul is our only hope," a California trucker wrote. "During the rule of the Bush administration," a Virginian chimed in, "my freedom has been stolen under the pretense of safety. Personally, I have concluded that freedom is more precious than safety." An Oregon woman, who claimed she no longer consumed mainstream news at all, wrote that she had "a hard time believing Congressman Ron Paul has only 1 percent of the voters. It sure does not appear that way on the Internet." If alternative media was "all abuzz" about Paul, she wrote, "Shouldn't television & newspapers be the same?"[18]

As was the case in the Dean campaign, supporters frequented digital alternative media platforms that promoted interest in Paul, giving them a misleading sense of their numbers and influence. As one partisan wrote to his local newspaper, supporters had posted over 84,000 videos to YouTube, a sign of their revolution's strength. "Search 'Barack Obama' and you'll find about 11,700 results," the writer pointed out. "John McCain? 3,690." The fundraising power of the movement also created a sense of momentum. Paul lagged well behind McCain and former Massachusetts governor Mitt Romney in the polls. But his campaign had raised the most money before the Iowa Caucuses in January 2008: over $20 million in the final quarter of 2007, mostly in small donations taken over the internet. In one twenty-four-hour internet "money bomb," as the campaign called it, supporters contributed $6 million.[19]

Paul partisans saw themselves as outsiders to a conservative intellectual and media establishment that wasn't listening. Even some Fox broadcasters let them down. "When you continually hear Fox TV personalities such as [Sean] Hannity, and guests such as neoconservative Bill Kristol from *The Weekly Standard*, refer to Congressman Ron Paul as a fringe candidate with no chance of winning, you begin to wonder just what is the agenda of Fox News," a Paul partisan wrote to his local newspaper. The truth was on the internet: they represented a majority of the American people. "Do a Google search on YouTube or go to *www.ronpaul2008.com*," he challenged readers. "You will find that Ron Paul represents the 70 percent of us who are dissatisfied with our president and Congress." The only honest coverage, Paul partisans believed, was in digital alternative media generated by the campaign. "Who is this man? Check him out on YouTube and MySpace and dailypaul.com," a Florida man wrote to his local paper, asserting that Paul had "more MySpace friends than all the other Republican candidates combined."[20]

An eclectic combination of old and new, the campaign's media integrated the intellectual history of the movement with novel, offline campaign tactics. In December 2007, supporters were asked to chip in to keep a blimp aloft that said on one side "Who is Ron Paul?," a reference to Ayn Rand's 1957 novel *Atlas Shrugged* that all Libertarians would surely recognize and with whom the candidate identified: in fact, Paul's son, Rand, was named after the controversial novelist and philosopher. On the other side the blimp read, "Google Ron Paul." Launched in North Carolina and headed to New Hampshire in time for that state's primary, the blimp planned a stop in Boston to dump tea into the harbor on the anniversary of the original Tea Party. The blimp had its own website, where donors had already contributed over half the $400,000 needed to keep it aloft. Supporters prided themselves on bolstering their fundraising by making homemade signs and videos, while groups like Homeschoolers for Paul and Veterans for Paul created their own websites.[21]

Paulites also became famous for trolling and doxing (posting private information about) their establishment enemies. In response to a blog post written by a *Wall Street Journal* political reporter, a man using the handle Taco John "posted a link to the piece as well as phone and email information for the newspaper's public editor and advertising department." A university professor who publicly stated that Paul was "unqualified to be president" was inundated with emails after his university address was published on a campaign site. Political blogs that normally prided themselves on not censoring the comments section started banning Paul partisans "for leaving incendiary comments."[22]

As the campaign progressed, it became clear that inspired by newsletters that attacked African Americans, some of these Paulites were migrating to the campaign from conspiracist, anti-government, and white supremacist digital alternative media. Those who saw the blimp and googled the candidate might stumble on the neo-Nazi site Stormfront.org, which sported a large Ron Paul banner. "Really, we haven't seen a candidate like Ron Paul in some time," said former Ku Klux Klan Wizard Don Black, of West Palm Beach, Florida, the owner of the site and a proud donor. While some Paul supporters found aggressive online tactics worrisome, others insisted that they were necessary because the establishment consistently lied about their candidate. David Chesley, a California lawyer who had taken leave from his job to work on the campaign, instructed supporters to "ceaselessly bombard" mainstream outlets that ignored Paul or gave him negative coverage. "You need to organize, call, boycott, protest and sue the media that is lying to us," Chesley wrote; "and if you don't, it is your own d- fault if Ron Paul loses."[23]

He did lose. But those supporters were now confirmed political junkies, roaming the internet for a new way to strike a blow for conservative populism and against "the left." After Obama won the election, philosophy professor Paul Gottfried, writing for the conservative blog *Taki's Magazine*, popularized the name for this new grassroots conservative populist energy powered by the internet. This "alternative right" had intellectual weaknesses, Gottfried felt, "particularly its utopian ideas about self-actualization and the retreat of government, something that would surely make the United States vulnerable to being physically displaced by the entire Third World, if its population chooses to settle on this continent[.]" And yet, Gottfried saw the potential for change in a right-wing populist movement that rejected the conservative establishment. An alt-right media ecosystem had matured to support this new movement, he noted: *Taki's Magazine*, the nationalist journal VDARE .com, and other sites "willing to engage sensitive, timely subjects." "We are convinced that we are right in our historical and cultural observations while those who have quarantined us are wrong," Gottfried proclaimed.[24]

By the end of 2009, another conservative alternative media site announced itself as the go-to alternative media destination for the Tea Party and the new alt-right coalition. It was time, an anonymous column in *Breitbart News* proclaimed in a manifesto, for a grassroots populist revolution. The marches, lobbying, crashing congressional servers with email dumps—none of that had stopped the political establishment. "Which party you decide to run on doesn't matter," the columnist wrote, because the party system was morally and intellectually bankrupt. "The system needs to be rebooted . . . 2010 is not the end game, neither is 2012. The end game is when we level the playing field and make America once again the land of opportunity."[25]

No one knows who wrote that column, but the author was suspected to be publisher and editor in chief Andrew Breitbart.

Breitbart News wasn't a new site in 2009, but by latching on to the Tea Party, it became newly relevant. Part of what made Andrew Breitbart compelling to populists was that regardless of how rich or powerful he became as the head of his own digital alternative media empire, he always seemed to be an ordinary guy, rarely seen in anything but a rumpled shirt, blue jeans, and a jacket, as if he was just too busy fighting the establishment to buy a suit or comb his hair. Breitbart insisted that he was just like the typical political junkie who read *Breitbart News*: a "Generation X slacker," a former sleepwalking liberal who "took the red pill" (alt-right lingo, borrowed from the 1999 film *The Matrix*, that meant waking up to reality) when he discovered conservative populism on talk radio.[26]

Breitbart believed that digital alternative media that made the case for conservative populism was not just a counterweight to the mainstream media's lies: it was a media revolution. On blogs, and in bite-sized chunks on Facebook, Twitter, and in text messaging, Breitbart argued, his generation's best ideas would be born. In a 2011 memoir, after *Breitbart News* had become a huge financial success and the hottest place for conservative populist and alt-right political junkies to gather, Breitbart declared that he, too, was addicted to online partisanship. "The internet jones I've acquired feels like what I hear a heroin or cigarette addiction is like," he wrote. The worst sin, in the world of Breitbart, was boredom. Anywhere without an internet connection was, by definition, boring. The mainstream media was boring. The political establishment was boring, and liberals were insufferably boring. "If the political left weren't so joyless, humorless, intrusive, taxing, over-taxing, anarchistic, controlling, rudderless, chaos-prone, pedantic, unrealistic, hypocritical, clueless, politically correct, angry, cruel, sanctimonious, retributive, intolerant," Breitbart wrote, "I would not be in your life."[27]

Becoming a political junkie in his mid-thirties had given Breitbart a purpose he had never known before. Born in Los Angeles on February 1, 1969, he described himself as having been ethically neglected by his moderate Republican parents and the liberal schools he attended. He chose to enroll at Tulane University in 1987, based on its reputation as a party school, and drank his way through an interdisciplinary major that many unfocused students embraced in the 1980s: American studies. Partying constantly and ignoring the "studies" aspect of the major had unexpected advantages, he later realized: he had avoided being brainwashed by his professors' "cultural Marxism."[28]

Breitbart graduated to the distressing news that unlike his friends, his parents expected him to support himself, a form of "decent conservatism" that arrested the moral drift of his college years. Breitbart became a waiter in Venice Beach, California, a "humiliation" that jolted him into a stark truth: he was a loser, with no accomplishments or abilities.[29] Slowly, he found his "values returning from exile." In October 1991, he watched the nationally televised hearings to confirm Clarence Thomas as an associate justice of the Supreme Court. Anita Hill, a law professor and former assistant to Thomas at the Equal Employment Opportunity Commission, testified that Thomas had sexually harassed her repeatedly. Both were African American, and both were conservative. Over the two days of testimony and Thomas's angry rebuttals, Hill became a hero to liberals and feminists, while conservatives mobilized to defend Thomas from what he angrily characterized as a "high-tech lynching."[30] Watching Thomas be battered by the establishment opened Breitbart's eyes, "perhaps for the first time, to the fact that something was awry in American political and media life."[31]

Breitbart had begun to date Susannah Bean, the daughter of conservative actor Orson Bean, who encouraged her future husband to read and listen to talk radio to develop his ideas. Breitbart became hooked on Rush Limbaugh's morning show as he spent hours crawling down the freeway to work. "I marveled at how [Limbaugh] could take a breaking news story and offer an entertaining and clear analysis that was like nothing I had ever seen on television," Breitbart recalled. The talk radio star was "the professor I had always wanted but never had the privilege to study under." As what Limbaugh called the "Democrat-Media Complex" lost its hold on him, Breitbart began to feel intellectually alive. Most of all, as Limbaugh's listeners called in to talk, Breitbart felt a community of conservative political junkies calling to him, one he could become part of by the simple act of listening, reading, and thinking.[32]

Breitbart began to explore what he called the "free-for-all Libertarian haven" on the internet. There were thousands of people who "desperately wanted to communicate with the world outside the Democrat-Media Complex," people who believed that conservative populist alternative media was the only "place where freedom of speech truly existed." On the internet, everyone was a social and intellectual equal. Breitbart's misspent college years, inability to concentrate, working-class job, and failure to achieve anything no longer mattered. His attraction to conservative ideas grew stronger, as did his addiction to antiestablishment newsgroups with a ".alt" designation, an acronym for "Anarchists, Lunatics and Terrorists" that was later repurposed as shorthand for alt-, or alternative, right. Free speech was an absolute value on the .alt web, Breitbart learned, its ideology to preserve the original freedom and creativity of the internet and resist corporate attempts to absorb it into the media establishment. Breitbart also started subscribing to conservative e-newsletters and websites. In 1995, he stumbled upon the *Drudge Report*, and it "really grabbed me."[33]

By 1997, Breitbart started work for Drudge: this is when the two became friends with Arianna Huffington, then a Libertarian journalist and blogger working out of her Brentwood home.[34] By 2005, however, she had moved decisively left to start the *Huffington Post* and Breitbart, who later claimed to have imagined himself as a secret agent in the liberal establishment (he was also one of a half-dozen people who claimed that the site was his idea), went to work for Huffington.[35] In mid-2007, after working on her project for two years, Breitbart launched his own website and video blog, Breitbart.com and *Breitbart TV*, sites devoted to challenging the Democrat-media complex. Over time, he added affiliates like *Big Government* and *Big Hollywood*, collectively known as the "Big" sites, dedicating himself to exposing "the false edifice that is the mainstream media, that is built on the false proposition of 'objective' journalism and the grotesque anti-American proposition of political correctness."[36]

Breitbart.com became a media home for conservative populists, Libertarians, and Tea Party activists, who collectively engineered a stunning set of victories in 2010 against both Democratic and establishment Republican politicians. While it has never been un-common for a president to lose Congress two years after taking office, Democrats lost sixty-three seats in the House and control of that chamber, their worst drubbing since 1948. They also lost seven Senate seats and twenty state legislatures. The Tea Party returned to Washington—this time as politicians who quickly identified them-selves as the Freedom Caucus. Four freshman Republican sena-tors, including Rand Paul, were Tea Party picks, as was Tim Scott, South Carolina's first black Republican Congressman in a hundred years.[37] The Republican leadership adapted to the insurgency and announced the midterm victory as a mandate to stop progressive governance in its tracks. "We're going to do everything—and I mean everything we can do—to kill it, stop it, slow it down, what-ever we can," vowed the new speaker of the House, Ohio's John Boehner. Yet, beyond extending the Bush tax cuts and repealing the ACA, it wasn't clear what the agenda of this new Republican ma-jority was—only that it was against Obama. The *New York Times* worried about what seemed to be a promise to create gridlock—which wasn't what these newly energized conservative populists had voted for. "Americans are fed up with that sort of gamesman-ship," a lead editorial noted a day after the election. "It's bad for the country."[38]

Breitbart was thrilled, both for the Tea Party's achievement and for the role his site played in mobilizing conservative populist vot-ers. "In less than two years I felt more allied to the Tea Party than to the GOP," he wrote later. The Tea Party was also making Breit-bart rich. *Breitbart News* now specialized in partisan "clickbait": sensational, deceptive, or misleading headlines that when posted to social media or by news aggregators, caused the reader's interest to spike, click through out of curiosity, drive advertising revenue, and give up user data that could be sold. These sensational stories, often fake news items that amplified political conspiracy theories, drew the interest of chaos-loving alt-right media entrepreneurs. In June 2009, Breitbart met James O'Keefe, a self-styled documen-tary filmmaker who specialized in creating free videos that made sensational charges against progressives. O'Keefe, impersonating a pimp, had secretly shot one of these in the Baltimore office of the Association of Community Organizations for Reform Now (ACORN), a powerful nationwide group that specialized in voter registration and organizing the poor. O'Keefe edited the video to make it seem as if ACORN organizers had given him, in his pimp persona, legal advice about how to traffic in underage girls and hide his illicit income.[39]

The short film emphasized hot-button issues that were driving conservative populists after the 2008 election: race, immigration, and government spending on social welfare programs.[40] Conservative populists had developed a particular hatred for community-based organizations like ACORN. Registering voters of color was partisan fraud, in their view, and provided the margin for Obama's 2008 victory. In the weeks before the election, Rush Limbaugh warned that ACORN was poised to commit "massive" voter fraud in Ohio and Pennsylvania, and that over one million voters had been illegally registered nationwide.[41] Releasing the O'Keefe video on September 10, 2009, was Breitbart's Monica Lewinsky moment, a piece of clickbait that galvanized the GOP's right wing, undermined ACORN's federal funding, and made *Breitbart News* a major player, not just in the conservative populist media environment, but on the national stage. The version posted to YouTube was captioned, "Your tax dollars fund ACORN members' thugs to allegedly develop an underage international prostitution ring. Call your congressman and senator and tell them that enough is enough."[42]

It didn't take a close examination of the video to see the choppy cutting and the responses intercut with a narrative recorded later: if there was impropriety, the film sequence did not prove it. But conservative populists felt it was true and deluged their representatives with demands to investigate, and defund, ACORN. The aftermath of the video's release was devastating to the organization. Amplified by Rush Limbaugh and *Fox News*'s Glenn Beck, the story migrated quickly into the mainstream media, and without investigating, the Obama administration refused to defend ACORN. Congress withdrew federal funding from the organization, private foundations backed away, and the Internal Revenue Service withdrew ACORN's 501(c)(3) status. The organizing giant, which had helped Obama get elected, collapsed in March 2010.[43]

It was a huge takedown for the Tea Party and its allies. The video made Breitbart a star among anti-Obama partisans, and the Republican establishment began to take notice of him. Breitbart and O'Keefe also introduced a sensibility into digital alternative media that was previously the province of a darker web: alt-right listservs, bulletin boards, and blogs. As it turned out, creating chaos with viral content that told a simple, deceptive story was more effective than the complex narratives even conservative alternative media like the *American Spectator* generated. Fake news could win quick political victories that might otherwise take years to accomplish in Congress. In the fall of 2010, Breitbart followed up with a second video, purportedly depicting Department of Agriculture employee Shirley Sherrod discriminating against a white farmer. Breitbart later explained that he had attacked Sherrod in revenge for the NAACP having passed a resolution that asked the Tea Party to renounce racism. He had intended to demonstrate that the establishment media had a "double standard" for African Americans and whites and would defend Sherrod when they had not defended the Tea Party. But Sherrod wasn't defended. She was hastily fired by the Obama administration, even though a subsequent investigation showed that she was blameless and the video doctored.[44]

Breitbart News became the meeting place for the alt-right by making assertions, often merely by insinuation, that confirmed partisans' core beliefs about the corruption of the establishment, publishing the assertions as news and pushing often baseless "scandals" into mainstream channels. Perhaps the most pervasive of these was aimed at Obama himself. This mix of Libertarians, white supremacists, nativists, nationalists, and Tea Party activists believed that the Obama presidency was not just objectionable, but unconstitutional. Obama, they asserted, had not been born in the United States, and the Constitution required the president to be "native born." Perhaps the most mainstream proponent of this view was New York's Donald Trump, who was toying with running against Obama in 2012. Political consultant Roger Stone had been urging Trump to get into politics since the 1990s, but Stone now believed that the New Yorker was positioned to lead the populist conservative insurgency that had formed around *Breitbart News* and the

Tea Party. Between April 2012 and November 2014, Trump trolled @BarackObama with twenty-three tweets containing the phrase "birth certificate," and six more praising the so-called birthers: "As I always said, the 'Birthers' were after the truth," one read, when in fact the birthers were peddling a lie. Trump sometimes retweeted fake news about Obama's birth originating on alternative media sites, but he also issued numerous original tweets that asked questions about Obama's birth ("Made in America?"); claimed that the president feared an investigation ("@BarackObama's birth certificate 'cannot survive judicial scrutiny'"); and asserted that he, Trump, had good information that the president's documentation was fraudulent ("An 'extremely credible source' has called my office and told me that @BarackObama's birth certificate is a fraud.").[45]

By incessantly focusing on Obama's national origin, Trump signaled his sympathy to Tea Party, alt-right, and conservative populist activists. As importantly, he moved their conspiracy theories onto mainstream media platforms as a legitimate topic of discussion. When *New York Times* columnist Gail Collins wrote an op-ed about his birther tweets on April 2, 2011, Trump responded with a letter to the editor asserting that there was "a large segment of our society who believe that Barack Obama, indeed was not born in the United States," writing the entire conspiracy theory, accompanied by well over a dozen lies, into the paper of record.[46] More alarmingly, on March 28, 2011, Trump aired it on *The View*, a daytime television show then hosted by comedians Joy Behar and Whoopi Goldberg, journalist Barbara Walters, and television personality Elisabeth Hasselbeck. In a rhetorical move that would soon become familiar, Trump interrupted a conversation about the federal deficit to declare that he was a Republican, but disliked the establishment in both parties. Behar then transitioned the conversation: "Are you a birther, Donald?" she asked.

Trump never responded yes or no, but he expressed outrage that birthers were misrepresented by the establishment as "the worst idiots." Then he asked why Obama did not produce his birth certificate (he had, in 2008). "And you know what? If you go back, if you go back to my first grade, people remember me," Trump continued. "Nobody from those early years remembers him."

"That's not true—" a shocked Goldberg blurted out.

"Okay, show me a picture," Trump fired back. "I haven't seen early pictures," following up by asserting that Obama "probably was" born in the United States. "But you know, the word probably—" he began, as all of the hosts immediately jumped in and drowned him out.[47]

In a signature alt-right media move, Trump continued to claim, without revealing how, that he had access to special knowledge that cast doubt on the president's constitutional legitimacy. When Obama released his long-form birth certificate on April 27, 2011, Trump claimed that he knew the document to be false, an assertion that may have contributed to a subsequent poll that named him as a leading candidate for the 2012 Republican nomination. An even more worrisome statistic emerged: even though the Republican establishment was distancing itself from birtherism, two-thirds of likely Republican voters believed that Obama was not native-born. Other politicians took notice. In October, Texas Governor Rick Perry, another 2012 prospect, said in two newspaper interviews he could not possibly know if the long-form birth certificate was genuine.[48]

These were early signs of how influential conservative populism, powered by digital alternative media and Tea Party success at the polls, was becoming in the Republican Party. It was also a sign of what disparate political realities partisans on the left and the right were living in. Breitbart News later insisted that it had never promoted birtherism, which was technically correct. However, what the site did promote were the conspiracy theories that made birtherism, and Trump's false narratives about Obama, plausible. In the spring of 2012, the site posted a literary agent's promotional booklet for an early version of Dreams of My Father that described Obama as having been born in Kenya, insinuating that he was either lying now about his birthplace or had lied then to sell a book. "I've got videos, by the way. I've got videos. This election we are going to vet him," Breitbart, now a star, assured a cheering crowd at CPAC in March 2012. "I've got videos, from his college days, to show you why—" The applause escalated, as Breitbart promised an O'Keefe-style investigation into Obama's past and the radical plot that had elevated him to the presidency. "The videos are going to come out, the narrative is going to come out, that Barack Obama met a bunch of silver ponytails," alt-right slang for aging 1960s radicals, "who said, one day, equally radical, we're gonna have the presidency," Breitbart explained. "The rest of us slept while they plotted, and they plotted, and they plotted," he continued. "Barack Obama is a radical. We should not be afraid to say that."[49]

The videos never appeared. And less than two months later, four days before a much-anticipated relaunch of *Breitbart News* that combined all the "Big" sites under one umbrella, Andrew Breitbart was dead of a heart attack at forty-three. Steve Bannon, a former vice president of Goldman Sachs, producer of conspiracy films, and a longtime member of the *Breitbart News* board, stepped forward as CEO. He vowed to finish Andrew Breitbart's work and take the alternative media site to the heart of the Washington and Hollywood establishments, by opening a new Los Angeles newsroom and a satellite office on Capitol Hill.[50]

———

Andrew Breitbart's body died, but his spirit did not. Two days after his fatal heart attack, an alt-right YouTube account titled ARSO-Nomics published Breitbart's CPAC speech under the title "Andrew Breitbart *Murdered*? Here's *Why*?!?" The video contained no real revelations. But it didn't have to. Conservative populist political junkies already knew the story: powerful and wealthy people would do anything to steal Americans' freedom, and murdering Breitbart was the least of it. Fittingly, Rush Limbaugh eulogized Breitbart, "an indefatigable bulldog for the conservative cause," on his show. The ACORN and Shirley Sherrod videos were notable accomplishments in a life, the broadcaster declared, that was "devoted to change." While Limbaugh did not support theories that Breitbart had been murdered, he did voice skepticism: "there were reports of health problems, but nothing like this." He also called out "well-known left-wing journalists" whose social media was "full of a callous and coarse mean-spiritedness today." That was true: several tweets joked that Breitbart had faked his own death as a publicity stunt. Another sniggered that it was a monument to

Andrew Breitbart's accomplishments that conspiracists who read the site regularly did not believe that he was dead.[51]

For Limbaugh, the partisan battle lines had been drawn: liberals had lost touch with how to behave in a decent society. How could anyone "compromise with these people?" Limbaugh asked. The attacks were "really vicious stuff, which, in the end, [Breitbart] would have loved, and was a testament to his effectiveness. And effective he was." Mocking Breitbart's death was a perfect example of liberal "mendacity." You would think that "speaking truth to power" would be universally applauded, Limbaugh said, "but the mainstream media has become part *of* the power, when that power is held by the Democrat party." Breitbart deserved the same respect, even "hero worship," that Bob Woodward and Carl Bernstein received after Watergate, Limbaugh continued, and "Breitbart's investigations were actually truthful."[52]

In fact, there really is no better way to describe the partisan world that Ron Paul, the Tea Party, and Andrew Breitbart made together than with accounts of Breitbart's death that proliferated on the populist right. "The most prevalent rumor goes something like this," proposed a site devoted to addiction and recovery, which also speculated that Breitbart may have died from the long-term effects of drug and alcohol abuse. "In reaction to Breitbart's pledge to release [a] video of a college-age President Obama appearing alongside a pair of notable 'Weather Underground terrorists,' the President's associates had Breitbart killed." A conservative member of Parliament in England took to social media to promote the belief that Breitbart had been murdered by Vladimir Putin. Another conspiracist declared that the "hit" on Breitbart was planned to prevent him from releasing exclusive evidence that Obama's birth certificate was false, but it was "probable" that Breitbart had faked his own death to go into hiding so that *Breitbart News* could continue its investigation. "Who besides the coroner has actually seen Breitbart's body?" asked art "counter-critic," conspiracist, and "foremost fake events researcher" Miles William Mathis in 2013, a voluminous internet writer who also believed that science and art were "managed" by the CIA. "Once again, the story must be taken on faith. Deaths are faked all the time, the government lies about almost everything all the time, so why believe this?"[53]

But to most conspiracy theorists Obama, and something they called "the deep state," were the most likely culprits. On March 5, a video was posted to YouTube that featured an interview with a woman who had purportedly worked for the CIA, titled: "Is this what killed Andrew Breitbart? The CIA Heart Attack Gun." In it, she explained that as a CIA employee, she had been part of a project to perfect an "undetectable poison," one that would mimic a natural heart attack. It was injected with a dart gun fired at "such a high speed" that the dart would melt inside the person and disappear. "How convenient for the Obamanochio that brave Andrew Breitbart died when he did," the poster wrote. "So, is it just lucky timing for Obama that Mr. Breitbart dropped dead so suddenly? Or, like me, do you suspect something more sinister at work here? I will let you decide."[54]

As conservative populists were deciding, the Obama administration was not sitting on its hands. It was fighting back. Coming out of the campaign, the Obama team had another vision for digital alternative media. It was one that did not just feed political junkies but, they hoped, had the potential to muster a majority around a progressive agenda—not by destroying the establishment, but by realizing the dream of making it transparent.

=10=

WHITE HOUSE 2.0

When the Obama transition team sat down in December 2008 to build the new White House website, Change.gov, they probably felt pretty cocky. Why? Because White House websites had a dismal history. It wouldn't be hard to do a lot better.

The Clinton administration built the first site, Whitehouse.gov, in 1992, following the Clinton–Gore team's having built the first internet platform for a presidential campaign. It was revised four times over the next eight years without ever becoming popular. Although it billed itself as an "Interactive Citizens Platform," Whitehouse.gov had few interactive features, except for the opportunity to sign a digital guest book. There was a comments page that urged visitors to "Speak Out!"—but not about anything in particular. A 1995 revision relaunched the site as the "Gateway to Government" with an "Interactive Citizens Handbook" that linked to federal agencies, directions about how to apply for a government job, policy statements, and a tool that allowed a visitor to "send electronic mail" to the president (who didn't read, or answer, email from anybody), the vice president, and their wives. The final two revisions, both done in 2000, emphasized the policy achievements of the Clinton administration as Vice President Al Gore mounted his unsuccessful campaign to remain in the White House.[1]

By the George W. Bush administration, Whitehouse.gov supported audio and video, and a digital team monitored interactive and online community pages. A section called "Ask the White House" occasionally offered live chat with members of the Bush Cabinet, and the "White House Interactive" page featured Cabinet secretaries explaining the administration's conservative agenda. "I believe many Americans are still paying a lot of income tax," asked "Kimberly," from Los Angeles. "Does Mr. President have a plan to reduce our taxes. I work hard every day and a lot of federal tax are taken in my paycheck. What can we do to reduce our taxes?" Secretary of the Treasury John Snow (or more likely, one of his aides) responded: "Kimberly, you and I think a lot alike, and I'm glad that you are looking at your paychecks to see how much of your money goes to pay taxes," and then he explained how much the Bush administration had done to reduce taxes.[2]

A sign of how little the site engaged real political junkies was that its second-most-popular offering was the kids' page devoted to the president's Scottish terriers, Barney and Miss Beazley. Dubbed Barney.gov, it featured activities intended to teach basic ideas about government and instill patriotism. The most frequently accessed feature of WhiteHouse.gov for the eight years of the Bush presidency also featured the dogs. The "Barney Cam" followed them as they explored backstage areas of the White House and celebrated holidays, sometimes with their friend Willie the Cat. Except for the First Pets, the staid White House web page was a tough sell compared to the vibrancy of the interactive, hyperpartisan social media and blogging scene. Over 80 percent of visitors to Whitehouse.gov never returned, even though, by 2004, 40 percent of Americans were getting some or all of their political information over the internet.[3]

It wasn't hard for the Obama digital team to imagine it could do better, particularly since its social media presence during the campaign had been modeled on the informality and interactivity of media personalities like Kim Kardashian and Paris Hilton. The biggest challenge, experts thought, would be for the administration to stay on message in the ways policy-making required, without disappointing supporters who had been repeatedly told that the election was about *them*. Obama partisans believed it and wanted to come to Washington. Almost 350,000 people, four times as many as in 2000, submitted résumés through the president-elect's partisan website, Change.gov, for 5,000 jobs. Informed that one hopeful applicant told CNN she "wanted to be a participant in this chapter," a transition team member gently suggested "broadening" her job search.[4]

During the campaign, the Obama administration used digital alternative media to create a new kind of bond with its supporters, but transferring partisans' sense of connection to governing was difficult and would ultimately be disappointing on both sides. The organizing spirit of the campaign had elevated transparency, even though maintaining the forms of privacy and confidentiality that government often demanded was not consistent with that goal. Nevertheless, as the new Whitehouse.gov site was being rolled out in January 2009, expectations that Americans would transition from a campaign about "you" to a government that was also about "you" were high. This was not just because electing an African American seemed like a historical metamorphosis to Obama partisans, but because Obama himself was thoroughly at ease on the internet and had cultivated millions of virtual followers on multiple platforms. "Judging by Obama's savvy use of social-networking sites during his campaign and the interactive nature of his transition team's Web site," journalist Brandon Griggs wrote at *CNN Politics* right before the inauguration, "Americans can expect a president who bypasses the traditional media's filters while reaching out to citizens for input[.]"[5]

The Obama team had been able to walk the tightrope of producing a vibrant alternative media presence while controlling a hyper-partisan narrative. There had been no more stunning example of this than Obama's speech on March 18, 2008, responding to criticism from all sides about his ties to Reverend Jeremiah Wright, a Chicago pastor whose vigorous criticism of American structural racism was condemned by some as anti-white. In "A More Perfect Union," delivered in the middle of the workday and broadcast on YouTube in time to make the evening news cycle, Obama directed Americans away from partisanship. He evoked the fierceness of the

African American struggle in the United States and offered himself up—the son of an interracial, international union—to bridge the racial divide. As the progressive political magazine *Mother Jones* put it, by going directly to the people, Obama "was not playing the race card. He was shooting the moon."[6]

Seizing the narrative from the mainstream media and appealing to voters themselves, Obama and his team relaunched the campaign. These digital alternative media strategies were part of what made Obama seem new, particularly by comparison to McCain, whose use of the internet was no longer new and whose still-maverick style was housed in an older, establishment body. As a study done in the weeks before the election showed, Obama benefited from journalists' perception that his opponent's time was past. Almost 60 percent of stories about McCain were negative, and only 14 percent positive, as opposed to the over 70 percent of stories that were positive or neutral about Obama. But President Obama, the media warned, could not expect such favorable treatment: it was one thing to run a campaign on alternative media, and another to try to govern without acknowledging the legacy press's responsibility for writing history's first draft. Bloggers disagreed. As Heather "Digby" Parton wrote, mainstream journalists did not seem to understand that the media was not about them anymore. Yes, journalists would criticize President Obama, but only because their street cred with each other demanded it, not because it was their civic responsibility. "The media could develop some self-awareness and not play out their adolescent psychodramas on American politics for a change," Digby chided them.[7]

However, all journalists may have underestimated what the Obama campaign team had accomplished by rebranding Obama, an actual politician, as a community organizer who *happened* to be a politician. As veteran pundit Mark Shields commented, internet-savvy candidates were not disrupters, only establishment politicians who adapted well to the digital alternative media environment. Yet Shields and others may have missed the significance of an election strategy that had capitalized on, and contributed to, social media's maturity as an alternative media news source. By 2008, digital strategies were part of every campaign, but Obama's had been the best: viral videos, a 5-million-strong email list, 2 million social media friends, and 1.7 million unique internet donors, with 25 percent of those donors having participated in face-to-face political organizing. This reflected the power of the candidate to inspire social and political community, one who, if not necessarily a technology expert, was nonetheless comfortable with digital culture.[8] But they also reflected a new kind of governance: the potential to bring that large, popular following, powered by handheld devices, into the business of partisan politics.

Populism, left or right, is partially defined by direct, emotional connections between leaders and followers. Although Obama did not define himself as a populist, the weeks before his inauguration featured speculation about whether he would, like other presidents, become walled off from the supporters he had cultivated. One of the big stories during the transition (other than his plan to quit smoking) was about Obama's insistence that he would not give up his beloved BlackBerry and, with it, direct access to friends, family, and baseball scores. "There is one addiction President Obama will not have to kick," the *New York Times* announced right after the inauguration: "his Blackberry." The candidate who had once caused a stir over his comment that some conservatives were "cling[ing] to their guns or religion" was now said to be clinging to a mobile computerized device. He won, but it was a temporary victory: by the time the Secret Service and the National Security Agency were done with it, the phone was so crippled with security software that, as he admitted on a visit to Jimmy Fallon's *Tonight Show* in 2010, it was "no fun" anymore.[9]

Minutes after an election, privacy and security changed the victorious candidate's life in ways that were hard to fully anticipate, effectively separating him from ordinary people until he was long out of office. Digital technology complicated but did not change that. The struggle over a phone symbolized a commitment made during the campaign to Obama's progressive populist base that he would find hard to fulfill. But the team would try to stay connected to partisans through Whitehouse.gov. "Just as candidate Obama used the Web to knock down rumors, deflect criticism, direct fire against his opponents, shape and retain his own campaign messages and knock down those of his primary and general election opponents," one journalist wrote, "President Obama clearly intends to utilize the official White House Web site in much the same way in dealing with Congress and the media." Obama's capacity to mobilize Americans' internet "addiction" to create a powerful and diverse political movement was "one area where Republicans didn't just miss the boat—they missed the entire ocean."[10]

———

The question that was never answered, perhaps even never asked, was this: Did the administration want to be connected to all Americans, or just some of them? Perhaps the sign that democracy was in trouble, even in the heady moment when the United States cast a resounding vote for an African American president, was that there were few questions about why large numbers of independent voters had voted for an almost completely untested politician, only pride and wonder that they had. "Barack Hussein Obama was elected the 44th President of the United States on Tuesday," Adam Nagourney of the *New York Times* wrote on November 4, 2008, "sweeping away the last racial barrier in American politics with ease as the country chose him as the first black chief executive." The election was "a national catharsis," Nagourney wrote, "a strikingly symbolic moment in the evolution of the nation's fraught racial history, a breakthrough that would have seemed unthinkable two years ago." Election Day, he wrote "shimmered with history."[11]

Yet there was little concern expressed about how an inexperienced, and untested, politician would cope with his historic role, much less a deepening recession that was enveloping the country after the financial crash. Instead, journalists pondered how Obama's powerful alternative media presence would enhance the project of governing. If the president-elect's brand was viewed as part of his appeal to youth and independent voters (Obama, his aides bragged, was "the king of branding"), what older and rural voters, many of whom were out of work and underwater on their mortgages, expected went uncovered and unbroadcast. Instead, analysts focused on Obama's power to lead the generation that had grown up on the internet. Millennials voted for Obama almost 2 to 1, providing

7- of the 9-million-vote margin that had swamped John McCain's campaign. Early comments from the transition team stayed on message with these young voters. The Obama administration would not be about the president, "but the people he was trying to reach," in other words—*you*.[12]

The role that digital alternative media would play in shaping this narrative was integral to a transition plan that needed to bridge more than race. White House strategists had to navigate a mainstream media environment, while retaining the loyalty of digital political junkies who believed that they, and they alone, had elevated Obama to the presidency.[13] Encouraged by the campaign, Obama's supporters imagined themselves as a social movement. The political pressure that these networks could bring to bear on the Congress, most prominently in relation to the Affordable Care Act, remained necessary to doing business in a Washington establishment where Obama was still a newcomer. But White House strategists knew the bigger risk: that these political junkies, new to the project of governing, might turn on a dime if foiled or disappointed; hence, they downplayed digital alternative media as a continuing connection to partisans. Significantly, Obama White House memoirs omit almost any mention of social media, whether in the campaign or in the transition to the presidency. David Axelrod, the communications director for the campaign and subsequently a senior advisor, claimed to be proud of the work he and his team did to "[harness] the power of the internet in ways that had never before been done, to build a grassroots campaign of millions, many of them new to politics." Yet the authenticity of this movement could also be compromised by its association with an increasingly corporate, multimillion-dollar social media establishment. Axelrod mentioned Facebook and YouTube only once each; MySpace and Twitter not at all.[14]

Social media had also not displaced the power of, and necessity for, a political establishment that would steer legislation. While the White House created a better alternative media infrastructure than any prior administration, predictably, the president's direct communication with the political junkies who had powered the campaign dissipated. Meanwhile, future presidential candidates maintained a vital social media presence, particularly on Twitter. Vice President Joe Biden joined in 2007, presumably because of his own primary bid. Donald Trump joined in 2009, and Hillary Clinton in 2013. But Obama did not launch a personal account until right before a presidential election cycle in which he would only play a supporting role. "Hello Twitter! It's Barack. Really!" read the first tweet from @POTUS in May 2015. "Six years in, and they're finally giving me my own account."[15]

The idea that the election had been "won on Facebook," a notion that was eagerly taken up by political scientists, was not a story that the Obama team wished to own or perpetuate into the presidency. For better or worse, they were the establishment now. During the first term, while his partisans continued to rally on digital alternative media and do battle with the rising tide of conservative populists, to the extent that they could, the White House distanced itself from these increasingly divisive digital struggles among political junkies. The same qualities that made social media effective—its brashness and highly unfiltered, public quality—were a potential hazard to a young and relatively inexperienced president as he prepared to grapple with a political establishment, and a Republican Party, that saw his progressive populist following as a political and cultural threat to the status quo.[16]

As presidents before him, most notably Jimmy Carter, had learned, it was hard to know how to implement transparency. *Wall Street Journal* publisher L. Gordon Crovitz, who had created an online edition for the paper only a year earlier, warned that it might have even been unwise to have promised transparency in the first place. Tom Schaller, a blogger at Nate Silver's progressive FiveThirtyEight.com, agreed. He also worried that the digitally mobilized partisans who had put Obama in the White House were not likely to turn out for establishment politicians in 2010. "Because there's never been an electorate assembled like the one Obama did in 2008," Schaller wrote, "we've also never had a post-Obama midterm cycle."[17]

Owning the internet, even if the White House chose not to advertise it, would be crucial. In 2008, only 39 percent of Americans read a physical or online newspaper every day. Over half of them, and two-thirds of internet users, went to social media for news, clicking through to stories on mainstream and alternative media sites recommended by friends and like-minded people via Twitter, Facebook, blogs, or email listservs.[18] In addition to Change.gov, by December 2008 the Obama transition team was building a new White House website where it hoped to assemble citizens and move its agenda. Every public document would be posted. Theoretically, Americans could access the day-to-day workings of the administration without ever entering a mainstream news environment or reading critical opinions by experts. "Presidential addresses on YouTube. Online chats with administration officials. And millions of energized Barack Obama backers ready for the next email or text message calling them to action," wrote Florida journalist David Ho. "It's been called White House 2.0, the first truly digital presidency. If the nascent effort succeeds, government and politics may never be the same." By early 2009, White House staff members were tweeting presidential speeches and press conferences live, and when Obama issued a warning to Iran, the speech was posted to Whitehouse.gov in both English and Farsi.[19]

It seemed that electronic democracy had finally arrived. Change .gov gave the president "powerful new tools that can rally public support for his agenda while bypassing traditional media," Ho continued. The site included "online communities that provide 'instant feedback' about Obama's top issues, starting with health care." All legislation would be made available to Americans on the site five days before it was scheduled to be signed into law. Those who registered could also be alerted when the president needed support from voters.[20] But conservative populists saw this new and unprecedented site for what it was: a continuation of the campaign, and they characterized it as divisive. "Such strong-arming irritates allies, infuriates fence-sitters and enrages opponents in Congress," conservative strategist Karl Rove warned in the *Wall Street Journal*. "Lawmakers dislike grass-roots lobbying by those representing people in their states or districts," he continued, without any reference to the Tea Party activists who had been pushing the Republican Party toward a conservative populist agenda. "They'll be livid if the White House facilitates it."[21]

Almost immediately, the Obama administration alerted supporters that they needed to prepare for the 2010 midterms. Paradoxically, Change.gov was imagined as the place where the establishment, and the progressive populist resistance to the old establishment, would bring home a collective victory. "Coming soon to a computer or cell phone near you! The Wired White House!" announced veteran reporters Steve and Cokie Roberts in an article about the site. The president would, as they described it, "use the internet to conduct an interactive conversation with voters and make them feel they own a stake in his success." The words "you" and "your" studded the home page. "It's Your America: Share Your Ideas," read one headline on Change.gov. A widget on the right labeled "The Agenda" laid out the Obama administration's plan for governing, and underneath were capsule biographies of Obama and Vice President Joe Biden labeled "Your Administration." A third widget, labeled "Open Government," with tabs named "Citizen Briefing Book," "Join the Discussion," "Your Seat at the Table," and "Open for Questions," solicited citizen feedback and promised responses.[22]

You, you, you. The Change.gov site reflected both the aspirations of the Obama team and the expectations of a personalized alternative media world that promised users infinite, deeper, and more meaningful forms of connection. There was no social media platform that represented these aspirations better than Facebook. Not surprisingly, Facebook cofounder Chris Hughes's role in the Obama campaign became an immediate object of mainstream press scrutiny. "At the age of 25," a reporter for *Fast Company* wrote in late January 2009, the tech entrepreneur had "helped create two of the most successful startups in modern history, Facebook and the campaign apparatus that got Barack Obama elected. Both were dedicated to the proposition that communities, and the way we share and interact within them, are vitally important." Hughes emphasized that Facebook did not manufacture personal connection; it activated real-life relationships. Mobilizing networks of people who were already committed to each other had been a natural evolution for the platform. "I just never think of myself as being in the business of building an *online* community," he said.[23]

What went unsaid was that no technology could give more than a few dozen people access to the president. In 1977, Jimmy Carter, one reporter remembered, "set a new standard for openness and accessibility in the Oval Office" by inviting the public to call him on the telephone, broadcasting those conversations on television and radio for two hours, with Walter Cronkite moderating the event. "Nine million people phoned the White House for a chance to jawbone with the leader of the free world, and 42 got through."[24]

About the same number of people, or fewer, had the opportunity to join a live forum with Obama in a March 2009 webcast. Citizens sent questions in and voted on which ones they wanted the new president to answer. Despite its limitations, the *Los Angeles Times* saw the live forum as a refreshing change from traditional press conferences, where reporters were often "so focused on inside-the-Beltway wrangling that they overlook the real-world issues that matter most to the general public." Counter to Rove's warnings that such events would be seen as automatically partisan, the response was generally quite positive. When a Maryland newspaper asked readers to evaluate the event, one wrote to say that as long as Obama listened to all points of view, he would be viewed as accountable. "People are downright angry with elected officials who continue to get great paychecks and benefits, continue to pass legislation without reading it, and say one thing but do another," wrote Carl Crumbacker. Another reader compared Obama to Reagan in his communication skills, and a third commented that a president who knew how to use the internet must be "a president who thinks out of the box."[25]

The positive feedback on the Obama administration's alternative media outreach concealed the fact that those who opposed the president had retreated to their own corners of the internet to voice their grievances. Aside from *Breitbart News* and the Tea Party, conservative populist and alt-right sites directed readers to assertions on bulletin boards like *4chan* where, by 2010, seven million users had gathered. Anti-Obama partisans seethed with resentment, creating memes that mocked the president and his allies that they then distributed on social media.[26] Partisans were more likely to take their politics online than alternative media users who were not politically engaged, but they were also far more likely to interact exclusively with those who shared their views.[27] In part, this tendency to cluster with the like-minded was chosen. But it was also produced by the growing practice of accessing news on social media, whose algorithmic designs directed "you" to the articles that they already knew "you" would like, and to potential friends who had similar opinions to "you." Unlike mainstream media, as MoveOn's Eli Pariser explained in 2011, algorithms did this invisibly.[28]

Members of Obama's staff were keenly aware of the ideological divide that was metastasizing in this online environment, and that even establishment media was now designed to grab political junkies' eyeballs by adopting and accentuating partisan alternative media styles. They understood this because their work, more so than the president's, depended on reading the daily barrage of partisan news. Speechwriter Ben Rhodes remembered that a typical Obama staffer's news day would begin with mainstream papers (the *New York Times* and the *Washington Post*, balanced with the *Wall Street Journal*), move to progressive alternative media focused on Capitol Hill, and end with scrutiny of key conservative populist and alt-right alternative media, including the daily dose of outrage served up in *Breitbart News*. After a morning briefing with the president, Rhodes read the *Politico Playbook*, a political news and gossip e-newsletter, that delivered "a handy BlackBerry and Treofriendly peek at the news driving each day." Launched in 2007 at the digital news site *Politico*, and emailed for free to the media and political establishment, it started arriving without Rhodes's having requested it. Throughout the day, he continued to monitor Twitter and Facebook for the same up-to-the-minute news that reporters monitored there, and to gauge responses to policy decisions in the White House. Rhodes read most of these sites on his BlackBerry as he went about his day.[29]

By 2009, the national health-care initiative, dubbed "Obamacare" by the right, made the divisions Rhodes was seeing online dramatically visible, as Tea Party activists mustered in Washington to stop it. The specter of "socialized" anything had always been a powerful issue for organizing conservative populists, and the Affordable Care Act (ACA) intensified anxiety about Obama's so-called socialist tendencies. Media figures also obliquely associated the ACA with a long-standing conservative concern, abortion, and what they believed to be liberals' disregard for human life. As firebrand Glenn Beck, newly arrived at Fox News from CNN, mischaracterized the bill, the Obama insurance plan would give the government the ability to ration health care, allowing some people to live and leaving others to die. This was, Beck ranted, a form of totalitarianism last seen in Nazi Germany: it would be achieved with government "death panels," where bureaucrats decided questions better left to the individual. Beck's attacks on the program taught viewers to "see" what was being concealed from them, something the president himself might not even be aware of. "Well-intentioned people can produce systems that raise serious questions," Beck admonished in an editorial that was then reproduced on YouTube, quoted on social media, and cited by online conservative and religious publications.[30]

The new White House media team found itself confronted with conservative populist activists who were disinclined to compromise over what they understood as matters of human dignity and freedom, and who declined to work from a common set of facts about the ACA. Minnesota Representative Michele Bachmann, chair of the new Tea Party Caucus in Congress, posted a speech on YouTube where she asserted that "decisions about our healthcare will be put in the hands of presidential appointees" when, in fact, the ACA supported consultations between doctor and patient. On Facebook, former vice presidential candidate Sarah Palin, speaking as the mother of a child with Down syndrome, claimed that to save money, government "death panels" would ration health care to the elderly, children, and the disabled. And an anonymous author at *Breitbart News* claimed that although the ACA did not cover undocumented Americans, a loophole provision would do just that.[31]

After several instances in which protests against Obamacare turned violent, White House blogger Macon Phillips inadvertently created an uproar by asserting that the president's critics were spreading "disinformation," rumors, half-truths, and outright lies that "often travel just below the surface via chain emails or through casual conversation." "Since we can't keep track of all of them here at the White House," Phillips continued, "we're asking for your help. If you get an email or see something on the web about health insurance reform that seems fishy, send it to *flag@whitehouse.gov*." Tea Party activists were outraged. This must prove that the health insurance initiative was the beginning of a new socialist regime dedicated to totalitarian control: after all, the Obama administration was encouraging Americans to inform on each other![32]

The Tea Party and alt-right media were succeeding in turning the terms of debate away from policy and toward the decline of democracy and freedom. Conservative populists charged that the Obama administration's commitment was not to transparency, but to concealing as much of its agenda as possible. As one Southern newspaper editorialized, Democrats "favor freewheeling debate only when the wheels are turning firmly to the left." Angry, the Democratic leadership then doubled down: holding up a piece of synthetic grass playing surface, generically known as Astroturf, as he spoke in the well of the Senate, Majority Leader Harry Reid charged that these were fake grassroots, or "Astroturf," movements, run and paid for by professional organizers. Activists, Reid charged, mindlessly took direction "from talk-show hosts, Internet rumormongers, and insurance rackets."[33]

Simultaneously, more and more Americans went to social media to feed their hunger for political news and opinion, and to talk to friends about what they were reading and thinking. There was an across-the-board surge in social media use in 2009: Facebook added 110 million users, making the community 350 million strong worldwide. Twitter exploded from 1 million to 30 million users, becoming "a true global phenomenon," as well as a new online culture of fast-breaking news, humor, and snark. Twitter brought partisans into intimate contact with populist conservative celebrities like Michele Bachmann and Donald Trump, and progressive media celebrities Oprah Winfrey and Ashton Kutcher. It also inspired a new language. Political junkies were now part of a "Twitterati" who engaged in "Tweet-ups" and "Twestivals." As one marketing blogger wrote, a sign of the platform's influence was that "Twitter beat out 'Obama,' 'Stimulus,' and 'Vampire,' as the most popular word of 2009."[34]

Social media made it possible to counter negative news coverage in the mainstream media, not by disproving a story with facts, but by flooding a platform with opinions and emotions. This not only changed the idea of what "news" was, but it also altered the political landscape that the Obama administration had hoped to build a progressive agenda on by turning Facebook, Twitter, and bloggers' comments sections into polarized shouting matches. It also made conservative populist politicians, with few legislative accomplishments, into opinion makers. "No story of the internet's ability to organize would be complete without talking about the Tea Party movement in the United States," one journalist pointed out after the Tea Party wave in 2010. After joining Twitter in 2009, former Republican vice presidential candidate Sarah Palin became a leading spokesperson for the group. Partisans like Palin preferred targeted social media to mainstream media outlets, where her idiosyncratic rhetorical style and thin grasp of many political issues, a real disaster during the 2008 campaign, often caused Palin to come off poorly in front of a politically mixed audience. "She only gives interviews to media outlets that are friendly to her message," wrote reporter Chuck Raasch, "so when she is not being thrown softballs by *Fox News* pundits, she can be found commenting from her Facebook page, Twitter account or email list."[35]

But the president could not avoid the mainstream media, and unfortunately, Whitehouse.gov was just as anemic as its predecessors: yet, as it turned out, a one-way stream of digital data strengthened Obama as he headed into the 2012 campaign. Social media had come to redefine what digital alternative media was, moving conversations that had happened on blogs onto Twitter and Facebook, where political junkies chose the news they wished to talk about and ignored the rest. Because of this, social media was also an increasingly critical source of accurate information about voters and how to reach them. Obama's 2012 Chicago headquarters now had an "innovation hub," with, as David Axelrod described it, "an iconoclastic army of young whiz kids—data-analysts, software designers, social media savants—who were inventing new products and programs to expand the reach and efficiency of all aspects of the campaign. From fund-raising and field organizing to rapid response and media placement, they were pushing the horizons of Big Data and the Internet to provide us with a critical edge."[36]

Meanwhile, aspiring Republican nominees were ready with their own social media plans. In 2012, voters would receive an unprecedented amount of information on their computers, and increasingly, they would read it on smartphones. "The slogan claiming the election is 'in our hands' has never been so literal," a Minnesota editorial noted about internet campaigns being mounted by Minnesota Governor Tim Pawlenty and former Massachusetts Governor Mitt Romney in the Republican primary season. All election news, from mainstream media outlets to campaign tweets and text messages, would literally be at voters' "fingertips"; it was "immediate, consistently relevant and many times interactive." But would that information be true? News emerging directly from campaigns had not been vetted by a reporter, editor, or fact-checker and increasingly, true news was the least effective news. What *felt* true was more likely to sway a voter. "How many Democrats know when to stop believing in some of the fallacies of MSNBC?" the editorial asked. "How many Republicans know when to step back from the misconceptions of Fox News?"[37]

Social media companies unveiled strategies for 2012 that went well beyond fundraising to emphasize the direct connections between politicians and political junkies that now drove campaigns. In April 2011, Facebook debuted the streaming service that it would launch in 2015 as Facebook Live, allowing candidates to broadcast directly to their followers without purchasing television time, relying on broadcast news producers, or engaging in moderated debates. Texas Senator John Cornyn and Governor Rick Perry, as well as President Barack Obama, all made the pilgrimage to Facebook offices in Washington and Palo Alto to conduct live town halls. In July, Obama hosted a town hall on Twitter, to which subscribers could send a question with the hashtag #AskObama. As politicians leaned on social media more and more, political junkies migrated their own debates to social media platforms. In January 2011, when rumors surfaced that Tea Party darling Michele Bachmann was exploring a presidential run; liberals scoffed and conservative Twitter exploded with support. In August, declaring that God (not Twitter) had called her to run for president, Bachmann won the Ames Iowa straw poll—edging out Ron Paul.[38]

But still, no one used social media quite like Obama. "Watching Barack Obama at the world's first Twitter town hall was like watching a slugger in a batting cage," wrote one political reporter in the summer of 2011. "If anything came even near the plate, he smacked it for a hit." When House Speaker John Boehner trolled him in the middle of the event about the deficit and unemployment, his message loaded with numerous typos, Obama responded drolly: "First of all, John obviously needs to work on his typing skills." Twitter, which the reporter admitted he was "hooked" on, was "a medium made for the wiseacre kid who was always made to stand in the hall because he talked too much in class." But again, it was not an unmediated connection to the candidate, it only *felt* that way. The 169,000 tweets submitted were carefully screened by journalists chosen from conservative and liberal newspapers, and only a small fraction was answered. And unlike a debate, there were no opportunities for follow-up questions, politicians' least favorite part of a debate or press conference and when reporters tore apart their polished talking points.[39]

White House 2.0 was determined to dominate every digital platform in 2012 and, at the same time, capture information about users that could be deployed for get-out-the-vote (GOTV) operations. In March, a blogger for the *Dallas Morning News* broke the story that Obama had joined Pinterest, an image-driven scrapbooking app that allowed users to share and "pin" items from pages they followed. Ann Romney, the wife of the eventual Republican nominee, was also on the platform: her popular page boasted campaign photos and favorite Romney family recipes. *Trail Blazers Politics* speculated that the president's page would probably duplicate his Tumblr, a re-blogging app that was particularly useful for disseminating memes and images rapidly. "Already, Obama's Pinterest page has some pep to it," the blog noted. "The page features photos of dogs wearing Obama gear, cakes shaped like Obama's campaign logo and even disarming photos of the president himself. Welcome to political campaigns circa 2012."[40]

In retrospect, it is astonishing how quickly, for the Obama administration, social media went from a way to establish transparency and consultation to a digital form of reality television. In April 2012, as the campaign was gearing up, voters could not only visit the White House web page, courtesy of Google, they could also take a virtual tour of the White House. Nicco Mele, former Howard Dean webmaster now teaching social media at Harvard's Kennedy School of Government, believed that the internet was still a great tool for political insurgents and disruptive to "the establishment." But digital news generated by the campaigns and by partisans became more prominent because there was less mainstream coverage of the 2012 campaign in 2012. The three major networks only broadcast an average of three hours per night of each convention, and NBC eliminated the first night of the Republican convention completely in favor of one of the most meaningless broadcast events possible, a preseason football game. A live convention was an overly scripted snooze, the editors of the *Arizona Republic* wrote. Voters' ways of interacting with politics were now "so varied, so interactive, that it no longer is precisely correct to use the passive verb 'watch' in regard to convention activities."[41]

Significantly, other mainstream news outlets felt marginalized by the White House's shift to digital platforms and its disregard for the historical role of newspapers. When the chair of the National Negro Press Association (NNPA) asked how the Obama campaign planned to use the black press, he received what he considered a haughty and thoughtless answer. "The audience your newspapers reach is not the demographic of the campaign," an Obama operative responded. As Walter Smith of the *New York Beacon* exploded in his column the next day, "What a ridiculous posture to take in regards to the Black Press, the father of progress of Black Americans." Of course, black youth were on social media just like everyone else. But what were social media companies doing to steer black voters to the Democratic Party, as the black press had since the 1930s, or to educate youth about how to deal with the obstacles black voters often faced at the polls? Nothing. "If Barack Obama expects to win this election, he must instruct his campaign managers to take a more realistic approach to the value of the Black Press," Smith wrote. "The Black Press is the only medium that is going to instruct its subscribers to get proper voter ID for themselves, their Black parents, grandparents and friends."[42]

Others were beginning to see social media as a dangerous form of partisan warfare that created news from insignificant errors and crowded out serious debates about the issues. When, in a debate a few weeks before the election, Republican nominee Mitt Romney announced his commitment to gender equity by referencing "binders full of women," when he meant binders of qualified women's résumés, a typical resource developed by a transition team, liberal social media exploded with the mocking hashtag #bindersfullofwomen. "The problem isn't only with the debates themselves, but the simultaneous critique by the world's largest party—social media," wrote Tennessee journalist Kathleen Parker about the newly "infantilizing" campaign process powered by populist partisans. "Our million-way conversation is a convention of Snarks Anonymous. The cleverest commenter gets a free, if short, ride on the Fame Wheel, usually at the expense of Mitt Romney, who, let's stipulate, is not the likeliest presidential choice of the Twitter generation." Social media, Parker grumbled, was turning us into "ninnies."[43]

The real digital story of 2012 was not, in fact, social media itself, but the data that could be derived from it. As Romney confidently believed he would win the election, Obama crashed to a massive victory using a data analytics approach that refined the Democratic ground game with never-before-seen precision. Known as Operation Narwhal, the digital team had, as *Time* magazine reported, crunched "information collected from pollsters, fundraisers, field workers and consumer databases as well as social-media and mobile contacts with the main Democratic voter files in the swing states," merging them into one massive database that allowed voters to be targeted more precisely than ever before. "The Obama campaign could identify the Planned Parenthood supporters living within largely Christian Zip codes," the *Washington Post* editorial page explained, "and send them emails about Romney's 'war on women' without the risk of alienating pro-life Reagan Democrats who might recoil from such language." The team could also track in real time how voters were responding to messages, using thirty times the sample size normally used in a typical Gallup poll, and "how events such as the presidential debates were moving the electorate—so they could respond effectively."[44]

Obama partisans tapping on their phones with their thumbs were, during the course of their normal social media day, doing the work that in the past would have been done by professional and volunteer campaign workers. The numbers of political junkies activated in 2012 from social media alone were staggering: 55 percent of voters said they had watched political videos online, almost 40 percent of users were sharing political content, and almost 35 percent were resharing it. During the campaign season, close to 35 percent of users logged on to either Facebook or Twitter to encourage everyone in their networks to vote. Over 10 percent of campaign donations had been received by mobile phone. Perhaps as importantly, however, candidates were held to a standard of instant accountability by the crowd. A study by the Pew Research Center showed that 11 percent of debate watchers were "dual screeners," people who watched on one device and fact-checked on another. "No one, not even politicians, can get away with lying about the facts for longer than it takes to ask Siri," Apple iPhone's voice-activated search, "or Google it," the blogger concluded.[45]

———

In its second term, the Obama White House continued to drive its agenda on alternative digital media, even as the administration's grip on governance slipped away to a Republican Party radicalized by the Tea Party and a powerful conservative populist media complex. In 2014, elections delivered both the Senate and the House to the Republican Party for the first time since 2004. Absent the ability to pass legislation, or even to bring a Supreme Court nominee to the Senate for confirmation, social media became less effective as a political tool. It also became more corporate, increasingly taken over by mainstream media outlets pushing their own stories out, rather than users sharing content that they wanted to debate with each other.[46]

But on July 13, 2013, when George Zimmerman, a self-appointed vigilante, was acquitted of murdering black teenager Trayvon Martin, the streets of Sanford, Florida, and cities all over the United States, exploded with rage—and anger at the first black president for not addressing the life-and-death issues faced by poor people of color. So did Twitter. Journalists, who once would have sought to seem objective regardless of the circumstances, joined celebrities and ordinary people in a mass Twitter protest. "Defense lawyers wrong and unwise for speculating about if Zimmerman had been black. Absurd. #zimmermantrial," tweeted *New Yorker* staff writer Jeffrey Toobin. "What are your thoughts? *@BarackObama* We're allowed to disregard 911 operators, pursue and kill ppl now? But send lauryn hill to jail 4 TAXES," singer Nicki Minaj pounded out angrily. "Trying to imagine the moment when some police officer or court employee hands the gun that killed Trayvon Martin back to George Zimmerman," MSNBC host Chris Hayes tweeted.[47]

A few days later, Alicia Garza, Patrisse Khan-Cullors, and Opal Tometi, three queer women of color and community organizers, gathered in a Facebook thread to comfort each other and vent their anger. Afterward, Garza wrote a Facebook post, which ended: "Our Lives Matter, Black Lives Matter." Cullors responded affirmatively in a comment:

"#BlackLivesMatter."

= 11 =

HASHTAG POPULISMS

Politicians' Twitter strategies now had one goal: influencing political junkies and the journalists who wrote for political junkies. Content was moving at an almost alarming velocity across mainstream and alternative media platforms. Journalists watched their mobile phones constantly for breaking news about world, and local, politics; or a tweet that might signal a human interest event. "What happens on Twitter informs what takes shape in other mediums," political scientist Dan Kreiss blogged on the *Monkey Cage* after the 2014 midterm elections, "and winning the news cycle is now defined all the way down to the half-hour." Prior to the first debate in 2012, Republican nominee Mitt Romney's digital team even rehearsed how, as their candidate was parrying questions on the stage, they would shape the conversation on Twitter to make it seem as if Romney was dominating Obama. Forty minutes into the event, mainstream journalists awarded Romney the win—also on Twitter. Realizing what had happened, in the second debate, the Obama campaign poised staffers to flood the platform with positive takes on their candidate. Even if Obama wasn't doing a great job, digital director Teddy Goff told Kreiss, journalists "would look at Twitter and see it was a lot more mixed than they expected and sort of second guess their own perception that the President wasn't doing that well."[1] With hired hands and "bots"—coded programs that spewed out tweets automatically—a political team could create an illusion, a feeling, and an online story that diverted partisans from what they were actually seeing.

But activists saw the radical potential in this technology. What if Twitter and Facebook could make Americans see, and feel, how marginalized people were experiencing the Obama administration? What if the hashtags that assembled tweets into a story about an event created space for a conversation that anyone could join, from anywhere?

Twitter told a story: not necessarily a true story, in the case of the birther movement, but a radically different story than the establishment was willing to tell about "you." By 2012, those stories could be told, and followed, more effectively, by using a hashtag, the # sign that—prior to Twitter—was known formally as an octothorpe, or pound sign, and was best known for its position on the bottom-right-hand corner of a telephone keypad. So when, on July 13, 2013, Patrisse Khan-Cullors wrote #BlackLivesMatter on Alicia Garza's Facebook page, it had several meanings. Khan-Cullors was, in the social movement language of the moment, "holding space" for Garza, not filling the feed up with unnecessary words that would drown out the emotions the two women were feeling. Holding space was as important as taking action. Khan-Cullors was also signaling, since numerous important political campaigns had already been powered by social media, that the time for organizing had begun. Most importantly, it was a topic sentence, the first line of a new story, in which African American people would speak back to the establishment. In the next day, #BlackLivesMatter would appear on social media 5,106 times. After Michael Brown was shot by police in Ferguson, Missouri, on August 9, 2014, the hashtag would be used 172,772 times in 24 hours. In the next three weeks, it would appear 1.7 million times. And by March 2016, #BlackLivesMatter had appeared on Twitter alone 11.8 million times.[2]

In a way, #BlackLivesMatter was the shortest, and most powerful, story ever written about racism in America. It was not just about ordinary black people who were suffering and dying at the hands of the police. It was a story about white supremacist violence. And it was about the first African American president, and his African American attorney general, and every other black politician, who had definitively failed to hold white supremacy to account. It told the story of young people building their lives, not around accumulating money and things, but around protest, social justice, and each other.[3] Most importantly, as scholar-activist Keeanga-Yamahtta Taylor wrote, it told the story of "hopes shattered like broken glass, the experiences of police abuse and intimidation" that "united young black people around the country."[4]

No account of the partisanship that crested in the 2016 presidential election is complete without explaining how hashtag activism, social justice movements that called activists together with the # and a phrase, split the Democratic Party in two as progressive populists amplified their own grievances about debt, war, and violence against people of color. Digital alternative media bound increasingly radicalized progressive populists together in new, often international, political formations that defied the world of politics as it had been. Evident in the social movements of the 1960s, left populisms gelled in the 1990s, in activist movements like ACT UP and in the protests against the World Trade Organization in Seattle. But the revolutionary activism that emerged between 2012 and 2016, particularly the anticapitalist #OccupyWallStreet encampments and #BlackLivesMatter, were, most importantly, attempts to tell a national story from the social and economic margins, where more and more Americans were living.

Twitter had not invented the hashtag. In the second week of March 2007, developer Chris Messina had been at Austin's South by Southwest (SXSW), the nation's premier film, music, and media conference. The hottest conversation that year was not about whether Hillary Clinton would be the first woman president, or Barack Obama the first African American president. Instead, everyone was talking about Twitter, then described as a "microblogging" platform. Released on March 21, 2006 as twttr (other names considered were Jitter and the more than mildly creepy Friendstalker), the spare platform gave each user 140 characters to express a thought.

At a moment when blogging was coming into its own as an alternative media platform to support long-form journalism, the question was: Who would use Twitter? And to what purpose? That, its creators decided, was for users to determine. Twitter was initially imagined by developers Jack Dorsey, Biz Stone, and Noah Glass as a messaging device that would connect groups of friends as they socialized on weekends and after work. But perhaps more quickly than any other social media platform, it came to define a way to produce conversations, not only within, but between, networks. "Tweets," as they were soon called, were broadcast by default to an open channel. The 2007 SXSW conference underlined this point. The app, downloaded to the iPhones that had just been introduced to great fanfare, was quickly adopted by attendees as a means to "broadcast" the event, both to those who were in different conference panels, and others who would have liked to be in Austin but were glued to their desks thousands of miles away. Twitter was "really blowing up" at SXSW, Messina recalled, "but there were a lot of people back in San Francisco frustrated that their Twitter feeds were full of stories from Austin that were not relevant to them. There was no way of organizing tweets so you knew what to pay attention to and what to ignore."[5]

How could Twitter be reorganized to tell a story? Messina was a longtime user of Internet Relay Chat (IRC), a text-based system for group communication and an early form of digital social media that sorted content into channels, each denoted by the pound key (programmers called it a hash) and a word. What if Twitter users similarly established channels, tagged with hashes and keywords? Messina wrote it up in a blog post. Later, he suggested the idea directly to Twitter, and the developers responded with a shrug: do it if you want to.[6]

Messina and his colleagues took up the challenge, and the idea percolated around the internet, an example of the kinds of experimentation and play that had always defined the digital alternative media world. Several months later, Messina's friend Nate Ritter was driving near San Diego when he saw smoke from a fire that had started, a potential calamity in Southern California. When he arrived at his destination, Ritter turned on the TV to try to get information about where the fire was so he could broadcast the information to other people who could then avoid driving in that direction, or evacuate if necessary. "The speed at which things were coming out was much too fast for me to blog about it," Ritter wrote, "so I started posting about it on Twitter." Messina suggested that he use #SanDiegoFire, which users on the photo-sharing app Flickr had already adopted.[7]

Hashtags took off organically and moved to all social media applications, sometimes as a deliberate way of telling stories and sometimes as a way to simply add emphasis to a remark with a word or phrase that expressed an attitude or feeling. The hashtag was also an invitation to community, beckoning others to chime in on the topic.[8] With its open network (as opposed to closed social media platforms like Facebook, which limited messaging by default to chosen friends), Twitter became a digital alternative news channel, expanding its user base quickly. In 2008, followers of both Barack Obama and John McCain took to the platform to receive breaking news from the campaigns. It was also an Olympic year. Tweeting spiked as new and old users in the United States broadcast their excitement about the record-breaking exploits of athletes like Michael Phelps and Usain Bolt, and digital fans around the globe followed their favorite sports in real time, rather than on a schedule dictated by television networks. In 2009, Twitter incorporated hashtags into the platform, making them instantly searchable by automatically converting them into hyperlinks.[9]

But digital alternative media, and particularly Twitter and Facebook, also became a way of organizing social media networks into progressive populist movements. Between 2010 and 2011, countries in the Middle East exploded with popular democratic revolutions, at least partially mobilized on social media platforms that were, as yet, not well understood by governments who had successfully dominated, or closed, all other forms of mainstream media. In February 2011, the world watched as Egyptian activists were galvanized into action by twenty-eight-year-old Khaled Mohamed Saeed's murder. Dragged out of a cybercafé in Alexandria for not showing police his identification card, Saeed was beaten to death. Following a Day of Rage, organized on Facebook, activists occupied and held Tahrir

Square in Cairo, continuing to demand democratic reforms, even after they were attacked by government troops mounted on camels. Activists organized an entire functioning community in Tahrir Square, sustaining it through a local, and a worldwide, network of digital activists who provided the protesters with food, clothes, books, shelter, medical, and sanitation supplies for the duration of the occupation, a pattern that would repeat itself in Istanbul's Gezi Park in 2013.[10]

Twitter was a grassroots newswire, one that helped activists stay organized and told their story to the world. After eighteen days of demonstrations in Tahrir Square, President Hosni Mubarak resigned and was later arrested and jailed. "I think we are all agreed," activist Ahdaf Soueif wrote in a book mostly compiled from tweets that had been posted during the insurgency, that "without the new media the Egyptian Revolution could not have happened the way it did." Young Egyptians converged on Tahrir from around the city, the region, and the globe. Expatriate Nadia Idle, driven from the country by the conditions of the dictatorship, left her job, booked a flight home to Egypt, and vowed to "not leave until justice was done." She appreciated the twenty-four-hour cable news coverage that kept the insurgency before the world. But the most truthful and "the most compelling coverage was on Twitter, coming directly from the people in the square."[11]

As progressive populists in the United States adopted Twitter, they were not just flocking to the lure of the new, or to channels that their elders did not yet fully understand. Nor were they only moving well-understood forms of community organizing pioneered in the New Left, the civil rights movement, and ACT UP to an on-line space. Activists were, once again, trying to realize the promise of electronic democracy, as they watched the Obama administration settle into a style of vertical establishment governance that failed to address pressing issues of social justice.

Similarly, other radical social movements around the globe blended the old with the new. Online communities of progressive populist political junkies activated on-site communities by organizing, telling their stories, and using the hashtags that signaled the topic of, and the emotion or analysis behind, a conversation.

Hashtag activism demonstrated a kind of fluidity, improvisation, and horizontal consciousness that mainstream electoral politics perhaps aspired to in the Obama years, but never realized. With the arrival of cheap mobile devices, hashtag activism also represented a revolutionary form of organizing among the poor and disenfranchised, people who might be homeless or who might be experiencing the same issues in different neighborhoods—or different cities.

It was an astonishing transformation. When #BlackLivesMatter (BLM) organizer and cofounder Patrisse Khan-Cullors found herself in the position of needing to raise bail money for her brother in 2006, she and her allies worked the phones and wrote letters, which they sent by email and through the postal service. By 2011, at the end of her brother's first sentence, they handed him his first cell phone because, "The world ha[d] turned over several times since 2006," and handheld digital devices were how a community of people protected each other.[12]

#BLM, and its predecessor, #OccupyWallStreet (#Occupy), repurposed digital alternative media to perform tasks that had been distinct in earlier forms of activism: organizing, recruiting, making decisions, creating a story about their movement, and pushing it out to other activists and to the mainstream media as events were unfolding. The technology was not just practical. It also reflected the leaderless organizing philosophies and collective decision-making that informed the political outlook of twenty-first century activists. Sometimes they were derided as "slacktivists" because of the misapprehension that these progressive populist movements largely consisted of people sitting at home and mindlessly reposting ideas and slogans. But that was far from the case. Hashtag activists were strategic technologists, not techno-utopians: alternative media was not just a way to tell a story, but to imagine and inspire change *by the act of telling that story*. As one #Occupy activist put it, modern grassroots movements combined "high-tech networking and low-tech gathering."[13]

Marginalized citizens who joined these movements had one foot in a material world of surveillance and inequality, a world where the media and political establishment did not represent their interests and refused to tell their stories. But the other foot was planted in a virtual world where they were in charge, where ideas moved rapidly, technology was agile and open, and they could call like-minded partisans together in spaces glowing with democratic possibility. Deliberately rejecting the establishment, these activists understood, as one media theorist put it in 2013, that "the nature of subjectivity and consciousness changes as media technologies change."[14] And when the Obama administration began to reveal itself as less the social movement it had represented itself as in the campaign and more a mainstream political establishment maintaining liberal government, young leftists armed with mobile devices literally took things into their own hands.

==

Hashtags, while they would come to be used for many kinds of events and emotions, became particularly associated with crisis situations where (often unwilling) participants reported news live. In November 2009, the sudden appearance of the hashtags #mumbai and #mumbaiattacks alerted the globe to a series of shocking, coordinated terrorist attacks in the heart of India's capital city. As police tried to reassert control over Mumbai, terrified victims broadcast the violence from their mobile phones, Twitter, and the photo-sharing service Flickr. The event demonstrated social media's effectiveness and its limits. Twitter got information out to journalists, and to the anti-terrorist squads trying to end the attack, but both services' internal safeguards proved inadequate to the task, locking accounts automatically when the volume of tweets triggered mechanisms designed to detect spammers. As one journalist commented, "conventional systems still seem to be the robust ones. But the strength of Twitter for passing on details of what's happening (if not for echoing it, which only added to the noise) may carry important lessons for larger organizations trying to keep track of widely-spaced emergencies."[15]

Perhaps it is unsurprising that Twitter's inherent appeal for electoral politics went unnoticed for as long as it did. Historically, each new form of digital alternative media seemed to bring first exhilaration, and then the disappointing realization that it failed to improve communication at all. In the spring of 2010, internet theorist

Evgeny Morozov declared that the promise of digital media for left movements, a source of excitement only a few years earlier, would probably go unrealized. "In the days when the internet was young, our hopes were high," he wrote in *Foreign Affairs*. "As with any budding love affair, we wanted to believe our newfound object of fascination was changing the world." But changing the world had turned out to be more complicated than that, and the political and media establishments far more adaptive and resilient than internet theorists imagined. Online organizing required focused and disciplined organizing on the ground too, and underfunded social movements had trouble sustaining both. Furthermore, as Morozov pointed out, transnational alternative media could connect and strengthen networks of reactionary and conservative populist movements as easily as progressive ones. "Establishing meaningful connections between information, transparency, and accountability will require more than just tinkering with spreadsheets," Morozov concluded. "It will require building healthy democratic institutions and effective systems of checks and balances. The internet can help, but only to an extent; it's political will, not more info, that is still too often missing."[16]

What Morozov left out of this explanation was the growing importance of digital alternative media in helping conservative and progressive populist movements tell their own stories, not just to the world, but also within their own circles. In the United States, conservative populists were not just using alternative media to get grassroots activists to the polls and elect Tea Party candidates to Congress, but also to craft a new story about liberty and freedom that might produce small government, preserve the constitutional right to bear arms, and prevent immigration to the United States.[17]

Similarly, progressive populist movements, often driven by feminists, LGBT activists, and activists of color, used alternative media to describe their present condition. Twitter and Facebook also linked young activists to veterans of radical, community-based civil rights and social justice movements like the AIDS Coalition to Unleash Power (ACT UP), the National Coalition of Black Lesbians and Gays, and the radical feminist of color organization INCITE!. These historical connections laid the groundwork for hashtag activisms staffed by a millennial generation who understood alternative media as only one tool among many, but one capable of telling a story that would never be told at the voting booth or promoted by establishment politicians and media figures. These stories, exchanged between organizers in a way that reflected their experience and values, and broadcast to the world, became real when activists used them to shape, and govern, their own chosen communities.[18]

Digital records allowed hashtag activists to mine recent history for information about what worked and what didn't work. From November 30 to December 3, 1999, radical protesters organized over the internet and assembled in Seattle to shut down the Third Ministerial Conference of World Trade Organization's meetings, battling police in the streets for four days. While neither smartphones nor app-based social media tools existed yet, independent journalists used digital alternative media like email, blogs, listserves, and chatrooms to get the protesters' story out. "As the national and international media arrange polite photo opportunities," *Wired* magazine reported, "upstart journalists at the Independent Media Center are pulling together reports on anti-WTO activities with two dozen donated computers, thousands of volunteer hours, and immeasurable pluck." Independent journalists flocked to the IMC, donating their time to create "content in video, audio, text, and photos. The stories are instantly published on the web using a system specifically developed by Free Speech TV for grassroots media efforts." As the protests intensified, the IMC became a resource for mainstream media outlets and syndicates like Reuters, whose reporters were, in many cases, unsure who to speak to or gain access from in this apparently leaderless but well-coordinated movement.[19]

It was hard to compare such activisms to the social movements that had moved history earlier in the twentieth century. Popular and community organizing, like the Southern Christian Leadership Conference or the National Organization for Women, was often inspired by a charismatic leader; their movements evolved into permanent institutions. But hashtag activists knew that because of this, these organizations had ultimately tied themselves to politics, becoming power brokers between the establishment and the people. Because hashtag activists sought to remain nimble, they were leaderless by design, movements called into being as if from nowhere, disappearing as quickly as they had been born, or popping up elsewhere without warning. In telling their story to a mass audience, they invited and called attention to conflicting experiences and points of view, documented in their alternative media platforms, rather than insisting on consensus. Alternative digital media played an important role in the WTO protests, not just in coordinating them, but in preserving and building on the activist networks and community organizations that had formed in person on streets filled with tear gas, broken glass from smashed storefronts, and police in military-style riot gear. "Activists in New York and Seattle read the same Web sites, magazines and newspaper articles discussing movement strategy," one observer wrote over a decade later, and stayed in touch with each other. "They were on the same email lists. Internet communities operated as sites for debate and enabled the distribution of news and information about various tactics."[20]

After the WTO demonstrations, progressive populist movements began to be characterized by political actions that were carefully planned but invisible to the establishment until they chose to emerge in public. These movements were variously socialist, anarchist, anti-racist, antiwar, queer, feminist—as well as any, or all, combinations of the above. A multicity antiwar protest launched on February 15, 2003, as the United Nations Security Council was debating the Bush administration's attempt to muster an international coalition to attack Iraq, was produced by coalitions of organizations around the globe that coordinated over digital alternative media. The antiwar protests helped activists learn how to coordinate global actions, trained individuals in social movement organizing, and created global networks of organizers who could spring into action from thousands of miles away to help others fight a local battle.[21]

Hashtags also alerted allies to an emergency or signaled a need for help. Movements could find comrades among the faceless collectives of anonymous alternative media activists. These keyboard warriors often devoted themselves to pranks and creating chaos, but saw their main job as protecting the freedom of the internet against censorship and surveillance. They would sometimes jump into a political struggle to disable establishment organizations through distributed denial of service (DDOS) attacks, by hacking into private collections of documents, or by altering websites. Visitors who came for routine business would find accusations against the organization, or a manifesto, instead. In 2003, a collective called Anonymous emerged from *4chan*, and joined forces with the anti-capitalist Adbusters collective, formed in Canada in 1989 to oppose the forms of corporate advertising that they believed were distorting, not just the internet, but all forms of mass culture and politics. Similarly, in 2006, Australian cyberpunk Julian Assange founded *WikiLeaks*, a site dedicated to radical transparency through the publishing of hacked documents. Registered as a journalism site to take advantage of first-amendment freedoms in the United States, *WikiLeaks* came to popular attention in February 2010, when Assange weighed in against the Iraq War. Publishing classified documents leaked by Chelsea Manning, a United States military intelligence specialist, Assange also leaked evidence of war crimes: a graphic video that went viral on YouTube of a US military gunship crew gleefully murdering a car full of journalists.[22]

Activists like Assange cared about something larger than holding government accountable. They wanted to tell a story about political power through primary documents that told the truth. They believed that unless progressive populists could establish a robust and truthful presence in digital alternative media, states, banks, mainstream media, and other establishment institutions would gradually foreclose what was politically possible. Assange himself imagined that the proliferation of digital alternative media promised a new and swift phase of transition from "an apathetic communications medium" used to facilitate commerce "to a *demos—a people*, with a shared culture, shared values, and shared aspirations." Political events, whether they occurred on the streets, in a war zone, or behind closed doors, could now be "witnessed by the whole world." News was no longer released on a timetable, or quantity, determined by the authorities, it "move[d] at internet speed."[23]

Hashtag activists sought to displace the story politicians, intellectuals, and finance told about them with a story they told about themselves. Challenging a power elite that was now global required a similarly global populist revolution, one that was flexible, ubiquitous, and beyond the reach of any single political establishment to discipline or restrain. It seemed possible. When governments did attempt to disable *WikiLeaks*, as the United States did following the 2010 release of the Chelsea Manning documents, what one observer has described as "a committed group of underage cyberfreaks and libertarians" jumped to Assange's defense. They launched DDOS attacks that disabled the websites of corporate institutions like Visa when, at the urging of the United States government, the credit card company withdrew *WikiLeaks*' ability to accept donations.[24] The Obama administration's ability to cajole a major corporation into shutting down an alternative digital media platform that legally, the government could not censor, sent an important signal to progressive populists that Obama, the so-called Facebook president, had lost his tolerance for political dissent.

While hashtag activists had never placed their faith in mainstream politics, the relationship between the Obama administration and the financial industry, already a source of progressive-populist anger, soured after the federal response to the 2008 recession continued to favor banks rather than debtors.[25] Almost immediately after the United States government moved against *WikiLeaks*, a surprising proposal circulated. On February 2, 2011, activist Kono Matsu posted an essay on the *Adbusters* site that called for an anticapitalist "people's revolt in the West" based on the design of the Arab Spring uprisings and powered by social media. "Could an uprising like this happen in America?" Matsu asked.[26]

It could. Across numerous platforms, alternative digital media was hosting a robust "nonviolent international," a reference to the Communist International, founded in March 1919 after the consolidation of the Russian Revolution. In this vast collective, linked by the internet, activists building left-populist movements circulated ideas, manuals, and trainings.[27] Furthermore, the conditions for a successful progressive populism in the United States were ripe: in the third year of the Obama presidency, twenty-five million Americans were still out of work, almost three million homes were foreclosed on by lenders, and people long out of college and graduate school were drowning in student loan debt. The financial class, which had cynically "brought this economic misery" on vulnerable Americans, Matsu wrote, had been bailed out by the government, and was rebuilding its wealth with "obscene bonuses and rewards," but ordinary people had not received any relief. "Blatant corruption rules at the heart of American democracy," he wrote.[28]

Most outrageously, Matsu fumed, since the Supreme Court had lifted restrictions on corporate political advertising in *Citizens United v. FEC*, progressive populists would find it even harder to be heard at the ballot box. Both establishment parties were driven by corporate money. "With corporations now treated as people, big business money dictates who is elected to Congress and what laws they shall pass," Matsu wrote. "America has devolved into a corporate state ruled by and for the megacorps." The system was, in short, rigged in favor of the haves, and rigged against the have-nots. "What would it take for the people of America to suddenly rise up and say 'Enough!'?" Matsu wrote. "A double dip recession? A crash on Wall St.? A war in the Middle East?" Borrowing terminology from the Million Man March on Washington that the Minister Louis Farrakhan had organized in 1995, Matsu called for "a million man march on Wall Street."[29]

Identifying with the anti-capitalist and anti-globalization forces emerging around the world, *Adbusters* launched the #Occupy-WallStreet hashtag on July 13, 2011, announcing that a march on and occupation of Wall Street would occur on September 17. The call asked for a "swarm" of activists with no leaders and no one following behind, an act of international solidarity that would be "a fusion of Tahrir with the *acampadas* of Spain." The movement would begin with twenty thousand protesters flooding lower Manhattan, setting up tents, feeding themselves, and creating a self-governing community. "The beauty of this new formula," the blog post continued, "and what makes this novel tactic exciting, is its pragmatic simplicity: we talk to each other in various physical gatherings and virtual people's assemblies . . . we zero in on what our one demand will be, a demand that awakens the imagination and, if achieved, would propel us toward the radical democracy of the future . . . and then we go out and seize a square of singular symbolic significance and put our asses on the line to make it happen."[30]

The demand would be, as the #OccupyWallStreet activists put it, uncomplicated: a people's democracy. The political system in the United States, they argued, was "currently unworthy of being called a democracy: we demand that Barack Obama ordain a Presidential Commission tasked with ending the influence money has over our representatives in Washington. It's time for DEMOCRACY NOT CORPORATOCRACY, we're doomed without it."[31]

The comments section of this post demonstrated that the organizers, to the extent that they represented a discrete political entity, were indeed part of a worldwide alternative media network sparkling with ideas. "You have all my support for your act of resistance," one comment read. "Greetings from Germany!" Other activists chimed in from Portugal, Spain, and Canada. A third posted an idea, which was quickly seized on by others. "hey adbusters and west coast jammers!" wrote jammer_jess. "I would really like to make it to new york but i don't think funds or my work schedule will allow me to . . . what I can make possible is an occupation of the financial district in san francisco. I would love to know if there are more people on the west coast interested in this occupation during the same time frame as the wallstreet occupation. I would also love to hear some advice and tactics from the adbuster folks and those running the wallstreet occupation. Thanks guys, I hope this westcoast plan can really happen!"[32]

Writing a new political story required meticulous advance planning and reflecting on the history of prior events. Supporters sent practical tips for signs, chants, and the location of the encampment itself and share links to alternative media sites that could serve as resources for the movement. "Tactically, it's easier to defend Times Sq from the NYPD than Wall Street," an anonymous commenter advised, suggesting that an organizer contact activists in Athens, Greece, for advice on how to strategize and occupy heavily policed urban areas. If activists chose Times Square, the protest would be better publicized and "more disruptive" because of the mainstream media outlets located there and its typical chaos. "ABC studios and Reuters are right there. It'll be easier to blend into the tourist crowd. It's easy to defend 8th Av/Broadway/the side streets from the police." A week later, someone built a site, Occupywallst.org, and someone else launched a Facebook page called "Take the Square," in honor of the Egyptian activists of Tahrir. Global coordination went through a second website called Takethesquare.com.[33]

By the time activists converged on Lower Manhattan during rush hour on September 17, 2011, #Occupy had borrowed, invented, planned, and executed a progressive political movement almost entirely on digital alternative media. It was one that surprised the mainstream media, the NYPD, and Wall Street financial institutions, even though it had been planned more or less in plain sight. #Occupy had also established a media team that broadcast events on Twitter, uploaded videos, and published their own newspaper, the *Occupy Wall Street Journal*. By the time its tent city was forced out of Zuccotti Park on November 15, #Occupy had put a new generation of progressive populists on the map. Its slogan, "We are the 99%," based on the notion that the wealthiest 1 percent of Americans hoarded the vast majority of wealth and political influence, went mainstream and pointed up the constant appeals to a "middle class" in the United States that no longer existed.[34]

Importantly, while there was news coverage of the encampment, #Occupy was more interested in broadcasting itself to its own audience. It generated over three million "likes" on its own Facebook page, and inspired similar encampments to spring up in numerous other cities around the globe. A year after the movement began, the digital Occupy Directory listed 1,518 encampments. Over a thousand were in the United States; 52 in Canada; 40 in the United Kingdom; and even 5 in Russia and Japan.[35]

MoveOn, which now boasted 6 million members, endorsed the protests. The movement's broad appeal stemmed from something rare in radical politics: that economic justice was not a class-specific demand, but spoke to the suffering of a range of Americans who were subjected to capitalist violence. The 99 percent, as #Occupy dubbed them, represented a range of potential activists: the homeless, military veterans, foreclosed-upon homeowners, and former students saddled with debt. Furthermore, the movement's visibility stimulated a conversation about the promise, and the difficulties, of grassroots democracy, both on-site and across the internet. As #Occupy organizer Mark Bray noted, the movement's performative politics, its heavy web presence (powered by activists at the encampments who rode stationary bicycle–powered generators night and day), and its self-organized community transmitted theories about anarchism to a broader public that prior to September 2011, was more associated with nineteenth-century assassins than with a twenty-first-century political agenda.[36]

Zuccotti Park and its sister encampments also told a story about democratic experimentation. While not all of its procedures and practices were successful, the vast majority of them—unlike the workings of the government—were fully transparent to anyone who visited, on-site or online. #Occupy was also mostly white, very male, and given to polarizing language. Community meetings were long, exhausting exercises in consensus building where an ethic of inclusion often collapsed as those with the most social power dominated the agenda. "Anyone who spent much time at the park and at the almost nightly meetings of the 'Spokes Council' (the body which became responsible for project funds)," wrote law professor and former Dean organizer Zephyr Teachout, "would be struck by how much time the Spokes Council spent on fairly arcane points of process, and how little time they spent on substantive discussions." Perhaps a grassroots movement that was committed to broad-based democratic principles became cumbersome almost by necessity. But instead of building on their story, meetings "tended to direct themselves to a discussion of rules and rule following," and whether those who contested these rules had fundamentally departed from the movement's core ethic.[37]

What often looked like chaos to others, however, had a logic that was difficult for those accustomed to the linear narratives of establishment politics to discern. Chaos, like the disruptions visited on chosen targets by Anonymous, often concealed design. It signified the refusal to do business as usual with a media and political establishment that collaborated to marginalize the disenfranchised. It is important to note that #Occupy, like #BLM, was a product of both long-term social justice struggles and disillusionment with the failure of establishment politics to transform in the wake of President Obama's appeal to progressive populists.[38] If #Occupy highlighted the violence of a rigged economic system, #BLM addressed the physical violence against black bodies that had continued unabated for centuries and the paradoxical hopes and disappointments in an African American president who had stormed the establishment, only to become part of it.[39]

Hashtag activism played a particularly important role in uniting young, trained activists in community organizations around the country in conversations with each other. In her memoir, #BLM's Khan-Cullors described Facebook as a critical space where young organizers from around the country maintained their ties in between conferences and trainings, and where they sometimes built intimate friendships with groups of people they had never met. While awaiting the decision in the Trayvon Martin case, Khan-Cullors remembered refreshing her Facebook over and over to get news, not from mainstream sources, but from friends on the ground who would tell her the truth and help her understand the story of a bewildering and traumatic live event. "I go on my Facebook page because that's where everyone is updating what's happening," she wrote. "I am nervous but Facebook keeps me connected."[40]

What seemed like a spontaneous movement marked by a hashtag was both the beginning of a story and its continuation. #BLM was the outcome of years of relationship building, organizing, education, strategizing, and trust. Digital alternative media was not just a form of communication, but a way for activists to clarify their radicalism, tell their stories to each other, create theory, and establish a position outside the mainstream political and media institutions that failed people of color repeatedly. "In the course of events," political philosopher Chris Lebron later wrote about the birth and naming of #BLM, "three women decided that not one more black person's life would be taken without America being forced to answer the question that black intellectuals have been asking for one-and-a-half-centuries: do black lives in America matter or not?" Furthermore, Garza, Khan-Cullors, and Tometi launched this phase of their activism with a clear vision for queer, feminist, and people of color struggles, imagining a democracy that set its agenda according to the needs of the most vulnerable members of their community.[41]

Hashtag activism was a site for writing about and reflection on, as well as a way of broadcasting, a revolutionary political culture. For #BLM organizers, Twitter and Facebook were organizing and community building tools, but as importantly, they were a means of establishing narrative authority over the stories that would be told about the movement and African American community resistance to white supremacy. As Lebron observes, #BLM drew on, and was consistent with a long intellectual history by which African Americans mobilized, through writing, speech, scholarship, and the arts, to tell a true story about themselves.[42]

Alternative digital media became a way of assembling and announcing a resistance, insisting on full personhood, bearing witness, and demonstrating, as abolitionist Frederick Douglass had done in his own writing, what democracy looked like. It signified "the potential power to rewrite the rules of the relationship" between oppressed and oppressor. Writing and publishing in the alternative media of her day, the African American press was, as turn-of-the-century journalist and publisher Ida B. Wells had understood, a method for graphically demonstrating "just how deeply entrenched white supremacy was, not only in the hearts of the average American but also in the practice of political elites." In its insistence on the complete humanity of African American people, #BLM also drew on the legacy of activist intellectual Anna Julia Cooper, the first feminist to point to the continuing oppression of black women by race and sex, and to insist on making them central to any narrative of American citizenship. The hashtag, Lebron notes, was also a form of "shameful publicity." Descended from the legacies of insisting on love and witnessing described by queer black writers Audre Lorde and James Baldwin, it was a sign of oppression that gestured to the possibility of a different future. It refused silence and called for an honest reckoning of harm.[43]

During the Obama years, the emergence of hashtag activism was both a call to arms and a way of seizing control of a story that was permitting structural violence to make logical sense. In the case of #BLM, it was a challenge to the political and media establishment to see democracy as it was experienced by people of color. Yet these movements raised uncomfortable questions: What did it mean for political groups to confine themselves to conversation with the like-minded? What would it look like for these hashtag activists to take their energies, and their media savvy, outside the electoral system entirely? As journalist Jelani Cobb wrote in 2016, #BLM's institutional indifference to the historic ascent of a black president was unsettling to many. Distinguishing themselves from a civil rights movement, some organizers had refused to attend a civil rights summit at the White House intended to bring together activists across generations in the year that Obama's successor would be chosen. "Until there was a black Presidency it was impossible to conceive of the limitations of one," Cobb observed. "Obama, as a young community organizer in Chicago, determined that he could bring about change more effectively through electoral politics; Garza is of a generation of activists who have surveyed the circumstances of his Presidency and drawn the opposite conclusion."[44]

It was in this atmosphere of rising partisanship—politics driven by hashtags, community organizers measuring radical aspirations against the ordinariness, and the disappointments of national politics—that Americans would turn the corner into the 2016 election.

=12=

DEMOCALYPSE NOW

On June 15, 2015, the reality TV star and his wife, a former model, floated down a gilded escalator into the lobby of Trump Tower in midtown Manhattan. Although it was a political event, mainstream journalists reported it almost as though it were a branding opportunity. Conservative populists who had been following the millionaire's hints at a presidential run since the 1980s would have been right to think that their candidate was not being taken seriously by the establishment. "Donald J. Trump, the garrulous real estate developer whose name has adorned apartment buildings, hotels, Trump-brand neckties and Trump-brand steaks announced on Tuesday his entry into the 2016 presidential race," read the first paragraph of the *New York Times* coverage, "brandishing his wealth and fame as chief qualifications in an improbable quest for the Republican nomination."[1]

The lobby was full. There weren't quite enough Trump fans, so the candidate's own employees, and paid actors, were brought in to fill the room.[2] Around the country, Trump watchers were thrilled. They had followed his career in the tabloids, read his popular books about how to get rich, and watched multiple seasons of his television franchise, *The Apprentice*. As Trump took his place behind the podium, he glared out from under his signature helmet of dyed blond hair. Trump looked around with satisfaction at the crowd. "Wow. Whoa," he said, as if they had all just spontaneously showed up. "That is some group of people. Thousands." He shook his head. "There's been no crowd like this." The next evening, comedian Jon Stewart's opening monologue analyzed the moment in a way that would turn out to be more accurate than the *New York Times*. "Like all of you, I heard some interesting, let's call it—news—today about a certain, let's say, gift from heaven"—the audience laughed— "entering the presidential race," Stewart began. "Because apparently," he continued, citing two conservative populists who were perennial contenders, "Huckabee–Santorum wasn't far-fetched enough. I gotta tell ya, the world right now is going"—Stewart made a sound and a gesture that indicated his head was exploding— "whites are black, blacks are white, Trump's running for president: Does gravity still work?" In a mockery of balanced coverage, Stewart ran a clip of presumptive Democratic candidate Hillary Clinton speaking over a chyron that said "Democalypse 2016."[3]

The 2016 election was the culmination of an alternative media journey, begun with attempts to get ideas to a public hungry for politics in the 1950s and ending with populist political junkies gorging on media that too often, entirely lacked ideas or even facts. Partisans, armed with digital devices, overwhelmed the ability of the mainstream political and media establishments to take control of the campaign narrative—or even know what that narrative was most of the time. Hillary Clinton expected to have a fairly easy path to the Democratic nomination. But the progressive populist insurgencies and hashtag activisms sparked during the Obama administration mobilized to back socialist Vermont Senator Bernie Sanders. Clinton won the nomination, but came into the general election wounded and surrounded by bickering, bitter Democrats, some of whom defected to support Green Party candidate Jill Stein. Trump, on the other hand, thrived in the hyper-partisan populist atmosphere that digital alternative media promoted, even as opponents imagined that his often vulgar antics would surely cause voters to turn away. The candidate and his supporters had mastered the art of digital alternative media. They had trained for this moment, through Tea Party activism, the birther movement, and following *Breitbart News* and *Fox News*. They nurtured an almost visceral hatred for Barack Obama and for all liberals, now collectively known in conservative circles as "the left." These voters were, as political psychologist Bart Rossi analyzed it, "typically individuals who are angry, even more so, they have contempt for the government. They're folks who feel that they're on the outside looking in, in American society. They don't feel that they're a part of American society as much as they'd like to be. They're angry at politicians."[4]

Digital alternative media brought these voters together as Trump supporters: it gave them a voice and a story to tell about themselves. Even the GOP establishment was caught off guard. As Trump knocked off one seasoned Republican after another over the next nine months, journalists, fact-checkers, fellow Republicans—many of whom had imagined that Florida Governor Jeb Bush would be the next member of his family to occupy the White House—and frustrated Democratic voters could not understand what was happening. Trump's extravagant, often false, claims about himself and his vicious personal attacks on others made him ever-more popular. The attacks were unprecedented. Primary opponent, CEO, and fellow millionaire Carly Fiorina, Trump noted, was ugly ("Look at that face!"). As he defended a false story about Muslims celebrating the 2001 terrorist attacks, Trump flapped his arms and jerked spasmodically, appearing to imitate *New York Times* reporter Serge Kovaleski, who had reported and then retracted the original story.[5]

Significantly, however, these attacks were on establishment figures. Whether Trump had—or had not, as he claimed—deliberately spoofed a disabled reporter was, in a sense, hardly the point. Nor was it shocking that he later lied and said his performance had been misunderstood. Politicians often lied, misstated, and inflated stories that were useful to them. But that Trump lied so much, so transparently, and about almost everything broke the democratic compact about what a campaign was for: earning public trust. According to one independent fact-checker, fewer than half of Hillary Clinton's statements selected for verification during the 2016 campaign were partially or completely true, but less than 30 percent of Trump's statements met that standard, and 15 percent of them were "pants on fire" false.[6]

Even more unusual was that Trump and his supporters insisted, on Twitter, that things journalists saw and heard with their own eyes and ears had never happened. Instead of apologizing to Kovaleski, Trump demanded in a tweet that the *New York Times* apologize to him and accused the paper of inventing the story because it was "rapidly going down the tubes." Trump enthusiasts cheered. "Tonight my dad said you should keep pointing out the lies," wrote @ellenEspence. "Everyone's catching on to these people." @faagifts shouted at the *New York Times*: "THERE IS NOTHING U CAN REPORT THAT WILL CHANGE OUR MINDS," and @ilovehiltonhead commiserated: "we all hate what reporters in general have become—left-wing propagandists."[7]

Trump's campaign style confounded primary opponents and journalists, who seemed not to know how to respond. In May 2016 Senator Ted Cruz was one of two remaining primary opponents, and Trump asserted that Cruz's Cuban father had been part of the JFK assassination plot, forcing Cruz, instead of campaigning, to debunk one of the oldest, and most incoherent, conspiracy theories in modern American history. "Let's be clear," a shaken Cruz said at a hastily called press conference, "this is nuts. This is not a reasonable position. This is just cuckoo."[8] Similarly, Trump often simply insulted his opponents with a blizzard of tweets in which, like Rush Limbaugh, he called opponents by disdainful nicknames. Cruz became "Lyin' Ted"; Jeb Bush, characterized as a "low energy person" by Trump, became "Low Energy Jeb"; and in the general election Hillary Clinton, the object of countless conspiracy theories herself, became "Crooked Hillary." As CNN correspondent Jeanne Moos pointed out, the insults were intended to make other politicians look helpless, since there was no dignified way to answer name calling. And they did. "I don't respond to a string of insults," Clinton said to Moos stiffly. "He can say whatever he wants to say about me. I could really care less." Bush was only able to muster responses like: "There's a big difference between Donald Trump and me. I'm a proven conservative with a record."[9]

Trump created a campaign narrative on Twitter, and then performed it at ever-larger rallies, designed themselves to circulate on social media. Clips of Trump's insulting people were so popular that CNN posted a "greatest hits" of Trump trolling Jeb Bush and posted it to a YouTube channel with over seven million subscribers.[10] After he won the nomination, a shaken Republican establishment still did not take seriously the proposition that Trump could become president. Yet the crowds of mostly white, working-class men and women wearing red "Make America Great Again" (MAGA) golf hats were growing, as were the social media partisans who defended Trump against all comers. The *Guardian* was the first major outlet to label the candidate a populist. Although numerous figures in American history promoted themselves with populist rhetoric and ideas, most recently Pat Buchanan in 1992, "no candidate," reporter Ben Jacobs wrote, "has combined all of those aspects with a level of celebrity rivaling a movie star or even a Kardashian."[11]

Repurposing hashtag activists' ability to tell a convincing anti-establishment story, the campaign had a dense presence on YouTube and Facebook. But Trump's alternative digital media of choice was always Twitter. There, he belted out multi-tweet attacks, often before dawn. His growing army of followers retweeted his utterances, added #MAGA to their profiles, and favorited anti-Clinton internet memes emanating from *4chan*. For journalists, who piped each wacky barrage onto mainstream media platforms, the candidate's tweets were mesmerizing, bypassing every filter that had ever existed in political campaigning. "The media and the establishment want me out of the race so badly," Trump tweeted four weeks before the election, after a series of boastful comments about molesting women, accidentally recorded by the television show *Access Hollywood*, leaked. "I will never drop out of the race, will never let my supporters down! #MAGA."[12]

Political junkies were all on social media now, reveling in, and responding angrily to, the most shocking headlines and political statements. As MSNBC reporter Katy Tur observed, the proliferation of digital alternative media, its intense use by candidates and partisans, and the need for reporters to both monitor and generate tweets, quickened the pace of the news cycle to the breaking point. Reporters were also less likely to be telling a story from a live event. During the March 3 debate between Republican candidates, the press was stashed in an off-site location with a televised feed, "a make-do place" as Tur characterized it, where "most of the working media" was simply regurgitating superficial observations on their social media feeds. "Now," Tur wrote, "we're all feeding the same multi-headed dog of digital: websites, social media, whatever's next."[13]

It was no accident that populist campaigns, driven by social media, were a global phenomenon by 2016. Pundits fretted that the democratic process in America, and everywhere else, was giving way to populism and authoritarianism. Foreign policy analyst Larry Diamond noted that between 2000 and 2015, "democracy broke down in 27 countries." Mike Lofgren of the *Guardian* mused that in the United States, the reality of establishment elites tightening their control on economics and politics actually made the populist conspiracy theories gushing out of Trump's community of supporters worth paying attention to. Right before Election Day, with a nod to a recent poll, Jason Grumet at *Roll Call* worried that the United States was in "real danger of becoming a nondemocratic, authoritarian country."[14]

Democracy was breaking: anyone on digital alternative media could see it. But depending on whether that person was a Clinton supporter, a Sanders partisan who was casting a protest vote for the Green Party's Jill Stein, or a Trump enthusiast, they either went to the polls on November 8, 2016, in a state of existential dread— or they straightened their MAGA hat and said it was about damn time.

The Democalypse had arrived.

———

A campaign promise to restore American greatness seems to be most effective at moments of economic decline. Thirty-five years before a Chinese factory ever stitched MAGA on a hat, in a campaign speech in New York City on July 4, 1980, Ronald Reagan promised to "make America great again." A decade later, Bill Clinton's team studied Reagan's speeches and revived the phrase for his campaign launch on October 3, 1991. "We can make America great again," Clinton said sincerely.[15] In 2012, political consultant Roger

Stone, who described Trump as a "populist with conservative instincts," revived it again.[16] A Libertarian populist himself, Stone was a former president of the Young Republicans, volunteered for Goldwater, and dropped out of college to work for the Nixon campaign in 1972. In 1980, he founded a successful political consulting firm with his friends Paul Manafort, Charles Black, and Peter Kelly. Stone had a bizarre sense of humor that played well on the internet, particularly on alt-right sites that favored crude lulz. After Hillary Clinton won the New Hampshire primary in 2008, Stone created an anti-Clinton PAC called "Citizens United Not Timid" because, as he explained, he couldn't come up with words for the acronym BITCH.[17]

Roger Stone hated Barack Obama, but Bush Republicans were more than he could stomach. On September 16, 2012, a few weeks after Mitt Romney accepted the party's nomination, Stone announced a grassroots movement to draft Trump as a third-party candidate. "Make America Great Again," he tweeted. "TRUMP HUCKABEE 2012 #nomormons." Although he decided not to run that year, Trump also adopted "Make America Great Again," or #MAGA, on Twitter too. In 2015, he reissued his book *Time to Get Tough: Making America #1 Again* with a revised subtitle: *Make America Great Again!* Two months after Stone's original tweet, Trump filed an application to trademark the phrase, a request approved on July 14, 2015. Later, he would claim to have invented it.[18]

Trump had no political experience and few policy ideas, but he knew media, he knew marketing, and he was a Twitter savant. In March 2011, Trump confided to the hosts of *Good Morning America* that he had "never been as serious" about running for president "as I am now." @realDonaldTrump became extremely active, quintupling his followers in 2011 and again in 2012. That year, nearly all politicians in House races were tweeting, and the more marginal the candidate, the more likely that person was to campaign on Twitter. Trump's tweets became increasingly aggressive and political. He picked fights with left-wing celebrities like lesbian actress Rosie O'Donnell and he began to attack President Obama as a whining slacker. "Obama's complaints about

Republicans are BS," he tweeted on September 2012. "He can never take responsibility."[19] Written in a personal voice, Trump's tweets were extreme and polarizing. He described his enemies as losers, failures, weak, fat, tired, and ugly. After Obama won re-election by a comfortable margin, despite much of the East being in disarray after Hurricane Sandy, Trump released a barrage of tweets that refused the outcome. "We are not a democracy!" he spluttered.[20] Trump's involvement with conspiracists, gun own-ers' rights, anti-immigrant and anti-Muslim politics, and the anti-Obama "birther" movement also intensified.[21]

As Hillary Clinton, the presumptive Democratic nominee, strove to address every flaw of her 2008 run—that she lacked authen-ticity, that her campaign had been fiscally undisciplined, that she had voted in favor of the Iraq War—Trump paid no attention to typical campaign organization, running a shoestring operation out of a vacant office suite in Trump Tower. Summoning large crowds to rallies, he ranted against immigrants, his opponents, and Pres-ident Obama. He rehearsed anti-Clinton conspiracy theories that had flourished on conservative populist media since the 1990s, and new ones from Clinton's years as a senator and secretary of state, repeatedly referring to her as a liar and a criminal. In the spring of 2015, as Trump was making his final decision to run for presi-dent, Clinton had also suddenly become vulnerable: the FBI opened an investigation into her use of a private email server as Secre-tary of State, and House Republicans summoned her to a hearing to explain her decisions prior to the 2012 massacre by terrorists of United States diplomatic staff in Benghazi, Libya.[22] At Trump rallies, where chants of "USA! USA!" had been popular, a darker dynamic emerged: Trump hinted that Clinton deliberately aban-doned the embassy staff and had effectively murdered them. On November 23, Trump posted a doctored video of a laughing Clin-ton superimposed on the ruins of the embassy on his Instagram, with the stern message: "Hillary, there is nothing to laugh about."[23]

Meanwhile, Clinton was also attacked from the populist left, where activists, energized by #Occupy and #BlackLivesMatter, ques-tioned her ties to Wall Street.[24] In February 2016, she was still locked in an unexpectedly fierce struggle with Vermont Senator

Bernie Sanders, one that must have triggered recurring nightmares in her Brooklyn campaign quarters about how 2008 had slipped away to an outsider. Sanders, a lifelong socialist, had tapped into the zeitgeist of the #Occupy movement's zeal for radical change and its distrust of the Clintons' move to the liberal center after 1992. Abandoning talk of compromise, Sanders spoke of his campaign as a "political revolution."[25] Although a veteran of the civil rights movement, Sanders struggled to speak with any depth to the contemporary struggle against violent racism that had galvanized #BlackLivesMatter. Yet in its calls for social justice, and its anticapitalist politics, his then largely white campaign reflected a fierce, progressive-populist critique of the Democratic Party establishment. Most notably, Sanders saw himself as a potential bridge between right and left populisms, even after he lost his bid for the nomination. "I do not think most of the people voting for Mr. Trump are racist or sexist," he tweeted, when it was fairly clear from social media feeds and the Confederate flags proudly displayed at Trump rallies that a great many of them actually were. "Our job is to reach out to Trump voters to tell them that we're going to create an economy that works for all of us, not just a few."[26]

Clinton found her campaign story constantly obscured by manufactured controversy, about her, her husband, and Trump. Democratic Facebook and Twitter feeds blossomed with revived criticisms of Bill Clinton's policies and his sexual affairs, her vote to authorize the Iraq War in October 2002, and speeches she had given at Goldman Sachs for large fees. Some female voters often outright repudiated her as a fellow woman, characterizing Clinton's attacks on Trump as nasty and unfair. "I think Hillary is a bully," a Minnesota woman told a reporter after Clinton called Trump "an evil person" for weight-shaming Alicia Machado, a former Miss Universe. Trump "calls it like it is," another female voter chimed in approvingly.[27]

With Sanders pressuring her from the left, it seemed impossible to fully re-create the magic of the Obama "first" for Clinton, also now a first. As in 2008, many left feminists were unmoved. "As first lady of Arkansas," socialist feminist Liza Featherstone wrote in January 2016, Clinton was no progressive. She opposed gay marriage and "led the efforts by her husband's administration to weaken teachers' unions and scapegoat teachers—most of them women, large numbers of them black—for problems in the education system, implementing performance measures and firings that set a punitive tone for education reform nationwide." Featherstone documented Clinton's support for mass incarceration, welfare means tests, and an aggressive United States foreign policy. Movie star, Hollywood fundraiser, #Occupy supporter, and Sanders partisan Susan Sarandon agreed. "Hillary's a good Republican," Sarandon said sarcastically in a Sirius XM radio interview.[28]

As Clinton struggled to win what should have been an easy, establishment-backed victory, Donald Trump swept primary after primary to take the Republican nomination.

Some thought that social media, once filled with democratic promise, was part of the problem. Digital alternative media had turned millions of Americans into political junkies by 2016, dividing voters into target audiences, harvesting their data, and training them to refresh their feeds dozens of times a day as they sat in front of computers at work and reflexively checked their smartphones. Pitched battles over politics divided friends, families, and communities on social media platforms, as partisans talked past each other. Twitter, which had added a live streaming service called Periscope and expanded its character limit from 140 to 280, had come alive with Trump followers retweeting memes, messages from Trump and his family, and stories from Fox, Breitbart, and sites they had never heard of before—but that a "friend" seemed to have shared. By May 2016, 61 percent of voters age 20 to 35 were getting the majority of their political news from Facebook. Users scrolled quickly through these items, opening news and sometimes bizarre opinion pieces, many of which were being promoted, not by friends, but by Facebook for a fee. Others came from foreign and domestic spam farms promoting sensational stories for advertising clicks. As a University of Pittsburgh student journalist complained during the campaign, the blurring of fake and real news, and the suppression of information by sensational stories promoted by algorithms, was "reinforcing a lack of tolerance, dialogue, and critical reasoning" that was essential to the democratic process.[29]

These struggles between Democrats were unexpectedly vicious, making it impossible for partisans to unify behind Clinton even after she had won the nomination. During the primary season, Sanders partisans responded to charges of extreme trolling by accusing Clinton partisans of dirty tricks too. "Members of Bernie Sanders' Facebook army have learned to be cautious," wrote one journalist, as if describing the Cold War. "Spies hide around every corner; infiltrators lurk behind even the friendliest friend requests." The Clinton campaign, Sanders partisans charged, was paying "hundreds of professional Internet trolls with the goal of sabotaging Sanders' Facebook groups. They sneak into closed communities with fake names and profiles, the rumors say, then post wild rants to make Sanders' supporters look bad. Or they file thousands of fake abuse reports to Facebook until the groups are overrun and their pages go black." Oddly, Clinton supporters made the same accusations: it was months before it became apparent that many of these trolls were probably sitting in basements in St. Petersburg, Russia. But by then the damage was done.[30]

The pace of social media exacerbated conflict, drawing users in and keeping them glued to repetitive arguments that no one could win, rather than promoting the informed conversations imagined by early proponents of electronic democracy. While a small group of "dedicated political junkies view the political discussions they encounter on social media in a much more positive light," researchers from the Pew Research Center noted shortly before the election, "a substantial share of social media users are worn out by the tone and volume of political material they encounter on these platforms and view social media as an inherently angry and disrespectful medium in comparison to other venues for discussing politics."[31]

The campaign also revealed a generational divide among Democrats about whether having a woman president necessarily represented democratic progress—if that woman was a member of the establishment. When former Secretary of State Madeleine Albright lectured Sanders supporters that there was "a special place in hell for women who don't help each other," feminist alternative digital media exploded with anger, forcing Albright to retract a statement she had been making without controversy for almost twenty-five years.[32]

Anger seemed to be the theme of 2016. Watching young people become devoted to a septuagenarian male socialist who had a modest portfolio of legislative accomplishments first appalled, then enraged, many Clinton supporters. They saw a woman who had more domestic and foreign policy experience than any candidate in the field being dismissed in favor of Sanders's calls for revolution. Yet there were good reasons for the success of a populist campaign among younger women: like most Americans, they were suffering economically too. Since the 1990s, Americans had "borrowed to make up for what their paychecks were lacking," progressive journalist Doug Henwood wrote in a book-length 2015 anti-Clinton polemic. Voters were desperate for "more equal distribution of income, investment in our rotting physical and social infrastructure, and a more cooperative ethic," and Clinton's so-called accomplishments were implicated in this decline.[33]

However, Clinton's fraught candidacy also revealed less about her as a politician than it did about the rise of populism in both parties, and about the divisions in the Democratic Party that had already begun to play out in alternative digital media in the Obama years. As former Obama adviser David Axelrod also analyzed it, digital alternative media, which consisted of multiple social media channels and thousands of platforms billing themselves as news sites, was vastly more labor-intensive than it had been in 2008 and 2012. Campaign staffs could barely keep up with the demands on their attention from the mainstream media. Now, engaging on, and monitoring, multiple social media and alternative news sites required endless staff hours. By 2016, the Clinton campaign found itself navigating a complex environment in which the alternative media "tail" was not only wagging the mainstream "dog," but also creating a blizzard of stories about Clinton it was impossible to respond to or correct.[34]

Clinton's was a story many women sympathized with, and for her loyal supporters, it hurt to watch her insulted and publicly degraded by Trump and his partisans, words that couldn't possibly be taken back in a symbolic call for reunification after the election. Successful professional women who still felt marginalized after distinguished careers resented the higher standard that they believed Clinton was being held to.[35] Some of us saw feminist friends and colleagues become less present in our social media feeds, slipping behind the walls of a private Facebook you had to be invited to join (although soliciting an invitation usually got a positive response). In the Obama tradition, these sites also became powerful fundraising and voter mobilization tools. The largest of what came to be erroneously called the "secret" Facebook groups, Pantsuit Nation, launched just two weeks before the election and raised $140,000 for Clinton's final push. After she lost, even more women joined: by early 2017, the group had four million members. For Clinton, the need for such groups was both emotionally moving and troubling. "I was taken aback by the flood of hatred that only seemed to grow as we got closer to Election Day," she later wrote, a hatred she felt had driven supporters into hiding.[36]

But hiding was not exactly what Clinton partisans were doing: it was a strategic retreat. Behind digital walls they could tell Clinton's story, and their own, in a way that seemed true and emotionally authentic. Annette Benedetti recalled having watched friends go silent about their enthusiasm for Clinton's candidacy because of the conflict with Sanders partisans that inevitably followed. It seemed that "every celebratory post I shared to my social media feed was immediately met with at least one angry commenter—most who identified as liberal," she wrote later. "Initially, I was easily drawn into arguments and lost hours to the endless exchange of 'supporting evidence,' but the online tension took a toll on real-life connections I valued." Pantsuit Nation and other groups were a relief from these angry exchanges, she recalled, and yes, after Clinton lost, she worried about that decision. "Imagine Election Day 2016 had every secret pro-Clinton group member chosen to stay out of the closet and fill their feeds with the information and excitement they so liberally shared in hiding," she wrote. "How many people could we have reached? How many minds and votes could we have changed?"[37]

But the rules for democratic engagement had changed. Other members of the private Clinton groups rejected the idea that joining these sites was a retreat to the echo chamber. Brooke Conti, an English professor, joined a secret group during the primary season "mostly because I liked the person who invited me," she remembers. "I was a strong supporter of Clinton, but didn't feel particularly silenced or inhibited on my regular Facebook feed." But she enjoyed it "so much & found it so affirming that I joined a second one—I did like having a separate space to talk politics exclusively, rather than filling up my own feed with that." Marilee Lindemann, another English professor, a former blogger, and a founder of the private group Bitches for Hillary, emphasized that people joined the groups for affirmation, not to hide.[38]

But some women did feel it was not safe to function as political junkies in their preexisting social media networks. "Months of getting trolled, dragged, lectured, and chastised by men of all political affiliations had finally worn me to my breaking point," wrote the cofounder of the #ImWithHer Facebook group. "All I wanted was a place to shout my love for Hillary Clinton without having to defend it or have it mansplained back to me." In a tradition dating back to nineteenth-century quilting circles, or the feminist conscious-raising groups of the 1970s, Clinton supporters used Facebook, a tool that was now old, to build new alternative digital media spaces where they were free to decide how they wanted to support Clinton. Lindemann and a friend formed Bitches for Hillary in response to the intense conflict they had experienced among friendship networks of Democrats. "Every time I said something positive about Hillary, I had to deal with my lefty friends arguing with me. It just drove me crazy," Lindemann told me. (Full disclosure: I was one of those lefty friends.)[39]

Being a political junkie was no fun anymore, and the election of 2016 seemed to have less and less to do with any democratic process that was familiar or desirable. "Wouldn't it be great," Lindemann characterized the conversation she and her friend had over coffee one day, "if we just had a space for like-minded people who didn't feel ambivalent about Clinton to strategize and work together?" But she emphatically rejected the notion that Bitches for

Hillary was a filter bubble or an echo chamber. Unlike some groups, it "was not a woman-only space," Lindemann emphasized. "Why? Because I don't live my life that way: we have a good group of gay, nonbinary, male-bodied people in the space. We had almost ten thousand in the group—we could have become Pantsuit Nation," had adding members to the group not been monitored meticulously to minimize trolling. Lindemann also observed people using Bitches for Hillary to support canvassing, door knocking, and mounting the occasional flash mob of pantsuit-clad partisans who took over public spaces with synchronized dance moves.[40]

The mainstream media's fascination with populism seemed to draw them back to the "secret Facebook" story repeatedly, but without any deeper understanding of what the stakes of the phenomenon were for democracy, or for the women who mustered there. In part, it was growing distrust of the establishment media. Many of the feminists who joined the groups opened their papers, or turned on the television, every day only to see more coverage of what Donald Trump had tweeted. They blamed mainstream media outlets for blunting the impact of their candidate and distorting her message. "Throughout the 2016 election," Susan Bordo wrote, "the pseudo-event ruled the airwaves, especially on the rolling news channels where leaks, poll results, gaffes, 'optics,' and concocted 'scandals' were immediately turned into high-voltage headlines and endlessly repeated, organizing people's perceptions into yet-to-be-analyzed 'narratives' of dubious factual status."[41]

Populist insurgencies on the left and the right were almost uninterested, and uninvested, in how the mainstream media was—or was not—responding to the pace of events because they didn't trust it or read it.[42] For Clinton supporters, perhaps no campaign issue epitomized the media's lack of judgment like the rolling stories about their candidate's alleged misuse of her personal email account. No harm or intent to deceive was found from Clinton's errors, but her supporters believed that the mainstream media should have reported that, rather than following the controversy, as if every viewpoint on the topic mattered. Clinton, they believed, was being held to account for what was, at best, a sign of her lack of digital sophistication common among male politicians of her generation as well.[43] Governors Howard Dean, Bobby Jindal, Rick Perry, and Jeb Bush had all used private email accounts for official business, and as president, George W. Bush, like Clinton, used a private server. Clinton, for her part, admitted that she should have used separate email accounts and even separate devices, but did not apologize for having erased thousands of emails that she asserted were personal. Instead of telling this story, the mainstream media rushed off to cover the next shiny, appalling thing. "Russia, if you're out there," Trump mocked his opponent at a July 27 rally, "I hope you're able to find the thirty thousand emails that are missing." The phrase was immediately tweeted out by CSPAN and rerun persistently on mainstream outlets throughout the campaign in such a way as to buttress the view that Trump's alternative media channels were promoting: that Clinton did have something to hide. Yet how could reporters have not been sympathetic to Clinton's email fumble, since they all struggled to keep their devices straight by the 2016 cycle? "I use one phone to talk to MSNBC," wrote Katy Tur. "I use another to text and call sources. Everyone in TV news has two phones. Add in your personal phone and some of us have three."[44]

The use of Twitter by mainstream reporters also meant that nearly every outrageous statement or claim that Trump made at his rallies was immediately broadcast by a reporter as a news item, with little context or critical commentary. Responses from Clinton partisans were often immediate, but they were only authoritative to other Clinton partisans. Actual fact-checking occurred back at the newsroom, or at nonprofit sites like Snopes .com or FactCheck.org, with a story correcting the lie emerging hours, or as much as a day, later—a story that went unread by the hundreds of thousands of people who had seen the tweet. For the Clinton campaign, which maintained a disciplined, top-down media operation, these battles over truth fought at the grass roots were unwelcome and distracted from communicating the candidate's policy experience. But for Trump supporters, whose hostility to the mainstream media was cultivated by the campaign, the public battle with the establishment on Twitter was energizing. Sometimes the campaign was even inadvertently hostile to its own alternative media supporters and able to turn potential disasters to its advantage. When Trump's then–campaign manager Corey Lewandoski manhandled a female reporter for *Breitbart* at a Florida rally in March 2016, the campaign denied that it had even occurred. "Wow, Corey Lewandowski, my campaign manager, and a very decent man, was just charged with assaulting a reporter," candidate Trump tweeted. "Look at tapes—nothing there!" But there was something "there": a surveillance video corroborated the victim's—and a nearby reporter's—account of the incident. But Trump's followers continued to repeat his falsehood and attack those who said otherwise. Reporters who understood the digital environment began seeing a sinister dynamic in the Trump echo chamber. "Crafting their own theories and banding together with other believers who will validate those ideas and troll the common enemy," a reporter for *Wired* observed, "it's become an all too predictable roadmap for how people respond to controversy online."[45]

It would be interesting to know how a reporter for *Breitbart News* ended up at the center of a violent encounter with a Trump campaign worker, since that publication, and its editor Steve Bannon, was central to promoting deceptive campaign materials, on and off the site. Bannon himself reviewed Trump's campaign book *Time to Get Tough*, calling it a "smart and serious" rebuttal to the candidate's critics. "Backed up with nearly 250 endnotes," Bannon wrote about a volume that had been ghostwritten by a *Breitbart News* employee, conservative populist Wynton Hall, "Trump's book clearly lays out serious policy solutions to vexing U.S. problems." The book covered "welfare reform, cyberwarfare, energy, illegal immigration and crime, taxes, healthcare, national defense—you name it," Bannon enthused. "Trump offers his plans, often including specific bills and amendments. Best of all, Trump does it all in his refreshingly blunt and authentic voice—the very voice now resonating with a citizenry fed up with the Political Class and its conceits."[46]

Breitbart News also promoted a second anti-Clinton book, Peter Schweizer's *Clinton Cash: The Untold Story of How and Why Foreign Governments and Businesses Helped Make Bill and Hillary Rich* (2015). A political attack in the guise of an investigative report, *Clinton Cash* was full of false assertions and published by a conservative press, but one owned by HarperCollins, and thus likely to reach an audience beyond committed Trump partisans and *Breitbart News* readers. The book collated a dizzying and complex set of charges against both Clintons that exported conspiracy theories from websites, blogs, and bulletin boards, where a general audience would never have read them, into a mass-market book. Schweitzer had come up through conservative intellectual channels such as Young Americans for Freedom, the Hoover Institution, and *Breitbart News*, and was now invited onto the mainstream news sites like NBC's *Today Show*, as a Clinton "expert." In fact, he was nothing of the kind: researchers employed by Schweizer were paid a collective $2.2 million to assemble the material for the book, two-thirds of which was paid for by conservative activist Rebecca Mercer. By 2016, the book had been reissued as both a film and graphic novel.[47]

And then on October 26, 2016, less than two weeks before Americans went to the polls, FBI Director James Comey suddenly reopened the investigation into Hillary Clinton's misuse of emails. For many, the assertions made in *Clinton Cash* that Hillary Clinton was congenitally dishonest seemed, miraculously, to have been acknowledged by the political establishment.

=

For seasoned political junkies, the grim look on James Carville's face had given it away early on the evening of November 8, 2016. Now an MSNBC commentator, the "Ragin' Cajun" who engineered Bill Clinton's victory in 1992 remembered later that when he saw that Trump had a 65 percent chance of winning Florida, "I knew right there, and the blood did go out of my face." Hope disappeared, state by state, then county by county, as Democrats watched the unimaginable. A little after 2:00 a.m., the election all but lost, Clinton campaign chair John Podesta told supporters gathered in the Jacob K. Javits Convention Center in New York City to go home and get some sleep. When her campaign manager told her it was over, Clinton is said to have responded, as if addressing the digital ghosts that rampaged from alternative media to the mainstream and back again: "I knew it. I knew this would happen to me. They were never going to let me be president."[48]

The sea of red MAGA hats at the Hilton Hotel, blocks away from Trump Tower, was listless for much of the evening. Even the most fervent partisans had not believed that Donald Trump could pull it off, and many were drinking heavily. But at 10:39 p.m. the announcement that Trump had won Ohio came through. At 10:53, Florida. At 1:35 a.m., Pennsylvania, where Hillary Clinton had held her final rally the night before the election, fell to Trump. At that announcement, fists started pumping in the air at the Hilton as the cries "USA! USA!" celebrated an electoral college lead that Clinton had virtually no chance of overcoming. At 2:30 a.m., Wisconsin sealed it. Donald Trump's victory in 2016 was a "complete earthquake," said MSNBC host Joe Scarborough the next morning. "This was an earthquake unlike any earthquake I have seen since Ronald Reagan in 1980. It came out of nowhere. Nobody expected it."[49]

Particularly, it is said, the candidate who, one observer speculated, imagined the presidential campaign as merely a platform for launching a mainstream media empire. And indeed, Trump reportedly "looked like a ghost" when it became clear he was going to win.[50] Whatever he did next Trump had, inadvertently perhaps, already changed history. As a writer for *Wired* magazine wrote in the aftermath of the election, the national debate moved decisively away from the mainstream media and onto alternative media during the 2016 election cycle.[51] Alternative media won a presidential election for a populist candidate—and in the history of the American presidency, a populist had never been elected.

After the election, the campaign never stopped. Trump's bombast and fury were transferred to a new America, one where a conservative populist president had no intention of abandoning his own political junkies to make himself appealing to the establishment. Similarly, Clinton partisans refused to stand down. In the months after the election, Bitches for Hillary, Pantsuit Nation, and other Clinton Facebook groups hung together to organize what many anti-Trump partisans began to call "the Resistance." Facebook's untrustworthiness as a vehicle for fake news and mismanagement of user data coexisted with real strengths that users were reluctant to abandon. If, by 2018, Clinton supporters were still bruised and angry about the loss, Facebook kept them organized for what came next. In January 2017, they mounted women's marches all over the world and gathered at airports to protest the Trump administration's Muslim ban. In the fall 2018 midterms, they ran for and won elected office in unprecedented numbers.[52]

Veteran Democratic activist and political consultant Donna Brazile later characterized Hillary Clinton's campaign as having been "haunted by ghosts." Brazile was forced to take over the Democratic National Committee in the middle of the campaign, when *WikiLeaks'* decision to unleash waves of emails hacked from the DNC servers revealed that Florida Congresswoman Debbie Wasserman Schultz had thrown the weight of the Democratic establishment behind Clinton. The document dump was intended to enrage Sanders' partisans with evidence that the party leadership had "rigged" the election, and it worked. Brazile became a one-woman rapid-response team on mainstream media, responding with calm and intelligence to the latest outrage pushed out from digital alternative media. But these cable television news appearances were not entirely about providing good information, either. They couldn't be, in a political atmosphere that was oversaturated with information that no one trusted. Instead, she knew it was all theater. "In the morning when I was getting ready to go to the studio I'd know if I was going to play the part of the bitch who stands up to the GOP talking points," Brazile recalled. "Or they might ask me to be the cool, calm Donna, the voice of reason and experience, who will just give it to you straight."[53]

Brazile's "ghosts" were not just the rumors stoked by Clinton conspiracists that had been churned back into the news. As it turned out, they were real people, and bots programmed by real people, that had infected alternative media with manifestos, insulting memes, and old conspiracies about Clinton that were then gleefully recirculated by Trump and Sanders partisans. Yet it was not just Hillary Clinton who had taken a beating: the concept of a fair election, and both political parties' understanding of how elections were won and lost, had been upended. The chaos was not just caused by the content circulated in digital alternative media, but by what Trump campaign operatives had learned to do with the data digital alternative media produced. "They knew how to size up voters, not by meeting them and finding out what they cared about, what moved their hearts and stirred their souls, but by analyzing their habits," Brazile wrote. "They could take all the things you bought while shopping online in the last six years, analyze them, and say they were confident that they knew pretty much all there was to know about you."[54]

The Democalypse had arrived. If they had run their own data on Election Day, would Facebook and Twitter have known, before any mainstream news agency did, that Donald Trump would win? They might have. Zoe Quinn, a feminist game designer who had spent the last two years hiding from trolls who were violently harassing her and other women as part of the #GamerGate controversy, watched the election unfold and what she saw wasn't about politics. For years, she had watched African American feminists harassed on Twitter and Facebook by people using fake accounts to sow dissension among racial justice advocates. She knew that the kind of sensational news the Trump campaign was creating would cause alternative digital media algorithms to drive this content up the search engine and social media ranks. After she became a victim of #GamerGate, she saw the growing connections "between online white supremacist movements, misogynist nerds, conspiracy theorists and dispassionate hoaxers who derive a sense of power from disseminating disinformation." And she saw the ways that these radicalized, populist communities migrated out of their own communities and into ever-greater contact with casual social media users, changing the behaviors of ordinary people who took on the obsessive, disruptive dark humor that these communities specialized in. And she saw how they flocked to *Breitbart News*, making that platform more prominent in the conservative populist community than it otherwise might have been.[55]

"I feel like one of the few people not surprised by Trump's election," Quinn concluded. "I called it the second he announced his candidacy. . . . I had just been years deep in the muck, and I saw my attackers shifting to support him."[56]

POST-TRUTH

On the evening of January 20, 2019, I, like millions of other Americans, was scrolling aimlessly through Twitter, clicking on links to the digital alternative media sites that supplement my newspaper and magazine reading. I checked for early reports on the March for Life, an annual anti-abortion protest, the third annual Women's March, and the Indigenous People's March, all in Washington, DC, that day. A short video, tweeted from an account I did not recognize, grabbed my attention. "This MAGA loser gleefully bothering a Native American protester at the Indigenous People's March," the caption read. In a tight shot filmed by a steady hand, a young, white man we now know as Covington Catholic High School student Nick Sandmann stood, smiling. Facing him was an older man, sixty-four-year-old Nathan Phillips, an Omaha Nation elder and military veteran. I clicked Play: Phillips sang and beat a drum rhythmically, inches from Sandmann's face. In the background, other young white men, some wearing MAGA hats and preppy clothes similar to Sandmann's, clapped, hollered, leaped around, laughed, and filmed the pair.

I watched the short video, which was traveling through social media rapidly under the hashtag #CovingtonBoys, looking unsuccessfully for specific evidence of when it had been filmed and where.

Aware of the retweet widget turning over rapidly, and the hundreds of replies accruing below, I could see that this video was going viral. It migrated quickly from an obscure site to Twitter and Facebook, and then onto mainstream news sites like *CNN*, *Fox News*, and the *Washington Post*, as well as onto alternative media platforms like the *Root*, an African American news and culture site. Some outlets reported the confrontation as it was clearly intended to be understood by the video's producers: a typical instance of Trumpian racism. My largely progressive social media feeds supported that narrative vociferously. But if I deliberately left that environment, I could find conservative populists telling a different story about how the "lamestream" liberal media accused white *boys* of racism, when it was clearly a racist Native American activist who was attacking *them*.

The real story was not initially clear from the video, although the political junkies on all sides who were spreading the footage were not conscious of that. "Tell me how you voted and I'll tell you what you think you saw," read the sub-headline of a *Politico* story published a few days later that warned of "our newly discovered infinite capacity for dispute."[1] But no one seemed interested in who had produced the video, why, and how it had been delivered so quickly to millions of people still energized, or enraged, about Donald Trump, two years after his inauguration.

The #CovingtonBoys video was an important cultural sign that, in the aftermath of the 2016 election, the logic of partisanship now overruled reason, fairness, and critical thought. In the world of political junkies, right and left, when a political narrative *felt true* it *was true*, and everyone who responded to this video was going with their gut.[2] A little digging on my part revealed that it seemed to have originated on a site run by progressive alternative media activists. Longer videos that emerged over the next few days showed that the original had been filmed and edited with the intention of eliminating information, such as the circumstances of how Sandmann and Phillips had come together in the first place, and who else was involved. Phillips had been surrounded by supporters, who were taunting Sandmann's classmates. The lack of context also distorted other kinds of visual cues, such as Sandmann's frozen, unmoving smile. The caption falsely inferred that Sandmann had deliberately interfered with Phillips's drumming, when in fact, he had not. Originating in a fake Twitter account, and proliferated by other fake accounts, the video seemed to be intended to disrupt and ignite widespread outrage across the political spectrum.

The video bore all the marks of having been designed to ignite political tensions that had been simmering since the last election. Phillips and Sandmann were shot in a close frame that excluded any identifying characteristics of when, or where, it had been shot. The alarmist, clickbait headline described Sandmann as a "MAGA loser," a phrase designed to activate partisans on both sides. When I cautioned them about sharing it, friends and acquaintances characterized my doubts about the video as deluded, politically disappointing, and a distraction from the urgency of what was, to them, an emergent racial justice crisis. I did not succeed in persuading anyone who did not already believe it that a campaign of online violence against the Covington students and their families, well underway hours after the video was posted, was disproportionate to the actual harm that had occurred; or that what my friends saw as breaking news might be a professional clickbait campaign. One white male interlocutor on a friend's Facebook feed even scoffed at the idea that anyone should fear online death threats "because they are never real."[3]

Spoken like someone who has never received a death threat, right?

Nevertheless, I persisted, culling evidence and insights from as many different sources as I could and writing an account of this pseudo-event on the digital alternative media platform I edit.[4] Predictably, my analysis made little impact, except among conservatives, who were shocked to see someone "on the left" take this position. In my networks, an interlocutor told me flat-out that I was lying about @2020fight, the Twitter account that had first distributed the video, even though I linked to the CNN investigation that confirmed that. Many of my friends also went on at length about how Nick Sandmann reminded them of Associate Justice of the Supreme Court Brett Kavanaugh, another Catholic school alumnus. This was a highly unfavorable comparison, given that

Kavanaugh had been recently confirmed amid allegations of serial sexual violence in his youth. My critics also rejected the possibility that data they had left behind during the Kavanaugh hearings might have been purchased and used to target them with the Covington video. Nor did it strike them as odd that partisan divisions might have been deliberately inflamed to distract. This was, after all, a weekend when the government had been shut down for over twenty days over a budget impasse, President Trump had delivered a major—and poorly received—address on border control, and three major political marches had occurred in Washington.[5]

As it turns out, I was right, and a good many people (or many good people, depending on how you want to think about it) were wrong about what happened in Washington that day, which is why this episode seemed like an important coda for a book that brings us into the history of the present. With less than two years to go before the 2020 election, political junkies were still selecting the versions of the news that supported their ideological predilections, many digital alternative media outlets were still shaping stories to create conflict among political junkies, and mainstream media outlets were still reacting to social media feeds before reporting a story in depth. These practices hurt all of us. And they will continue to hurt all of us until we grapple with what digital alternative media has become, what role it plays in our political imagery, and why we are so unwilling to put our responsibility to be truly informed citizens ahead of the pleasure and excitement of being political junkies.

As these chapters show, if the mainstream media once imagined itself as creating a sense of nationhood, and alternative media was created in the effort to do that better, with a few exceptions, neither is really doing its job anymore. Divided, proud of our political identities, we political junkies now persistently search for "scoops" that reaffirm our own views at the expense of understanding a whole debate. The search for inside information that made *I. F. Stone's Weekly* so powerful; the commitment to ideas that helped Paul Weyrich and Richard Viguerie change the history of the Republican Party; and the desire for informed conversation that made the *MacNeil-Lehrer NewsHour* a destination for those eager to learn about politics encouraged Americans to develop a critical perspective on the political and media establishment. Experiments in electronic democracy, blogging, born-digital platforms, and social media enhanced the possibility that ideas and events occurring on the margins could be pushed into the mainstream, and that mainstream media outlets would be increasingly held accountable for their failures. But at the same time, as alternative media moved online, it became more unfiltered and friendly to partisan propaganda. As alternative media became part of the process of producing mainstream news, critical forms of truth-seeking—fact, expert opinion, and principled disagreement—all necessary to maintaining democracy, began to fail. Populism, both progressive and conservative, now dominates the spirit and objectives of alternative media across the political spectrum in the twenty-first century. And it is also dominating our political life, unchecked by trusted voices that give us real information—not a *feeling* that we are informed.[6]

Alternative media depended on assembling and encouraging political junkies as early as the 1950s. But when political consultants and activists learned that platforms for discussing politics could actually be tools for *doing* politics, they learned how to not just assemble, but create, partisans. After 2004, the work of the next national campaigns began as soon as the last ones ended: by 2016, the presidential campaign became merely a punctuation point in an ongoing political war.

The #CovingtonBoys story shows that while alternative media was once marginal to the mainstream news environment, it became the tail wagging many establishment dogs. Celebrities, politicians, journalists, the Covington Diocese leadership that rebuked their own students before speaking to them, and entire news outlets were forced to apologize. Within days, more deliberate investigations revealed that the high school students had not instigated the conflict: they had been waiting for their bus when two separate groups of activists, one with Phillips and the other a group of Black Hebrew Israelites, harassed them persistently.[7]

The story also underlines a new phenomenon that gripped our nation of political junkies during the 2016 election. So-called fake news not only reflects partisan divides, it creates them, and this function has replaced the desire for true and complete information that shaped the aspirations of early alternative media. From talk radio to Twitter, alternative media increasingly became a source of information that was partial at best, completely false at worst, and one that often aspired to tell a partisan story. Contemporary political junkies now view all mainstream news, regardless of its origin, as partisan and all information coming from the "other" side as fatally suspect. Investigative reporting by citizen journalists was a valuable check on a mainstream media establishment that if it was not intentionally dishonest, also saw maintaining relationships to the political establishment as a critical feature of professional journalism. But these same platforms also created a market for speculation, gossip, alternative realities, and conspiracy theories masquerading as news. By 2012, Donald Trump's signature phrase—"a lot of people are saying"—was enough to launch crackpot theories born on conservative populist news sites into the mainstream as "news."[8]

As citizens of a democracy, we should be outraged, not entertained, by fake news, and even more outraged when real news is said to be fake. The stakes are too high. Twentieth-century mass media technology made it possible, as philosopher Hannah Arendt observed, to erode "factual reality" with anti-Semitic propaganda, making Europeans willing—even eager—to abandon fellow citizens to their deaths.[9] More recently, deliberately fake news was reborn on television as a form of comedy devised to undermine authority. In the 1960s, late-night hosts like Johnny Carson performed opening monologues that among other things, offered a critical perspective on the news. In the 1970s, ABC's *Saturday Night Live* debuted a segment called "Weekend Update," a darkly humorous send-up of establishment journalism featuring anchors who were at ideological loggerheads, or didn't fully understand the news they were reading. By the turn of the century, Stephen Colbert and Jon Stewart gave us acerbic political humor styled as news. The point of these shows was, in the aftermath of 9/11 and a war on Iraq launched on the basis of false intelligence, to skewer the failure of the mainstream news and political establishments to do their job—but also to inform, using satire and other forms of performance associated with entertainment.[10]

By 2019, it was not unusual for political satire from alternative media sites like the *Onion* to be mistakenly retweeted or reposted as factual on the strength of a headline, a situation that reflects how attenuated the bullshit meters of many political junkies have become.[11] But this also reflects our now-common belief that politicians routinely lie, reporters print those lies, and that fake news reported by an establishment media outlet can change history. After all, following 9/11, President George W. Bush and his advisors believed that the decision to go to war with Iraq, and the absence of facts that would justify that policy, existed in separate universes. In their view, historians and journalists, otherwise known by the Bush White House as the "reality-based community," were free to make corrections after the fact. But the terrorism crisis, the Bush White House believed, demanded forceful messaging that although false, would control the news cycle and move Americans, and Congress, toward war. It did. In 2004, the *New York Times* admitted that their reporter Judith Miller had actually promoted some of these falsehoods, fed to her by a political opponent of Iraq's president, Saddam Hussein.[12] But now politicians hardly need a top reporter from a mainstream media outlet to promote their version of events. In alternative media, disinformation mimics reliable information. False scientific reports and paid experts are circulated to partisans, and cycle into the mainstream media as, in the words of Trump White House advisor Kellyanne Conway, alternate facts.[13]

Since the 1950s, our political debates have been reshaped by alternative media, in good ways and bad. They created forms of investigative reporting that defied authority with the truth, and they amplified conservative and progressive populisms that are as concerned with feelings than facts. But they have also demonstrated how reporting has been displaced by opinion journalism, editorializing, and political storytelling designed for "you." Intended to attract an audience of political junkies and create new ones, by selecting information for niche audiences, digital alternative media has undermined a common idea of what news really is and whether truth can even exist outside the mind of the beholder. We don't need to romanticize the public square, or nightly news broadcasts that lasted for fifteen minutes on only three channels, to imagine that agreeing on basic facts would be a path to a more productive debate about what our democratic future should look like.

Thus, one takeaway for readers, progressive and conservative, should be to imagine what true political news could look like again, how the story of a candidate could be told in a way that is both factual and compelling, and what the useful function of the establishment is in stabilizing a political culture undone by alternative media. In 2005, Stephen Colbert proposed a neologism that captured the slide between truth and untruth that had already occurred in politics: "truthiness." A statement is "truthy," Colbert explained, when it is "stating concepts or facts" that the speaker "wishes or believes to be true, rather than concepts or facts known to be true." Truthiness was a key attribute of alternative media created and sold to the political junkie, because the story it told was intuitive and emotionally true. To understand a given truth, "you" did not require a broader knowledge of evidence, context, or the larger political debate. All you needed was a feeling about what was true: college teachers know that it is now not uncommon for students to make an assertion in class that begins with "I feel," rather than "I think." As a genre, despite some of the good investigative reporting that it promoted, each stage of alternative media history actually pushed us closer to a world where truthiness would replace the truth, all news was fake to someone, and ideology would be privileged as the primary source and context for political news.[14]

There seem to be four kinds of people now in the United States. There are political junkies and people who have tuned out altogether. There are populists, left and right, who see a broken democracy as fertile ground for revolutionary changes; and citizens, left and right, who are determined to rebuild a political system based on liberal values. Throughout this book, I have investigated a long history that began by promising Americans better reporting, and deeper political knowledge, and ended with a nation whose ideological divisions are expressed as alternative realities. Our political conversations often do not rest on the same set of basic facts, let alone on shared assumptions about what democracy is and how it is sustained. As he did before and during the 2016 campaign, President Donald Trump continues to use Twitter for daily briefings about his views and policies that go straight to his partisans, without offering what he came to call "the fake news media" an opportunity to ask questions. On April 23, 2019, *Newsweek* noted that then–Press Secretary Sarah Huckabee Sanders had gone forty-three days without formally briefing the press, longer than any of her thirteen predecessors.[15]

Like Trump, Huckabee-Sanders often went straight to Trump supporters with the news by tweeting her press releases, controlling the narrative among the president's base directly from the White House. While this created opportunities for partisans to criticize and troll her, it also established a historically low bar for government transparency, something that Americans still believe they value.[16] The White House often has access to facts withheld from the media and general public, and both mainstream and alternative journalists have sometimes seen revealing those facts as their civic responsibility. Yet the Trump administration has become an unprecedented factory of manufactured news, distributed to supporters by mainstream outlets like *Breitbart News* and *Fox News*, dozens of alternative digital media outlets that specialize in opinion pieces and clickbait. These sites, in turn, become "evidence" of what Trump partisans already know: mainstream journalists cannot be trusted. Hashtags created by Trump and his aides have also emphasized this as a conservative populist article of faith: #FakeNews, #WitchHunt, #FailingNYTimes, and #FakeMSM all signaled to the Trump base that only information coming from the White House and its allies was reliable.

═══

We cannot know how Izzy Stone would have responded to the trajectory of the alternative media history he initiated in 1953, but I would guess that he would've been astonished by how freely we speak online, and, at the same time, how little what we say contributes to the project of knowledge and human freedom. The right to publish whatever comes across our desktops, regardless of whether it happened or not, and to reproduce these items without asking questions about where they came from and why would have astonished, and I suspect, angered him. Stone might have pointed out that the role of alternative media was to be more responsible, not more free of constraint, and to make the establishment better, not to tear it down. He would have understood that the #Covington Boys video was not news, but propaganda; and that while the distribution networks that sent it spinning out to digital devices at warp speed did not distinguish between news and propaganda, readers and mainstream journalists should have. Speed, Stone would have insisted, is not an alternative news value: slowing down the story is. Outlets like *I. F. Stone's Weekly* and the *PBS NewsHour* (the current name for the *MacNeil-Lehrer NewsHour*) were alternative outlets that improved the news not because they were fast, but because stories were selected by a trusted friend, produced with care, packed with facts and well-considered opinions, and curated for an audience that valued information over sensationalism.

It was this same impulse to improve news that motivated the architects of electronic democracy and the first generation of political bloggers, whose merits are as valuable to remember as their failures. Whether on the left or the right, these political junkies believed in facts—but they also believed in the importance of conversation and the power of digital alternative media to inspire conversation that was inherently self-correcting, because the weight of public opinion would lead the entire *demos* to a common set of facts. As Arianna Huffington told an interviewer in 2011 when she first began blogging, "I fell in love with the online conversations that ensued," and she created *Huffington Post* because the internet was where the most important conversations took place. These conversations were typically well informed, sometimes because they were written by experts, but more often because they were written from vetted news accounts that bloggers then re-vetted with new research. As Libertarian blogger Tyler Cowan reflected in 2011, the best blogs were "self-critical and self-reflective"; a blogger needed to cultivate a sense of "your own weaknesses, where you were wrong last time, and where you can do better."[17]

While some political junkies are born, others are made. Alternative media became financially successful after 2006 by establishing partisan narratives that felt true, not that were new or necessarily better informed. The #CovingtonBoys incident played heavily into the media skepticism established by Paul Weyrich, Richard Viguerie, and Phyllis Schlafly; by decades of talk radio and cable news hosts; by the conservative populist Tea Party; and by the progressive populists of #OccupyWallStreet and #BlackLivesMatter. Although all of these partisans are politically different in their standpoints and their objectives, their achievement was to tell their own stories, network existing political junkies who cared about those stories, and persuade new partisans to question authority. But too often, populists did not seek to provide new information, but to change the narrative to express a singular, exclusive, and passionate point of view. Andrew Breitbart's path to success, publishing doctored videos that "proved" the liberal conspiracy against "the people," is but one example.

That said, populist narratives can be aspirational and truth-seeking too. The Obama campaign called a world into being where an African American man could be president of the United States, and it merged the alternative media world and political organizing, bringing progressive populisms onto the national political stage. #BlackLivesMatter imagined a society in which black lives really did matter, and white people acknowledged African Americans' "basic human rights and dignity." #OccupyWallStreet, for a few weeks, called into being a leaderless community to demand that political and economic power was more fairly distributed between the 99 percent and the 1 percent.[18] All of these movements set the stage for a 2020 Democratic primary campaign in which not just candidates on the left like Bernie Sanders and Elizabeth Warren, but liberals like Joseph Biden, Amy Klobuchar, Pete Buttigieg, and Kamala Harris, appealed to "the people" primarily by telling their stories on alternative media.

What are the lessons at a moment when political talk has never been so pervasive, but voting, and the belief that political and media institutions matter, has never been more fragile? In 2019, on the brink of another election, in the midst of a conservative populist resurgence and unprecedented organizing by progressive partisans, Americans believed that Washington heard them less than ever before and was more impermeable to change than ever. And according to one study, they were right.[19]

Worse, it is difficult to organize for change when it seems like all we do is reassure each other, within our partisan bubbles, that "we" are right and "they" are fatally wrong. Across the political spectrum, our views are often produced in the spur of the moment and shaped by others who are not sufficiently different from us to prompt the kinds of reflection that politics requires. In *The Destruction of Hillary Clinton* (2016), literary critic Susan Bordo described how writing and conversation, in a range of alternative media, helped her to analyze the forces that she believed had kept her candidate out of the White House. "I found I had a lot more to say than could be contained in a Facebook post," Bordo wrote, "so I began to blog for the *Huffington Post* and for a website of my own." Eventually she edited what she had written into a book. Social media, Bordo wrote, created a "running, virtually daily record of the 2016 election."[20] It is also worth noting that Bordo, an experienced and well-regarded scholar, was holding herself to fundamentally different rules as a political junkie than she would have as an academic professional. Her thoughts were formed in a partisan environment where, except for strident trolls, she would have encountered few ideas that were different from her own.

When every political junkie gets news tailored to their taste, it's not just our candidates that lose: democracy does. But the other lesson of this book is that it's not over. *Political Junkies* is not a history of cynicism and despair: it is a history of optimism, hope, innovation, improvement, and the desire to promote new ideas that sometimes go wrong and require correction. Alternative media fueled a crisis of political civility and distrust, as well as contempt for traditional forms of cultural and social authority. But alternative media also played a role in holding mainstream media accountable, and it revolutionized political organizing and fundraising. It confronted mainstream media's relationship to the political establishment and won. It helped new grassroots movements thrive. And it opened personal channels of communication between leaders and supporters, as well as between networks of people who believe that they know something about the world they want to live in, if not always how to get there.

The #CovingtonBoys video and its aftermath was always a bigger story than Donald Trump and his MAGA followers: it was a story about us. It was a story about the nation that alternative media gave us, but it was also a lesson about how we tend to retreat into our partisan corners in the shock of the present, rather than step forward and question the "information" we receive. But that isn't how it has to be. American political junkies, and our counterparts around the world, now find ourselves living in a political culture that snuck up on us while we were tweeting, Facebooking, and watching YouTube videos. It is not unlike that moment, almost 250 years ago, when all American media that didn't belong to the king of England was alternative media, and to paraphrase a historian of the American Revolution, "the sheer explosiveness of the controversies" catapulted eighteenth-century minds "toward a mode of understanding altogether new, altogether modern."[21] Yet those early Americans reacted and reflected. They fought a war, and they wrote pamphlets. They clamored in coffeehouses, and they dueled. They settled, often grudgingly, for compromises and imperfect solutions, acted on them, and then started writing, reading, and listening some more. And their descendants kept doing it, generation after generation, creating new, alternative media in which they upbraided each other, resolved their differences, and gathered like-minded folks together to imagine new futures.

So can we.

ACKNOWLEDGMENTS

A book that covers seven decades, and has to tell that story concisely, cannot be written without ongoing feedback, tough love, huge leaps of faith, and many friends.

Thanks to the New Haven "groupies"—Edward Ball, Beverly Gage, and Paul Sabin—who read the book proposal and sample chapter and helped me get *Political Junkies* to Basic Books; and to the Upper West Side writing gang, who spent a solid evening talking to me about Joe Trippi. Other friends and colleagues who read and commented on chapters of the manuscript include Elaine Abelson, Eric Alterman, Nancy Barnes, Federico Finchelstein, Oz Frankel, David Greenberg, Aaron Jakes, Jill Lepore, Marilee Lindemann, Laura Palermo, Emma Park, David Perlmutter, Natalia Mehlman Petrzela, James Traub, Jeremy Varon, Eli Zaretsky, and Julian Zelizer. Juan Cole, Brooke Conti, Howard Dean, Ryan Girdusky, Michael Isikoff, and Brendan Nyhan generously answered questions over email and telephone. Robert MacNeil sat for a ninety-minute interview.

The New School has embraced and supported me since 2012; all funding for this project was provided by them. It was exactly the institutional home I needed in 2012 to take the next step in my writing life. I cannot possibly thank everyone who has welcomed and supported my research in the past eight years at the Schools for Public Engagement, Eugene Lang College, and the New School for Social Research. Special thanks go to Laura Auricchio, Seth Cohen, Julia Foulkes, Jeffrey Goldfarb, Dara Levendosky, Tim Marshall, Will Milberg, Jim Miller, Julia Ott, Bryna Sanger, and Mary Watson. Research assistance for the book was provided by Preston Charles and Kenny Dillon. Christopher Howard-Woods was my general assistant for three years, and not only made all the trains run on time, but did it with unmatched good humor.

My editor at Basic Books, Brian Distelberg, pushed hard to make this the best book it could be, to clarify its vision and argument, and to get it to the audience it was written for. Thanks also to Basic's Alex Colston, Ian Gibbs, Katie Lambright, and Brynn Warriner. My sister, Dorothy Potter-Snyder, proofread the manuscript at a key moment: thanks so much, Piglet. Ryan Girdusky, my fellow political junkie, conservative populist polling expert, and late-night text message writing buddy, proves that there really are bridges between the left and the right. Roz Foster has been the agent of my dreams and is always ready with great comments and a sincere "You've *got* this!" I also want to thank the Sandra Dijkstra Agency for everything they have done to support me.

And finally, to Nancy Barnes, fellow writer, organizer of vacations, and heart's companion: I couldn't do anything, much less write books, without you. Thank you for everything. And yes, it's finished now.

NOTES

Introduction: Press Pass

1. Nicole Hemmer, *Messengers of the Right: Conservative Media and the Transformation of American Politics* (Philadelphia: University of Pennsylvania Press, 2016), 50–51; Nicco Mele, *The End of Big: The Internet Makes David the New Goliath* (New York: St. Martin's Press, 2013), 60, 80–84.

2. Lee McIntyre, *Post-Truth* (Cambridge: MIT Press, 2018), xiv.

3. Amina Dunn, John Laloggia, and Carol Doherty, "In midterm voting decisions, policies took a back seat to partisanship," *Pew Research Center*, November 29, 2018.

4. Benedict Anderson, *Imagined Communities: Reflections on the Origin and Spread of Nationalism* (New York: Verso Books, 1983), 4.

5. Joseph M. Adelman, *Revolutionary Networks: The Business and Politics of Printing the News, 1763–1789* (Baltimore: Johns Hopkins University Press, 2019), 3–4; Benjamin Fagan, *The Black Newspaper and the Chosen Nation* (Athens: University of Georgia Press, 2016), 3–8; Amanda Frisken, *Victoria Woodhull's Sexual Revolution: Political Theater and the Popular Press in the Nineteenth Century* (Philadelphia: University of Pennsylvania Press, 2004), 24–25.

6. Peter Novick, *That Noble Dream: The Objectivity Question and the American Historical Profession* (New York: Cambridge University Press, 1988), 47–60; Michael Schudson, *Discovering the News: A Social History of American Newspapers* (New York: Basic Books, 1981), 3–10.

7. Michael Schudson, *Discovering the News*, 49; Charles Ponce de Leon, *That's the Way It Is: A History of Television News in America* (Chicago: University of Chicago Press, 2016), 27, 50–52, 71.

8. Richard Forgette, *News Grazers: Media, Politics and Trust in an Information Age* (Thousand Oaks, CA: Congressional Quarterly Press), 60; Eric Alterman, *What Liberal*

Media? The Truth about Bias and the News (New York: Basic Books, 2003), 15, 30, 111; Jill Abramson, *Merchants of Truth: The Business of News and the Fight for Facts* (New York: Simon and Schuster, 2019), 80–81.

9. Joshua D. Atkinson, *Journey into Social Activism: Qualitative Approaches* (New York: Fordham University Press, 2017), 173.

10. Viguerie, *The Establishment vs. the People: Is a New Populist Revolt on the Way?* (Chicago: The American Populist Institute/Regnery Press, 1983), 11.

11. Richard Hofstadter, *The Paranoid Style in American Politics* (New York: Alfred A. Knopf, 1965), 61, 150.

12. John Cassidy, "Bernie Sanders and the New Populism," *New Yorker*, February 3, 2016; David Freedlander, "There Is Going to Be a War within the Party. We Are Going to Lean into It," *Politico*, February 4, 2019.

13. Jeff Stein, "9 Questions about the Democratic Socialists of America You Were Afraid to Ask," *Vox*, August 5, 2017; Doug Henwood, "The Socialist Moment: Inside DSA's Struggle to Move into the Political Mainstream," *New Republic*, May 16, 2019.

14. Frank Friedel, "The Old Populism and the New," *Proceedings of the Massachusetts Historical Society* 85 (1973): 78–90.

15. Chantal Mouffe, *For a Left Populism* (New York: Verso, 2019), 4–6, 22, 131–4; Steve Hilton, *Positive Populism: Revolutionary Ideas to Rebuild Economic Security, Family and Community in America* (New York: Crown Forum, 2018), 131–34, 178.

16. Kathleen Hall Jamieson and Joseph N. Cappella, *Echo Chamber: Rush Limbaugh and the Conservative Media Establishment* (New York: Oxford University Press, 2008), 18; Eli Pariser, *The Filter Bubble: How the New Personalized Web Is Changing What We Read and How We Think* (New York: Penguin Books, 2011), 88–9.

17. Benedict Anderson, *Imagined Communities: Reflections on the Origin and Spread of Nationalism* (London and New York: Verso Books, 1983), 1–36; Pariser, *The Filter Bubble*, 9–10.

18. Joshua A. Tucker, Yannis Theocharis, Margaret E. Roberts, and Pablo Barberá, "From Liberation to Turmoil: Social Media and Democracy," *Journal of Democracy* 28, no. 4 (October 2017): 46–59; Jay David Bolter, "Social Media Are Ruining Political Discourse," *Atlantic*, May 19, 2019.

19. Marshall McLuhan, "Electronics and the Changing Role of Print," *Audio-Visual Communication Review* 8, no. 5 (1960): 76.

20. Susan Douglas, *Listening in: Radio and the American Imagination* (Minneapolis: University of Minnesota Press, 2004), 5.

21. John Herrman, "Online, Everything is Alternative Media," *New York Times*, November 10, 2016.

22. Hunter S. Thompson, *Fear and Loathing on the Campaign Trail '72* (New York: Simon and Schuster, 1973), 3, 256.

23. See Google Ngram, https://books.google.com/ngrams/graph?content=politics +junkie%2C+political+junkie&year_start=1800&year_end=2000&corpus=15 &smoothing=3&share=&direct_url=t1%3B%2Cpolitics%20junkie%3B%2Cc0%3B .t1%3B%2Cpolitical%20junkie%3B%2Cc0#t1%3B%2Cpolitics%20junkie%3B %2Cc0%3B.t1%3B%2Cpolitical%20junkie%3B%2Cc0. Charted February 13, 2019.

24. Joseph S. Miller, *The Wicked Wine of Democracy* (Seattle: University of Washington Press, 2008), 3; Mary Alice Kellogg, "Washington's Star Stargazer," *New York*

Times, January 16, 1977; Bob Baker, "What's the Rush?," *Los Angeles Times*, January 20, 1991.

25. Russell Baker, "At Rope's End," *New York Times*, August 12, 1987; James Traub, "Inyourface the Nation," *New York Times Magazine*, September 20, 1998; Frank Rich, "The Weight of an Anchor," *New York Times Magazine*, May 19, 2002; Corey Kilgannon, "Watching the News, Not Reporting It," *New York Times*, April 16, 2010.

26. Richard Viguerie and David Franke, *America's Right Turn: How Conservatives Used New and Alternative Media to Take over America* (Chicago: Bonus Books, 2004); Tanni Hass, *Making It in the Political Blogosphere: America's Top Bloggers Share the Secrets to Success* (Cambridge, UK: The Lutterworth Press, 2011), loc. 245, 460, 513, 2,529, 2,948, 3,056–60, 3,200, Kindle.

27. Matthew Pressman, *On Press: The Liberal Values That Shaped the News* (Cambridge: Harvard University Press, 2018), 23–4; Paul Goodman, *Growing up Absurd: Problems of Youth in the Organized Society* (New York: New York Review of Books, 1972. Orig. 1956), loc. 635, Kindle.

28. Jon Schwarz, "I. F. Stone's One Weird Trick to Do Great Journalism," *Intercept*, May 7, 2015.

Chapter 1: The Political Newsletter

1. "PM Gets Another Stay: Marshall Field to Continue Publication Through April," *New York Times*, April 14, 1948; "The Daily Compass Ends Publication: Left Wing Paper Runs Out of Funds—Equipment Is Sold after Lamont Forecloses," *New York Times*, November 4, 1952; "Mrs. Anita Blaine Is Dead in Chicago: Daughter of C. H. McCormick Financed *The Compass*; Here Noted as Philanthropist," *New York Times*, February 13, 1954.

2. David M. Oshinsky, *A Conspiracy So Immense: The World of Joe McCarthy* (New York: Oxford University Press, 2005), 108–10, 182–95; Edwin R. Bayley, *Joe McCarthy and the Press* (Madison: University of Wisconsin Press, 1981); Victor S. Navasky, *Naming Names* (New York: Hill and Wang, 1980), 58–68; Myra McPherson, "The Secret War Against I. F. Stone," *Washington Post*, August 21, 1994; I. F. Stone, FBI File #37078, folders 21–30, Victor S. Navasky Papers, The Tamiment Library, New York University.

3. Marc Fisher, "Who Did Trump Borrow His Press Tactics from? Joe McCarthy," *Washington Post*, August 11, 2017; Walter Bernstein, *Inside Out: A Memoir of the Blacklist* (New York: Da Capo Press, 2000), 257.

4. Matthew Pressman, *On Press: The Liberal Values That Shaped the News* (Cambridge: Harvard University Press, 2018), 23, 113; Richard and Phyllis Kluger, *The Paper: The Life and Death of the New York Herald Tribune* (New York: Vintage Books, 1989), 276, 481.

5. Robert Cottrell, *Izzy: A Biography of I. F. Stone* (New Brunswick: Rutgers University Press, 1992), 68; Peter Osnos, "I. F. Stone, a Journalist's Journalist," *New York Times*, June 20, 1989; D. D. Guttenplan, *The Life and Times of I. F. Stone* (Evanston, IL: Northwestern University Press, 2012), 233–5.

6. George Seldes, *Tell the Truth and Run* (New York: Greenberg Press, 1953), 5, 273; William Dicke, "George Seldes Is Dead at 104; An Early, Fervent Press Critic," *New York Times*, July 3, 1995.

7. Myra McPherson, *"All Governments Lie": The Life and Times of Rebel Journalist I. F. Stone* (New York: Scribner's, 2004), 24; Andrew Patner, *I. F. Stone: A Portrait* (New York: Pantheon Books, 1988), 10; advertisement, *New York Times*, November 25, 1952.

8. Ralph Young, *Dissent: The History of an American Idea* (New York: NYU Press, 2015), 43–126; Jill Lepore, *These Truths: A History of the United States* (New York: W. W. Norton, 2018), 126.

9. For newsletters as a feature of the civil rights movement, see John Lewis and Michael D'Orso, *Walking with the Wind: A Memoir of the Movement* (New York: Simon and Schuster, 1998), 128, 249; for an early typewritten newsletter, see Rabbi Charles and Anna Mantinband to friends, typewritten newsletter (December 1954), box 2, folder 6, M327 Mantinband (Rabbi Charles) Papers, McCain Library, University of Southern Mississippi; Dario Fazzi, *Eleanor Roosevelt and the Anti-Nuclear Movement: The Voice of Conscience* (New York: Palgrave Macmillan, 2016), 16.

10. Martin Meeker, *Contacts Desired: Gay and Lesbian Communications and Community, 1940s–1970s* (Chicago: University of Chicago Press, 2006), 34, 44, 46, 54; Marcia Gallo, *Different Daughters: A History of the Daughters of Bilitis and the Rise of the Lesbian Rights Movement* (San Francisco: Seal Press, 2007), 18, 25, 154.

11. Douglass Cater, *The Fourth Branch of Government* (New York: Houghton Mifflin, 1959), 73.

12. Publications Director, Mattachine Society, Inc., *Mattachine Review*, no. 1 (January/February 1955).

13. McPherson, *"All Governments Lie,"* 65, 115; Max Holland, "I. F. Stone: Encounters with Soviet Intelligence," *Journal of Cold War Studies* 11, no. 3 (summer 2009): 177; I. F. Stone, "I. F. Stone Interviews I. F. Stone at 70," *New York Times*, January 22, 1978; Cottrell, *Izzy*, 87, and McGrory quote is from 6.

14. *I. F. Stone's Weekly* 1, no. 1 (January 17, 1953): 3.

15. Peter Dreier, "In Praise of I. F. 'Izzy' Stone," *Common Dreams*, June 18, 2019.

16. Dreier, "In Praise of I. F. 'Izzy' Stone."

17. *I. F. Stone's Weekly* 1, no. 2 (January 24, 1953): 3.

18. Eric Alterman, "The Ironies of Izzymania," *Mother Jones*, June 1988.

19. Patner, *I. F. Stone*, 10, 78–9, 99, 105; McPherson, *"All Governments Lie"*, 290, 331–3, quote is from 329; I. F. Stone, "I. F. Stone Interviews I. F. Stone at 70," *New York Times*, January 22, 1978; "Capsule Capitol Commentary," *I. F. Stone's Weekly*, February 14, 1953, 3; "Vital Statistics," *I. F. Stone's Weekly*, March 28, 1953.

20. "Claque on Capitol Hill," *I. F. Stone's Weekly*, April 4, 1953, 3.

21. Patner, *I. F. Stone*, 17; McPherson, *"All Governments Lie,"* 101–2, 115.

22. "Capsule Capitol Commentary," *I. F. Stone's Weekly*, February 14, 1953, 3; McPherson, *"All Governments Lie,"* 333; "Vital Statistics," *I. F. Stone's Weekly*, March 28, 1953.

23. "A Word to Our Readers," *Dissent* (winter 1954): 3; *Village Voice*, October 26, 1955, 1, 7.

24. Holland, "I. F. Stone," 183, 200; John McMillian, *Smoking Typewriters: The Sixties Underground Press and the Rise of Alternative Media in America* (New York: Oxford University Press, 2011), 33.

25. "Another Underground Triumph for Dr. Teller?," *I. F. Stone's Weekly*, January 12, 1959; Cottrell, *Izzy*, 202; "The Case History of Another Nuclear Deception," *I. F. Stone's Weekly*, March 2, 1959.

26. McPherson, "The Secret War against I. F. Stone," *Washington Post*, August 21, 1994.

27. Pressman, *On Press*, 32.

28. Seymour M. Hersh, *Reporter: A Memoir* (New York: Knopf, 2018), 43, 54, 61, 138–44.

29. Niraj Choksi, "Behind the Race to Publish the Secret Pentagon Papers," *New York Times*, December 20, 2017.

30. Neil Sheehan and Hedrick Smith, ed., *The Pentagon Papers: The Secret History of the Vietnam War* (New York: Quadrangle Books, 1971), xiv, xvii.

31. Eric Alterman, *What Liberal Media? The Truth about Bias and the News* (New York: Basic Books, 2003), 1–2; David Greenberg, *Nixon's Shadow: The History of an Image* (New York: W. W. Norton, 2004), 51, 158.

32. Lisa McGirr, *Suburban Warriors: The Origin of the New American Right* (Princeton, NJ: Princeton University Press, 2001), 95; Cas Mudde and Cristobal Rovira Kaltwasser, *Populism: A Very Short Introduction* (New York: Oxford University Press, 2017), 11.

33. Phyllis Schlafly, *A Choice Not an Echo* (Alton, IL: Pere Marquette Press, 1964), 107–10.

34. Nicole Hemmer, *Messengers of the Right*, 168–71.

35. Donald Critchlow, *Phyllis Schlafly and Grassroots Conservatism: A Woman's Crusade* (Princeton, NJ: Princeton University Press, 2005), 123–25; Marjorie Spruill, *Divided We Stand: The Battle over Women's Rights and Family Values That Polarized American Politics* (New York: Bloomsbury Press, 2017), 78–9.

36. McGirr, *Suburban Warriors*, 35–7; Kim Phillips-Fein, *Invisible Hands: The Businessman's Crusade against the New Deal* (New York: W. W. Norton, 2009), 67, 71.

37. Alan Brinkley, *Voices of Protest: Huey Long, Father Coughlin and the Great Depression* (New York: Vintage Books, 1983), 83, 95.

38. Alan F. Westin, "An Arsenal of Facts," *New York Times*, October 25, 1964.

39. Arnold Forster and Benjamin Epstein, *Danger on the Right* (New York: Random House, 1964), xvi–xvii; Alan F. Westin, "An Arsenal of Facts," *New York Times Sunday Book Review*, October 25, 1964.

40. Westin, "An Arsenal of Facts"; Forster and Epstein, *Danger on the Right*, 9, 112–14.

41. Dylan Byers, "National Review Goes Nonprofit," *Politico*, March 31, 2015; Forster and Epstein, *Danger on the Right*, 123–7, 130–1.

42. Forster and Epstein, *Danger on the Right*, 132–5, 142.

43. These stereotypes seem to have entered the national conversation in the wake of Nixon's defeat in the 1960 presidential campaign: see Stanley Mosk and Howard H. Jewel, "The Birch Phenomenon Analyzed," *New York Times Magazine*, August 20, 1961.

44. Forster and Epstein, *Danger on the Right*, 241–3.

45. Hemmer, *Messengers of the Right*, 76.

46. Forster and Epstein, *Danger on the Right*, 200–3, 230, 234; "Talk by Walker is Cancelled Here," *New York Times*, February 13, 1962.

47. Corey Robin, *The Reactionary Mind: Conservatism from Edmund Burke to Sarah Palin* (New York: Oxford University Press, 2011), loc. 140–53, Kindle.

48. Dan Smoot, *Dan Smoot Report* 10, no. 21 (broadcast #457), "Discrimination in Reverse," May 25, 1964. YouTube, www.youtube.com/watch?v=8eEBK9X0T00. Accessed April 21, 2019.

49. Dan Smoot, *The Invisible Government* (Dallas, TX: Dan Smoot, 1962), iv, 173.

50. McPherson, *"All Governments Lie,"* 191, 201; Schlafly, *A Choice Not an Echo,* 120.

51. Cottrell, *Izzy,* 227, 243, 259.

52. "Will New Chances for Peace Be Another Lost Opportunity?," *I. F. Stone's Weekly,* October 28, 1963.

53. Christopher Lyon, "I. F. Stone to Suspend 19-Year-Old Leftist Biweekly," *New York Times,* December 7, 1971; Jack Newfield, Nat Hentoff, I. F. Stone, and William L. Kunstler, "LNS," *New York Review of Books,* September 21, 1972.

54. I. F. Stone, "I. F. Stone Interviews I. F. Stone at 70," *New York Times,* January 22, 1978; Pressman, *On Press,* 191; Cottrell, *Izzy,* 261, 265–6, 283–5.

55. Aimai, "One Hundred Years of I. F. Stone," *If I Ran the Zoo,* November 17, 2008, http://tehipitetom.blogspot.com/2008/11/one-hundred-years-of-if-stone.html#0. Accessed September 21, 2019.

56. "Notes in Closing but Not in Farewell," *I. F. Stone's Bi-weekly,* December 21, 1971.

Chapter 2: Public Broadcasting

1. Interview with Robert MacNeil, September 11, 2019; in author's collection, 1.

2. Robert MacNeil, *The Right Place at the Right Time* (Boston: Little, Brown and Company, 1982), 3–5.

3. Interview with Robert MacNeil, 6; Joel Achenbach, "Did the News Media, Led by Walter Cronkite, Lose the War in Vietnam?," *Washington Post,* May 25, 2018.

4. Douglas Martin, "Walter Cronkite, 92, Dies; Trusted Voice of TV News," *New York Times,* July 17, 2009.

5. Robert MacNeil, *The People Machine: The Influence of Television on American Politics* (New York: Harper and Row, 1968), 66; interview with Robert MacNeil, 7.

6. Oscar Patterson III, "Television's Living Room War in Print: Vietnam in the News Magazines," *Journalism & Mass Communication Quarterly* 61, no. 1 (March 1, 1984): 35.

7. Charles Ponce de Leon, *That's the Way It Is: A History of Television News in America* (Chicago: University of Chicago Press, 2016), 97–99, 103–4, 108; Robert MacNeil, *The People Machine: The Influence of Television on American Politics* (New York: Harper and Row, 1968), 189, 219, 320; Alex Storozynski, "Fred Friendly, the High Road," *New York Daily News,* October 21, 1999; Steve Behrens, "Fred Friendly: A Tough Man, but My God, Full of Ideas," *Current,* March 16, 1998; Heather Hendershot, *Open to Debate: How William F. Buckley Put Liberal America on the Firing Line* (New York: Broadside Books, 2016), 140, 151–5, 200.

8. Howard Rosenberg, "MacNeil-Lehrer: Newsy-News," *Los Angeles Times,* July 4, 1978.

9. Matthew Pressman, *On Press: The Liberal Values That Shaped the News* (Cambridge: Harvard University Press, 2018), 186; Jeff Cohen, "The Legacy of I. F. Stone," (White Pine Pictures, 2015); "What Few Know about the Tonkin Bay Incidents," *I. F. Stone's Weekly,* August 24, 1964; Michael Schudson, *Discovering the News: A Social History of American Newspapers* (New York: Basic Books, 1978), 164; Newfield

paraphrase is from a quote in John McMillian, *Smoking Typewriters: The Sixties Underground Press and the Rise of Alternative Media in America* (New York: Oxford University Press, 2011), 84.

10. Ruth Marion-Baruch, Pirkle Jones, and Kathleen Cleaver, *Black Panthers, 1968* (Ann Arbor: Greybull Press, 2002), 14; Todd Gitlin, *The Whole World Is Watching: The Mass Media in the Making and Unmaking of the New Left* (Berkeley: University of California Press, 2003. Orig. 1992), 27–8.

11. Bill Ayers, *Fugitive Days: Memoirs of an Antiwar Activist* (Boston: Beacon Press, 2001), 166–7.

12. Gitlin, *The Whole World Is Watching*, 25–6.

13. McMillian, *Smoking Typewriters*, 82–5.

14. MacNeil, *The Right Place*, 204, 217–19, 228–9.

15. Nan Robertson, *The Girls in the Balcony: Women, Men and the New York Times* (New York: Random House, 1992), 130–31; Charlayne Hunter-Gault, *To the Mountaintop: My Journey through the Civil Rights Movement* (New York: The New York Times Company, 2012), 37; Art Sears Jr., "Lawyer Asks to Defend Hunter's Mixed Race Marriage in Georgia Court," *Jet*, September 19, 1963.

16. Gay Talese, *The Kingdom and the Power: Behind the Scenes at the New York Times, The Institution That Influences the World* (New York: Random House, 1969), 6.

17. Joe McGinnis, *The Selling of the President, 1968* (New York: Penguin Books, 1969), xi–xiv.

18. Roger Ailes, *You Are the Message: Getting What You Want by Being Who You Are* (New York: Doubleday, 1989), xiii.

19. David Greenberg, *Nixon's Shadow: The History of an Image* (New York: W. W. Norton, 2004), 137; McGinnis, *The Selling of the President*, 37.

20. McGinniss, *The Selling of the President*, 26–9, 39, 63, 123; Greenberg, *Nixon's Shadow*, 137–40.

21. Daniel J. Boorstin, *The Image: A Guide to Pseudo-Events in America* (New York: Atheneum Publishers, 1961), 9.

22. Interview with Robert MacNeil by author, 4–6.

23. Ponce de Leon, *That's the Way It Is*, 7, 60; MacNeil, *The People Machine*, 3, 12–13, 19, 30, 40, 58, 67.

24. Ponce de Leon, *That's the Way It Is*, xii.

25. Interviews with MacNeil by Don Carleton, Archive of American Television, Syracuse University, conducted on November 18, 2000 and May 15, 2001; interviews with MacNeil by Don Carleton; David Halberstam, *The Best and the Brightest* (New York, Random House, 1969), x, xiv, 46; Clarence R. Wyatt, *Paper Soldiers: The American Press and the Vietnam War* (Chicago: University of Chicago Press, 1993), 140, 200; Sydney Schanberg, "The Saigon Follies, or Trying to Head Them off at the Credibility Gap," *New York Times*, November 12, 1972.

26. Interview with Robert MacNeil by author, 18–19; MacNeil, *The Right Place*, 244.

27. MacNeil, *The People Machine*, ix, xiii, 191, 208, 223, 328.

28. Ponce de Leon, *That's the Way It Is*, 13; MacNeil, *The People Machine*, 96, 98, 100, 102, 110, 114.

29. MacNeil, *The Right Place*, 237, 239–40.

30. Ponce de Leon, *That's the Way It Is*, 51–2, 85, 89; MacNeil, *The People Machine*, 37, 59.

31. MacNeil, *The Right Place*, 185; Ponce de Leon, *That's the Way It Is*, 81; John J. O'Connor, "Want to Play Discredit the Press?," *New York Times*, January 7, 1973; Albin Krebs, "1971–72 Crisis in Broadcast Journalism, DuPont-Columbia U. Survey Reports," *New York Times*, February 14, 1973.

32. Greenberg, *Nixon's Shadow*, 99.

33. MacNeil, *The Right Place*, 279, 281, 283–4.

34. John J. O'Conner, "Want to Play Discredit the Press?"; MacNeil, *The Right Place*, 286.

35. Ponce de Leon, *That's the Way It Is*, 16–17, 110; interview with Jim Lehrer by Don Carleton, May 21, 2001, Archive of American Television, the Television Academy, Los Angeles, CA.

36. Interview with Jim Lehrer by Don Carleton.

37. "Covering Watergate: 40 Years Later with MacNeil and Lehrer," interview by Jeffrey Brown, *PBS NewsHour*, May 16, 2013.

38. MacNeil, *The Right Place*, 286–88.

39. Brown, "Covering Watergate."

40. MacNeil, *The Right Place*, 293, 298–9, 300–306; Ponce de Leon, *That's the Way It Is*, 67, 114–15.

41. MacNeil, *The Right Place*, 309.

42. "The Robert MacNeil Report," 1975–1976, Brown Media Archives and Peabody Award Collection, Television Archive, University of Georgia.

43. MacNeil, *The Right Place*, 311.

44. John J. O'Connor, "The 'MacNeil Report,'" *New York Times*, November 11, 1975.

45. "MacNeil Will Go National," *New York Times*, December 13, 1975; John Carmody, "The 'MacNeil Report' is Here," *Washington Post*, March 22, 1976; Rosenberg, "MacNeil-Lehrer: Newsy-News."

46. Henry Regnery, *Perfect Sowing: Reflections of a Bookman* (Wilmington, DE: ISI Books, 1999), 132–6.

Chapter 3: Creating Partisans

1. Alvin S. Felzenberg, *A Man and His Presidents: The Political Odyssey of William F. Buckley, Jr.* (New Haven: Yale University Press, 2017), 31, 152–3.

2. Leah M. Wright Rigueur, *The Loneliness of the Black Republican: Pragmatic Politics and the Pursuit of Power* (Princeton, NJ: Princeton University Press, 2016), 68–71; Rick Perlstein, *Before the Storm: Barry Goldwater and the Unmaking of the American Consensus* (New York: Nation Books, 2001), 223–5.

3. Critchlow, *Phyllis Schlafly and Grassroots Conservatism: A Woman's Crusade* (Princeton, NJ: Princeton University Press, 2005), 127; Lisa McGirr, *Suburban Warriors: The Origins of the New American Right* (Cambridge: Harvard University Press, 2001), 112–13, 135; William F. Buckley, "The Young Americans for Freedom," *National Review*, September 24, 1960; Perlstein, *Before the Storm*, 59–63.

4. Richard A. Viguerie, *The New Right: We're Ready to Lead* (Falls Church, VA: Viguerie Books, 1981), 72.

5. Morton C. Blackwell, "A Tribute to Paul Weyrich," *Leadership Institute*, October 6, 2015; Julian Zelizer, *Governing America: The Revival of Political History* (Princeton, NJ: Princeton University Press, 2012), 269.

6. Election administration assignments sheet; advertisement for WISN, November 1964, box 2, folder 5, Paul Weyrich Scrapbooks, Library of Congress, Washington, DC.

7. Walter Hixson, *Search for the American Right-Wing: An Analysis of the Social Science Record, 1955–1987* (Princeton, NJ: Princeton University Press, 1992), 211; Michael Kazin, *The Populist Persuasion: An American History* (Ithaca, NY: Cornell University Press, 1995), 248.

8. Irving Molotsky and Warren Weaver, Jr., "On Sin and Dissent," *New York Times*, July 18, 1986; *Globe* staff, "Interview with Paul Weyrich," *Boston Globe*, December 13, 1980.

9. Roger E. Wyman, "Agrarian or Working-Class Radicalism: The Electoral Basis of Populism in Wisconsin," *Political Science Quarterly* 89, no. 4 (winter 1974–1975): 835, 845–6; birth certificate, box 1, folder 1, PWS; typed worksheet, n.d., box 1, folder 1, PWS; Sara Diamond, *Spiritual Warfare: The Politics of the Christian Right* (Boston: South End Press, 1999), 56–79; "Circular Number 1, The Eagle Patrol," October 12, 1955; Ad Altare Dei folder, n.d., box 1, folder 1, PWS.

10. Ticket to the Senate Chamber; Lawrence Smith to PMW, June 29, 1953; box 1, folder 4, PWS; Governor Vernon W. Thomson to PMW, September 24, 1958; box 1, folder 5, PWS.

11. Eleanor J. Smith to PMW, November 19, 1958, box 1, folder 5, PWS; Racine *Journal Times*, May 8, 1959; "PMW, The Young Republican Creed," n.d., box 1, folder 5, PMW.

12. Andrea Friedman, *Citizenship in Cold War America: The National Security State and the Possibilities of Dissent* (Amherst and Boston: University of Massachusetts Press, 2014), 81–3.

13. David Oshinsky, *A Conspiracy So Immense: The World of Joe McCarthy* (New York: Oxford University Press, 2005), 151–5.

14. "Top Teen Announcer," *Milwaukee Sentinel*, July 3, 1959; Racine *Journal Times*, September 23, 1958, box 1, folder 5; debate roster, n.d., box 1, folder 3; St. Catherine's *Shield* (November 1959), box 1, folder 1, PWS.

15. Program for Young Republicans National Federation Fourth Annual Leadership Training School, January 17–22, 1960; photograph of PMW with Barry Goldwater, January 1960; *Varsity Voice*, n.d. [spring 1962], box 1, folder 6, PWS; Felzenberg, *A Man and His Presidents*, 133.

16. PMW, letter to the Railroad Club of Racine, June 19, 1962; Susan J. Douglas, *Listening: Radio and the American Imagination* (Minneapolis: University of Minnesota Press, 2004), 5.

17. Schadeberg to PMW, July 7, 1961, box 1, folder 7, PWS; Dennis W. Johnson, *Democracy for Hire: A History of American Political Consulting* (New York: Oxford University Press, 2017), 82–105.

18. *Milwaukee Sentinel*, June 22, 1961; Racine *Journal Times*, June 23, 1961; Kenosha *Evening—News*, June 23, 1961.

19. Racine *Journal Times*, January 9, 1962, February 6, 1962, March 9, 1962, March 11, 1962; Invitation, box 1, folder 7, PWS; Milwaukee *Journal*, March 11, 1962; Milwaukee *Journal*, March 11, 1962; *Sheboygan Press*, May 12, 1962; Kenosha *News*, May 14, 1962.

20. "YGOP Elects J.F. Rench," Racine *Journal Times*, January 22, 1963; "2 From Racine Help Form Cuban Liberation Group," Racine *Journal Times*, May 7, 1963; PMW to Fritz Rench, Chairman, Racine County YGOP, June 1, 1963, box 2, folder 1, PWS.

21. Advertisement for WAXO, n.d., Henry Schadeberg to PMW, October 24, 1962, box 1, folder 7, PWS; Photographs of Weyrich interviewing these politicians on March 9 and 23, 1963, box 2, folder 1, PWS.

22. William Proxmire to PMW, June 14, 1963; Schadeberg to PMW, June 17, 1963, box 2, folder 1, PWS.

23. Kenosha County press pass, 1963; flyer, n.d., Rae E. Krueger, program director of the Republican Party of Waukesha County to PMW, November 12, 1963; PMW to Roy Ambrose, December 6, 1963, box 2, folder 1, PWS; Catherine E. Rymph, *Republican Women: Feminism and Conservatism through the Rise of the New Right* (Chapel Hill: University of North Carolina Press, 2006), 59–60.

24. PMW to Sonneborn, October 16, 1964, box 2, folder 3; "WISN-TV Reporter Paul Weyrich Received Milwaukee Common Council Award," November 3, 1964, box 2, folder 5, PWS.

25. The Southwest Suburban Republican Club newsletter no. 18 (March 1965); "A Program of Interest at the Elm Grove Women's Club," April 13, 1965; *Glendale Republican Club Newsletter*, May 10, 1965, box 2, folder 6, PWS.

26. Viguerie, *The New Right*, 27–8.

27. Homer Bigart, "Cuba Crisis May Blunt Hard GOP Drive in Texas," *New York Times*, October 28, 1962.

28. Viguerie, *The New Right*, 28–30.

29. "The Star and Lamp of Pi Kappa Phi," May 1963, 4; Gregory L. Schneider, *Cadres for Conservatism: Young Americans for Freedom and the Rise of the Contemporary Right* (New York: New York University Press, 1999), 44.

30. John Farrell, *Richard Nixon: The Life* (New York: Vintage Books, 2017), 294–8.

31. Ithiel de Sola Pool, Robert Abelson, and Samuel Popkin, *Candidates, Issues and Strategies: A Computer Simulation of the 1960 Presidential Election* (Cambridge, MA: MIT Press, 1964), 2, 17, 24, 58.

32. De Sola Pool, Abelson, and Popkin, *Candidates, Issues and Strategies*, 10, 18, 20.

33. De Sola Pool, Abelson, and Popkin, *Candidates, Issues and Strategies*, 1.

34. Viguerie, *The New Right*, 32.

35. Andrew N. Case, "'The Solid Gold Mailbox': Direct Mail and the Changing Nature of Buying and Selling in the Post-war United States," *History of Retailing and Consumption* 1, no. 1 (2015): 28, 31.

36. Lester Wunderman, *Being Direct: Making Advertising Pay* (New York: Random House, 1996), 13–15.

37. Douglas Martin, "Robert Moon, an Inventor of the Zip Code, Dies at 83," *New York Times*, April 14, 2001.

38. Wunderman, *Being Direct*, 155–6; Devin Leonard, *Neither Snow nor Rain: A History of the United States Postal Service* (New York: Grove Press, 2017), 212–13.

39. Emily Langer, "Lester Wunderman, Advertising Executive Who Perfected Direct Marketing, Dies at 98," *Washington Post*, January 15, 2019; Wunderman, *Being Direct*, 164–66.

40. Langer, "Lester Wunderman, Advertising Executive Who Perfected Direct Marketing, Dies at 98"; Elizabeth Kolbert, "Technology Brought in to Add Personal Touch," *New York Times*, June 9, 1992.

41. Michael MacDonald, "National General Election VEP Turnout Rates, 1789–Present," United States Elections Project, www.electproject.org/national-1789-present. Accessed July 29, 2019.

42. Ray E. Hiebert, Robert F. Jones, John d'Arc Lorenz, and Ernest Lotito, *The Political Image Merchants: Strategies for the Seventies* (Washington, DC: Acropolis Books, 1975), 21–23.

43. Case, "'The Solid Gold Mailbox,'" 33; Viguerie, *The New Right*, 33–4.

44. Blackwell, "A Tribute to Paul Weyrich"; Nancy MacLean, *Democracy in Chains: The Deep History of the Radical Right's Stealth Plan for America* (New York: Penguin Books, 2018), xxi, 174.

45. Jennifer S. Butler, *Born Again: The Christian Right Globalized* (London: Pluto Press, 2006), 160–61.

46. Craig Allen Smith, "Leadership, Orientation and Rhetorical Vision: Jimmy Carter, 'The New Right,' and the Panama Canal," *Presidential Studies Quarterly* 16, no. 2 (spring 1986): 318–19.

47. Rick Perlstein, "The Long Con: Mail Order Conservatism," *Baffler*, no. 21 (2012): 22–32.

48. Paul Weyrich, "The White House, the Elections and the Right," and Richard Viguerie, "An Open Letter to President Reagan," *Conservative Digest* (July 1982), 45–7.

49. Bill Peterson, "For Reagan and the New Right, the Honeymoon Is Over," *Washington Post*, July 21, 1981.

50. Richard A. Viguerie to President-elect Ronald Reagan, January 14, 1981; Gregory J. Newell to RAV, February 5, 1981; Viguerie, box 6, Ronald Reagan to Roy Brewer, November 17, 1983; Viguerie (7), RR to RAV, May 30, 1984; Viguerie, box 6, RRPL.

51. Viguerie, *The Establishment vs. The People*, iv, 1, 10, 27.

52. Viguerie, *The Establishment vs. The People*, 111–13, 115–16, 153.

53. Viguerie, *The Establishment vs. The People*, 181, 234–5, 237.

54. Kathy Sawyer, "Linking Religion and Politics," *Washington Post*, August 24, 1980; Paul Weyrich, remarks delivered to the Religious Roundtable, August 1980, YouTube, www.youtube.com/watch?v=8GBAsFwPglw. Accessed June 18, 2019. For "goo-goo" as a way of mocking Republican reformers, see Kevin Murphy, *Political Manhood: Red Bloods, Mollycoddles, and the Politics of Progressive Era Reform* (New York: Columbia University Press, 2008), 3, 39, 64.

55. Viguerie, *The New Right*, 1, 4, 6.

Chapter 4: Electronic Democracy

1. "Apple 1984 Super Bowl Commercial Introducing Macintosh Computer" (Chiat /Day: dir. Ridley Scott, 1983).

2. "Steve Jobs Presenting the First Mac in 1984," January 24, 1984, YouTube; uploaded by bavaritalian, October 6, 2011, www.youtube.com/watch?v=8bepz UM1x3w. Accessed September 28, 2019.

3. Julian Zelizer and Kevin Kruse, *Fault Lines: A History of the United States Since 1974* (New York: W. W. Norton, 2019), 14–17.

4. Carol Doherty, Jocelyn Kiley, and Bridget Johnson, "Public Trust in Government Remains Near Historic Lows as Partisan Attitudes Shift," Pew Research Center, May 3, 2017.

5. Milton Lodge and Ruth Hamill, "A Partisan Schema for Political Information Processing," *American Political Science Review* 80, no. 2 (June 1986): 505–20.

6. Bernard Weinraub, "Reagan, Taking 49 states and 59% of Vote, Vows to Stress Arms Talks and the Economy," *New York Times*, November 8, 1984; Arnold Sawislak, "1984 Voter Turnout up Slightly, but Down after TV Projections," United Press International, November 11, 1984.

7. Jack Pittman, "But Who's Watching 'Big Brother'?," *Variety*, June 15, 1983; David Gelman, "Slouching Towards 1984," *Newsweek*, February 21, 1983; Gregory N. Joseph, "USD Professor Says Orwell Based His Warning on Hope," *San Diego Tribune*, December 8, 1983; Rita Calvano, "Few Believe Big Brother Is Watching: Orwell's '1984' Still Considered a Work of Fiction," *San Diego Tribune*, December 29, 1983.

8. Heinz C. Luegenbiehl, "'1984' and the Power of Technology," *Social History and Practice* 10, no. 3 (fall 1984): 289–300.

9. James Poniewozick, *Audience of One: Donald Trump, Television and the Fracturing of America* (New York: Liveright Publishing Company, 2019), 146.

10. Evan Comen, "Check out How Much a Computer Cost the Year You Were Born," *USA Today*, June 22, 2018.

11. Edward Snowden, *Permanent Record* (New York: Metropolitan Books, 2019), 44.

12. Heather McPherson, "Who Kicked off the Tradition," *Orlando Sentinel*, February 2, 2005; "Apple '1984' Sledgehammer Startles TV-viewing Nation," *Philadelphia Inquirer*, January 28, 1984.

13. "Macintosh 1984 Promotional Video," YouTube, https://youtu.be/-5zeJyQ31rM; "Bill Gates, Computer Standard in 1984," YouTube, https://youtu.be/Uau0aIbrzkQ. Accessed June 21, 2019; Thomas C. Hayes, "Strong Sales Seen in '84 for Apple's Macintosh," *New York Times*, February 25, 1984.

14. Snowden, *Permanent Record*, 106.

15. Fred Turner, *From Counterculture to Cyberculture: Stewart Brand, the Whole Earth Network and the Rise of Digital Utopianism* (Chicago: University of Chicago Press, 2006), 104–5, 117, 131, 213; Heathkit Company catalogue (fall 1978): 66; "What You See Is Pretty Close to What You Get: New Pagination Program for IBM PC," *Seybold Report on Publishing Systems* (February 13, 1984): 21–2; Kate Eichorn, *Adjusted Margin: Xerography, Art, and Activism in the Late Twentieth Century* (Cambridge, MA: MIT Press, 2016).

16. Reuters, "Fast IIc Plus Computer Is Introduced by Apple," *New York Times*, September 17, 1988.

17. Michael Banks, *On the Way to the Web: The Secret History of the Internet and Its Founders* (New York: Apress, 2008), 29–35; Bloomberg News, "America Online Stock Advances by 14%," *New York Times*, January 29, 1994.

18. Mark Nollinger, "America, Online!," *Wired*, September 1, 1995; "Times Raises Price for Sunday Paper," *New York Times*, March 22, 1995.

19. Marshall T. Poe, *A History of Communications: Media and Society from the Evolution of Speech to the Internet* (New York and Cambridge: Cambridge University Press, 2011), 245, 263; Turner, *From Counterculture to Cyberculture*, 213; Mike Godwin, "Technologies of Freedom," *Whole Earth Review*, December 1994.

20. "Cable News Subscribers by Channel," Pew Research Center, March 12, 2007; Bill Carter, "With America Well Wired, Cable Industry Is Changing," *New York Times*, July 9, 1989.

21. Gabriel Sherman, *The Loudest Voice in the Room: How the Brilliant, Bombastic Roger Ailes Built Fox News—and Divided a Country* (New York: Random House, 2014), 167–8, 175, 185.

22. Benj Edwards, "The Lost Civilization of Dial-up Bulletin Board Systems," *Atlantic*, November 4, 2016.

23. Turner, *From Counterculture to Cyberculture*, 131–2, 146; Christine Lagorio-Chafkin, *We Are the Nerds: The Birth and Tumultuous Life of Reddit, the Internet's Culture Laboratory* (New York: Hachette Books, 2018), 74–6.

24. Poniewozik, *Audience of One*, 147.

25. Charles Ponce de Leon, *That's the Way It Is: A History of Television News in America* (Chicago: University of Chicago Press, 2016), 127; Peter Stark, "Something Else," *San Francisco Chronicle*, January 19, 1991.

26. Wolfgang Saxon, "Ted Turner, 66; Helped Build 24 Hour News," *New York Times*, April 2, 2001; N. R. Kleinfeld, "Making 'News on the Cheap' Pay Off," *New York Times*, April 19, 1987; Ponce de Leon, *That's the Way It Is*, 233; Lionel van Deerlin, "'Sixty Minutes' Clock Stops," *San Diego Tribune*, October 4, 1984; "Judge Refuses Dentist Plea to Block 'Sixty Minutes,'" *Chicago Tribune*, December 26, 1987.

27. Quoted in Fred Turner, *From Counterculture to Cyberculture*, 117.

28. Fred Turner, *From Counterculture to Cyberculture*, 3–6, 80–81, 104; Katie Hafner, *The Well: A Story of Love, Death and Real Life in the Seminal Online Community* (New York: Carroll & Graf, 2001), 109.

29. Turner, *From Counterculture to Cyberculture*, 183, 281.

30. "Pages Created or Hosted by Members of the WELL," *Internet Archive*, https://web.archive.org/web/19961103044513/www.well.com/community/. Accessed July 18, 2018; Charles Bowen and David Peyton, *The Complete Electronic Bulletin Board Starter Kit* (Des Plaines, IL: Bantam Books/Direct Sales, 1989), reviewed by Robert Horvitz in *Whole Earth Review*, June 1991; Dan Perkins, "Reader Alert for residents of Chicago, Washington DC, Los Angeles and Miami," *WELL*, October 21, 1998, *Internet Archive*. https://web.archive.org/web/19990508192705/www.WELL.com/user/tomorrow/. Accessed July 17, 2018.

31. "Feminism and Free Speech: The Internet," Feminists for Free Expression, *Internet Archive*, https://web.archive.org/web/19981205014100/www.well.com/user/freedom/. Accessed July 14, 2018.

32. Betsy Culp, "Chip Shots," *SF Flier*, May 28, 1999. https://web.archive.org/web/20010114103000/www.well.com/user/sfflier/jeopardy-slippage-chip.html#anchor465433. Accessed July 17, 2018.

33. Howard Rheingold, *The Virtual Community: Homesteading on the Electronic Frontier* (Menlo Park, CA: Addison-Wesley Publishing Company, 1993), 43.

34. Hafner, *The Well*, 18, 41; Turner, *From Counterculture to Cyberculture*, 132–3; Sally Gearheart, "Questioning Technology," *Whole Earth Review*, March 1, 1989.

35. Lorenzo Milam, "The Real, Honest, True Deregulation of Broadcasting," *Whole Earth Review*, October 1990.

36. Duane Elgin, "Conscious Democracy through Electronic Town Meetings," *Whole Earth Review*, June 1991; Robert F. Larson, "Public TV and Community Service," *Broadcasting*, December 14, 1987.

37. Horvitz review of *The Complete Electronic Bulletin Board Starter Kit*; Barry Horstman, "High-Tech Linkup to Add Far-flung Look to Meetings of San Diego Supervisors," *Los Angeles Times*, July 27, 1987; Michele Wittig, "Electronic City Hall," *Whole Earth Review*, June 1991.

38. Rheingold, *Virtual Community*, 255–58, 264–5.

39. Howard Rheingold, "Electronic Democracy," *Whole Earth Review*, June 1991.

40. Howard Rheingold, "Politics," *Whole Earth Review*, March 1991.

41. Brock N. Meeks, "The Global Commons," *Whole Earth Review*, spring 1991.

42. Kevin Kelly, "Soros Backs Media Revolution," *Wired*, April 1, 1993.

43. Howard Rheingold, "Civic Networking: If You Had an Information Highway, Where Would You Go?," *Whole Earth Review*, March 1994; Clay Shirky, *Here Comes Everybody: The Power of Organizing without Organizations* (New York: Penguin Press, 2008), 21–22.

44. Kristin Spence, "Getting Wired on Capitol Hill: Charlie Rose and the New Digital Democrats," *Wired*, February 1, 1993; David Kupfer, "Jerry Brown Committed," *Whole Earth Review*, January 1995.

45. Robert Putnam, "Bowling Alone: America's Declining Social Capital," *Journal of Democracy* 6, no. 1 (1995): 65–7.

46. Robert Putnam, *Bowling Alone: The Collapse and Revival of American Community* (New York: Simon and Schuster, 2000), 38–9, 46, 344.

Chapter 5: Scandal

1. Matthew Drudge, "Newsweek Kills Story on White House Intern x x x x x Blockbuster Report: 23-Year Old, Former White House Intern, Sex Relationship with President," *Drudge Report*, January 17, 1998, www.drudgereportarchives.com/data/2002/01/17/20020117_175502_ml.htm. Accessed October 6, 2019.

2. Drudge, "Newsweek Kills Story."

3. Greg Price, "After Bill and Monica, Drudge Report Continued with Scoops Almost as Big for Twenty Years," *Newsweek*, January 13, 2018.

4. Andrew Morton, *Monica's Story* (New York: Macmillan, 1999), 17–18, 94–101.

5. McKenzie Wark, *A Hacker Manifesto* (Cambridge: Harvard University Press, 2004), 2–7.

6. When I asked if he had leaked his own story Michael Isikoff replied: "Everything I know I put in the book"; email from Isikoff to author, October 6, 2019. For an account of Drudge's visit to *Newsweek* and his conversation with Isikoff, see 146–9; and for an account of Isikoff's contact with Goldberg and Moody after the story was spiked, see 337. For "The Elves" and for George Conway's prior connection to Drudge, see Ben Terris, "George Conway Is the Man at the Center of Everything," *Washington Post*, May 14, 2017.

7. Phone conversation, Ryan Girdusky, October 6, 2019.

8. Matt Drudge, *Drudge Manifesto* (New York: New American Library, 1998), 25–6.

9. Felicity Barringer, "What Hath Drudge Wrought?," *New York Times*, March 8, 1999.

10. Susan B. Glasser, *Covering Politics in Post-Truth America* (Washington, DC: Brookings Institution Press, 2016), 14.

11. Drudge, *Drudge Manifesto*, 27.

12. Tribute to Doug Bailey, *Congressional Record* 159, no. 86 (Senate—June 17, 2013); Breanna Edwards, "Hotline Founder Doug Bailey Dies," *Politico*, June 10, 2013; Glasser, *Covering Politics in Post-Truth America*, 14.

13. Matt Drudge, "Pop Music Is Back," *Wired*, November 12, 1996; "Chelsea Meets Butt-head," *Wired*, November 18, 1996; "Oprah vs. Rosie for the Oscars," November 18, 1996.

14. Byron York, "The Life and Death of the American Spectator," *Atlantic*, November 2001.

15. *Drudge Report*, December 7, 1997; Matt Drudge, "Internet President Finally Logs On," *Wired*, April 18, 1997.

16. *Drudge Report*, December 7, 1997; *Internet Archive*, https://web.archive.org/web/19971210093544/www.drudgereport.com/. Accessed September 5, 2018.

17. Arianna Huffington, "Frightening Words: 'President Gore,'" reprinted in *SFGate*, October 16, 1997.

18. Drudge, *Drudge Manifesto*, 55–62.

19. Neal Gabler, *Walter Winchell: Gossip, Power and the Culture of Celebrity* (New York: Vintage Books, 1995), 207–209; 275–80.

20. Gabler, *Walter Winchell*, 130; William H. Chafe, *Bill and Hillary: The Politics of the Personal* (New York: Farrar, Straus and Giroux, 2012), 174.

21. Michael Isikoff, *Uncovering Clinton: A Reporter's Story* (New York: Crown, 1999), xv.

22. Eric Alterman, *What Liberal Media? The Truth about Bias and the News* (New York: Basic Books, 2003), 141–2.

23. Matt Bai, *All the Truth Is Out: The Week Politics Went Tabloid* (New York: Vintage Books, 2014), 32–5, 120.

24. Critchlow, *Phyllis Schlafly and Grassroots Conservatism*, 295; Jeffrey B. Gaynor, *The Contract with America: Implementing New Ideas in the U.S.* (Washington, DC: The Heritage Foundation, October 12, 1995); Rick Perlstein, "How Wily Newt Pulled the 'Contract with America' Scam," *Rolling Stone*, January 26, 2012.

25. Julian Zelizer and Kevin Kruse, *Fault Lines*, 204–14; Oral history of Alice Rivlin, Budget Director, interviewed December 13, 2002, Presidential Oral Histories, Bill Clinton Presidency, The Miller Center, University of Virginia.

26. David Shedden, "New Media Timeline," Poynter Institute, www.poynter.org/archive/2004/new-media-timeline-1980/. Accessed October 1, 2019. Peter H. Lewis, "The New York Times Introduces a Website," *New York Times*, January 22, 1996; "The Los Angeles Times' History," *Los Angeles Times*, September 21, 2012; Dave Kindred, *Morning Miracle: Inside the Washington Post; A Great Newspaper Fights for Its Life* (New York: Anchor Books, 2011), 50.

27. Steve Silberman, "A Portal to the Heart," *Wired*, July 1, 1998.

28. Catherine McKercher, "Computers and Reporters: Newsroom Practices at Two Canadian Daily Newspapers," *Canadian Journal of Communication* 20, no. 2 (1995), https://cjc-online.ca/index.php/journal/article/view/867/773. Accessed January 6, 2020.

29. McKercher, "Computers and Reporters"; David Corn, "Cyberlibel and the White House," *Nation*, January 12/19, 1998; Denise Caruso, "The Law and the Internet Beware," *Columbia Journalism Review*, May/June 1998.

30. Alicia C. Shepard, "The Incredible Shrinking News Cycle," *The World & I* 13, no. 6 (June 1998), 80–85; Caitlin Anderson, "Can Traditional Media Compete with the New Kids on the Block?," *Nieman Reports* (winter 1998).

31. Janet Wiscombe, "What Hath the Web Wrought?," *Los Angeles Times*, August 6, 1988; Charles Laurence, "Drudging the Rumor Mill," *Ottawa Citizen*, August 24, 1998.

32. "Matt Drudge Brings Internet Report to TV," *Charleston Gazette*, June 26, 1998; David Hinkley, "With Drudge, Hats All Folks!," *New York Daily News*, June 28, 1998.

33. Bill Kovach, "Public Pressure for a Responsible Press," *Nieman Reports* (winter 1998).

34. Morton, *Monica's Story*, 342.

35. David Karpf, *The MoveOn Effect: The Unexpected Transformation of American Political Advocacy* (New York: Oxford University Press, 2012), 10.

36. Karpf, *The MoveOn Effect*, 27; Katie Hafner, "Online Petition Solicits Outrage at Congress," *New York Times*, September 24, 1998.

37. "Censure and Move On," MoveOn.org, screenshot from December 12, 1998, *Internet Archive Wayback Machine*, http://web.archive.org/web/1998 1212015742/http://moveon.org/. Accessed October 5, 2019.

38. Eric C. Newburger, "Home Computers and Internet Use in the United States, August 2000," United States Department of Commerce (Washington, DC: Government Printing Office, 2001); "The Internet News Audience Goes Ordinary: Online Newcomers More Middlebrow, Less Work Oriented," Pew Research Center, January 14, 1999.

39. Neil Selwyn and Kate Robson, "Using Email as a Research Tool," *Social Research Update* (summer 1998); Katie Hafner, "Online Petition Solicits Outrage at Congress"; Deborah Fallows, "Email at Work: Few Feel Overwhelmed and Most Are Pleased with the Way Email Helps Them Do Their Jobs," *Pew Internet & American Life Project*, December 8, 2002.

40. Gabriel Sherman, *The Loudest Voice in the Room: How the Brilliant, Bombastic Roger Ailes Built Fox News—and Divided a Country* (New York: Random House, 2014), 225.

41. Monica Lewinsky, "Roger Ailes's Dream Was My Nightmare," *New York Times*, May 22, 2017; Morton, *Monica's Story*, 342; Kovach, "Public Pressure for a Responsible Press."

42. "Matt Drudge at the National Press Club," C-SPAN, June 2, 1991, www.c-span.org/video/?c4455026/matt-drudge-national-press-club. Accessed March 3, 2018; Drudge, *Drudge Manifesto*, 25.

43. David Carr, "How Drudge Stays on Top," *New York Times*, May 15, 2011.

44. Henry Blodgett, "It's Time People Realized That the Drudge Report Is a Major Media Property Worth Hundreds of Millions of Dollars," *Business Insider*, October 10, 2012.

45. Ryan Holiday, *Conspiracy: Peter Thiel, Hulk Hogan, and the Anatomy of Intrigue* (New York: Portfolio/Penguin, 2018), 15, 20.

Chapter 6: Netroots

1. Alison Mitchell, "With 'Patriotic Challenge' McCain Makes Run Official," *New York Times*, September 8, 1999; Thomas B. Edsall, "Buchanan Bolts GOP for Reform Party," *Washington Post*, October 26, 1999; "Senator John McCain Attacks Pat Robertson, Jerry Falwell, Republican Establishment as Harming GOP Ideals," CNN transcript, February 28, 2000.

2. Anthony Ramirez, "McCain's Ethnic Slur: Gone, but Not Quite Forgotten," *New York Times*, March 5, 2000; C. W. Nevius, Marc Sandalow, and John Wildermuth, "McCain Criticized for Slur: Says He'll Keep Using Term for Ex-captors in Vietnam," *San Francisco Chronicle*, February 18, 2000; Ian Haney-Lopez, *Dog Whistle Politics: How Coded Racial Appeals Have Reinvented Racism and Wrecked the Middle Class* (New York: Oxford University Press, 2015), 3–5.

3. Alison Mitchell, "By Opening up, McCain Gets His Message Out," *New York Times*, December 25, 1999.

4. Bob Somerby, "They'll Have Fun, Fun, Fun," *Daily Howler*, February 25, 2000, www.dailyhowler.com/h022500_1.shtml. Accessed January 18, 2019.

5. Declan McCullagh, "McCain on the Stump, on the Web," *Wired*, June 8, 1999.

6. Lindsey Arent, "Let the Mudslinging Begin," *Wired*, October 25, 1999.

7. Alison Mitchell, "Fate of McCain Campaign Today Rests on Today's Vote," *New York Times*, February 1, 2000.

8. Mike McCurry, "Straight Talk Is Overrated," *New York Times*, March 14, 2000.

9. Dan Nowicki and Bill Muller, "John McCain's 2000 Presidential Run Saw Challenges, 'Ugly' Politics," *Arizona Republic*, April 2, 2018, originally October 1999; Pew Research Center, "New Audiences Increasingly Politicized," June 8, 2004; Somerby, "They'll Have Fun, Fun, Fun," *Daily Howler*, February 25, 2000, www.dailyhowler.com/h022500_1.shtml. Accessed on January 18, 2019.

10. Robert Draper, *Dead Certain: The Presidency of George W. Bush* (New York: Free Press, 2008), 72–3.

11. Richard Gooding, "The Trashing of John McCain," *Vanity Fair*, November 2004.

12. Charlotte Moore, "Click the Vote: From Gore's Town Hall E-meetings to Bush's Tax Calculator, the Presidential Candidates Are Finding the Web a More Personal Way to Connect with People," *American Statesman*, October 20, 2000.

13. "Senate Campaign Expenditures: Major Party General Election Candidates, 1974–2016," Table 2, The Campaign Finance Institute, www.cfinst.org/data/historicalStats.aspx. Accessed October 3, 2019.

14. Gary Hart, *The Thunder and the Sunshine: Four Seasons in a Burnished Life* (Golden, CO: Fulcrum Publishing, 2010), 44; Susan Yoachum, "At the Other End of Brown's 800 Line," *San Francisco Chronicle*, April 2, 1992.

15. Dennis W. Johnson, *Democracy for Hire: A History of American Political Consulting* (New York: Oxford University Press, 2017), 334–5.

16. David Karpf, *The MoveOn Effect: The Unexpected Transformation of American Political Advocacy* (New York: Oxford University Press, 2012), 14.

17. Don Van Natta, Jr., "McCain Gets Big Payoff on Website," *New York Times*, February 4, 2000.

18. Henry C. Kenski, "The Rebels Revolt and the Empires Strike Back: A Tale of Two Insurgencies in the Presidential Nominations of 2000," in *The 2000 Presidential Campaign*, ed. Robert E. Denton Jr. (Westport, CT: Praeger Press, 2000), 53; David Corn, "The McCain Insurgency," *Nation*, February 10, 2000.

19. Alison Mitchell, "The Maverick: Fate of McCain Campaign Rests on Today's Vote," *New York Times*, February 1, 2000; Van Natta, Jr., "Courting Web-Head Cash," *New York Times*, February 4, 2000; Thomas Streeter, "Redefining the Possible," in *Mousepads, Shoe Leather and Hope: Lessons from the Howard Dean Campaign for the Future of Internet Politics*, eds. Zephyr Teachout and Thomas Streeter (New York: Routledge, 2007), 3.

20. David Foster Wallace, "The Weasel, Twelve Monkeys and the Shrub," *Rolling Stone*, April 13, 2000.

21. Joe Trippi, *The Revolution Will Not Be Televised: Democracy, the Internet and the Overthrow of Everything* (New York: HarperCollins, 2004), loc. 1,273, Kindle.

22. David Weinberger, *Small Pieces Loosely Joined: A Unified Theory of the Web* (New York: Basic Books, 2003), 100; Astra Taylor, *The People's Platform: Taking Back Power and Culture in the Digital Age* (New York: Henry Holt, 2014), 14.

23. Trippi, *The Revolution Will Not Be Televised*, loc. 344, Kindle.

24. Trippi, *The Revolution Will Not Be Televised*, loc. 396–414, Kindle.

25. Trippi, *The Revolution Will Not Be Televised*, loc. 440, 463, Kindle; Markoff, *What the Dormouse Said*, 58–68; Trippi, *The Revolution Will Not Be Televised*, loc. 430–71, Kindle.

26. Trippi, *The Revolution Will Not Be Televised*, loc. 634–62, Kindle.

27. Trippi, *The Revolution Will Not Be Televised*, loc. 829, Kindle.

28. Trippi, *The Revolution Will Not Be Televised*, loc. 543, 467, Kindle; Matt Bai, *All the Truth Is Out: The Week Politics Went Tabloid* (New York: Vintage Books, 2014), 129; Howard Rheingold, "Are Virtual Communities Harmful to Civil Society?," "Tomorrow" thread, The WELL, last modified September 4, 1995, www.well.com/~hlr/tomorrow/vccivil.html. Accessed January 23, 2017.

29. Trippi, *The Revolution Will Not Be Televised*, loc. 1,177, Kindle.

30. Jon Margolis, "Howard's End," *New York Times*, February 19, 2004; Howard Dean, "Health Care That Will Work," *New York Times*, August 20, 1993; Bob Zelnick, *Gore: A Political Life* (Washington, DC: Regnery Publishing, 1999), 361; Carey Goldberg, "No, Says Vermont Chief, He Is No Gore Threat (Yet)," *New York Times*, December 12, 1997.

31. David Wallis, "Questions for Howard Dean: Is It 2004 Yet?," *New York Times*, July 14, 2002; Trippi, *The Revolution Will Not Be Televised*, loc. 1,570, Kindle.

32. Eric Boehlert, *Bloggers on the Bus: How the Internet Changed Politics and the Press* (New York: The Free Press, 2009), 48; Daniel Kreiss, *Taking Our Country Back: The Crafting of Networked Politics from Howard Dean to Barack* Obama (New York: Oxford University Press, 2012), 6, 33–60; Ryan Lizza, "Dean.com," *New Republic*, June 2, 2003.

33. Michael Powell, "Dean a Tax-and-Spend Liberal? Hardly," *Washington Post*, August 3, 2003.

34. Lizza, "Dean.com"; Linda, "Get Active: U.S. Representative David Price at Town Meeting on the Federal Budget," *Deaniacs* blog, http://deaniacs.blogspot.com /2003/08/,

August 7, 2007. Accessed August 5, 2019.

35. Jeff Howe, "What Were They Thinking?," *Wired*, August 1, 2005; Robert Mac-Neil, *The People Machine: The Influence of Television on American Politics* (New York: Harper and Row, 1968), 133; for Facebook data collection, see email with Julian Zelizer, in author's notes, July 17, 2019.

36. Pam Paul, "Experiences of a Grassroots Activist," in *Mousepads, Shoe Leather and Hope: Lessons from the Howard Dean Campaign for the Future of Internet Politics*, eds. Zephyr Teachout and Thomas Streeter (New York: Routledge, 2007), 130–46.

37. Kreiss, *Taking Our Country Back*, 9.

38. Howe, "What Were They Thinking?," *Wired*, August 1, 2005.

39. Clay Shirky, *Here Comes Everyone: The Power of Organizing without Organizations* (New York: Penguin Books, 2009), 86–7, 158.

40. Streeter and Teachout, "Interview with Howard Dean," January 25 and March 6, 2007, in *Mouse Pads, Shoe Leather and Hope*, 19; Streeter and Teachout, "Theories: Technology, the Grassroots, and Network Generativity," in *Mouse Pads, Shoe Leather and Hope*, 27.

41. Streeter and Teachout, "Interview with Howard Dean," 18.

42. "The Dean Activists: Their Profile and Prospects," Pew Research Center, April 6, 2005; Bart Cammaerts, "Critiques on the Participatory Potential of the Blogosphere," *Communication, Culture and Critique* 1, no. 4 (2008): 10.

43. "Road Trippi," campaign blog, May 16, 2003, http://deancalltoaction .blogspot.com/2003_05_11_archive.html. Accessed February 5, 2016.

44. Robert Robb, "Understanding the Dean Phenomenon," *Arizona Republic*, February 20, 2004.

45. Robb, "Understanding the Dean Phenomenon"; Zephyr Teachout, "Something Bigger Than a Candidate," in *Mouse Pads, Shoe Leather and Hope*, 56; Jerome Armstrong, "How a Blogger and the Dean Campaign Discovered Each Other," in *Mouse Pads, Shoe Leather and Hope*, 39.

46. Jim Ruttenberg, "Distrust of Media Takes a Role in Campaigns," *New York Times*, October 12, 2003; Steve Carney, "In Rush Limbaugh's World He's Always Right," *Los Angeles Times*, August 1, 2003.

47. Email from Juan Cole to author, August 5, 2019; in the author's collection.

48. Glen Justice, "Mix of Donors adds to Dean Coffers," *New York Times*, October 2, 2003.

49. Ginia Bellafante, "Footwear Politics; Just Who, Really, Is a Birkenstock Voter?," *New York Times*, October 5, 2003.

50. Bellafante, "Footwear Politics."

51. Glen Justice, "Dean Rejects Public Financing in Primaries," *New York Times*, November 9, 2003; Adam Nagourney and Jodi Wilgoren, "Gore to Endorse Dean; Remaking Democratic Race," *New York Times*, December 9, 2003.

52. "The Dean Scream: What Really Happened," a short film directed by Bryan Storkel (produced by *FiveThirtyEight* and ESPN), *FiveThirtyEight*, February 4, 2016.

53. "The Dean Scream: What Really Happened."

54. Blake Morrison, "Dean Scream Gaining Cult-like Status on Web," *USA Today*, January 22, 2004.

55. Jodi Wilgoren, "In Second Defeat, Dean Lowers Volume as Crowd Roars," *New York Times*, January 28, 2004.

56. Jodi Wilgoren, "The Doctor Makes a Visit to Aid His Own Ailing Campaign," *New York Times*, February 8, 2004.

57. Annette Marotta, "A Contest and a Debt," Letters to the Editor, *New York Times*, February 20, 2004.

58. "Wisconsin Marks End of Line for Dean," CNN.com, February 18, 2004; Bob Kelleher, "Howard Dean's Last Stand," *Minnesota Public Radio*, February 10, 2004.

59. Juan Williams, "What Happened to Howard Dean?," NPR.org, February 9, 2004.

60. Glen Justice, "Report Shows Dean Campaign Spent $31.7 Million in 2003," *New York Times*, February 1, 2004; Don Van Natta and Leslie Wayne, "Gore Campaign Manager Wears Many Hats," *New York Times*, April 8, 2000.

61. Ben Hammersley, "Audible Revolution," *Guardian*, February 11, 2004.

62. Ryan Lizza, "Howard's End," *New Republic*, February 16, 2004.

63. Lizza, "Howard's End."

64. Andres Martinez, "Will We Remember 2004 as the Year of the Dean Bubble?," *New York Times*, January 30, 2004.

65. Karl Rove, "The Democrats' Tech Cash Machine," *Wall Street Journal*, June 26, 2019.

66. Kreiss, *Taking Our Country Back*, 82.

67. Nicco Mele, *The End of Big: How the Internet Makes David the New Goliath* (New York: Macmillan, 2013), 88.

68. "Goodbye, Candidate Dean," *New York Times*, February 19, 2004.

69. Jodi Wilgoren, "Dean Makes His Exit from Campaign but Vows, 'We Are Not Going Away,'" *New York Times*, February 1, 2004.

70. Wilgoren, "Dean Makes His Exit."

71. David Brooks, "A Short History of Deanism," *New York Times*, February 5, 2005.

72. "Post-Scream Strategizing," *New York Times*, February 22, 2005.

73. As of 2016, Mark Zuckerberg was registered to vote as an independent and described himself as nonpartisan; most of his political activity seems to occur through lobbying and donating money to major party candidates: see Tom Murse, "Is Mark Zuckerberg a Democrat or a Republican?," *ThoughtCo*, July 13, 2019.

74. Ben Mezrich, *The Accidental Billionaires: The Founding of Facebook: A Tale of Sex, Money, Genius and Betrayal* (New York: Doubleday, 2009), 43; David Kirkpatrick, *The Facebook Effect:The Inside Story of the Company That Is Connecting* the World (New York: Simon and Schuster, 2011), 126.

Chapter 7: Blogging the News

1. Max Blumenthal, "Beyond Macaca: The Photograph That Haunts George Allen," *Nation*, August 29, 2006; David A. Graham, "The White Supremacist Group That Inspired a Racist Manifesto," *Atlantic*, June 22, 2015; Ira Forman, "George Allen's Twelve Days of Refusal," *Philadelphia Jewish Voice* (October 2006); "George Allen

Claims He Made up 'Macaca,'" NBC *Meet the Press*, September 17, 2006, YouTube, https://www.youtube.com/watch?v=wRfP3vj8Gl8. Accessed January 7, 2020.

2. "The People Are Applauding George Allen, and for Good Reason," *Richmond Times-Dispatch*, December 28, 1997; "Nobody Much Snickers at 'Boy George' Anymore," *Roanoke Times*, January 12, 2000; Lon Wagner, "The Real George Allen Is Not Just a Good Ol' Boy," *Norfolk Virginian—Pilot*, September 27, 2007.

3. Oliver Burkeman, "Bloggers Catch What *Washington Post* Missed," *Guardian*, December 20, 2002.

4. Jeff E. Schapiro, "Lott's Problems Call to Mind Record of Others, Like Allen," *Richmond Times-Dispatch*, December 22, 2002; "Senator George Allen's Star Rises," Associated Press, November 5, 2004; "Senators Introduce Lynching Apology," *New York Times*, February 2, 2005.

5. Brendan Nyhan, "George Allen and the Noose," February 2, 2005; "George Allen's Ugly History on Racial Issues," Brendan-nyhan.com, May 15, 2005; "Does 'Macaca' Hurt George Allen for 2008?," August 15, 2006, https://www.brendan-nyhan.com. Accessed October 15, 2019.

6. Fred Bernstein, "An Online Peek at Your Politics," *New York Times*, October 4, 2000.

7. "Justin Hall's Personal Site, Growing and Breaking Down Since 1994," spring 1995, http://links.net/vita/web/story.html. Accessed January 5, 2019.

8. S. R. Sidarth, "I Am Macaca," *Washington Post*, November 12, 2006.

9. zkman, "George Allen Introduces Macaca," YouTube, August 15, 2006, www.youtube.com/watch?v=r90z0PMnKwI. Accessed June 30, 2019.

10. "The Meaning of Macaca," *Angry Asian Man*, August 14, 2006, http://blog.angryasianman.com/2006/08/meaning-of-macaca.html. Accessed June 26, 2019; Jeff Yang, "Mad Man: Meet Blogger Phil Yu," *KoreAm: the Korean American Experience*, November 1, 2010, https://web.archive.org/web/20101108013932/http://iamkoream.com/angry-asian-man/. Accessed June 25, 2018.

11. Email from Brendan Nyhan to author, October 14, 2019, in author's collection; Brendan Nyhan, "Scandal Potential: How Political Context and News Congestion Affect the President's Vulnerability to Media Scandal," *British Journal of Political Science* 45, no. 2 (April 2015): 435–566.

12. "Blogger Beta," *Blogger: The Latest News and Tips from the Blogger Team*, August 14, 2006, https://blogger.googleblog.com/2006/08/blogger-in-beta.html. Accessed June 29, 2019; Siva Vaidhyanathan, *Antisocial Media: How Facebook Disconnects Us and Undermines Democracy* (New York: Oxford University Press, 2018), 47.

13. Bob Garfield, "YouTube vs. Boob Tube," *Wired*, December 1, 2006; Lena Dunham, "Pressure," 2006, YouTube, April 14, 2012, https://youtu.be/WRZhZiA5q9o. Accessed May 12, 2019.

14. Sheryl Gay Stolberg, "Under Fire, Lott Apologizes for His Comments at Thurmond's Party," *New York Times*, December 10, 2002; David D. Perlmutter, *Blog Wars* (New York: Oxford University Press, 2008), 63.

15. Oliver Burkeman, "Bloggers Catch What *Washington Post* Missed," *Guardian*, December 2002.

16. Lawrence Lessig, *Free Culture: How Big Media Uses Technology and the Law to Lock down Culture and Control Creativity* (New York: Penguin Press, 2004), 42–4; Vaidhyanathan, *Antisocial Media*, 53, 67; Myra McPherson, *"All Governments Lie": The Life and Times of Rebel Journalist I. F. Stone* (New York: Scribner's, 2004), xii.

17. Andrew Sullivan, "Here Comes the Groom: A Conservative Case for Gay Marriage," *New Republic*, August 28, 1989.

18. Andrew Sullivan, "A Blogger Manifesto: Why Online Weblogs Are One Future for Journalism," *Sunday Times of London*, February 24, 2002.

19. Sullivan, "A Blogger Manifesto."

20. Amanda Lenhart and Susannah Fox, "Bloggers," Pew Research Center, July 19, 2006.

21. Thomas J. Johnson, Barbara K. Kaye, Shannon L. Bichard, and W. Joanne Wong, "Every Blog Has Its Day: Politically-Interested Internet Users' Perceptions of Blog Credibility," *Journal of Computer-Mediated Communication* 3, no. 1 (October 2007): 100–22.

22. Bryant Gumbel, CBS News special report, September 11, 2001: posted on YouTube as CBS News "09.11.01: The Towers Are Hit," www.youtube.com /watch?v=9eTzV7HvKHU; Peter Jennings, ABC News special edition, September 11, 2001: posted on YouTube as bigblue999, "Peter Jennings Crying on Television during 9/11," n.d., www.youtube.com/watch?v=UZdL_XNBcyo. Accessed October 13 2019.

23. David Weinberger, *Small Pieces Loosely Joined: A Unified Theory of the Web* (New York: Basic Books, 2003), 97, 105.

24. Weinberger, *Small Pieces Loosely Joined*, 120, 126–7, 142, 170; Brian Stelter, "Mainstream News Outlets Start Linking to Other Sites," *New York Times*, October 12, 2008; Jonathan Stray, "Why Link out? Four Journalistic Purposes of the Noble Hyperlink," *Nieman Lab*, June 8, 2010.

25. Marlon Manuel, "Covering the Conventions: Boston E-party, Trash-mouthed, Opinionated, Relentless Political Bloggers Are Bound for Both This Week's Democratic Convention and the GOP's in August," *Atlanta Journal-Constitution*, July 25, 2004.

26. Walter V. Robinson, "One Year Gap in Bush's National Guard Duty," *Boston Globe*, May 23, 2000.

27. Rebecca Leung, "New Questions on Bush Guard Duty," *CBS News: Sixty Minutes*, 2004; Bob von Sternberg, "From Geek to Chic: Blogs Gain Influence; a Web site Based in Minneapolis Was Key to Igniting the Furor at CBS," *Minneapolis Star-Tribune*, September 22, 2004; Perlmutter, *Blog Wars*, 90–2.

28. Perlmutter, *Blog Wars*, 69.

29. Jim Rutenberg, "Web Offers Hefty Voice to Critics of Mainstream Journalism," *New York Times*, October 28, 2004.

30. Paul Burka, "That Blog Won't Hunt," *Texas Monthly*, March 2005.

31. Eric Boehlert, *Bloggers on the Bus: How the Internet Changed Politics and the Press* (New York: The Free Press, 2009), 98–100.

32. Rush Limbaugh, *See, I Told You So* (New York: Pocket Books, 1994), 186.

33. Glenn Beck, *An Inconvenient Book: Real Solutions to the World's Biggest Problems* (New York: Threshold Editions, 2007), 108–10; Nicole Hemmer, *Messengers of the Right: Conservative Media and the Transformation of American Politics* (Philadelphia: University of Pennsylvania Press, 2016), 264–5; Lilla, *The Once and Future Liberal*, 51.

34. Tom Rosenstiel, "The End of 'Network News,'" *Washington Post*, September 12, 2004.

35. Sherrie Gossett, "Good vs. Bad Bloggers," *Accuracy in Media*, April 1, 2005.

36. Tim Reid, "Citizen Journalists Relish Their Power to Overthrow Press," *London Times*, February 15, 2005.

37. Richard Davis, "Interplay: Political Blogging and Journalism," in *iPolitics*, eds. Richard L. Fox and Jennifer M. Ramos, 81; Adam C. Smith, "Florida's New Political Blog Wars," *St. Petersburg Times*, June 12, 2005; Jonathan Darman, "I'm Real. Really," *Newsweek*, February 19, 2007.

38. Dick Polman, "Hey, Al Gore Is Back," *Philadelphia Inquirer*, May 29, 2006; Al Gore, *The Assault on Reason* (New York: Penguin Press, 2007), 134, 266–9.

39. Jeffrey Boase, John B. Horrigan, Barry Wellman, and Lee Rainey, "The Strength of Internet Ties," *Pew Internet and Media Life Project*, January 25, 2006; Tunku Varadarajan, "Happy Blogiversary," *Wall Street Journal*, July 14, 2007.

40. Brooks Jackson and Kathleen Hall Jamieson, *Unspun: Finding Facts in a World of Disinformation* (New York: Random House, 2007), viii–xi, 73, 128.

41. Burka, "That Blog Won't Hunt."

42. Jeri Freedman, *Arianna Huffington: Media Mogul and Internet News Pioneer* (New York: Cavendish Square Publishing, 2018), 51–4; Matt Drudge, *The Drudge Manifesto*, 52–4; Andrew Breitbart, *Righteous Indignation, Excuse Me While I Save the World* (New York: Grand Central Publishing, 2011), 100–101.

43. Katharine Q. Seelye, "A Boldface Name Invites Others to Blog with Her," *New York Times*, April 25, 2005.

44. Jennifer L. Lawless, "Twitter and Facebook: New Ways for Members of Congress to Send the Same Old Message?," Richard L. Fox and Jennifer M. Ramos, *iPolitics: Citizens, Elections and Governing in the New Media Era* (New York: Cambridge University Press, 2012), 210–11; Jake Tapper and Betsy Kulman, "The Macaca Heard Round the World," *ABC News*, August 13, 2006, https://abcnews.go.com/Nightline/story?id=2322630&page=1&page=1. Accessed October 12, 2018.

45. Carrie Budoff, "Senators Fear Having a 'Macaca' Moment," CBSnews.com, February 2, 2007, www.cbsnews.com/news/senators-fear-having-a-macaca-moment/. Accessed June 14, 2019.

46. Arrowhead77, "Conrad Burns' Naptime," YouTube, August 17, 2006, www.youtube.com/watch?v=a_B0i2LukP4; powerclam, "Joe Biden's Racist Slip," YouTube, July 6, 2006, www.youtube.com/watch?v=sM19YOqs7hU. Accessed June 3, 2018; Jessica Clark, "YouTube in MeWorld," *In These Times*, October 2006.

47. David Karpf, "Macaca Moments Reconsidered: Electoral Panopticon or Grassroots Mobilization?," *Journal of Information Technology & Politics* 7 (2010): 143–62; Ivan Carter, "Allen and 'Macaca' Needs to Stay in the News," *Daily Kos Community*, September 1, 2006; David Stout, "Verbal Gaffe from a Senator, then an Apology," *New York Times*, August 15, 2006; Carl Hulse, "Senator Apologizes to Student for Remark," *New York Times*, August 24, 2006; Associated Press, "Sen. Allen Denies Using a Racial Slur in the 1970s," *Los Angeles Times*, September 26, 2006; David Shuster, "Woman Says Allen Used Racial Slur Repeatedly," NBCNews.com, September 26, 2006; David D. Kirkpatrick, "2 Ex-Acquaintances of Senator Allen Say He Used Slurs," *New York Times*, September 26, 2006; Max Blumenthal, "Beyond 'Macaca': The Photograph That Haunts George Allen," *Nation*, August 29, 2006.

48. John Sides, "Did Macaca Lose the Election for George Allen," *Monkey Cage*, December 24, 2007.

49. Nate Silver, "A Gaffe Can Matter When It Motivates the Base," *FiveThirty Eight*, April 1, 2014, https://fivethirtyeight.com/features/a-gaffe-can-matter-when-it-motivates-the-base/. Accessed February 1, 2019.

Chapter 8: MyBarackObama

1. Patrick Healey and Jeff Zeleny, "At Debate, Two Rivals Go after Defiant Clinton," *New York Times*, January 6, 2008.

2. "The New Hampshire Debates," *ABC News*, St. Anselm's College, Goffstown, New Hampshire, January 5, 2008, www.youtube.com/watch?v=K3DeCLP wxXI. Accessed February 10, 2019.

3. Dave Bry, "People Have Been Misunderstanding Barack Obama's Friendly Teasing of Hillary Clinton for Four Years," *Awl*, October 3, 2012; Suzanne Goldenberg and Richard Adams, "The Tears over Coffee That Turned around the Poll," *Guardian*, January 10, 2008.

4. Goldenberg and Adams, "The Tears over Coffee"; David Axelrod, *Believer: My Forty Years in Politics* (New York: Penguin Books, 2014), 252–3; "Stunner in N.H.: Clinton Defeats Obama," *NBC News*, January 9, 2008; "Hillary Clinton Tears up during Campaign Stop," YouTube, January 7, 2008, www.youtube.com /watch?v=6qgWH89qWks. Accessed August 10, 2019.

5. Aaron Smith, "The Internet's Role in Campaign 2008," Pew Research Center, April 15, 2009; Brian Stelter, "Finding Political News Online, the Young Pass It On," *New York Times*, March 27, 2008.

6. Aaron Smith, "Obama's YouTube Moment," Pew Research Center, January 4, 2008.

7. Eric Boehlert, *Bloggers on the Bus: How the Internet Changed Politics and the Press* (New York: The Free Press, 2009), 99; Axelrod, *Believer*, 276–7.

8. Rush Limbaugh, "Tuesday Quotes: The One You've Been Waiting For," *The Rush Limbaugh Show*, rushlimbaugh.com, April 15, 2008.

9. Aaron Smith, "The Internet's Role in Campaign 2008," Pew Research Center, April 15, 2009.

10. Rachel Sklar, "A Crush on Obama and an Eye on the Prize," *Huffington Post*, March 28, 2008.

11. Joe Rospars, "Howard Dean's Scream Helped Obama Land the Presidency," *Time*, July 1, 2014.

12. Julie Bosman and Jeff Zeleny, "Edwards Drops out of Democratic Race," *New York Times*, January 30, 2008; Adam Nagourney, "Strategy, Not Drama, in 'I Intend to Run in '08,'" *New York Times*, December 27, 2006.

13. Leon Neyfakh, "The 10 Essential News and Politics Podcasts That Shaped the Genre," *New York*, October 2, 2019.

14. "Republican Funded Group Attacks Kerry's War Record," FactCheck.org, August 6, 2004.

15. Kathleen Hall Jamieson and Joseph N. Cappella, *Echo Chamber: Rush Limbaugh and the Conservative Media Establishment* (New York: Oxford University Press, 2008), 6; "Rove Derangement Syndrome," *The Rush Limbaugh Show*, August 14, 2007.

16. Chris Cillizza, "The Vast Conspiracy Rides Again," *Washington Post*, March 14, 2007; Linda Hirshman, "Hillary and Women Voters—Don't Count on It," *Washington Post*, January 29, 2007.

17. Robin Ghivan, "Hillary Clinton's Tentative Dip into New Neckline Territory," *Washington Post*, July 20, 2007; for cleavage stories, see Kristina Horn Sheeler, *Woman*

President: Confronting Post-Feminist Political Culture (College Station, TX: Texas A&M Press, 2017), 202, fn. 71; Jim Geraghty, "Message from Hillary Clinton's Campaign: 'Cleavage,'" *National Review*, July 27, 2007.

18. Peter Levine, "Three Forms of Populism in the 2008 Campaign," *A Blog for Civic Renewal*, February 7, 2007; Ben Smith, "Obama Echoes Legendary Populist Wallace," *Politico*, December 24, 2007.

19. Ann E. Kornblut, "For This Red Meat Crowd, Obama's '08 Choice Is Clear," *New York Times*, September 18, 2006; Ron Formisano, "Populist Currents in the 2008 Presidential Campaign," *Journal of Policy History* 22, no. 2 (April 201): 237–55.

20. Matt Bai, "The Clinton Referendum," *New York Times Magazine*, December 23, 2007; "Edwards Slams Clintons, 'Establishment Elites,'" *CNN Politics*, August 23, 2007; Sam Stein, "Bloggers Could Be Dead Link for Clinton," *Politico*, May 10, 2007.

21. "Hillary Clinton 2008 Presidential Announcement," January 2007, www.youtube.com/watch?v=GPMhQmHFXAw. Accessed February 28, 2018.

22. Adam Nagourney and Jeff Zeleny, "Obama Formally Enters Presidential Race," *New York Times*, December 11, 2007; "Barack Obama's Presidential Announcement," December 10, 2007, YouTube, www.youtube.com/watch?v=gdJ7Ad15WCA. Accessed January 3, 2019.

23. Ben Smith, "Hardball Fun," *Politico*, December 13, 2007; @davidaxelrod, profile; Ben Wallace-Wells, "A Star Strategist Offers Democrats a New Vision," *New York Times*, March 30, 2007.

24. Axelrod, *Believer*, 62, 65, 74; Chris Hughes, *Fair Shot: Rethinking Inequality and How We Earn* (New York: St. Martin's Press, 2018), loc. 1,188, Kindle; Ben Rhodes, *The World as It Is: A Memoir of the Obama White House* (New York: Random House, 2018), 28; Boehlert, *Bloggers on the Bus*, 31–45.

25. Axelrod, *Believer*, 177–78.

26. Zephyr Teachout, "CB's, MeetUp and Visible Volunteers: From the Dean Campaign to the Future of Internet Organizing," *Social Policy* (winter 2004/5); 7–8; Hughes, *Fair Shot*, 1, 213; Ellen McGirt, "How Chris Hughes Helped Launch Facebook and the Barack Obama Campaign," *Fast Company*, April 1, 2009.

27. James Wolcott, "When Democrats Go Post-Al," *Vanity Fair*, June 2008.

28. Susan Bordo, *The Destruction of Hillary Clinton* (New York and London: Melville House, 2017), 38; Diana B. Carlin and Kelly L. Winfrey, "Have You Come a Long Way, Baby? Hillary Clinton, Sarah Palin, and Sexism in 2008 Campaign Coverage," *Communication Studies* 60, no. 4 (September–October 2009): 326–43; "Vote Different," March 5, 2007, www.youtube.com/watch?v=6h3G-lMZxjo. Accessed January 15, 2018; "Apple '1984' Ad Gets Makeover," Associated Press, March 24, 2007; Boehlert, *Bloggers on the Bus*, 19–29, 124–26; Chuck Tryon, "'Why 2008 Won't Be like 1984,' Viral Videos and Presidential Politics," *Flow: A Critical Forum on Media and Culture*, March 21, 2007.

29. Susan Morrison, ed., *Thirty Ways of Looking at Hillary: Reflections by Women Writers* (New York: HarperCollins, 2008), xi–xii.

30. Morrison, ed., 31, 50, 71, 73, 78, 174, 186, 240.

31. Mike Allen, "Study Finds New Strain of E-activism," *Politico*, September 19, 2007; United States Federal News Service, "YouTube Redefines Terms of Presidential Debates," *U.S. State News*, August 29, 2007. Marketing experts, and certainly Chris Hughes, were already aware that the largest group of Facebook users were not young,

but middle-aged people: see Dick Stroud, "Social networking: an age-neutral commodity—social networking becomes a mature application," *Journal of Direct Marketing and Digital Practice* 9, no. 3 (2008): 278–92.

32. Boehlert, *Bloggers on the Bus*, 35; Tim Johnson, "Professor Keeps an Eye on the Election," *Burlington Free Press*, October 26, 2007.

33. Charlie Fisher, "Child's Pay," MoveOn.Org, March 10, 2008, www.youtube.com/watch?v=A9WKimKIyUQ. Accessed October 1, 2018; Jonah Lehrer, "Why Do Viral Videos Go Viral?," *Wired*, July 25, 2011.

34. Matthew W. Ragas and Spiro Kiousis, "Intermedia Agenda Setting and Political Activism: MoveOn.org and the 2008 Presidential Election," in *New Media, Campaigning and the 2008 Facebook Election*, eds. Thomas J. Johnson and David Perlmutter (New York: Routledge, 2011), 8, 14.

35. Dan Kennedy, "Highway Robbery," *Missoula Independent*, November 29, 2007; Will Thomas, "Matt Damon, Ben Affleck, John Legend Join MoveOn for 'Obama in 30 Seconds,'" *Huffington Post*, December 6, 2017; Ragas and Kiousis, "Intermedia Agenda," 14–16; David Gaw and Lance Mungia, "Obamacan," MoveOn.org, May 11, 2008, www.youtube.com/watch?v=YvO1xELHp3k. Accessed October 1, 2018.

36. Axelrod, *Believer*, 219–21, 316.

37. Deirdre Conner, "Election 2008 Campaign Web Sites: What Clicks?," "Barack Obama: Candidate Cycle 2008," and "Hillary Clinton: Candidate Cycle 2008," *Florida Times-Union*, January 20, 2008, OpenSecrets.org, Center for Responsive Politics, www.opensecrets.org/. Accessed October 5, 2018; Axelrod, *Believer*, 303.

38. Katie Couric and Brian Goldsmith, "What Sarah Palin Saw Clearly," *Atlantic*, October 8, 2018.

39. Randy Salas, "Technobabble," *Star-Tribune*, November 4, 2008.

40. David Pennock, "Yahoo! Election 2008 Political Dashboard," *Oddhead Blog*, December 17, 2007, http://blog.oddhead.com/2007/12/17/yahoo-election-2008-political-dashboard/#comments. Accessed July 15, 2018.

41. "Senator Obama Campaign to Change Election Strategy, University of Illinois Professor Says," University of Illinois Press Release, US Federal News Service, March 26, 2008; Adam Nagourney, "Obama Elected President as Racial Barrier Falls," *New York Times*, November 4, 2008.

42. Reuters, "*Time* magazine's 'Person of the Year' Is . . . You," NBCNews.com, December 17, 2006.

43. Barack Obama, "Remarks on Election Night," November 4, 2008, Presidential Speeches, Barack Obama, The Miller Center, University of Virginia, https://millercenter.org/the-presidency/presidential-speeches/november-4-2008-remarks-election-night. Accessed November 18, 2018.

44. "McCain's Concession Speech," *New York Times*, November 5, 2018; Martina Stewart, "Palin Hits Obama for 'Terrorist' Connection," *CNN Politics*, October 5, 2008, www.cnn.com/2008/POLITICS/10/04/palin.obama/. Accessed November 18, 2018.

45. Axelrod, *Believer*, 306.

46. Axelrod, *Believer*, 314; William Moyet, "Tax Critics Speak Out at 'Binghamton Tea Party,'" Binghamton *Press & Sun-Bulletin*, January 25, 2008.

Chapter 9: Tea Party Time

1. Zev Chafetz, "The Limbaugh Victory," *New York Times*, May 19, 2010; Kenneth Vogel and Mackenzie Weinger, "The Tea Party Radio Network," *Politico*, April 17, 2014; "From Waco to Nietzsche," *Wisconsin State Journal*, January 23, 2000; Michelle Mittelstadt, "Waco Movie Puts Blame on Feds," *Washington Post*, November 3, 1999.

2. David Kirby and Emily Elkins, "Libertarian Roots of the Tea Party," Policy Analysis, August 6, 2012.

3. Richard D. Elliott, "It's Just a Jump to the Right: The Tea Party's Influence on Conservative Discourse," *European Journal of American Studies* 12, no. 2 (summer 2017): 3; Richard Viguerie, "Tips for a Proper Tea Party," *Dallas Morning News*, May 6, 2010.

4. Sharron Angle, "Tea Party Primary Candidates: The GOP's Worst Nightmare," *Guardian*, September 22, 2010.

5. Rebecca Mead, "Rage Machine: Andrew Breitbart's Empire of Bluster," *New Yorker*, May 17, 2010.

6. Theda Skocpol and Vanessa Williamson, *The Tea Party and the Remaking of Republican Conservatism* (New York: Oxford University Press, 2012), 7–8, 129; Nick Carey, David Stoddard, and David Morgan, "Brewing Tensions between the Tea Party and GOP," *Reuters*, March 18, 2010; Joshua B. Freeman and Steven Fraser, "The Strange History of Tea Party Populism," *Salon*, May 4, 2010.

7. Gabriel Sherman, *The Loudest Voice in the Room: How the Brilliant, Bombastic Roger Ailes Built Fox News—and Divided a Country* (New York: Random House, 2014), 354.

8. Christopher Beam, "You Lie! Among the Protesters at the 9/12 March on Washington," *Slate*, September 13, 2009; Sherman, *The Loudest Voice in the Room*, 355; Rush Limbaugh, "Gibbs on Tea Parties, DHS Report," *The Rush Limbaugh Show*, April 15, 2009; "Representative Wilson Shouts 'You Lie!' to Obama during Speech," *CNN Politics*, September 9, 2009.

9. Mark Hemingway, "Obama Lied about Health Insurance, but Let's Blame Glenn Beck," *Washington Examiner*, November 7, 2013; Alex Leo, "Meet Your Newest Internet Meme: Rep. Joe Wilson," *Huffington Post*, November 10, 2009; Alex Leo, "Joe Wilson is Your Pre-existing Condition: New Website Takes Shots at 'You Lie' Congressman," *Huffington Post*, November 10, 2009.

10. Ben Rhodes, *The World as It Is: A Memoir of the Obama White House* (New York: Random House, 2018), 298.

11. @realDonaldTrump, Twitter, November 7, 2012.

12. "Then and Now," *The Rush Limbaugh Show*, December 3, 2009; David Corn, "Hard Right Burning for Bush?," *Nation*, July 27, 2000; "Republicans Cave to Obama and Left at Their Own Peril," *The Rush Limbaugh Show*, January 15, 2009.

13. Skocpol and Williamson, *The Tea Party and the Remaking of Republican Conservatism*, 28; "Keep It in the Open," *Denver Post*, June 30, 1999; conversation with journalist Ryan Girdusky, March 1, 2018; notes in author's collection.

14. "The No-choice Election," *The Rush Limbaugh Show*, May 2, 2008.

15. David Batty, "'You Lie': Republican Joe Wilson's Outburst at Obama's Health Speech," *Guardian*, September 10, 2009; Claire Potter, "Professor Radical Goes to Washington to Preview the Apocalypse," *Tenured Radical*, September 13, 2009,

www.chronicle.com/blognetwork/tenuredradical/2009/09/professor-radical-goes-to
-washington-to/. Accessed July 2, 2019.

16. Ronald Formisano, *The Tea Party: A Brief History* (Baltimore: Johns Hopkins University Press, 2012), 5–14; Kate Zernike, "With No Jobs, Plenty of Time for Tea Party," *New York Times*, March 27, 2010; David Kirby and Emily Elkins, "Libertarian Roots of the Tea Party," *Policy Analysis*, August 6, 2012.

17. Skocpol and Williamson, *The Tea Party and the Remaking of Republican Conservatism*, 35; "An Article about Presidential Candidate Ron Paul," *Pittsburgh Post-Gazette*, May 24, 2007; Mark Lisheron, "In Austin, Resonance with Paul's Off-beat Run," *Austin American-Statesman*, December 16, 2007; Sonya Smith, "'Warcraft' Avatars Rally for Ron Paul," *Orange County Register*, January 1, 2008.

18. "An Article about Presidential Candidate Ron Paul"; Michelle Mittelstadt, "Paul Draws Backers Alienated from Parties," *Houston Chronicle*, August 26, 2007.

19. Sam Holley-Kline, "Ron Paul Fascinates with Online Presence," *Anchorage Daily News*, February 1, 2008.

20. Anonymous, *Norfolk Virginian-Pilot*, December 8, 2007; Larry Flinchpaugh, "The Real Threat," *St. Joseph New Press*, January 12, 2008; Randy Henning, "Paul vs. Machan," *Northwest Florida Daily News*, June 7, 2008.

21. "Look up in the Sky! Blimp Lifts Ron Paul's Name to New Heights," *Concord Monitor*, December 9, 2007.

22. Amy Schatz, "Paul's Supporters Clash with Media," *Wall Street Journal*, November 24, 2007.

23. Michael Brendan Dougherty, "The Story behind Ron Paul's Racist Newsletters," *Atlantic*, December 22, 2011.

24. Paul Gottfried, "The Decline and Rise of the Alternative Right," *Taki's Magazine*, December 1, 2008.

25. "Code Tea: Tea Parties Go Home! All Politics Is Local," *Breitbart News*, December 21, 2009.

26. Andrew Breitbart, *Righteous Indignation: Excuse Me While I Save the World* (New York: Grand Central Books, 2011), 7–10.

27. Breitbart, *Righteous Indignation*, 13.

28. Jeremy W. Peters, "Andrew Breitbart, Conservative Blogger, Dies at 43," *New York Times*, March 1, 2012; Breitbart, *Righteous Indignation*, 13, 18–19; Jonathan Tilove, "Andrew Breitbart, Conservative Blogger, Often Focused on New Orleans," *Times-Picayune*, March 6, 2012.

29. Conor Friedersdorf, "Why Breitbart Started Hating the Left," *Atlantic*, April 18, 2011; Breitbart, *Righteous Indignation*, 25–7.

30. Anna Quindlen, "Public and Private; Listen to Us," *New York Times*, October 9, 1991.

31. Breitbart, *Righteous Indignation*, 29.

32. Breitbart, *Righteous Indignation*, 40.

33. Breitbart, *Righteous Indignation*, 40–3; Katherine Brooks, "A Brief History of America's Most Controversial Prefix," *Huffington Post*, November 22, 2016; Turner, *From Counterculture to Cyberculture*, 2; David Barr, "So You Want to Create an Alt Newsgroup," 1995, www.faqs.org/faqs/alt-creation-guide/. Accessed August 18, 2018.

34. Breitbart, *Righteous Indignation*, 43, 46–8, 53.

35. Caitlin Johnson, "Arianna Huffington's About Face," *CBS Sunday Morning*, October 15, 2006.

36. Breitbart, *Righteous Indignation*, 100.

37. Michael Kazin, "Criticize and Thrive," in *The Presidency of Barack Obama*, ed. Julian Zelizer (Princeton, NJ: Princeton University Press, 2018), 247–8.

38. "Election 2010," *New York Times*, November 23, 2010.

39. Jeff Zeleny, "G.O.P. Captures House, but Not Senate," *New York Times*, November 2, 2010; Breitbart, *Righteous Indignation*, 162–3, 218.

40. Breitbart, *Righteous Indignation*, 3; Push Back Now, "ACORN Prostitution Investigation," YouTube, September 10, 2009, www.youtube.com/watch?v=9UOL9 Jh61S8. Accessed December 5, 2018.

41. Mead, "Rage Machine"; "Nut Cracking," *The Rush Limbaugh Show*, October 27, 2008.

42. Push Back Now, "ACORN Prostitution Investigation—James O'Keefe and Hannah Giles—Part 1," YouTube, September 10, 2009, www.youtube.com/watch?v=9UOL 9Jh61S8. Accessed October 17, 2019.

43. Ian Urbina, "ACORN on Brink of Bankruptcy, Officials Say," *New York Times*, March 19, 2010; Peter Dreier and John Atlas, "Lessons from the Right's Attack on ACORN and Planned Parenthood," *New Labor Forum* 21, no. 3 (fall 2012): 88–93.

44. Peter Dreier and Christopher Martin, "How ACORN Was Framed: Political Controversy and Media Agenda Setting," *Perspectives on Politics* 8, no. 3 (September 2010): 761–92; Robin Abcarian, "Andrew Breitbart: The Man behind the Shirley Sherrod Affair," *Los Angeles Times*, September 2, 2010; Frank James, "Andrew Breitbart: Not about Shirley Sherrod but NAACP," *NPR*, July 20, 2010.

45. Roger Stone, *The Making of the President 2016: How Donald Trump Orchestrated a Revolution* (New York: Skyhorse Books, 2017), 37–8; Charles Babbington, "'Birther' Claims Force GOP Leaders to Take a Stand," Associated Press, April 22, 2011; @realDonaldTrump "birther" tweets can be found at the searchable Trump Twitter Archive; quoted tweets are from April 24, 2012, July 23, 2012, and August 6, 2012. Accessed August 6, 2019.

46. Donald J. Trump, "Donald Trump Responds," *New York Times*, April 8, 2011.

47. *The View*, ABC, March 28, 2011.

48. Michael D. Shear, "Perry's Emphasis on Birther Issue: A Wink at the Right?," *New York Times*, October 25, 2011.

49. Joel B. Pollak, "The Vetting—Exclusive—Obama's Literary Agent in 1991 Booklet: 'Born in Kenya and raised in Indonesia and Hawaii,'" *Breitbart News*, May 17, 2012; ARSONomics, "Andrew Breitbart MURDERED?: Here's WHY?!?," YouTube, March 3, 2012, www.youtube.com/watch?v=EBAoBsldgns. Accessed December 3, 2017.

50. Joshua Green, *Devil's Bargain: Steve Bannon, Donald Trump, and the Storming of the Presidency* (New York: Penguin Press, 2017), 92; Keach Hagey, "Breitbart to Announce New Management," *Politico*, March 19, 2012.

51. Tom McGeveran, "Some Tweets upon the Death of Andrew Breitbart, Conservative Digital-media Pugilist," *Politico*, March 1, 2012.

52. MercuryOneMemphis, "Rush Limbaugh Attacks Media over Breitbart Death Coverage," YouTube, March 1, 2012, https://www.youtube.com/watch?v=lmqkLX EEHu8. Accessed January 6, 2020.

53. Maer Roshan, "What Killed Andrew Breitbart?," *Fix*, March 4, 2012; Jon Stone, *Independent*, March 12, 2017; Miles William Mathis, "Proof from Breitbart that Obama Was Born in Kenya," http://mileswmathis.com/breit.pdf. Accessed December 4, 2018.

54. *Apparently Apparel*, "Is This What Killed Andrew Breitbart? The CIA Heart Attack Gun," YouTube, March 5, 2012, www.youtube.com/watch?v=yrrdtICFQUI. Accessed July 20, 2018.

Chapter 10: White House 2.0

1. Diana Owen and Richard Davis, "Presidential Communication in the Internet Era," *Presidential Studies Quarterly* 38, no. 4 (December 2008): 662; "Welcome to the White House," version 1, https://clintonwhitehouse1.archives.gov/; version 2, https://clintonwhitehouse2.archives.gov/; version 3, https://clintonwhitehouse4.archives.gov/; version 4, https://clintonwhitehouse4.archives.gov/; Archived Presidential White House Websites, National Archives and Records Administration (NARA), www.archives.gov/presidential-libraries/archived-websites. Accessed August 23, 2018.

2. "The White House: President George W. Bush," White House Interactive, March 22, 2006, https://georgewbush-whitehouse.archives.gov/interactive/interactive06.html#March; "Barney," https://georgewbush-whitehouse.archives.gov/barney/; Archived Presidential White House Websites, NARA. Accessed August 24, 2018.

3. Owen and Davis, "Presidential Communication," 664.

4. Kate Bolduan and Larry Lazo, "Obama Administration Job Seekers Face Tough Odds," *CNN Politics*, January 11, 2009.

5. Brandon Griggs, "Obama Poised to Be First 'Wired' President," CNN, January 15, 2009.

6. "Barack Obama's Speech on Race," *New York Times*, March 18, 2008; David Corn, "'Black and More than Black': Obama's Daring and Unique Speech on Race," *Mother Jones*, March 18, 2008.

7. "Winning the Media Campaign: How the Press Reported the 2008 General Election," Pew Research Center, October 22, 2008; Jon Friedman, "Mr. Obama, Enjoy the Media Adulation While You Can," *Media Watch*, November 28, 2008, www.marketwatch.com/story/obama-remorse-sweeps-through-the-media?print=true&dist=print MidSection. Accessed June 28, 2019; Heather Parton, "Kewl Kid Kabuki," *Hullabaloo*, November 28, 2008.

8. Mark Shields, "Obama's 'Gimmick,'" Ocala *Star-Banner*, March 4, 2008.

9. Jeff Zelemy, "For a High-Tech President, a Hard Fought E-victory," *New York Times*, January 22, 2009; Jacob Kastrenakes, "Obama Finally Upgraded from His BlackBerry," *Verge*, June 11, 2016.

10. Owen and Davis, "Presidential Communication," 665, 669; Sid Salter, "New Look for White House Website," *Hattiesburg American*, January 22, 2009.

11. Adam Nagourney, "Obama Wins Election," *New York Times*, November 4, 2008.

12. Tom Rosenstiel, "Newspapers Face a Challenging Calculus," Pew Research Center, February 26, 2009; Michael Hais and Morley Winograd, "It's Official: Millennials Realigned American Politics in 2008," *Huffington Post*, December 18, 2018.

13. Ben Rhodes, *The World as It Is: A Memoir of the Obama White House* (New York: Random House, 2018), 109.

14. Ragas and Kiousis, "Intermedia Agenda Setting and Political Activism," 26; David Axelrod, *Believer: My Forty Years in Politics* (New York: Penguin Books, 2014), 315; Rhodes, *The World as It Is*, 129.

15. Niela Orr, "Hello Twitter! It's Barack!," *Baffler*, May 22, 2015.

16. Mary Paulsell, "The Entrepreneur Next Door," *Columbia Daily Tribune*, November 22, 2008; Emily Steele, "Obama's Digital Campaign Allies Seek to Cash In," *Wall Street Journal*, December 31, 2008.

17. L. Gordon Crovitz, "Can We Trust Anyone over 30?," *Wall Street Journal* (Europe), November 10, 2008; Tom Schaller, "The Big 2010 Question," FiveThirty Eight.com, November 5, 2009.

18. Aaron Smith, "The Internet's Role in Campaign 2008," Pew Research Center, April 15, 2009, https://www.pewresearch.org/internet/2009/04/15/the-internets -role-in-campaign-2008/. Accessed January 6, 2020; Rosenblum and Muirhead, *A Lot of People Are Saying*, 52.

19. David Ho, "Bits of Digital Obama Presidency Emerge," *Palm Beach Post*, December 1, 2008; Scott Wilson, "Obama in Farsi, on Twitter and Whitehouse.gov," *Washington Post*, June 24, 2009.

20. Ho, "Bits of Digital Obama Presidency Emerge."

21. Ho, "Bits of Digital Obama Presidency Emerge"; Tannette Johnson-Elie, "Obama Took Soap-box to Computer Screen," *Milwaukee Journal Sentinel*, December 31, 2008; Jann S. Wenner, "How Obama Won," *Rolling Stone*, November 27, 2008.

22. Steve and Cookie Roberts, "Coming Soon to a Computer Near You!," syndicated column, *Burlington County Times*, November 13, 2008; "Change.gov: Office of the President-Elect," Library of Congress Web Archives Collection, http://webarchive.loc .gov/all/20081111041617/http://change.gov/. Accessed October 15, 2018.

23. Siva Vaidhyanathan, *Antisocial Media: How Facebook Disconnects Us and Undermines Democracy* (New York: Oxford University Press, 2018), 33; Ellen McGirt, "How Chris Hughes Helped Launch Facebook and the Barack Obama Campaign," *Fast Company*, April 1, 2009.

24. "Online with Obama," *Los Angeles Times*, March 26, 2009.

25. "What Do You Think of Obama's Style of Outreach?," Letters to the Editor, Salisbury (MD) *Daily Times*, March 29, 2009.

26. John D. Sutter, "4chan Founder Defends Online Pranks," CNN, February 22, 2010.

27. Lee Rainie and Aaron Smith, "Politics on Social Media," Pew Research Center, September 4, 2012.

28. Eli Pariser, *The Filter Bubble: How the New Personalized Web Is Changing What We Read and How We Think* (New York: Penguin Books, 2011), 10–11.

29. Rhodes, *The World as It Is*, 129, 166.

30. Paul Starr, *Remedy and Reaction: The Peculiar American Struggle over Health Care Reform* (New Haven: Yale University Press, 2013), 45; Gaby Wood, "Glenn Beck: The Renegade Running the Opposition to Obama," *Guardian*, November 28, 2009; Amanda Turkel, "Glenn Beck Agrees with Palin's 'Death Panel' Claim: 'I Believe It to Be True,'" *Think Progress*, August 10, 2009; Peter J. Smithy, "Glenn Beck Exposes Three Scary ObamaCare Czars," *Catholic Exchange*, September 2, 2009.

31. Michele Bachmann, "The President's Health Care Advisers," YouTube, July 29, 2009; Sarah Palin, Facebook, August 7, 2009, www.facebook.com/note.php?note_id =113851103434. Accessed October 20, 2019; Big X, "Debunking the Great Debunker: Obamacare Covers Illegals," Breitbart, August 29, 2009.

32. Kathleen Hall Jamieson and Joseph N. Cappella, *Echo Chamber: Rush Limbaugh and the Conservative Media Establishment* (New York: Oxford University Press, 2008), 99; "Health Care: Snitching for Obama," *Savannah Morning News*, August 20, 2009.

33. "Second Opinions," Worcester (MA) *Telegram & Gazette*, August 9, 2009.

34. Mike O'Toole, "Social Media Dreamin': The 2009 Edition," *MarketingProfsDaily*, January 15, 2010.

35. Sarah Palin, *Going Rogue: An American Life* (New York: HarperCollins, 2009), 274–7; 305; Chuck Raasch, "Social Media Boosts the Candidacy of Ron Paul," *Home News Tribune*, December 17, 2011.

36. Axelrod, *Believer*, 451.

37. Axelrod, *Believer*, 451; Eric Loehr, "Fact Check Social Media Claims," *St. Cloud Times*, April 11, 2011.

38. "Cornyn to Talk Social Media during Live Facebook Town Hall," *Trail Blazers Politics*, April 12, 2011; Iain Thompson, "President Obama Hosts First Twitter Town Hall Meeting," *Silicon Valley Sleuth*, July 6, 2011; Randy Krebs, "Will Social Media Reach Moderates in '12?," *St. Cloud Times*, April 24, 2011; Jonathan Martin and Mike Allen, "Bachmann Wins Ames Straw Poll," *Politico*, October 13, 2011.

39. Roger Simon, "Obama Meets the Tweeple," *Asheville Citizen-Times*, July 12, 2011.

40. "Barack Obama Joins Pinterest. The Question Is: Now What?," *Trail Blazers Politics*, March 27, 2012.

41. Amit, "Take a Virtual Tour of the White House," *Digital Inspiration*, April 3, 2012; Kevin J. Kelley, "Seven Questions for Nico Mele, Howard Dean to Web Guru," *Seven Days*, May 9, 2012; "Less on TV; More on Social Media," *Arizona Republic*, August 23, 2012.

42. Walter Smith, "What Are President Obama's Campaign Managers Thinking?," *New York Beacon*, August 23, 2012.

43. Kathleen Parker, "Exhausting the Insignificant," *Leaf Chronicle*, October 22, 2012.

44. "Obama's 'Moneyball' Campaign," *Washington Post*, November 12, 2012; quotes from *Time* are from this article.

45. "New Tools Become the Norm: Social Media and the Presidential Race," *MarketingProfsDailyFix*, December 6, 2012.

46. Julian E. Zelizer, "Tea Partied," in *The Presidency of Barack Obama*, ed. Julian Zelizer (Princeton, NJ: Princeton University Press, 2018), 12.

47. "Reactions to Zimmerman Not Guilty Verdict Flood Social Media," *Wall Street Journal*, July 13, 2013.

Chapter 11: Hashtag Populisms

1. Daniel Kreiss, "The Real Story about How the Obama and Romney Campaigns Used Twitter," *Monkey Cage*, December 9, 2014.

2. Jeremy Rodriguez, "Black Lives Matter Cofounder Speaks on Activism, New Memoir," *Philadelphia Gay News*, January 25, 2018; Monica Anderson, "The Hashtag #BlackLivesMatter Emerges: Social Activism on Twitter," Pew Research Center, August 15, 2016.

3. Zeynep Tufekci, *Twitter and Tear Gas: The Power and Fragility of Networked Protest* (New Haven, CT: Yale University Press, 2017), 84.

4. Keeanga-Yamahtta Taylor, "Five Years Later, Do Black Lives Matter?," *Jacobin*, September 30, 2019.

5. "We Look Back at Famous First Tweets as Twitter Turns Ten," *BBC Newsbeat*, March 21, 2016; Lexi Pandell, "An Oral History of the #Hashtag," *Wired*, May 19, 2017.

6. Pandell, "An Oral History of the #Hashtag."

7. Pandell, "An Oral History of the #Hashtag."

8. Belle Beth Cooper, "The Surprising History of Twitter's Hashtag Origin and 4 Ways to Get the Most out of Them," *Buffer*, September 24, 2013.

9. Pandell, "An Oral History of the #Hashtag."

10. Tufekci, *Twitter and Tear Gas*, 49–66; Nadia Idle and Alex Nunns, *Tweets from Tahrir* (New York: OR Books, 2011), loc. 70, Kindle; Liz Else, "The Revolution Will Be Tweeted," *New Scientist*, February 1, 2012.

11. Idle and Nunns, *Tweets from Tahrir*, 41, 70.

12. Patrisse Khan-Cullors and Asha Bandele, *When They Call You a Terrorist: A Black Lives Matter Memoir* (New York: St. Martin's Press, 2017), 129, 132.

13. Barbara Ransby, *Making All Black Lives Matter: Reimagining Freedom in the 20th Century* (Berkeley: University of California Press, 2018), 100–101; Todd Gitlin, *Occupy Nation: The Roots, the Spirit and the Promise of Occupy Wall Street* (New York: itbooks, 2012), 4.

14. Gary Hall, "#Mysubjectivation," *New Formations: A Journal of Culture/Theory/Politics* 79 (2013): 85.

15. Doriano "Paisano" Carta, "The Year in Tweets: Ten Most Memorable Twitter Moments of 2008," *Mashable*, December 19, 2008; Charles Arthur, "How Twitter and Flickr Reported the Mumbai Terror Attacks," *Guardian*, November 27, 2008.

16. Evgeny Morozov, "The Internet," *Foreign Policy* 179 (May/June 2010): 40–44.

17. Julian Zelizer and Kevin Kruse, *Fault Lines: A History of the United States Since 1974* (New York: W. W. Norton, 2019), 309–10, 314.

18. Ransby, *Making All Black Lives Matter*, 11–28.

19. Zosha Millman, "19 Years Later: Looking Back at the Battle in Seattle, the WTO Riots," *Seattle Pi*, November, 30 2018; Steve Boozin, "Taking Media to the WTO Streets," *Wired*, November 30, 1999; Dan Brekke, "What's behind the WTO Ruckus?," *Wired*, December 2, 1999.

20. Lesley J. Wood, *Direct Action, Deliberation and Diffusion: Collective Action after the WTO Protests in Seattle* (New York: Cambridge University Press, 2014), 2, 26–30.

21. Phyllis Bennis, "February 15, 2003: The Day the World Said No to War," Institute for Policy Studies, February 15, 2013; Tufekci, *Twitter and Tear Gas*, 83–6.

22. Gabrielle Coleman, *Hacker, Hoaxer, Whistleblower, Spy: The Many Faces of Anonymous* (New York: Verso, 2015); Parmy Olson, *We Are Anonymous: Inside the Hacker World of Lulzsec, Anonymous and the Global Cyber Insurgency* (New York:

Back Bay Books, 2013); Elizabeth Bumiller, "Video Shows U.S. Killing of Reuters Employees," *New York Times*, April 5, 2010.

23. Julian Assange, *When Google Met Wikileaks* (New York: OR Books, 2016), 9, 29.

24. David Leigh and Luke Harding, *Wikileaks: Inside Julian Assange's War on Secrecy* (New York: PublicAffairs, 2011), 203–4.

25. Amy Goodman interview with Glenn Greenwald, Democracy Now!, October 26, 2011.

26. Kono Matsu, "A Million Man March on Wall Street: How to Spark a People's Revolt in the West," *Adbusters*, February 2, 2011, https://web.archive.org/web/20150402104218/www.adbusters.org/blogs/adbusters-blog/million-man-march-wall-street.html#comments. Accessed December 13, 2018.

27. Gitlin, *Occupy Nation*, 125.

28. Matsu, "A Million Man March on Wall Street."

29. Gitlin, *Occupy Nation*, 85; Matsu, "A Million Man March on Wall Street."

30. Gitlin, *Occupy Nation*, 15–16.

31. Culture Jammers, "#OccupyWallStreet: A Shift in Revolutionary Tactics," *Adbusters*, July 13, 2011, www.webcitation.org/63DZ1nIDl?url=www.adbusters.org/blogs/adbusters-blog/occupywallstreet.html. Accessed January 2, 2019.

32. Culture Jammers, "#OccupyWallStreet: A Shift in Revolutionary Tactics."

33. Culture Jammers, "#OccupyWallStreet: A Shift in Revolutionary Tactics."

34. Gitlin, *Occupy Nation*, 4–5, 87.

35. These numbers are from the Occupy Directory at directory.occupy.net. Accessed September 30, 2019.

36. Gitlin, *Occupy Nation*, 28, 148.

37. Zephyr Teachout, "Legalism and Devolution of Power in the Public Sphere: Reflections on Occupy Wall Street," *Fordham Urban Law Journal* 39 (2012): 1,868–70; Gitlin, *Occupy Nation*, 73–9.

38. Ransby, *Making All Black Lives Matter*, 22.

39. Khan-Cullors and Bandele, *When They Call You a Terrorist*, 177–81; Lindsey Weedston, "12 Hashtags That Changed the World in 2014," *Yes!*, December 19, 2014.

40. Khan-Cullors and Bandele, *When They Call You a Terrorist*, 216.

41. Ransby, *Making All Black Lives Matter*, 5; Christopher Lebron, *The Making of Black Lives Matter: A Brief History of an Idea* (New York: Oxford University Press, 2017), 10.

42. Lebron, *The Making of Black Lives Matter*, 105.

43. Lebron, *The Making of Black Lives Matter*, 10, 27, 29, 83, 95, 114, 132, 142; Vaidhyanathan, *Antisocial Media*, 130–31, 136.

44. Lebron, *The Making of Black Lives Matter*, 34; Jelani Cobb, "The Matter of Black Lives," *New Yorker*, March 6, 2016; Keeanga Yamahatta-Taylor, *From #BlackLivesMatter to Black Liberation* (Chicago: Haymarket Books, 2016), 16.

Chapter 12: Democalypse Now

1. Alexander Burns, "Donald Trump, Pushing Someone Rich, Offers Himself," *New York Times*, June 16, 2015.

2. Henry Farrell, "This Is How Donald Trump Engineers Applause," *Washington Post*, January 23, 2017.

3. "Here's Donald Trump's Presidential Announcement Speech," *Time*, June 16, 2015; opening monologue, *The Daily Show*, Comedy Central, June 16, 2015.

4. "The Hard Line," *NewsmaxTV*, August 14, 2015.

5. Maggie Haberman, "Donald Trump Says His Mocking of New York Times Reporter was Misread," *New York Times*, November 26, 2015.

6. "Hillary Clinton's File," Politifact.com, www.politifact.com/personalities/hillary-clinton/; "Donald Trump's File," Politifact.com, www.politifact.com/personalities/donald-trump/. Accessed October 12, 2019.

7. @realDonaldTrump, Twitter, November 26, 2015. Accessed October 19, 2019.

8. "Trump Links Cruz's Father to Kennedy Assassination," *BBC News*, May 3, 2016; "Ted Cruz Responds after Donald Trump Attacks His Father," *CBS News*, May 3, 2016.

9. "When Trump Attacks with a Nickname," CNN, April 18, 2016.

10. "The Best of Donald Trump vs. George Bush," CNN, August 24, 2015.

11. Ben Jacobs, "Donald Trump's Candidacy: A Populist, Celebrity-Driven First in US Politics," *Guardian*, August 10, 2015.

12. @realDonaldTrump, Twitter, October 8, 2016. Accessed October 19, 2019.

13. Katie Tur, *Unbelievable: My Front Row Seat to the Craziest Campaign in American History* (New York: HarperCollins, 2017), 144; @CSPAN, July 27, 2016, https://twitter.com/cspan/status/758320094619381760?lang=en. Accessed April 4, 2019.

14. Larry Diamond, "Democracy in Decline: How Washington Can Reverse the Tide," *Foreign Affairs*, July/August 2016; Mike Lofgren, "An Oligarchy Has Broken Our Democracy. It Must Be Dislodged," *Guardian*, January 16, 2016; Jason Grumet, "Whatever Happens Tuesday, Democracy Is Banged up but Not Broken," *Roll Call*, November 5, 2016.

15. Sam Dangremond, "Who Was the First Politician to Use 'Make America Great Again' Anyway?," *Town & Country*, November 4, 2018; Ronald Reagan, "Labor Day Speech at Liberty State Park, Jersey City, New Jersey, September 1, 1980," Ronald Reagan Presidential Library and Museum, www.reaganlibrary.gov/9-1-80. Accessed June 14, 2018; "Text of Ronald Reagan's Speech Accepting Republican Nomination," July 18, 1980, Don Baer, "Smart Speeches," Clinton Digital Library, https://clinton.presidentiallibraries.us/items/show/34671. Accessed January 30, 2019; "Talking Points for CEO Event—Chicago," September 24, 1992, box 4, folder 3, Speechwriting Office—Boorstin, Clinton Presidential Records, National Security Council, William J. Clinton Presidential Library, Little Rock, AR.

16. Roger Stone, *The Making of the President 2016: How Donald Trump Orchestrated a Revolution* (New York: Skyhorse Books, 2017), 322.

17. David Niewert, *Alt-America: The Rise of the Radical Right in the Age of Trump* (New York: Verso Books, 2017), 256; Matt Labash, "Making Political Trouble: Roger Stone Gets It Done—Again," *Weekly Standard*, January 28, 2008.

18. Jess Joho, @RogerJStoneJr, tweet, September 16, 2011. Stone's Twitter account was suspended in October 2018 and is no longer available for citation; the text can be retrieved from "Sorry Trump: 'The Handmaid's Tale' Was Saying MAGA before You," *Mashable*, January 14, 2018; Carlos Lozada, "Donald Trump's 'Time to Get

Tough' Is out in Paperback. You'll Never Guess the New Subtitle," *Washington Post*, August 21, 2015; Emi Kolawole, "Huckabee Claims Inaccurately That Obama Was Raised in Kenya," *Washington Post*, March 1, 2011; facsimile of the application is in Alex Kasprak, "Did Donald Trump Register 'Make America Great Again' in 2012?," Snopes.com, February 21, 2018; Sam Dangremond, "Who Was the First Politician to Use 'Make America Great Again' Anyway?" *Town & Country*, November 14, 2018.

19. Heather K. Evans, Victoria Cardova, Savannah Sipole, "Twitter Style: An Analysis of How House Candidates Used Twitter in Their 2012 Campaigns," *Political Science and Politics* 47, no. 2 (April 2014): 456; Peter Singer and Emerson T. Brooking, *Like War: the Weaponization of Social Media* (New York: Eamon Dolan/Houghton Mifflin Harcourt, 2018), 3; @realDonaldTrump, Twitter, September 26, 2012.

20. Marina McIntyre, "Donald Trump Launches Twitter Tirade over Barack Obama's Victory," November 7, 2012.

21. P. W. Singer and Emerson T. Brooking, "The Little-Known Story of Donald Trump's First Tweet," *Time*, October 2, 2018; Kendra Marr, "Donald Trump, Birther?," *Politico*, March 17, 2011.

22. Casey Hicks, "Timeline of Hillary Clinton's Email Scandal," *CNN Politics*, November 7, 2016.

23. Peter W. Stevenson, "A Brief History of the 'Lock Her up' Chant by Trump Supporters against Clinton," *Washington Post*, November 22, 2016; @realdonaldtrump, Instagram, November 23, 2015.

24. John Cassidy, "Bernie Sanders and the New Populism," *New Yorker*, February 3, 2016.

25. "The Bernie Sanders Revolution," *New York Times*, March 12, 2006.

26. @BernieSanders, Twitter, November 5, 2016.

27. Jared Goyette, Julia O'Malley, and Nicole Puglise, "The Republican Women Unfazed by Trump's Sexism," *Guardian*, October 2, 2016.

28. Liza Featherstone, "Why This Socialist Feminist Is Not Voting for Hillary," *Nation*, January 5, 2016; "Susan Sarandon Says She Doesn't Support Trump—but Calls Clinton a 'Really Good Republican,'" *SiriusXM Blog*, April 19, 2016.

29. Hadas Gold, "Twitter CEO Dick Costolo Steps Down," *Politico*, June 11, 2015; Marlo Safi, "Facebook's News Suppression Misleads Users," *Pitt News*, May 18, 2016.

30. Caitlin Dewey, "Inside Democratic Facebook's Vicious Civil War," *Washington Post*, May 5, 2016.

31. Maeve Duggan and Aaron Smith, "The Tone of Social Media Discussions around Politics," Pew Research Center, October 25, 2016.

32. Katie Reilly, "Madeleine Albright Apologized for 'Special Place in Hell' Comment," *Time*, February 12, 2016.

33. David E. Sanger, "Foreign Policy Questions Push Bernie Sanders out of Comfort Zone," *New York Times*, February 8, 2016; Doug Henwood, *My Turn: Hillary Clinton Targets the Presidency* (New York: OR Books, 2015), 6–7, 9.

34. David Axelrod, *Believer: My Forty Years in Politics* (New York: Penguin Books, 2014), 345.

35. Samantha Smith, "A Gender Gap in Views of Hillary Clinton, Even among Her Supporters," Pew Research Center, November 5, 2016.

36. Jessica Bennett, "Hillary Supporters Can Now Be 'Public' on Facebook," *New York Times*, June 14, 2016; Hillary Clinton, *What Happened* (New York: Simon and Schuster, 2017), 162–3.

37. Annette Benedetti, "Why I Regret Joining 'Secret' Pro-Hillary Clinton Facebook Groups," *Bust*, October 13, 2017.

38. Interview with Marilee Lindemann, December 9, 2018. The letter to Hillary became a blog post: see Marilee Lindemann, "A Bitch's Love Letter to Hillary," *Madwoman with a Laptop*, November 14, 2016, https://madwomanwithalaptop .com/2016/11/14/a-bitchs-love-letter-to-hillary/. Accessed March 4, 2019.

39. Kate Spencer, "Why I Started a Secret, Pro-Hillary Facebook Group," *Cosmopolitan*, November 2, 2016; interview with Marilee Lindemann, December 9, 2018; Lindemann, "A Bitch's Love Letter."

40. Interview with Marilee Lindemann, December 9, 2018; Siva Vaidhyanathan, *Antisocial Media: How Facebook Disconnects Us and Undermines Democracy* (New York: Oxford University Press, 2018), 90–91; Cass Sunstein, *Republic 2.0* (Princeton, NJ: Princeton University Press, 2009), 116.

41. Susan Bordo, *The Destruction of Hillary Clinton* (New York and London: Melville House, 2017), 117.

42. Matt Kapko, "Twitter's Impact on 2016 Presidential Election Is Unmistakable," *CIO*, November 3, 2016.

43. James Comey, *A Higher Loyalty: Truth, Lies, and Leadership* (New York: Flatiron Books, 2018), 3.

44. Michael S. Schmidt, "Hillary Clinton Asks State Department to Vet Emails for Release," *New York Times*, March 5, 2015; Domenico Montenaro, "Hillary Clinton's Email Defense Is a Mixed Bag," *It's All Politics: Political News from NPR*, September 11, 2015; Will Cabaniss, "Howard Dean: 'Tremendous' Number of Public Officials Have Done What Hillary Clinton Did with Email," *Punditfact*, August 18, 2015; Tur, *Unbelievable*, 73.

45. Jill Lepore, *These Truths: A History of the United States* (New York: W. W. Norton, 2018), 161–4; @realDonaldTrump, Twitter, March 29, 2016, https://twitter. com/realdonaldtrump/status/714855025055514624?lang=en. Accessed February 13, 2019; Issie Lapowsky, "In Video of Trump's Campaign Boss, the Internet Sees What It Wants," *Wired*, March 29, 2016.

46. Steven K. Bannon, "Time to Get Tough: Trump's Blockbuster Policy Manifesto," *Breitbart*, July 12, 2015; Joshua Green, "This Man Is the Most Dangerous Political Operative in America," *Bloomberg Businessweek*, October 8, 2015.

47. Zachary Mider, "Clinton Cash Book Got Most of Its Funding from One Hedge Fund Star," *Bloomberg News*, January 18, 2017.

48. James Carville, "It's Not Going to Be a Blue Wave Election," MSNBC, November 6, 2018, YouTube, www.youtube.com/watch?v=84MdgR7Ip7Q; Amy Chozick, *Chasing Hillary: Ten Years, Two Presidential Campaigns, and One Intact Glass Ceiling* (New York: Harper, 2018), 362–3.

49. Clara McCarthy and Claire Phipps, "Election Results Timeline: How the Night Unfolded," *Guardian*, November 9, 2016; "Morning Joe," MSNBC, November 9, 2016, YouTube, www.youtube.com/watch?v=VgYphOJ7qiw.

50. Michael Wolff, *Fire and Fury: Inside the Trump White House* (New York: Henry Holt, 2018), 18; David Greenberg, *Nixon's Shadow: The History of an Image* (New York: W. W. Norton, 2004), 267–8; Adam Howard, "What Do Losing Politicians Do Next?," *NBC News*, November 13, 2016; "Richard Nixon's Concession Speech," November 8, 1960, YouTube, www.youtube.com/watch?v=yn1FOyaM_c4. Accessed January 3, 2019; Harold Jackson and Alex Brummer, "Aides Tell Tearful Jimmy Carter

That 'It's All Over,'" *Guardian*, November 5, 1980; "The Election Infection," September 12, 1984; "Interview with George W. Bush," *Face the Nation, CBS News*, November 9, 2014.

51. Graeme MacMillan, "Want a Preview of Trump's America? Watch Twitter," *Wired*, November 11, 2016.

52. Telephone interview with Marilee Lindemann, December 9, 2018. In author's collection.

53. Donna Brazile, *Hacks: The Inside Story of the Break-ins and Breakdowns That Put Donald Trump in the White House* (New York: Hachette Books, 2017), xix, 5.

54. Brazile, *Hacks*, 28, 42, 54.

55. Zoe Quinn, *Crash Override: How Gamergate (Nearly) Destroyed My Life, and How We Can Win the Fight against Online Hate* (New York: PublicAffairs, 2017), 4–5, 43–5, 74.

56. Quinn, *Crash Override*, 235.

Conclusion: Post-Truth

1. Jack Shafer, "I Know the Truth about the Covington Catholic Story," *Politico*, January 22, 2019.

2. Lee McIntyre, *Post-Truth* (Cambridge, MA: MIT Press, 2018), 5.

3. Frances Stead Sellers and Kevin Williams, "Death Threats and Protests: Kentucky Town Reels from Fallout over Lincoln Memorial Faceoff," *Washington Post*, January 22, 2019.

4. Claire Potter, "How I Knew the #CovingtonBoys Video Was Clickbait: And Why You Should Care That It Is," *Public Seminar*, January 24, 2019, www.public seminar.org/2019/01/how-i-knew-the-covingtonboys-video-was-click-bait/. Accessed February 25, 2019.

5. While both conservative and liberal media have picked up on how the two cases map onto each other in their details and the audiences they engage, the question of whether purchased social media data was implicated in the virality of the original video has not been established: see Brian Flood, "Media Treatment of Covington Students 'Way Worse' Than Kavanaugh Coverage, Critic Says," *Fox News*, January 22, 2019; Jonathan Capehart, "Time to Take on the Covington 'Smirk,'" *Washington Post*, January 25, 2019.

6. Yochai Benkler, Robert Faris, and Hal Roberts, *Network Propaganda, Disinformation, and Radicalization in American Politics* (New York: Oxford University Press, 2018), 39–40.

7. Caitlin Flanagan, "The Media Botched the Covington Catholic Story," *Atlantic*, January 23, 2019; Frances Stead Sellers, "Investigation Finds No Evidence of 'Racist or Offensive Statements' in Mall Incident," *Washington Post*, February 14, 2019; Bruce Haring, "Washington Post Issues Editor's Note on Flawed Coverage in Covington Teens vs. Nathan Phillips Confrontation," *Deadline*, March 2, 2019.

8. Rosenblum and Muirhead, *A Lot of People Are Saying*, 32–3.

9. Hannah Arendt, *The Origins of Totalitarianism* (New York: Harcourt, Inc., 1973. Orig. 1951), xv, 264, 306.

10. Michael C. Munger, "Blogging and Political Information: Truth or Truthiness?," *Public Choice* 134, nos. 1 & 2 (January 2008): 125–38; Amarnath Amarasingam, ed.,

The Stewart/Colbert Effect: Essays on the Real Impact of Fake News (Jefferson, NC: McFarland and Company, 2011), 11, 20.

11. Amanda Mead, "*The Onion* in the Age of Trump: 'What We Do Becomes Essential When Its Targets Are This Clownish,'" *Guardian*, August 27, 2017.

12. Eric Boehlert, "NY Times Echoes Judith Miller's Iraq War Excuse by Blaming Sources, Not Reporters," *Media Matters*, July 29, 2015.

13. Kathleen Hall Jamieson, "Implications of the Demise of Fact in Political Discourse," *Proceedings of the American Philosophical Society* 159, no. 1 (March 2015): 66, 69–71; Eric Bradner, "Conway: Trump White House Offered 'Alternative Facts' on Crowd Size," CNN.com, January 23, 2017.

14. Mark K. McBeth and Randy S. Clemons, "Is Fake News the Real News? The Significance of Stewart and Colbert for Democratic Discourse, Politics, and Policy," in *The Stewart/Colbert Effect: Essays on the Real Impact of Fake News*, ed. Amarnath Amarasingam, 81; Munger, "Blogging and Political Information: Truth or Truthiness?," 125–6.

15. Alexandra Hutzler, "Sarah Sanders Has Not Had a Formal Press Briefing in 43 Days, Setting a New White House Record," *Newsweek*, April 23, 2019, www.news week.com/sarah-sanders-press-briefing-record-1403781. Accessed July 3, 2019.

16. The Cato Institute, "Government Transparency," *Handbook for Policymakers*, February 16, 2017, https://www.cato.org/cato-handbook-policymakers/cato-handbook -policy-makers-8th-edition-2017/government-transparency. Accessed January 6, 2020.

17. Tanni Haas, *Making It in the Political Blogosphere: The World's Top Political Bloggers Share the Secrets to Success* (Cambridge, UK: The Lutterworth Press, 2011), loc. 320, 1,773, 1,848, Kindle.

18. Alicia Garza, "A Herstory of the #BlackLivesMatter Movement," *Feminist Wire*, October 7, 2014, https://thefeministwire.com/2014/10/blacklivesmatter-2/?fb clid=IwAR07O0IFkxovFoRFKRLgDgkiDmMXiF6T_tQGoPitthec3u4_aZ4WP2z PF0g. Accessed June 4, 2019; Josh Sternberg, "Occupy Wall Street and Narratives," *Sternberg Effect*, November 22, 2011, https://joshsternberg.com/2011/11/22/occupy -wall-street-and-narratives/. Accessed June 4, 2019.

19. Joshua Kalla and Ethan Porter, "Politicians Don't Actually Care What Voters Want," *New York Times*, July 11, 2019.

20. Susan Bordo, *The Destruction of Hillary Clinton* (New York and London: Melville House, 2017), 22.

21. Bernard Bailyn, *The Origins of American Politics* (New York: Vintage Books, 1967), 125.

INDEX

343

Wolcott, James, 190
Wolf, Naomi, 193
women, Weyrich's focus on,
    72–73
Wonkette, 167
Woodruff, Judy, 62–63
Woodward, Bob, 56, 220
World Economic Forum, 171
World Magazine, 133
World Trade Organization, protests
    against, 247, 254–255
Worthy, William, 72
Wright, Jeremiah,
    225–226
Wright, Jim, 61
Wunderman, Lester, 76–79

Young Americans for Freedom (YAF),
    74–75
YouTube
    during 2008 election cycle, 176–177
    Allen video on, 161–162, 176
    campaign events on, 180, 181
    Clinton's campaign announcement
        on, 187
    Democratic debate and, 192
    growth of, 163
    Obama's campaign and, 190
Yu, Phil, 161–162

Zimmerman, George, 243
zip codes, 77–78
Zuckerberg, Mark, 155
Zuniga, Markos Moulitsas, 143, 167

CLAIRE BOND POTTER is a political historian at the New School for Social Research. She is executive editor of *Public Seminar* and was the author of the popular blog *Tenured Radical* from 2006 through 2015. She lives in New York City and Northampton, Massachusetts.